"LINCOLN'S HUMOR" AND OTHER ESSAYS

Benjamin P. Thomas

BENJAMIN P. THOMAS

"*Lincoln's Humor*"
and Other Essays

EDITED BY MICHAEL BURLINGAME

UNIVERSITY OF ILLINOIS PRESS

URBANA AND CHICAGO

The Library of Congress cataloged the cloth edition as follows:
Thomas, Benjamin Platt, 1902–1956.
"Lincoln's humor" and other essays / Benjamin P. Thomas ;
edited by Michael Burlingame.
p. cm.
Includes bibliographical references and index.
ISBN 0-252-02708-6 (alk. paper)
1. Lincoln, Abraham, 1809–1865.
2. Presidents—United States—Biography.
I. Burlingame, Michael, 1941– .
II. Title.
E457.8.T44 2002
973.7'092—dc21 2001003094

PAPERBACK ISBN 978-0-252-07340-3

For Sarah Thomas

Contents

Acknowledgments

Sarah Thomas, the younger daughter of Benjamin P. Thomas, has provided invaluable guidance and information as I edited this volume. When I learned that she had donated her father's papers to the Illinois State Historical Library in Springfield, I immediately scrutinized them and discovered several unpublished essays. She graciously granted me permission to publish them and supplied biographical data about her father. As I rummaged through the collections of the State Historical Library in search of yet more information, she also extended hospitality above and beyond the call of duty, enabling me to spend long periods conducting research in Springfield not only for this volume but also for several other Lincoln-related projects. I am deeply in her debt.

In Springfield I have enjoyed kind hospitality at the hands of many others, most notably Jim and Mary Patton, Tom and Cathy Schwartz, Wayne and Sandy Temple, Cullom and Ann Davis, and Amy Slocombe. Their friendship and generosity have made my research binges in Springfield a pleasure. At the Illinois State Historical Library, Kim Bauer, Kathryn Harris, Jill Blessing, Cheryl Schnirring, Cheryl Pence, George Heerman, and Linda Oelheim have been remarkably helpful and generous, making me appreciate why Harry E. Pratt used to refer to that facility as "the fun house."

The staff at the Harry Ransom Humanities Research Center at the University of Texas provided photocopies of the extensive correspondence by and about Benjamin Thomas from their Alfred A. Knopf archive. Librarians at Rutgers University, the Chicago Historical Society, and the Library of Congress also helped locate Thomas correspondence in their holdings. John Hoffmann of the University of Illinois Library shared copies of the Thomas letters he had tracked down in the Carl Sandburg Papers.

The R. Francis Johnson Faculty Development Fund at Connecticut College has helped defray the costs of research and travel involved in editing this volume.

My sister, Sue Burlingame Coover, and her husband, Edwin R. Coover, have been unusually generous in hosting me for long stretches while I conduct research in Washington, D.C.

For many years the lovely and long-suffering Lois McDonald has uncomplainingly provided indispensable support and encouragement as I have pursued the historical Lincoln.

MICHAEL BURLINGAME

Introduction

The essays gathered here complement Benjamin P. Thomas's
Abraham Lincoln: A Biography, which since its publication in 1952 has
been widely (and justly) considered the best single-volume life of America's sixteenth president.[1] Written in Thomas's limpid style and with a
profound understanding of Lincoln and his times, these essays include
unpublished items found among the research files of the Abraham Lincoln Association and the papers that Thomas's family donated to the Illinois State Historical Library. Several other essays first appeared in periodicals or in pamphlet form.

For good reason, the historian John A. Garraty called Thomas "a great
biographer."[2] Although other full-length, single-volume Lincoln biographies have appeared since 1952, Thomas's study remains "the definitive
work" for "the reader looking for Lincoln at once in full and in brief," as
critic Jonathan Yardley observed in a review of David Herbert Donald's
Lincoln, published in 1995. Yardley declared that "in no significant way
does Donald's *Lincoln* supplant Benjamin Thomas's."[3] In 1999 Allen C.
Guelzo, author of *Abraham Lincoln: Redeemer President,* described
Thomas's *Lincoln* as "the finest one-volume survey biography" of the sixteenth president.[4] Seven years earlier, James Hurt, a literary scholar, praised
Thomas's biography for its restraint: "There is no sentimentalizing in the
book. . . . Powerfully emotional scenes such as the First and Second Inaugural ceremonies and the deaths of Lincoln's children are told crisply and
economically and thereby earn their emotional power by suggestion rather
than by rhetorical violins in the background." Upon rereading the 548-page
biography, Hurt was surprised by "how short it seemed," for "the organi-

zation is so straightforward and the style so bare and lucid that it moves quickly and purposefully." Hurt was especially impressed that four decades after its publication, it did not feel dated: "for the most part the book could have been written yesterday."[5] In 1986 the Civil War historian Stephen W. Sears concurred, observing that scholarly "reassessments of the past few decades have not invalidated his portrait of Lincoln—indeed, in some cases they have strengthened it."[6] Four years previously, Mark E. Neely, Jr., had called *Lincoln* "wonderful," a "masterpiece," and an "elegant and balanced synthesis" resting on "the best research" and written in a "fluid and readable style."[7] In 1962 David M. Potter, a leading scholar of the Civil War era, praised *Abraham Lincoln: A Biography* as "a masterly summary of a vast amount of scholarship."[8]

Even before Thomas's biography was officially released, it impressed knowledgeable readers. The former executive secretary of the Abraham Lincoln Association, Paul M. Angle, who had seen the galley proofs, declared that the book's "proportions are perfect," synthesizing "modern scholarship so unobtrusively that the general reader will never even notice it—which is the way it should be done." The writing, Angle thought, "has the pace of fiction," with prose "always straightforward, and often vivid, even eloquent." He confessed that "most Lincoln books, even the good ones, bore me, but every page of this held my interest." He told Thomas: "Yours is going to be *the* biography for a generation. . . . You've made yourself a reputation, boy, and I suspect a lot of dough too."[9]

In 1951 Allan Nevins, dean of American Civil War historians, wrote Thomas that his biography "seemed to me quite beyond criticism" and that he had "read it with great enjoyment . . . and with much real instruction." Nevins had feared "that the heavy compression required will crush the life out of the story, leaving it pemminanized—nutritious but flavorless." He was relieved that Thomas had "admirably surmounted" that danger and that the "book has real narrative flow and color, and the portrait of Lincoln emerges slowly (as it should: no man ever did more *growing*) but surely and convincingly." Nevins predicted accurately that Thomas's biography "will at once be recognized as *the* one-volume life of Lincoln, for which there is so crying a need. . . . No other book can be compared with it at all." Nevins thought that Thomas rendered the presidency "very ably" but was most impressed with his "treatment of the Lincoln of Illinois, and of Lincoln as a human being rather than as a statesman." Nevins doubted that "anybody who picks up the book, however familiar he is with the subject, will lay it down."[10] The following year, Nevins declared, "Thomas has done the world a notable service in writing a single-volume life of Lincoln which combines the latest and most expert scholarship with real interpretive power and literary finish. Henceforth this is the work with which the general reader should begin his studies in the Lincoln field; and even those who know the field well will find much which is new and arresting."[11] He congratulated Thomas "with real fervor" for "completing just what I knew you would give us, by far the best short life of Lincoln ever written. . . . You have written one of the Lincoln classics, and I predict a long career of worldwide scope for that volume."[12]

As Nevins anticipated, Thomas's biography has endured largely because the author captured the spirit of "Lincoln the human being" so well. More recent scholarship has cast doubt on a few of Thomas's interpretations, such as his contention that Lincoln's "father was always a respectable, industrious man" and that Lincoln and Mary Todd "seem to have had a reasonably happy home life."[13] In fact, abundant evidence suggests that the contrary is true.[14] In addition, Thomas's mildly revisionist hostility to the Radical Republicans betrays the book's age.[15] But on the whole, Thomas succeeds better than any other biographer in portraying Lincoln as a three-dimensional, living, breathing figure.

Although the short, chubby-cheeked, portly, and balding Thomas did not look like Lincoln, he strongly resembled the sixteenth president in many other respects.[16] As Thomas's editor and close friend Earl Schenck Miers observed, there "was a simple goodness in Ben, the same simple goodness that was in his hero, and it brought to his *Abraham Lincoln* a success such as few books enjoy."[17] Thomas's "Lincoln-like humility" impressed the editor of the Springfield *State Register*, who observed in 1952 that "Ben's personal charm, calm understanding, . . . warm heart, kindly hand, tender voice and magnetic smile write a book into the lives of his countless admirers."[18] Paul Angle noted that Thomas, like Lincoln, "made no effort to impress or to be ingratiating; he was simply himself—kindly, gentle, humorous, interesting."[19] George W. Bunn, Jr., recalled that "so unassumingly did he carry his wide and constantly ripening scholarship that it surprised his friends to realize that, all of a sudden, he was famous."[20]

Thomas's ideology strongly resembled Lincoln's. Both "abhorred the oppression" of blacks.[21] In 1932 he left a teaching post in Alabama, for "he was not too fond of living in the South partly because of their prejudices against Negroes," as Sally Thomas, his wife, recalled.[22] According to Paul Angle, Thomas "was deeply disturbed by the failure of many Southern communities to follow the Supreme Court's [1954] desegregation decision, and seriously considered canceling an important trip to New Orleans not long before his death [in 1956] because of his revulsion at what he took to be human retrogression."[23] Thomas, a registered Re-

publican, often declared that blacks should, by rights, become commu-
nists in protest against racial discrimination in the United States. He was
dismayed by neighbors who banded together to prevent blacks from
moving into their section of Springfield. Often he admonished his children never to generalize about racial, ethnic, or religious groups.[24]

At the graduation of his daughter Sarah from Ferry Hall School, he
urged her and her classmates to eschew bigotry. He echoed Lincoln's
celebrated Peoria speech of 1854, in which the future president expressed
hatred for slavery expansion "because it deprives our republican example of its just influence in the world; enables the enemies of free institutions, with plausibility, to taunt us as hypocrites; [and] causes the real
friends of freedom to doubt our sincerity." Thomas said, "Every one of
us knows men and women who would be sincerely shocked to be accused
of being enemies of democracy, yet who, by their intolerant thinking and
their intolerant actions, put democracy at greater risk than all the secret
agents the Russians could ever send against us. Because unwittingly, but
no less effectively, by denying some classes of our people the chance for
self-advancement which democracy promises them, they are preparing
a fertile seed-bed for communist propaganda."[25] In 1953 Thomas declared:

> [A] fundamental law of life gears my personal welfare with the welfare
> of mankind. I can move onward and upward only with the progress of
> humanity. Thus self-interest, of itself, if I can command no higher mo-
> tive, demands that I aid my fellow man. But to help him I must know
> him. Only with understanding can I trust and respect him, and grant him
> tolerance. With understanding, I do not blame his offenses on his race
> or his creed or his color, remembering that I, and men of my race, creed
> and color also fall short and offend. I must recognize that the desire for
> life, liberty, and the pursuit of happiness of all our people, of all people
> the world over, is no less valid than mine.[26]

Carl Sandburg praised Thomas's idealism, noting that in "his talk, in his
dealings with men, in his reach of compassion for the less lucky of the
family of man, he was rare."[27]

Thomas "hated—literally hated" the apostle of anticommunism, Sen.
Joseph McCarthy, for "his tactics and for the cleavage he rived in what
had generally been a tolerant and unified people," Paul Angle remembered.[28] Thomas's minister, Richard Graebel of the First Presbyterian
Church of Springfield, said, "The thing that made us friends, and the thing
that won his respect, was our shared detestation of that awful thing called
'McCarthyism,' the limitation of true freedom and honesty, the fear
among many Americans that the commonwealth was not safe in the
hands of the common people."[29]

Like Lincoln, Thomas had a knack for friendship.[30] According to George W. Bunn, Jr., Thomas's neighbors in Springfield thought him "a lovable companion and active associate in the everyday life of the community."[31] Thomas "had friends everywhere," Angle observed. "Everyone liked him—businessmen, cattlemen, historians, writers, publishers."[32] As an undergraduate at Johns Hopkins University, his fellow students chose Thomas president of the senior class. In middle age, when he devoted several years to business and farming, colleagues elected him president of both the Springfield Chamber of Commerce and the Illinois Polled Hereford Association.[33]

Also like Lincoln, Thomas was ambitious.[34] "Ben's ambition had a driving intensity," according to Earl Schenck Miers, who ascribed that ambition in part to Thomas's need to prove to the skeptical burghers of "provincial and back-bitish" Springfield that he could achieve fame and fortune as a professional writer: "By God, his manner said, some day he would make Springfield sit up and take notice."[35] Paul Angle believed that by quitting business to become an independent scholar Thomas "knew he would raise some eyebrows, for Springfield would never quite understand why a man who could make money in an orthodox occupation would turn to something of such doubtful legitimacy as writing."[36] Sally Thomas recollected that her husband was "bitter" because "all Springfield worships is money."[37] He also longed for recognition outside Springfield. In 1949, for example, he confessed that he was "nettled" by his failure to be listed in *Who's Who*.[38] As he told a friend seven years later, "Inclusion in or omission from *Who's Who* is a poor measure of a man, as I see it. Many stuffed shirts manage to get into *Who's Who*, whereas many able men are omitted."[39]

Thomas shared Lincoln's sense of humor and love of mimicry.[40] Paul Angle recalled his "uncanny ear not only for peculiarities of English speech but also for dialect." Angle sent him to a Chicago barber who spoke "the most amusing blend of English, Italian, and American profanity." When Thomas returned, he reproduced the barber's conversation "to the last mixed syllable." According to Angle, Thomas was also celebrated for delivering "a monologue in pseudo-Russian that would bring tears of laughter to any audience. The dialect itself was amusing enough, but the real attraction of the performance was the wise, witty, and ever-changing commentary that he clothed in comic language." That monologue "sometimes produced an epigram or a hit that surprised even Ben," who "would burst into laughter, and the performance would stop until the performer recovered his composure." Thomas was also "adept at pantomime." Angle described his memorable imitation of a "batter facing a

pitcher who could smoke a ball in so fast that it would thud into the
catcher's glove before the batter could take the stick from his shoulder."
Thomas would skillfully imitate "all the orthodox practices of the batter—knocking the dirt from cleats, hitching up pants, stepping out of the
box a split second before the pitcher delivers—as well as facial expres-
sions denoting amazement at the pitcher's speed and disgust at the um-
pire's ball-and-strike calls."[41]

Thomas was especially fond of baseball, which he played at Johns
Hopkins. His younger daughter Sarah believes, "His first love was baseball and his unfulfilled dream was to play professional baseball." He regularly attended games of the Springfield minor league club as well as those
played in the public parks, including girls' softball contests. As Sarah
Thomas recalls, if the family was "out driving and he saw the lights on
at that little park, we always had to go see who was playing." On the front
yard of the family home he organized children's softball games, using
three evenly spaced trees for bases.[42] When attending the annual meetings of the Mississippi Valley Historical Association, he would sneak off
to the local ball park.[43] Lincoln, too, enjoyed athletic contests in his
youth, when he outwrestled, outjumped, and outran most of his contemporaries. He also played "corner ball," a precursor of modern baseball. As
an adult, he enjoyed handball and bowling and, like Thomas, took his
children to baseball games.[44]

Lincoln was not saintly—and neither was Thomas. His daughter
Sarah testifies that he "liked bawdy stories and loved his martinis and
cigarettes." (Lincoln shared his enthusiasm for off-color humor if not for
liquor and tobacco.) "I know I should stop smoking," he once said, "but
what if I should stop smoking and then get run over by a car. Think of
all the good smokes I would miss!"[45] After Thomas's biography of Lincoln appeared, his friends Chuck and Louise Lanphier composed a lim-
erick about his drinking habits:

> There once was a shortstop named Ben
> Who achieved great fame with his pen
> He wrote of Abe Lincoln
> Who never got stinkin'
> Though Benjamin did now and then.[46]

When attending historical association conventions, Thomas and Paul
Angle would slip away not only to ball games but also to burlesque
houses.[47] The speaker of the U.S. House, Schuyler Colfax, reported that
he and Lincoln "often went to Ford's opera house," where they found "real
relaxation" while watching "those southern girls with their well rounded

forms, lustrous hair and sparkling voices. We thought it a veritable treat to see them dance and hear their song."[48] At that same theater, Lincoln and his assistant personal secretary, John Hay, flirted with showgirls when the First Lady was out of town.[49]

Thomas's prose style calls to mind Lincoln's way with words. Thomas believed that "history was worthless if it was not readable," as Paul Angle put it. "In his own writing," Angle recalled, Thomas "developed the faculty of self-criticism, revising repeatedly for clarity and movement, especially movement."[50] Thomas regretted that "all too often, academic biographers, and academic historians, too, refuse to face up to the fact that they work in a literary medium, and pay far too little attention to literary craftsmanship." He urged that universities "teach our future historians how to write. Unless things have changed since my days in graduate school, it might almost be said that a man must slough off the ponderosity that adheres to him from graduate training before he can hope to write well."[51]

Because both Lincoln and Thomas shared much in common, the biographer was able to empathize with his subject to an unusual degree and thus create a remarkably lifelike study.

———————

In an autobiographical sketch, Thomas declared that anyone "of normal discernment might have predicted my future field of usefulness while I was still in rompers; for with that skepticism that marks the true historian I refused to credit my parents' claim that they found me one wintry morning in 'the old apple tree' in our backyard at Pemberton, New Jersey," a town where, according to an amazed traveling salesman, "everybody ate good without seemin' to do nothin'." Thomas's father, "a successful general storekeeper" after whom he was named, died when Ben, an only child, was two years old. Ben's mother, née Martha Johnson, soon thereafter was courted by a Baptist theology student, Ernest Ward Pickering. The young suitor used Ben as an excuse to call on the widow. Thomas recalled that Pickering "would come to our house in his buggy and ask if 'Ben' could go driving, whereupon my howls would echo through the house: 'Want to go with the preacher! Want to go with the preacher!'" After marrying Martha Thomas, Pickering completed his studies and settled in Baltimore following brief stays in Collingwood and Newark, New Jersey. Pickering, who was tall, handsome, and good-natured, provided the kind of loving solicitude for his stepson that Sarah Bush Johnston Lincoln gave her stepson Abraham.[52]

Upon graduating from Baltimore City College High School, Thomas attended the Johns Hopkins University. "I had no special aim in college," he recalled. "My mother thought I should consider dentistry—I suspect because it would enable me to sport the title of doctor—and I went along with that for awhile." Ultimately, he majored in economics and received his bachelor's degree in 1924. A scholar-athlete, Thomas captained the baseball team while earning a Phi Beta Kappa key. "I aspired to play professional baseball during my college years," he remembered, "but a few summers of semi-pro ball in New Jersey convinced me that I belonged in that large and undistinguished company described by the Cuban, Mike Gonzales, as 'good field, no hit.'"[53]

After graduation, Thomas, as he later wrote, "felt pretty much at loose ends, but got a job teaching Latin and history and coaching baseball and football at St. Paul's School near Baltimore. To take on Latin was sheer daring, but by keeping a few pages ahead of the class I managed to get by." Although classroom instruction was agreeable, he found "the confining nature" of the job, "especially the 'nursemaid' chores that it involved," very "irksome." Thomas's widow, Sally, reported that while he was at St. Paul's, "One night of taking care of a boy with an ear ache and another with a stomach ache at the same time changed his mind about teaching in a boys' school."[54] Therefore, he permitted himself "to be beguiled into selling bonds in Baltimore, a vocation which few college graduates of the lush 'twenties' seem to have escaped." He soon "wearied of it" and found "nostalgia" drawing him "once again to the academic cloisters."[55]

In 1926 he returned to Johns Hopkins to study history, a subject that had intrigued him since his mother had given him children's books on the American Revolution, the Civil War, and the Spanish-American War. But his curiosity, as he remembered, "had been almost obliterated by the genius of my high school teachers for making history dull." In his undergraduate days, however, John H. Latané, an American diplomatic historian, restored his enthusiasm for the study of the past. Resolved to become a teacher, Thomas applied to the Ph.D. program in history at his alma mater: "An interview with kindly Doctor Latané led not only to my admission to the graduate school at Johns Hopkins but also to a scholarship, which was renewed through my three years of study." Thomas remembered his graduate career as a "wonderfully rewarding" experience. Hopkins "had great teachers in those days," among them Latané and Edward Raymond Turner in history and two political scientists, Westal W. Willoughby and Frank Johnson Goodnow, president of the university.[56]

In 1929 Thomas received his doctorate after completing a dissertation on nineteenth-century Russian-American diplomatic relations, which the Johns Hopkins University Press published.[57] "Teaching jobs were not plentiful in 1929," he recalled, "but I landed a position at Birmingham-Southern College in Birmingham, Alabama. It was vital that I get a job, for love had entered my life . . . in the person of a girl at Goucher College, whom I met on a blind date," Salome (Sally) Carpenter Kreider. A native of Springfield, Illinois, she had a "Lincoln background. When Lincoln engineered the removal of the capital of Illinois from Vandalia to Springfield, a condition of removal was that Springfield should provide $50,000 toward the erection of a new state house. And Sally's grandfather, an early Illinois landowner, was one of those who kicked in."[58]

At Birmingham-Southern, Thomas "formed many delightful friendships" but felt uncomfortable, not only because of the pervasive racial bigotry but also because he had to teach European history. Lacking proficiency in the relevant languages, Thomas envisioned no future as a historian of Europe. In 1932, while vacationing at Sally's family's summer home in Old Mission, Michigan, Thomas met Logan Hay, a prominent Springfield attorney and grandson of Lincoln's second law partner, Stephen T. Logan. As president of the Abraham Lincoln Association, Hay was looking for a scholar to replace Paul M. Angle, who was about to step down as executive secretary of the Lincoln Association. When Hay asked Thomas if he would be interested in the job, the young man hesitated at first. "What I knew about Lincoln could have been written on one page," Thomas recalled. Assured by Hay and Angle that he could learn on the job, he accepted the offer.[59] Angle recommended that he ignore Lincoln biographies and read the sixteenth president's own writings first. Thomas later acknowledged that Angle "gave me good advice. We can learn a good deal about Lincoln from what has been written about him, but one only learns to *know* him from what he himself wrote and said."[60]

As executive secretary of the Abraham Lincoln Association, Thomas managed its business affairs, conducted research, and edited a bulletin. His first article in that periodical was "Old New Salem."[61] It won praise from the editor of the *Illinois State Journal:* "Mr. Thomas is master of a most pleasing literary style and he has dressed an old subject in attractive new garments. In a long time I have not read a better written or more interesting bit of history."[62] Thomas expanded the article into a book, *Lincoln's New Salem*, which the Abraham Lincoln Association published in 1934. The central theme of that slender volume was the influence on Lincoln of frontier conditions, which "made life hard for him" but which also "gave him strength, courage, and confidence."[63] In a talk included in this volume (chapter 7), Thomas summarized his thoughts on Lincoln and New Salem.

One reviewer called *Lincoln's New Salem* a "fascinating piece of Lincolniana" and a "contribution to the Lincoln saga of the first order."[64] The *Boston Herald*'s reviewer rated it far and away "the best study of the hamlet and of Lincoln's life there."[65] Equally enthusiastic was the Lincoln biographer Ida Tarbell, who told Thomas, "It is just the kind of book that I have been hoping for many a day somebody would write, but I confess I did not conceive that anybody would ever do it as well as you have done it. You have put so much sober care into it and shown what is dear to me—an appreciation of the reality and dignity of the life in that little settlement."[66] In *A Shelf of Lincoln Books,* Paul Angle praised *Lincoln's New Salem* as "readable, even captivating—clear, straightforward, and sprinkled with humor." The author, he noted, "was not content with tradition, as nearly all his predecessors had been. Instead, he searched court records and contemporary newspapers, and hunted out the letters of Lincoln's friends and neighbors in order to supplement and verify the old-age recollections of the villagers. As a result, his book has an authority that other studies lack." Angle singled out for special commendation Thomas's "keen, succinct appraisal of the effect of Lincoln's New Salem years on his growth and character." On that subject, Thomas concluded that although Lincoln availed himself of "the opportunities that the frontier afforded," he "avoided the frontier's weaknesses or, learning from experience, outgrew them. He became self-reliant without becoming boastful and without overestimating himself; analytical and conservative rather than opportunistic and impulsive."[67]

It was a theme some historians had slighted. In 1907 Ezra M. Prince had observed of Lincoln: "The pioneer life broadened him instead of narrowed him as much of our industrial life does our artizans. The farmer's life still gives much of that general mental & physical training that is necessary to make real men. That is an aspect of Mr. Lincoln's life that has been entirely missed especially by his eastern biographers."[68] Thomas was endorsing a theme that a historian from the Midwest, Frederick Jackson Turner, had popularized in his sweeping interpretation of American history.[69] Ida Tarbell and Carl Sandburg had taken a similar approach to Lincoln's frontier background. More recently, some scholars have complained, with justice, that Thomas portrayed the rude hamlet too glowingly, giving insufficient attention to the darker side of frontier life.[70]

While writing *Lincoln's New Salem,* Thomas benefited from the mentorship of Logan Hay, whom he described vividly: "Although Mr. Hay always insisted that the various Association secretaries should have full credit for the books that bore their names as author, a great deal of him went into everything they wrote. Constantly peering over their shoulders as they worked were his kindly but questioning eyes. As a critic he was unexcelled; with loose writing or loose thinking he was merciless. When one made a statement or offered a conjecture in his presence, he had better be prepared to back it up."[71]

Thomas recalled that writing *Lincoln's New Salem* "almost drove me nuts" and "disfigured me for awhile":

> Mr. Hay took such a keen interest in it that he scrutinized every phase of the research and weighed and pondered over every word I wrote. It had such possibilities, he said, that we must spare no effort on it. . . . I became so nervous before the thing was finished that my beard began to drop out. It wouldn't have been so bad if it had dropped out all at once. But it came out in patches, leaving shiny spots, and I looked like hell. The doctor diagnosed this startling phenomenon with some Latin medical term, and assured me that it was quite common to people under nervous strain—a woman patient of his who suffered from it had found all her hair lying on the pillow when she woke up one morning. Although I had begun to lose the hair on my head some years before, my ailment didn't seem to speed that process, and my beard grew back after while. I hadn't foreseen an occupational hazard when I entered the Lincoln field.[72]

"Damn it, I can't be that bad!" Thomas exclaimed to a friend after Hay had criticized his manuscript during a particularly grueling editorial meeting. After regaining his composure, however, he "would manfully meet Mr. Hay's objections. In the end he would admit . . . that the book was far better than it would have been without those sessions that so severely taxed his patience. Ben was particularly grateful for Logan Hay's tutelage because he believed that through it he learned a great deal about historical writing."[73]

Thomas next turned his hand to *Lincoln: 1847–1853*, a volume in the "Lincoln Day by Day" series that the Abraham Lincoln Association had launched in 1933:

> [The book] involved an enormous amount of tedious, dirty work in newspaper collections, court files, congressional records, and any number of miscellaneous sources; but it also brought thrills and satisfactions. I can well remember the days I spent in dingy central Illinois courthouses, often in the basement, turning the interminable pages of dusty ledgers and poring through grimy files long undisturbed. Invariably the clerks declared it was a waste of time, no Lincoln documents had been found for years. Yet in every instance I did find documents and records, and in more than one courthouse the documents ran into the hundreds. Usually they were in Lincoln's handwriting without his signature; those that he signed had disappeared. In each instance I obtained permission to photostat them, then returned them to the incredulous custodians.[74]

Of the four volumes in the Day by Day series, Thomas's was the only one with "an outstanding introduction" in the opinion of Paul Angle, who commended it to the attention of the "reader who wants the best account of these eight years in Lincoln's life, when the future President realized his long-standing ambition to serve in Congress only to see his political career fade out in failure."[75] In addition, that introduction (chapter 9 of this volume) was "colorful as well as factual—a fine filling-out of the chronological framework."[76] Lloyd Lewis, author of *Myths after Lincoln*, was so impressed with the introduction that he called its author "an independent researcher . . . whose discernment and originality of approach have long entitled him to greater recognition in the field."[77]

In 1936 Thomas and Angle planned to write a study of Lincoln the lawyer.[78] Thomas had already published a long article on "Lincoln and the Courts, 1854–1861" (chapter 11 of this volume).[79] He also considered doing a study of Lincoln's career as a state legislator.[80] He abandoned these schemes, however, in part because of dissatisfaction with his job at the Abraham Lincoln Association. "Routine work cut deeply into time for research, and personal responsibilities were making increasing demands," Paul Angle explained.[81] (Angle wrote pungently—and with authority—about the drudgery of the secretaryship that he had once held. Duties included arranging the annual Lincoln's birthday banquet, dealing with irate members who objected to their table assignments, and leading tours of Lincoln sites for schoolchildren and VIPs.)[82] In addition, Thomas felt intellectually isolated. "Springfield," he recalled, "while distinguished by the presence of many cultured people, is primarily a business town; most of my friends were business men, and I sometimes became both lonesome in my work and discouraged because my salary was necessarily small—those were depression years and the resources of the Association were limited."[83]

In 1936 he "succumbed to the money-making urge" and abandoned his career as a Lincoln specialist to establish a successful general insurance and property management firm.[84] He also took charge of a farm that his wife had inherited. In addition, he began breeding cattle—hornless ("polled") Herefords—which, he believed, were "the greatest agricultural innovation since seedless oranges."[85] "It is a relaxing contrast to discard city polish and swap yarns with other cattlemen on the summer fair circuit," Thomas reported.[86] Moreover, he became a director of the First National Bank and the head of the Chamber of Commerce. Despite his financial success, however, Thomas was uneasy. "I began to write in my spare time," he recalled, "but found it difficult going with so many business distractions."[87]

By 1945 Thomas was finding the siren song of Lincoln scholarship irresistible. As he told a journalist, "If you want to get away from Lincoln for good, you have to leave this part of the state."[88] To Harry E. Pratt he confided that for people trained as professional historians, "it is pretty hard to derive a full measure of satisfaction" from anything other than research and writing.[89] "It feels good to get back" to "full time writing" he declared in 1946.[90] Because he had remained on the board of directors of the Abraham Lincoln Association, Thomas "found it easy to return to the Lincoln field full swing." He became an associate editor of the *Abraham Lincoln Quarterly* and later an editorial advisor for the *Collected Works of Abraham Lincoln*, which was published in 1953. He did not regret spending time on the historical sidelines:

> Although my business career robbed me of a possible ten years of productive literary work, those were not wasted years. My partners were congenial, and I made many friends. I learned where my true happiness and interest lie. And, in deserting history temporarily, I read widely in general literature, learning how a good novelist builds up his plot and something about literary grace and artful writing. I returned to history with a new perspective, a new appreciation of good writing, and a resolve to avoid the stuffiness and rigidity that are more of an occupational hazard to historical writers than the malady that took my beard.[91]

In his leisure time, Thomas had been gathering information on Lincoln's biographers, mostly from the files of their unpublished correspondence at libraries in Washington, D.C., Pennsylvania, and California, as well in Springfield and Chicago. The result was *Portrait for Posterity: Lincoln and His Biographers*, which the Rutgers University Press published in 1947. "That book was fun," he remembered, "for I found much more material than I expected to, and the letters I unearthed were sometimes bitter, sometimes humorous, sometimes gossipy, and often keen and penetrating, as the biographers feuded with one another."[92] He was proud of it. As he told Harry E. Pratt, "I think it is the most original Lincoln book to appear for a long time, and it should certainly enable one to read the more important biographies with more discernment."[93]

Portrait for Posterity won critical praise.[94] Arthur M. Schlesinger, Jr., called it "a valuable and readable contribution to the Lincoln literature."[95] Allan Nevins said, "For a highly specialized subject, Mr. Thomas's book is both entertaining and rewarding."[96] Carl Sandburg deemed it "a rather wonderful book" that "flows as a story." He told Thomas, "You not only absorbed all the materials at the source, but you brooded over them, and I go along with nearly all of your delicately shaded judgments as to persons and issues."[97] Thomas thanked Paul Angle for his favorable review, which made him "forget the hours of drudgery that go into any book."[98] A reviewer in a South Carolina newspaper especially pleased Thomas by declaring that although he had once regarded Lincoln as "considerably less than a God," he had to confess after reading *Portrait for Posterity* that the sixteenth president became "more human and appealing than many biographers had made him."[99] Reviewers admired Thomas's style, which was deemed "graphic and lively," "ludid," "refreshing and authentic," "entertaining," "racy," and "unacademic."[100] A critic who thought the book read "like an absorbing tale" exclaimed, "O, rare it is to find a man who can make his material sing on the page like this!"[101] A professor of English, Roy P. Basler, thought that Thomas was the obvious scholar to write the long-needed one-volume biography of Lincoln.[102] "Although I didn't realize it at the time," Thomas later said, "the writing of that book was probably my apprenticeship in the high minor leagues of literature or at any rate as a rookie on the bench; without having written it, I could scarcely have written *Abraham Lincoln: A Biography.*"[103] Highlights of *Portrait for Posterity* are contained in "Backstage with the Lincoln Biographers," chapter 13 in this volume.

As much as he enjoyed its critical success, the book's poor sales disappointed Thomas, who ruefully called *Portrait for Posterity* "that flop of mine."[104] He was angry at Rutgers University Press: "I think I have sucked the hind tit with them ever since I turned my book over to them," he told Paul Angle.[105] He also complained to his editor, Earl Schenck Miers, that Rutgers had promoted his book too little compared to its bestselling *Lincoln Reader:* "You concentrated on it to the detriment of POR-TRAIT."[106] Miers replied that the publisher had given Thomas's volume "a far better than average promotion effort" and had spent more "than a commercial publisher would have spent on this type of book." He also lamented that "splendid book that it is," *Portrait for Posterity* "simply did not have a popular appeal." Gently he admonished, "You must not expect a book without universal appeal in subject matter . . . to sky-rocket into best sellerdom."[107] To Paul Angle, who had edited *The Lincoln Reader*, Miers confided, "Poor old Ben, he still refers to the success of THE LIN-COLN READER. I guess he is griped as the devil over the fact that his own book did not do as well. My God, nobody expected it would—except Ben. What a wonderful person he would have been to have collaborated with Billy Herndon; they could have spent endless hours damning all the publishers, all booksellers, and all stupid people who buy books."[108]

So discouraged was Thomas that he was "thinking rather seriously of going back into teaching." "If I thought I could make anything by writing alone," he told Angle, "I'd stick to it, but if I can't, I would be tempted to combine it with a teaching job. I feel like a parasite with Sal producing all the income. And with three kids to educate over the next eight or ten years, I hardly feel justified in indulging in an activity which brings in only about $1,000 for two years work."[109]

But Thomas did not resume a career in academia. For all his disappointment, he declared to Miers, "I want to join your writing stable if you'll have me."[110] When Miers urged him to do a study of the abolitionists in order to prove his versatility, Thomas agreed, but after a few months decided to narrow his focus to a single antislavery champion, Theodore Dwight Weld.[111] In March 1948 he informed Rutgers University Press:

> I just got to the point in the Abolitionists where I concluded that the subject was too big to write a worthwhile book without spending a lot more time than either you or I would care to have put into it. It is a great subject, but any book that I could finish by the end of this year would be so superficial that it would be no credit to you or me. On the other hand, I do feel that I can do an interesting study of Weld and finish it this year. A large number of the other abolitionists and interesting characters of the period will come into it naturally. . . . I don't know how a life of Weld will sell, but after much soul-searching I have concluded the hell with sales, inasmuch as there is only a very remote possibility of ever selling very many copies of historical books anyway. I now have three books to my credit, all of which are recognized as books of permanent value. It seems to me that the thing for me to do is try to write books that measure up to that standard, and forget the sales angle.[112]

By July 1948, however, he had undergone a change of heart. "I am severing my relations with the Rutgers Press," he told Miers.[113] He intended to approach the firm of Alfred A. Knopf, which had earlier that year asked him to write a biography of Charles Sumner.[114] An editor at Knopf had read the Weld biography and "enjoyed it thoroughly," but, ultimately, Thomas decided to stay with Rutgers.[115]

"I should have the first draft of my new book done by the end of this month, and ready to go sometime in October or November," Thomas confided to Angle in the summer of 1948. "I'm probably prejudiced, but I really think the life of this Theodore Weld is one hell of a fascinating story."[116] By Christmas he had finished the manuscript of *Theodore Weld: Crusader for Freedom*, which offered "a new conception of the abolitionists." Flying in the face of the "modern antiabolition prejudice" that was so conspicuous in the works of James G. Randall and other members of the dominant school of Civil War revisionism, Thomas asserted that "we need a reappraisal" of the abolitionists. "It has too long been the fashion to scoff at them, to write them off as humorless fanatics, to ignore their rich humanity, and to minimize the tremendous impact of the moral convictions they avowed. And to misjudge the force of moral humanism invites distortion of history." Despite their faults:

> We must credit the abolitionists with striving to perfect the American ideal, and to vitalize the precepts of our Declaration of Independence. . . . Our present sensitivity to the rights of racial and religious minorities . . . is in no small degree a heritage from the antislavery impulse. . . . A reappraisal of the abolitionists is all the more in order inasmuch as the struggle for equal human rights is still a vital issue in our day. . . . there is a restless stirring in the land, reminiscent of the antislavery days, testifying to the eternal validity of the equalitarian principles to which the abolitionists were dedicated, foretokening, we may hope, a new era of enlightenment in human relationships.[117]

Abolitionists of all varieties shared in common an "unselfish consecration to a high ideal. They were dangerous to be sure, dangerous to counterfeit democracy, dangerous to all institutions and concepts that denied a portion of mankind its natural birthright." While attacking the anti-abolitionism of the revisionist school, Thomas also called into question another central revisionist theme: "Perhaps it [the Civil War] was avoidable, as some historians insist—who can be sure?"[118]

Thomas was not alone in urging reconsideration of abolitionism. In 1933 Gilbert Hobbs Barnes had made similar arguments in his study *The Anti-Slavery Impulse, 1830–1844,* which portrayed Weld and his western colleagues as more influential than their eastern counterparts such as William Lloyd Garrison. Thomas, according to Weld's biographer, gave "a livelier, more humane, and more comprehensive view of Weld than [did] Barnes."[119]

Thomas hoped that the Weld biography, like *Portrait for Posterity,* would be a critical success. "From the reaction of those who have read it, I do not think it beyond the realm of possibility to aspire to the Pulitzer Prize," he said hopefully.[120] "I don't know when I have had more pleasure from writing a book," he told a friend. "To me, the man [Weld] became fascinating."[121] Paul Angle credited Thomas with having "proved that the abolitionist movement outside New England has never had its just deserts."[122] Carl Sandburg was enthusiastic: "There was urgent need for a biography of the great, lovable and picturesque figure of Theodore Weld. Ben Thomas meets this need in the story of a bashful, publicity-shy abolitionist who nevertheless was a storm-bird in the making of American history."[123] Marion Bonzi, an editor of *The Collected Works*

Benjamin Platt Thomas. In the background is the old Illinois State Capitol, where Abraham Lincoln served as a legislator and where he delivered his "House Divided" speech in 1858.

of Abraham Lincoln, thought "Thomas did a swell job—except that I wish that he had fought to let his footnotes stay."[124]

Not all critics were so favorable. In the *American Historical Review*, Louis Filler complained that Thomas did not "succeed in limning Weld's personality, or explaining such personal influence as he exerted."[125] In 1980 Robert H. Abzug observed in a psychologically subtle biography of Weld that "Thomas's book lacks depth and is not really a complete account of Weld's life."[126]

To earn some money, Thomas in 1949 wrote part of a history of Springfield's Sangamo Electric Company, a task for which "the pay was mighty good."[127] When a leading university press appeared ready to offer him an editorial post, he turned to Earl Schenck Miers, who had recently moved from Rutgers University Press to Alfred A. Knopf, Inc., in New York: "As you know, I have done a great deal of editorial work in connection with the Abraham Lincoln Association's books and Quarterly, and I like that sort of work. But I also like to write, and if you have anything in mind for me, . . . I should appreciate hearing from you."[128]

In November 1949 Thomas met with Miers and discussed possible projects. "Why don't you write a biography of Abraham Lincoln?" queried Miers. "Oh, there's been too much written about Lincoln" came the reply.[129] As Thomas recalled:

> I hesitated, because it impressed me at first as an awesome undertaking. It meant the compression into some five hundred pages of an enormous store of information about Lincoln, the product of the last thirty years of research plus all the reminiscent and factual material that had originated previously. It would mean, if the book was to serve its true purpose, assuming the responsibility of interpreting this greatest of Americans to the American people. It would mean putting a fresh glint on a story most of which was known, although perhaps not as well known as some of us close to Lincoln had thought.[130]

Miers persisted, reporting in late November that Knopf was "quite willing to offer Ben a contract for a one-volume life of Lincoln."[131]

Ultimately, Miers convinced Thomas to accept the daunting challenge. Before starting work, Thomas asked Carl Sandburg if he intended to condense his six-volume Lincoln biography into one volume: "You can count upon a clear track so far as I am concerned, if you plan to undertake it. . . . I shall do nothing whatever in the matter without a green light from you."[132] Sandburg, "a notoriously bad correspondent," replied a few weeks later: "It will be so long a time, somewhere between two to five years, before I have finished [my] one-vol[ume] Lincoln—if at all—that I would say you go ahead for Knopf. Each book will be distinctive, supplementing each other."[133] Elated, Thomas told Miers, "I believe we can produce a good book, giving the people an up-to-date account of Lincoln that will incorporate the latest scholarship and at the same time make Abe a living figure." Eager to get to work, he began writing even before Sandburg's answer arrived. "I believe I can do the job in two years," he estimated in December 1949.[134]

In mid-January, Knopf sent Thomas a contract providing for a $1,500 advance and establishing a February 1, 1953, delivery date. Miers explained that Knopf had faith not only in Thomas's ability as a researcher but also his literary skills: "There is no question in my mind about the scholarly background which you can give to this manuscript, but it is not on the basis of this virtue alone that we want you to do this book. When the Charnwood biography [*Abraham Lincoln* by Godfrey Rathbone Benson, first baron Charnwood] appeared [in 1916] its strength rested largely on the impact it made as a piece of fine writing. I believe that any one-volume life of Lincoln that you write can have the same quality, in addition to its scholarly attribute, and it is on this basis that we want you to proceed."[135] When Thomas returned the contract, Miers was delighted: "Over a long period of time, with some stormy but mostly pleasant sailing, I have had great faith in your ability, and now, by god, I am going to have a chance, personally, to see that promise completely fulfilled! . . . it must be the beginning of your career as one of the country's top-notch literary historians, and you are not to tackle it as anything less. Brother, this is the big time, and you are in it."[136]

Thomas flung himself into the project "with the will of a man possessed," working twelve-to-fourteen-hour days week in and week out.[137] Above his desk hung Boris Riedel's caricature of Lincoln, mouth agape, eyes radiating incredulity, with the caption "My God! Another book!"[138] By the end of January, he had taken the story up through the Lincolns' wedding in 1842; by mid-March he had progressed to 1854. "Making very satisfactory progress," he reported in May to Sandburg, "and trying to say a whole lot in a very few words." As he worked away, Thomas developed "even a greater appreciation" of Lincoln.[139] By June he had Lincoln elected president, and by the following May, scarcely eighteen months after beginning, Thomas completed a draft of the entire biography.[140]

Editors at Knopf were ecstatic about the first half of the manuscript, which arrived nine months ahead of schedule. Harold Strauss heaped encomiums on it: "This is an absolutely magnificent book, first-rate in every way. It is beautifully and even movingly written. It is continuously absorbing. It is authoritative, but wears its learning gracefully. Thomas is so much the master of his material that he never has to struggle with it. It is no small feat to make a life of Lincoln seem fresh and new, but fresh and new it was to me."[141]

Miers praised several features of the manuscript. Thomas had, in portraying "young Lincoln as a callow, opportunistic politician who gave no promise of future greatness," presented the facts "with genuine skill and objectivity." In "interpreting Lincoln as a product of the Midwest, as a personality that could not have been produced in either the North or South," Thomas had foreshadowed "the essential conflict of the nation that Lincoln symbolized." In dealing with such familiar subjects as the Lincoln-Douglas debates and Lincoln's relationship with Mary Todd, Thomas had achieved "a clarity of viewpoint that becomes surprisingly refreshing and exciting." In presenting the Civil War through Lincoln's eyes, Thomas's would "be the first Lincoln biography that keeps a singleness of impression . . . by putting the horse and cart of history in their proper relations." By portraying Lincoln as "the first great champion of an imperiled democracy," Thomas would illuminate "Lincoln's proper relation to history."[142]

At the same time, however, Miers worried that a glut of inferior Lincoln books might hurt the market for Thomas's biography:

> The day has come in publishing books in this field when the slight book or the semi-monograph-trade book is doing definite harm. Even the remainder market is becoming overloaded with Lincoln material, and booksellers everywhere are beginning to shy away from any Lincoln books that cannot justify their existence as valid books. It may be that we have come to a day when even The Abraham Lincoln Association should stick to its Quarterly and forget its book publishing program; too often books like LINCOLN'S VANDALIA [by William E. Baringer] and the book by F. Lauriston Bullard [*Lincoln and the Widow Bixby*], which we did at Rutgers, amount to nothing more than puffed-up journal articles. Both the Lincoln specialists and the public have grown wise. . . . [if] this type of publishing goes on, the tragedy is that when a book like Ben's one-volume biography comes along, a great deal of unjustified buyer-resistance already exists. The book, therefore, does not get its fair chance, or requires a tremendous amount of over-advertising to convince everyone that it is legitimate merchandise. In Ben's case the principal way to break down this resistance is to start now—two years in advance of publication—to stimulate the experts into discussing the book behind the scenes, and thus creating the feeling that here is a book for which they have been longing.[143]

Miers was less enthusiastic about the second half of Thomas's manuscript, which covered Lincoln's presidency. "Ben seems to make rather dry reading" of policy decisions, he complained. Moreover, revisions were needed to give Union generals "stronger personalities." A military historian himself, Miers urged Thomas to etch more sharply the major campaigns, to criticize Lincoln's appointment of political generals, to analyze more fully Lincoln's military genius, and to keep the focus steady, telling the story consistently from Lincoln's perspective.[144]

Thomas replied defensively that "we have a fundamental difference of opinion with respect to our views of Lincoln as a military leader." Denying that Lincoln's "selection of generals was political at first," Thomas argued that "he picked generals regardless of their politics in the hope of finding those who could do the job." Although "not oblivious of the political necessities of the situation," Lincoln "hoped that his nonpartisan attitude would hold the loyalty of the democrats." Indeed, all his top commanders were West Point graduates. Thomas contested Miers's argument that "Lincoln was the great military man." To be sure, the president had "quickly grasped the fundamental strategic concept that the North was [compelled to] make effective use of this superior manpower and resources if it was to win; that he must fight an aggressive war." In addition, he had "a very quick, sometimes an uncanny perception of where and when to strike or where and when the enemy might strike." Citing U. S. Grant's memoirs to clinch his argument, Thomas declared that he wished "to give Lincoln every bit of credit he deserves," but "I do not want to join the superman school. That, I think, would be fatal to the book." Thomas had asked other readers "to pay particular attention to the balance between battles and the man in the White House, since I realized that a proper balance here was one of my major problems." Those readers "expressed the opinion that in this respect I had achieved a real triumph, that one got the feel of the war and yet never got too far away from Lincoln." While reveling in their praise, Thomas was "jolted" by Miers's opinion "that this was one of the major weaknesses of the manuscript." He was willing to "shorten up the battle scenes" but reluctant "to be too drastic in these cuts."[145]

Alfred A. Knopf also raised some questions. "It seems to me that the reader gets no idea from you as to what an average day in Lincoln's life was like when he wasn't at the War Office or receiving callers, and so forth," Knopf observed. "How did he manage to write in his own hand all those letters? What time did he spend with the family? What were meals like? Who frequently ate lunch or dinner with the Lincolns, and so on? . . . Of course this isn't the main story . . . but it's awfully helpful human stuff and I don't think the average reader can help but ask . . . such questions."[146]

Thomas acknowledged that he should include "more human interest stuff" and agreed to pull together bits and pieces from throughout the book to create a separate chapter to be entitled "The Man in the White

House" or "Life in the White House."[147] Although he had originally hoped that the book would appear in February 1952, Thomas told Angle, "I could do it hastily and still make the deadline, but believe it would be better to take my time. Moreover, with no deadline imposed, I think I'll do some more browsing in the Lincoln Papers with the idea of finding more colorful stuff that has not been used elsewhere."[148]

In September, after a summer at the Library of Congress combing through the Robert Todd Lincoln Collection of Abraham Lincoln Papers, which had first been opened for public inspection four years earlier, Thomas informed Knopf: "I found much new material for an additional chapter, 'Profile of a President.'"[149] His examination of the Lincoln Collection was "the aspect of the research I enjoyed most," Thomas said. "It was a tedious job, and I put it off until I reached a point where I knew what I could and could not use; but there was a lot of satisfaction in it. Like panning for gold, I guess; you have to process a lot of earth to find the nuggets. But plenty of them can be found, and students will be bringing them out of that collection for a long time."[150] As well as adding a new chapter (the most eloquent one in the book), Thomas fleshed out the human interest material in "Shadows on the White House."[151] In the summer of 1951 he had also examined the John G. Nicolay Papers at the Library of Congress and then tinkered more with the manuscript, especially the passages of military history.

The revised manuscript was forwarded to Allan Nevins, who responded most positively, although he did suggest that "the book would gain in organization if you broke up your longer chapters," especially those on Lincoln's presidency. He also advised Thomas to "strive to get more generalizations into the book—generalizations, or deductions, upon the frontier as a school, upon democracy Jacksonian and Lincolnian, upon the inner nature of the sectional struggle, upon Lincoln's place in politics, in literature, in the folk-history of Americans, upon 'man's vast future' as Lincoln saw it, and so on, and so on. We have all the facts we need; more rays of cosmic illumination would be helpful."[152]

Perhaps, Thomas conceded, "in an effort to avoid eulogy and encomiums," he had "leaned too far the other way and failed to bring out Lincoln's greatness as strongly as I should have. I shall certainly re-read with that in mind. I know that I consciously tried to avoid being overly adulatory and to let the facts speak for themselves, but I don't want the reader to miss the point and put the book down, when he finishes, with an under-estimation of Lincoln's greatness."[153] In January 1952 he heeded Nevins's advice by adding "paragraphs at proper points amounting to perhaps ten pages in all."[154] The pithy summaries that conclude many chapters, probably what Thomas refers to, are among the strongest passages in the biography.

In the spring of 1952, Miers reported that Thomas was "floating on the clouds now with his new book coming out, and I can't blame him much. Knopf predicts an advance somewhere between twenty-five thousand and fifty thousand copies of it and the book is, I understand, an 'A' book at the B[ook] O[f the] M[onth] C[lub]. Ben, who doesn't need the money, is going to make a lot of money."[155] In September, Miers advised, "Ben, it is a magnificent piece of work—every word of it gets across with vigor and with verve. It has a good style. It is, I suspect, a monument in the field of contemporary literary history, and I know that I, for one, am immensely proud and pleased to know the guy who wrote it. The book will be an enormous success. Both you and the Department of Internal Revenue will do well."[156]

When the biography appeared in bookstores in the fall of 1952, reviewers praised it extravagantly. Many echoed Bruce Catton's verdict: "by far the best one-volume biography of Abraham Lincoln," a "truly excellent piece of work."[157] Sterling North called it "a keen, perceptive, reliable, complete" work "which should be in every home and school in America."[158] In the *New York Times*, Orville Prescott declared Thomas's book "an altogether superb biography."[159] Harry E. Pratt hailed it as "an excellent job of distillation" and "a masterful synthesis."[160] Paul Angle added, "It is the best one-volume life of Lincoln ever written. And I'm not at all sure that that assertion needs the 'one-volume' qualification."[161] William B. Hesseltine concurred: "The credible picture of the man and his growth makes this one of the important biographies of Lincoln of any length."[162] Dumas Malone considered the biography to be "illuminated by a genuine understanding of [Lincoln's] personality."[163] "Your personality [is] there," Sandburg told Thomas, "your vast coverage of materials and your long broodings over those materials. It will always be one of the more companionable and requisite books for the Lincoln student."[164]

As similar praise appeared, Thomas reportedly was "purring like a kitten over the success of his book."[165] "What a heady wine fame is!" he exulted. "I'm loving it but trying to keep sober."[166] As he said shortly after the biography was published, "All this acclaim has left me feeling like Noah Webster, the famous dictionary man, who devoted his life to the precise use of words. One day Mrs. Webster came into the kitchen and found him embracing the maid. 'Mr. Webster!' said she, 'I'm surprised.' 'Oh, no, Mrs. Webster,' he corrected her, 'I'm surprised. You're amazed.' I'm both surprised *and* amazed." He declared that it was "a unique experience for me to be on the best seller lists and I have mixed emotions about it." Alluding to other best-sellers of the day—Tallulah Bankhead's *Tallulah: My Autobiography*, Norman Vincent Peale's *The Power of Positive Thinking*, and the Anchor Bible—he added, "It has been exciting, and at the same time rather embarrassing to find myself, week by week, creeping up on *Tallulah* before a nation-wide audience. Of course the Bible has stood between us most of the time, with *The Power of Positive Thinking* also coming in there now and then."[167]

Thomas's fame astonished him, according to George W. Bunn, Jr., who noted that "in a wholesome and unaffected manner he enjoyed it immensely. He enjoyed the speaking engagements and autographing parties, all of which gave him a new fund of stories to tell with himself as the target of his own quiet humor."[168] In March 1953, while *Abraham Lincoln: A Biography* was still atop the best-seller lists, Thomas and his family vacationed in Florida, where he hoped that his fame had spread. Sarah Thomas recalls that her father "did love the attention that being a best-selling author brought and he was rightfully proud of himself." On the Florida trip, "whenever we checked into a hotel and the desk clerk asked him his name, he would say 'Benjamin P. Thomas,' and then stand there with a little smile on his face. I think he expected the hotel clerks to recognize who Benjamin P. Thomas was. I could tell by the look on his face. He wasn't a hard person to read. Of course a hotel clerk down South wasn't about to know who Benjamin P. Thomas was. His face would fall when it became evident that, to them, he was just another overnight guest."[169]

Thomas was more upset when a negative critique by Donald Riddle appeared in the *Mississippi Valley Historical Review*. "The chapters on Lincoln's early life are too conventional," Riddle complained, and "the book continues the myth that Lincoln after his congressional term retired from politics, to emerge when the Kansas-Nebraska Act repealed the Missouri Compromise." Lincoln "was, in fact, never out of politics, and the Kansas-Nebraska Act was the occasion for Lincoln to rehabilitate himself and to run for office on the slavery issue." Moreover, Riddle continued, Lincoln's contemporaries "play hardly more than supporting roles." Stephen A. Douglas "appears to have served no more useful purpose than Lincoln's opposite. Surely he deserves more than this." In Thomas's treatment of the presidential years, "the war eclipses all else—hardly anything is said of Lincoln's administration as far as economic developments are involved." By virtually ignoring banking, tariff, and homestead legislation, Thomas distorted the picture: "The reader of this book will be assured that Lincoln saved the Union, but he will not learn what kind of a Union Lincoln's party leaders were creating." Thus, "while Dr. Thomas has given us an excellent chronicle of Lincoln's life he does not 'explain' him; to the reader of this book Lincoln is still an enigma."[170]

As a boy, Thomas had a temper, which he managed to keep under control in adulthood.[171] When attacked, however, his old feistiness re-emerged. Bristling, he told Riddle that many readers "have commented either in print or to me that the book 'explains' Lincoln better than any other they have read," although he conceded that if Lincoln "did not come clear to you in its pages, you are surely entitled to say so." Thomas doubt-ed that "Lincoln's character is susceptible of perfect understanding by any one" and objected strenuously to Riddle's comments about Lincoln's retirement from politics. "I believe," he said, "I have made the most thor-ough study ever of the years 1849 through 1853 in Lincoln's life, and it certainly seemed to me that for all practical purposes he was out of pol-itics. I learn now, for the first time, that this is myth. If you are prepar-ing a book or article to prove this point, I shall be interested in reading the supporting facts, whenever they appear." Riddle's use of the term *chronicle* wounded Thomas, who complained, "You could scarcely have found a word that more forcefully conveys the idea that a book is dry and dull. If my book is no more than a chronicle, I have certainly fallen far, far short of what I tried to do."[172]

Thomas wrote a similar letter to the editor of the *Mississippi Val-ley Historical Review*, asking why he had assigned Riddle "to review what is generally regarded as an important Lincoln book?"[173] To Alfred Knopf, Thomas explained, "Riddle is a third-rate professor of history at the U[niversity] of I[llinois]'s Navy Pier school in Chicago" who had written *Lincoln Runs for Congress*, which the Abraham Lincoln Asso-ciation had published in 1948. When Thomas, acting as an editor, ex-tensively revised Riddle's manuscript, the author allegedly became "re-sentful." "I think I have as few enemies as anyone in the profession but I always seem to fall afoul of one of them in these so-called 'learned jour-nals,'" Thomas lamented.[174]

A more telling criticism than Riddle's was made by William B. Hes-seltine, who observed that Thomas did not "psychologize Lincoln."[175] Hesseltine meant to praise the author for his reticence in examining Lin-coln's inner life, but that reticence constitutes a weakness rather than a strength in an otherwise outstanding biography.

Thomas mulled over several projects for his next book: a child's life of Lincoln; a volume of Lincoln's writings; a brief history of the Civil War; a study of the northern home front during that conflict; or a biography of Edwin M. Stanton, or Andrew Carnegie, or Stephen A. Douglas, or Woodrow Wilson, or Adlai Stevenson.[176] He was a conspicuous admirer of Stevenson and occasionally acted as a ghostwriter for him.[177]

While considering his long-term options, he decided in the short run to edit the memoirs of a Civil War journalist, Sylvanus Cadwallader. The idea came to him one day in 1950 while reading a slender volume of letters by Lloyd Lewis in which the Chicago-based historian-journalist, who was working on a biography of Grant, related his discovery of "a highly valuable mss. by Cadwallader" that contained "much new stuff—very vivid and anecdotal—with very full statement in detail of Grant's drinking."[178]

Although Lewis failed to identify the location of the valuable document, Thomas inferred that it might be in the Illinois State Historical Library in Springfield. "Early the next morning," Thomas recalled, "I went to the library. And sure enough. There it was." It had been reposing undisturbed, save by Lewis, for two decades. Thomas "dug it out of a filing cabinet and began to read it" and, as he recalled, "soon became absorbed. It was indeed a find! I went back to the library day after day until I finished it." But "there was dross as well as color and originality in the nine hundred or so handwritten pages." It was obvious to Thomas that "the manuscript needed the sort of editing that would tighten it up and keep it essentially an eye-witness account."[179]

In the fall of 1952, Thomas began paring down the voluminous manuscript, weeding out repetitive passages and stretches of canned history and providing annotations and an introduction. He enlisted the help of a noted Civil War expert, E. B. Long, who offered many useful suggestions.[180] In 1954 he submitted the final draft to Knopf, which published *Three Years with Grant: As Recalled by War Correspondent Sylvanus Cadwallader* to critical acclaim from the likes of Bruce Catton, who called it "the most valuable bit of source material on the Civil War to attain book publication in a long while."[181]

Not all reviews were so positive. Thomas had anticipated an angry response from some readers, especially U. S. Grant III, who, he feared, "may not like us for revealing his grandfather's drinking habits. But I don't suppose he would have any grounds for a law suit, and the matter is scarcely a secret any longer."[182] As predicted, Grant's grandson did object to what he deemed Cadwallader's "fantastically untrue and scurrilous" account of his ancestor's bibulous habits.[183]

What Thomas had not anticipated was a contemptuous assault from Kenneth P. Williams, a mathematician at Indiana University who was writing a multi-volume study entitled *Lincoln Finds a General.* "I always considered him a friend and have often helped him when he was working in Springfield," Thomas told Knopf.[184] Williams had praised Thomas's Lincoln biography as "well-balanced and judicious," "readable and stimulating," "authoritative," and offering "not only an understanding portrayal of Lincoln, but an equally comprehensive account of great and complex events."[185] By addressing primarily Grant's alleged inebriation during the Vicksburg campaign, however, Williams suggested that Thomas had neglected to read any of Cadwallader's wartime dispatches, had been hoodwinked by an old man with an inventive memory, had failed to compare Cadwallader with other contemporary observers, and in general had demonstrated incompetence as an editor.[186]

Thomas, who thought Williams's letter "vicious," replied that although some of the criticisms were "valid," there were several weaknesses in its argument.[187] In 1996 Brooks D. Simpson corroborated Thomas's analysis, noting that "Williams's denunciation of Cadwallader's entire manuscript erred on the side of excess, for subsequent research has negated a good number of his criticisms."[188]

Thomas eventually chose as the subject for his next project a biography of Edwin M. Stanton, Lincoln's secretary of war. Thomas told Miers that his wife, Sally, "a level-headed little cuss in many matters . . . thinks that . . . my real forte is personalities. She favors another biography. . . . Stanton seems like rather a logical follow-up after Lincoln—he is surely challenging."[189] Sandburg agreed about the challenge a Stanton biographer would face: "He was stormy, dramatic, with a genius allied to insanity and you will have a merry ride with his snarls, sneers, struts, assumptions—he could be so vehemently loyal and subtly treacherous. Of civilians in the cast of the play he is perhaps, next to Lincoln, the most titanic."[190] Miers feared the project was a mistake. To a mutual friend he gloomily predicted in 1953: "A book on Stanton might sell five thousand—Ben hasn't learned yet that the subject can be bigger than the author. Apparently, in this case, neither has Alfred [Knopf]. About five years from now someone will have to pick up the pieces with Ben."[191] Much later Miers said that Thomas "would never completely understand" someone like Stanton, "a mysterious mixture of quirk and human contradiction: a man who for months carried around the coffin containing his daughter's corpse. 'How could he do that?' Ben asked. 'How do you probe that kind of mind?'" Miers hoped in vain that Thomas "would chuck the whole business that so plainly dulled the edge of his creative drive."[192]

Aware that Fletcher Pratt had also undertaken a Stanton biography, Thomas at first worried that Pratt might scoop him.[193] When he saw Pratt's book in galley proofs, however, Thomas was relieved. As he told Knopf, "His treatment of Stanton's early life is extremely skimpy and during the war his book is four-fifths a rehash of military events and one fifth Stanton. Stanton the man doesn't come out at all. . . . Pratt simply hasn't done the necessary digging."[194]

Thomas called the Stanton project "a mighty big and a mighty puzzling job."[195] Particularly bothersome were Stanton's "inconsistencies of character, which will not be easy to untangle."[196] Beginning work early in 1953, Thomas proceeded with customary industriousness. By June he reported that his subject "is surely a man of mystery and the book will be a hard job."[197] Making the task somewhat less difficult were the notes on Stanton assembled by a Princeton University scholar, Edward S. Corwin, who rented them to Thomas for $500.[198] Also helping speed the work was Robert V. Bruce, Thomas's research assistant. In the summer of 1953, Bruce, who had recently completed his dissertation, "Lincoln and the Tools of War," met Thomas when they both were conducting research in Washington.[199] Bruce had discovered many previously unknown Lincoln letters and other documents, which he called to the attention of the editor of Lincoln's collected works, Roy P. Basler, who invited him to lunch. Joining them was Thomas, who was on the lookout for a research assistant and offered Bruce $300 per month plus expenses for a stint of five or six months. Unemployed and having difficulty finding a teaching job, Bruce accepted the proposal and searched manuscript collections in Boston and Washington for Stanton materials.[200] "You have done a great job," Thomas told him, "one that will save me no end of time, and that has unearthed much valuable stuff. I can't tell you how much I appreciate your work."[201]

With Thomas's help, Bruce obtained a publisher for his dissertation, for which Thomas provided a generous introduction: "I can vouch at first hand for Bruce's expertness in tracking down elusive facts," he wrote, "because for some six months . . . he worked for me in Washington as a research assistant. . . . I am pleased and proud to help give it [the book] a healthy start in life. With something of the same sense of satisfaction an obstetrician must feel in ushering a sound, sturdy, appealing creation of another sort into the world, I slap it heartily on the backside of the cover and commend it to your careful attention."[202]

In the fall of 1953, Thomas reported to his publisher that the "Stanton project gets more interesting all the time and you can be sure that the story of the Civil War from the War Department point of view has never been adequately told. I am digging up a lot of new backstage stuff."[203] By November 1954, Thomas had taken Stanton up to his entry into President Buchanan's cabinet. "There I find confusion worse confounded with all sorts of contradictory statements about what he did or did not do," he told Knopf. "It is probably the roughest going that I shall encounter in the book."[204] Thirteen months later, Thomas had gotten his subject "just about through 1863."[205] In September 1956 he reported that the "biography is coming along, though slowly, and I estimate that I have about one more year's work to do."[206] What slowed him somewhat was his work on television scripts.[207]

When Robert V. Bruce visited Springfield in July 1956, Thomas showed him what he had so far written of the Stanton biography. As Bruce recalled, "I sensed some apprehension on his part, not unusual in an author at that stage." After six hours of reading, Bruce was disappointed. "It didn't come up to his *Lincoln* in empathy and literary distinction. Not trusting to my acting ability, I didn't feign high delight, though I didn't express dissatisfaction either. The best I could do was to praise it as likely to be definitive. He probably took that as faint praise."[208]

Four months later, when Thomas was diagnosed with throat cancer, he abruptly killed himself. A friend suffering with the same form of cancer had recently died after a long and painful illness that caused his family hardships that Thomas wanted to spare his wife and children.[209] Harold Hyman was chosen to complete the Stanton biography, which Knopf published in 1962. In his suicide note, Thomas said of the manuscript: "There may be some talk of having someone finish this. I don't object but I'm not proud of this job. So often I couldn't be sure about Stanton."[210] He had evidently finished thirteen chapters.[211] The volume, as Bruce noted, lacked literary and historical distinction.

Abraham Lincoln: A Biography is, however, a masterful work for which Benjamin Thomas is widely noted and will be long remembered. Soon after it appeared, he explained what he had tried to accomplish:

> First of all, I hope I have produced a living Lincoln, not a statue, a Lincoln that people can believe in. I think we make a mistake in idolizing Lincoln—he was human, just as we are human; to maintain our kinship with him, we must keep him real. I think he would want it that way. To me Lincoln was a man of amazing growth through self-effort, and I have tried to depict that growth. Take for example, his power with words. It was no accident. As a young lawyer Lincoln tried to write poetry; he liked to read poetry, too. One of his favorite poems was "Mortality" by William Knox, a Scotsman. Lincoln once sent a copy of that poem to a fellow lawyer, and when this friend asked if Lincoln had written it himself, Lincoln replied that he hadn't, but that he would give all that he owned and go into debt to be able to write such a poem. So here we have a young lawyer, yearning and striving for the power to coax beauty from language, teaching himself to write well and to speak well. Consequently, it was not by mere chance or sudden inspiration that later, under deep

emotion, he could utter imperishable words. The roots of the Gettysburg Address and the Second Inaugural were in the prairie soil of Illinois.

   Another thing that I tried to do was to relate Lincoln to his own and to our own times, and there is a close relationship between the two. Because democracy was under challenge in Lincoln's day, just as it is in ours. And since he probably understood the true meaning of democracy better than any of our other leaders, his life holds great significance for us and the world today. In fact, his vision was so far reaching that I sometimes think we are just now catching up with him, just now beginning to appreciate the lessons his life holds for us.[212]

Thomas provided few annotations and source citations for these essays. Where I could identify persons and events as well as the sources of quotations, I have done so in notes. The handful of notes written by Thomas are identified as such at the beginning of the citation.

Notes

   1. Benjamin P. Thomas, *Abraham Lincoln: A Biography* (New York: Alfred A. Knopf, 1952).

   2. John A. Garraty, dedication of *The Nature of Biography* (New York: Alfred A. Knopf, 1957).

   3. Jonathan Yardley, "The Enigma behind the Icon," *Washington Post Book World*, 1 Oct. 1995, 3. The other full-length, single-volume biographies published since 1952 are marred by plagiarism and superficiality: Stephen B. Oates, *With Malice toward None: The Life of Abraham Lincoln* (New York: Harper and Row, 1977) and Reinhard Luthin, *The Real Abraham Lincoln: A Complete One-Volume History of His Life and Times* (Englewood Cliffs: Prentice-Hall, 1960).

   4. Allen C. Guelzo, *Abraham Lincoln: Redeemer President* (Grand Rapids: Eerdmans, 1999), 469.

   5. James Hurt, "Benjamin Thomas: A Portrait for Posterity," talk given in Springfield, 5 March 1992, and included in *Illinois Libraries* 74 (1992): 307–8.

   6. Stephen W. Sears, introduction to a reprint of Benjamin P. Thomas, *Abraham Lincoln* (New York: Book of the Month Club, 1986), xxiv–xxv.

   7. Mark E. Neely, Jr., *The Abraham Lincoln Encyclopedia* (New York: McGraw Hill, 1982), 309.

   8. David M. Potter, *Lincoln and His Party in the Secession Crisis* (New Haven: Yale University Press, 1962), xxxiii.

   9. Paul M. Angle to Alfred A. Knopf, Jr., (Chicago), 25 April 1952, copy, and Angle to Thomas, ca. 25 April 1952, quoted in Thomas to Alfred Knopf, Jr., Springfield, 30 April 1952, copy, Paul M. Angle Papers, Chicago Historical Society.

   10. Allan Nevins to Benjamin P. Thomas, New York, 10 Dec. 1951, Benjamin P. Thomas Papers, Illinois State Historical Library, Springfield.

   11. Allan Nevins to Alfred Knopf, Jr., 5 May 1952, copy, Benjamin P. Thomas Papers, Illinois State Historical Library, Springfield.

12. Allan Nevins to Benjamin P. Thomas, New York, 19 Jan. 1952, Benjamin P. Thomas Papers, Illinois State Historical Library, Springfield; cf. Allan Nevins, "Captain from Illinois," *Saturday Review of Literature*, 8 Nov. 1952, 15–16.

13. Radio broadcast chaired by Luther Evans at the Library of Congress, with Benjamin P. Thomas, Roy P. Basler, and David C. Mearns, 29 Dec. 1952, copy of transcript, Benjamin P. Thomas Papers, Illinois State Historical Library, Springfield.

14. John Y. Simon, *House Divided: Lincoln and His Father* pamphlet (Fort Wayne: Louis A. Warren Lincoln Library and Museum, 1987); Rodney O. Davis, *Abraham Lincoln: Son and Father* pamphlet (Galesburg: Knox College, 1997); Michael Burlingame, *The Inner World of Abraham Lincoln* (Urbana: University of Illinois Press, 1994), 20–56, 268–355.

15. Thomas, *Lincoln*, 291, 351, 357, 410.

16. Both men did, however, think themselves homely. Sarah H. Thomas, "Random Thoughts about My Father, Benjamin P. Thomas," typescript in possession of the author, 1.

17. Earl Schenck Miers, *The Trouble Bush* (New York: Rand McNally, 1966), 232.

18. V. Y. Dallmann, "Assorted Smiles," *Illinois State Register*, 10 Nov. 1952, 6.

19. Paul M. Angle, "Benjamin Platt Thomas, 1902–1956," *Journal of the Illinois State Historical Society* 50 (1957): 23.

20. George W. Bunn, Jr., "Benjamin P. Thomas," *Lincoln Library Bulletin*, Jan. 1957, 1. Margaret Flint, assistant state historian of Illinois, called this piece "the finest tribute that appeared after his death, even surpassing Sandburg." Flint to John J. Duff, New York, 2 May 1958, Duff Papers, Illinois State Historical Library, Springfield.

21. Abraham Lincoln to Joshua Speed, Springfield, 24 Aug. 1855, in *The Collected Works of Abraham Lincoln*, ed. Roy P. Basler, Marion Dolores Pratt and Lloyd A. Dunlap, asst. eds., 8 vols. plus index (New Brunswick: Rutgers University Press, 1953–55), 2:323.

22. "Mrs. Benjamin P. Thomas Memoir," 6, transcript of an interview conducted by Virginia Bomke, 30 Sept. 1972, for the Oral History Office of Sangamon State University, Springfield, Benjamin P. Thomas Papers, Illinois State Historical Library, Springfield.

23. Angle, "Benjamin Platt Thomas," 18–19.

24. Author interview with Sarah Thomas, Springfield, 13 April 1997.

25. Speech at Peoria, 16 Oct. 1854, in *Collected Works*, ed. Basler et al., 2:255; Benjamin P. Thomas, "The Education of Women in a Troubled World," undated typescript, Benjamin P. Thomas Papers, Illinois State Historical Library, Springfield.

26. Thomas's statement prepared for Edward R. Murrow's "This I Believe" series presented by CBS and included in *Illinois State Journal*, 19 Jan. 1953.

27. Carl Sandburg, eulogy at Thomas's funeral, included in *Illinois State Journal*, 2 Dec. 1956.

28. Angle, "Benjamin Platt Thomas," 18.

29. Richard Graebel, eulogy for Thomas, copy, Benjamin P. Thomas Papers, Illinois State Historical Library, Springfield.

30. As a young man starting out in the world, "Lincoln *had nothing only plenty of friends,*" according to an associate. George Close, interview with James Q.

Howard [May 1860], emphasis in the original, Lincoln Papers, Library of Congress. Cf. William H. Herndon to Jesse W. Weik, Springfield, 15 Jan. 1886, in *The Hidden Lincoln: From the Papers and Letters of William H. Herndon*, ed. Emanuel Hertz (New York: Viking, 1938), 134.

31. Bunn, "Benjamin P. Thomas," 1.

32. Angle, "Benjamin Platt Thomas," 23.

33. Ibid., 12.

34. Lincoln's law partner William Henry Herndon called him "inordinately ambitious," "a man totally swallowed up in his ambitions," and "the most ambitious man in the world." Herndon remarked on "his general greed for office" and "his burning and his consuming ambition," declared that his "ambition was never satisfied" and "was a consuming fire which smothered his finer feelings," and stated flatly that any "man who thinks Lincoln calmly sat down and gathered his robes about him, waiting for the people to call him, has a very erroneous knowledge of Lincoln. He was always calculating, and always planning ahead. His ambition was a little engine that knew no rest." William H. Herndon, "Analysis of the Character of Abraham Lincoln" [lecture of 26 Dec. 1865], *Abraham Lincoln Quarterly* 1 (Dec. 1941): 410–11; Herndon, "Lincoln's Ambition," essay in Herndon-Weik Papers, Library of Congress; Herndon to Unidentified Member of the New York Clergy, Springfield, 24 Nov. 1882, *New York Tribune*, 21 Jan. 1883; Paul M. Angle, ed., *Herndon's Life of Lincoln: The History and Personal Recollections of Abraham Lincoln as Originally Written by William H. Herndon and Jesse W. Weik* (Cleveland: World, 1942), 304.

35. Miers, *Trouble Bush*, 202, 199–200.

36. Angle, "Benjamin Platt Thomas," 13.

37. Richard Graebel Diary, 30 Nov. 1956, Richard Graebel Papers, Illinois State Historical Library, Springfield. Sally Thomas observed that he "really felt that most people in Springfield were more interested in making money than in historical things." "Mrs. Benjamin P. Thomas Memoir," 2.

38. Benjamin P. Thomas to Robert L. Kincaid, Springfield, 11 April 1949, Lincoln Museum, Lincoln Memorial University, Harrogate, Tenn.

39. Benjamin P. Thomas to Marion Pratt, Springfield, 28 Sept. 1956, copy, Benjamin P. Thomas Papers, Illinois State Historical Library, Springfield.

40. According to Herndon, Lincoln was unequaled as a storyteller and mimic. "His power of mimicry . . . and his manner of recital, were in many respects unique. . . . His countenance and all his features seemed to take part in the performance. As he neared the pith or point of the joke or story every vestige of seriousness disappeared from his face. His little gray eyes sparkled; a smile seemed to gather up, curtain like, the corners of his mouth; his frame quivered with suppressed excitement; and when the point—or 'nub' of the story, as he called it—came, no one's laugh was heartier than his." Angle, ed., *Herndon's Lincoln*, 249–50.

41. Angle, "Benjamin Platt Thomas," 19–20.

42. Thomas, "Random Thoughts about My Father," 2.

43. Angle, "Benjamin Platt Thomas," 21.

44. Gabor S. Boritt, "The President at Play," *Civil War Times Illustrated* 34 (Dec. 1995): 14–18, 122–23.

45. Thomas, "Random Thoughts about My Father," 1–2.

46. Sarah Thomas to Author, undated letter ca. 1996.

47. Angle, "Benjamin Platt Thomas," 21–22.

48. Franz Mueller, "Lincoln and Colfax," enclosed in Mueller to Ida Tarbell, Spokane, 13 Feb. 1896, Ida M. Tarbell Papers, Allegheny College, Meadville, Pa.

49. In 1864 Hay told a friend that he and the president attended a performance at Ford's, where they "occupied [a] private box & . . . carried on a hefty flirtation with the Monk Girls in the flies." John Hay to John G. Nicolay, Washington, 20 June 1864, in *At Lincoln's Side: John Hay's Civil War Correspondence and Selected Writings*, ed. Michael Burlingame (Carbondale: Southern Illinois University Press, 2000), 86.

50. Angle, "Benjamin Platt Thomas," 23.

51. See "The Art of Biography," chapter 16 in this volume.

52. Benjamin P. Thomas, autobiographical sketch [Oct. 1952], Benjamin P. Thomas Papers, Illinois State Historical Library, Springfield; author interview with Sarah Thomas. For a thoughtful overview of Thomas's life, see John Hoffmann, "Benjamin P. Thomas," *Journal of the Abraham Lincoln Association* 19 (Summer 1998): 15–54.

53. Benjamin P. Thomas, autobiographical sketch.

54. *Historico* [newsletter of the Sangamon County Historical Society] (Jan. 1985): 2.

55. Benjamin P. Thomas, autobiographical sketch.

56. Ibid.

57. Benjamin P. Thomas, *Russo-American Relations, 1815–1867*, Johns Hopkins University Studies in Historical and Political Science, series 48, no. 2 (Baltimore: Johns Hopkins University Press, 1930).

58. Benjamin P. Thomas, autobiographical sketch.

59. Angle himself had read but little about Lincoln before accepting the post of secretary of the Lincoln Association. Paul M. Angle, *On a Variety of Subjects* (Chicago: Chicago Historical Society, 1974), 70.

60. Benjamin P. Thomas, autobiographical sketch.

61. Benjamin P. Thomas, "Old New Salem," *Bulletin of the Abraham Lincoln Association* 29 (Dec. 1932): 3–9.

62. Quoted in Angle, "Benjamin Platt Thomas," 9–10.

63. Benjamin P. Thomas, *Lincoln's New Salem* (New York: Alfred A. Knopf, 1954), vii.

64. Herschel Brickell, "Books on Our Table," *New York Evening Post*, 27 Aug. 1934, 9.

65. John Clair Minot, quoted on the dustjacket of the edition of *Lincoln's New Salem* published in 1954 by Alfred A. Knopf.

66. Ida M. Tarbell to Benjamin P. Thomas, n.p., n.d., quoted on the dustjacket of the edition of *Lincoln's New Salem* published in 1954 by Alfred A. Knopf.

67. Paul M. Angle, *A Shelf of Lincoln Books* (New Brunswick: Rutgers University Press, 1946), 73–74; Thomas, *Lincoln's New Salem*, 136.

68. Ezra M. Prince to Truman H. Bartlett, Bloomington, Ill., 2 Oct. 1907, Bartlett Papers, Boston University.

69. Frederick Jackson Turner, *The Frontier in American History* (New York: Holt, 1920).

70. Richard S. Taylor and Mark L. Johnson, "Reinventing Lincoln's New Salem:

The Reconstruction of a Pioneer Village," 14–15, draft of an unpublished essay dated 10 April 1994, copy provided by Richard S. Taylor.

71. Benjamin P. Thomas, *Portrait for Posterity: Lincoln and His Biographers* (New Brunswick: Rutgers University Press, 1947), 273–74.

72. Benjamin P. Thomas, autobiographical sketch.

73. Angle, "Benjamin Platt Thomas," 22–23.

74. Benjamin P. Thomas, autobiographical sketch.

75. Angle, "Benjamin Platt Thomas," 11.

76. Angle, *A Shelf of Lincoln Books*, 72.

77. Quoted in Angle, "Benjamin Platt Thomas," 11.

78. James G. Randall to Allan Nevins [Urbana, Ill.], 28 Feb. 1936, copy, Randall Papers, Library of Congress.

79. Benjamin P. Thomas, "Lincoln and the Courts, 1854–1861," *Abraham Lincoln Association Papers, Delivered before the Members of the Abraham Lincoln Association at Springfield, Illinois, on February 13, 1933* (Springfield: Abraham Lincoln Association, 1934), 47–103.

80. Benjamin P. Thomas, "Executive Secretary's Report," *Bulletin of the Abraham Lincoln Association* 42 (March 1936): 8.

81. Angle, "Benjamin Platt Thomas," 18.

82. Angle, *On a Variety of Subjects*, 70–84.

83. Benjamin P. Thomas, autobiographical sketch. Earl Schenck Miers (*Trouble Bush*, 199) said that to "appreciate Ben one had to understand Springfield, a funny town in many ways. Despite its flood of tourists and legislators, Springfield remained provincial and back-bitish, if not a Peyton Place on the prairies at least a Main Street. Springfield had its circle of prosperous business executives who took a heady pleasure in the money they had made and Ben did not quite fit their pattern."

84. Benjamin P. Thomas, autobiographical sketch.

85. A. J. Liebling, "Abe Lincoln in Springfield," in *A Springfield Reader*, ed. James Krohe, Jr. (Springfield: Sangamon County Historical Society, 1976), 44.

86. *The Senator Speaks* [published by Springfield High School], 24 Feb. 1956.

87. Benjamin P. Thomas, autobiographical sketch.

88. Liebling, "Abe Lincoln in Springfield," 44.

89. Benjamin P. Thomas to Harry E. Pratt, Springfield, 5 Dec. 1949, Harry E. Pratt Papers, University of Illinois at Urbana-Champaign.

90. Benjamin P. Thomas to William H. Townsend, Springfield, 18 Nov. 1946, William H. Townsend Papers, University of Kentucky, Lexington.

91. Benjamin P. Thomas, autobiographical sketch.

92. Ibid.

93. Thomas to Pratt, Springfield, 5 Dec. 1949.

94. One exception was Henry Steele Commager, who complained that Thomas "ignores wholly the innumerable monographs, the vast and laborious documentary publication, [and] the swarm of biographies of contemporaries." Commager, "Lincoln in Myth and History," *New York Herald Tribune Book Review*, 7 Dec. 1947, 44.

95. Arthur M. Schlesinger, Jr., "A. Lincoln and His Biographers," *New York Times Book Review*, 21 Sept. 1947, 3.

96. Allan Nevins, "The Lincoln Image," *Saturday Review of Literature*, 25 Oct. 1947, 14, 39.

97. Carl Sandburg to Benjamin P. Thomas, n.p., 24 June 1953, copy, Carl Sandburg Papers, University of Illinois at Urbana-Champaign.

98. Benjamin P. Thomas to Paul M. Angle, Springfield, 22 Aug. 1947, Paul M. Angle Papers, Chicago Historical Society.

99. Angle, "Benjamin Platt Thomas," 14.

100. Ernest Cady, "Reader's Note Book," *Columbus Dispatch*, 5 Oct. 1947, A4; Jay Monaghan, "The Story behind the Lincoln Books," *Chicago Sun Book Week*, 21 Sept. 1947, 3; David V. Flets, *Decatur* (Ill.) *Herald*, 23 Sept. 1947; Willard Hallam Bonner, "Sixty-five Biographers of Lincoln Undergo Scrutiny," *Buffalo Evening News Magazine*, 20 Sept. 1947, 5.

101. Kelsey Guilfoil, "A Keen Appraisal of Lincoln's Biographers," *Chicago Tribune*, 21 Sept. 1947, pt. 4, 3.

102. Roy P. Basler, "Scholarly Work on Lincoln," *Nashville Banner*, 24 Sept. 1947, 16.

103. Benjamin P. Thomas, autobiographical sketch [1953], Benjamin P. Thomas Papers, Illinois State Historical Library, Springfield.

104. Benjamin P. Thomas to Paul M. Angle, Springfield, 19 Jan. 1948, Paul M. Angle Papers, Chicago Historical Society.

105. Benjamin P. Thomas to Paul M. Angle, Springfield, 16 July 1948, Paul M. Angle Papers, Chicago Historical Society.

106. Benjamin P. Thomas to Earl Schenck Miers, n.p., 22 July 1948, copy, Paul M. Angle Papers, Chicago Historical Society.

107. Earl Schenck Miers to Benjamin P. Thomas, n.p., 27 July 1947, copy, Paul M. Angle Papers, Chicago Historical Society.

108. Earl Schenck Miers to Paul M. Angle, New Brunswick, N.J., 27 July 1947, Paul M. Angle Papers, Chicago Historical Society.

109. Thomas to Angle, Springfield, 19 Jan. 1948.

110. Miers, *Trouble Bush*, 199. This appeal was made in 1947, Miers remembered.

111. Benjamin P. Thomas, autobiographical sketch.

112. Benjamin P. Thomas to Alan E. James, Springfield, 27 March 1948, Benjamin P. Thomas Papers, Illinois State Historical Library, Springfield.

113. Thomas to Miers, n.p., 22 July 1948.

114. Benjamin P. Thomas to Paul M. Angle, Springfield, 22 July 1948, Paul M. Angle Papers, Chicago Historical Society.

115. Benjamin P. Thomas to Carl Sandburg, Springfield, 27 Jan. 1949, Carl Sandburg Papers, University of Illinois at Urbana-Champaign.

116. Thomas to Angle, Springfield, 16 July 1948.

117. Benjamin P. Thomas, *Theodore Weld: Crusader for Freedom* (New Brunswick: Rutgers University Press, 1950), vi–vii. Thomas had some unflattering things to say (215, 63) about "[c]austic, vengeful Thaddeus Stevens" and William Lloyd Garrison ("Cloaked in a hidebound righteousness, Garrison was incapable of entertaining the thought that he might be unfair").

118. Thomas, *Theodore Weld*, vii, 238.

119. Robert H. Abzug, *Passionate Liberator: Theodore Dwight Weld and the Dilemma of Reform* (New York: Oxford University Press, 1980), 362.

120. Undated memo, filed 1950, Benjamin P. Thomas Papers, Illinois State Historical Library, Springfield.

121. Benjamin P. Thomas to Harry E. Pratt, Springfield, 17 Sept. 1950, Harry E. Pratt Papers, University of Illinois at Urbana-Champaign.

122. Paul M. Angle to Benjamin P. Thomas, Chicago, 3 Nov. 1950, Benjamin P. Thomas Papers, Illinois State Historical Library, Springfield.

123. Carl Sandburg to Benjamin P. Thomas, n.d., Benjamin P. Thomas Papers, Illinois State Historical Library, Springfield.

124. Marion Bonzi to Harry Pratt, Springfield, 6 Nov. 1949, Harry E. Pratt Papers, University of Illinois at Urbana-Champaign.

125. Louis Filler, review of Benjamin P. Thomas's *Theodore Weld*, in *American Historical Review* 56 (July 1951): 914.

126. Abzug, *Passionate Liberator*, 362.

127. Benjamin P. Thomas to Earl S. Miers, Springfield, 13 Sept. 1949, Alfred A. Knopf Archive, University of Texas at Austin. The book was entitled *Sangamo: A History of Fifty Years* (Chicago: privately printed, 1949). The first 103 pages of the 145-page volume were written by Robert C. Lanphier in 1936 and entitled "Forty Years of Sangamo." The rest of the book, by Thomas, was "Sangamo in Peace and War." The unsigned preface stated that Thomas had "free access to company records and has also profited from numerous conversations with those most intimately acquainted with company affairs" (vi).

128. Thomas to Miers, Springfield, 13 Sept. 1949.

129. "Mrs. Benjamin P. Thomas Memoir," 3; Benjamin P. Thomas to Earl S. Miers, 1, 7 Nov. 1949, Alfred A. Knopf Archive, University of Texas at Austin.

130. Benjamin P. Thomas, autobiographical sketch [1953].

131. Earl Schenck Miers to Paul M. Angle, New York, 24 Nov. 1949, Paul M. Angle Papers, Chicago Historical Society.

132. Benjamin P. Thomas to Carl Sandburg, Springfield, 27 Nov. 1949, Carl Sandburg Papers, University of Illinois at Urbana-Champaign.

133. Benjamin P. Thomas to Earl Schenck Miers, Springfield, 9 Dec. 1949, Alfred A. Knopf Archive, University of Texas at Austin; quoted in Thomas to Miers, Springfield, 20 Dec. 1949, also in Alfred A. Knopf Archive. In fact, Sandburg did publish a one-volume condensation of his multi-volume biography in 1954.

134. Thomas to Miers, Springfield, 20 Dec. 1949.

135. Earl Schenck Miers to Benjamin P. Thomas, New York, 11 Jan. 1950, Benjamin P. Thomas Papers, Illinois State Historical Library, Springfield.

136. Earl Schenck Miers to Benjamin P. Thomas, New York, 18 Jan. 1950, Benjamin P. Thomas Papers, Illinois State Historical Library, Springfield.

137. Miers, *Trouble Bush*, 231; Benjamin P. Thomas to Earl Schenck Miers, Springfield, 27 May 1951, Alfred A. Knopf Archive, University of Texas at Austin.

138. Benjamin P. Thomas, "Why I Wrote a New Lincoln Book," *McClurg's Bookseller*, undated clipping, Benjamin P. Thomas Papers, Illinois State Historical Library, Springfield.

139. Benjamin P. Thomas to Carl Sandburg, Springfield, 11 May 1950, Sandburg Papers, University of Illinois at Urbana-Champaign.

140. Benjamin P. Thomas to Earl Schenck Miers, Springfield, 18 March, 11 June, 27 June 1950, 7 May 1951, Alfred A. Knopf Archive, University of Texas at Austin.

141. Report by Harold Strauss dated 13 Sept. 1950, Alfred A. Knopf Archive, University of Texas at Austin.

142. Report dated 20 July 1950, Alfred A. Knopf Archive, University of Texas at Austin.

143. Earl Schenck Miers to Roy P. Basler, New York, 1 Aug. 1950, Roy P. Basler Papers, Library of Congress.

144. Miers's report is dated 22 May 1951, Alfred A. Knopf Archive, University of Texas at Austin; Earl Schenck Miers to Benjamin P. Thomas, New York, 24 May 1951, Benjamin P. Thomas Papers, Illinois State Historical Library, Springfield.

145. Thomas to Miers, Springfield, 27 May 1951.

146. Alfred A. Knopf to Benjamin P. Thomas, New York, 1 June 1951, Benjamin P. Thomas Papers, Illinois State Historical Library, Springfield.

147. Benjamin P. Thomas to Alfred A. Knopf, Springfield, 6 June 1951, Alfred A. Knopf Archive, University of Texas at Austin.

148. Benjamin P. Thomas to Paul M. Angle, Springfield, 10 June 1951, Paul M. Angle Papers, Chicago Historical Society.

149. Benjamin P. Thomas to Alfred A. Knopf, Springfield, 12 Sept. 1951, Alfred A. Knopf Archive, University of Texas at Austin.

150. Benjamin P. Thomas to Mr. Kalb, ca. Sept. 1952, draft, Benjamin P. Thomas Papers, Illinois State Historical Library, Springfield.

151. Benjamin P. Thomas to Earl Schenck Miers, Springfield, 27 March 1952, Earl Schenck Miers Papers, Rutgers University, New Brunswick, N.J.

152. Nevins to Thomas, New York, 10 Dec. 1951.

153. Benjamin P. Thomas to Allan Nevins, Springfield, 17 Dec. 1951, Allan Nevins Papers, Columbia University.

154. Benjamin P. Thomas to Earl Schenck Miers, Springfield, 6 Jan. 1952, Earl Schenck Miers Papers, Rutgers University, New Brunswick, N.J.

155. Earl Schenck Miers to David C. Mearns, New York, 24 May 1951, David C. Mearns Papers, Library of Congress.

156. Earl Schenck Miers to Benjamin P. Thomas, Stelton, N.J., 15 Sept. 1952, copy, Earl Schenck Miers Papers, Rutgers University, New Brunswick, N.J.

157. Bruce Catton, in *Cleveland News*, 3 Dec. 1952.

158. Sterling North, in *New York World-Telegram and Sun*, 10 Nov. 1952.

159. Orville Prescott, in *New York Times*, 11 Nov. 1952.

160. Harry E. Pratt, in *Journal of the Illinois State Historical Society* 45 (1952): 409. Pratt did detect a dozen minor errors. Pratt to Wayne C. Temple, n.p., 5 Aug. 1953, copy, Harry E. Pratt Papers, University of Illinois at Urbana-Champaign.

161. Paul Angle, in *Chicago Sunday Tribune Book Review*, 9 Nov. 1952, part 4, 3.

162. William B. Hesseltine, clipping in Benjamin P. Thomas Papers, Illinois State Historical Library, Springfield.

163. Dumas Malone in *History Book Club Review*, June 1953.

164. Carl Sandburg to Benjamin P. Thomas, Flat Rock, N.C., 30 March 1953, copy, Carl Sandburg Papers, University of Illinois at Urbana-Champaign.

165. C. H. Wilhelm to Paul M. Angle, New York, 12 Feb. 1953, Paul M. Angle Papers, Chicago Historical Society.

166. Benjamin P. Thomas to David C. Mearns, Springfield, 7 Dec. 1952, David C. Mearns Papers, Library of Congress.

167. Benjamin P. Thomas, autobiographical sketch [1953].

168. Bunn, "Benjamin P. Thomas," 1.

169. Thomas, "Random Thoughts about My Father," 4.

170. Donald Riddle, review of Benjamin P. Thomas's *Abraham Lincoln*, in *Mississippi Valley Historical Review* 39 (Dec. 1952): 564–65.

171. Author interview with Sarah Thomas.

172. Benjamin P. Thomas to Donald Riddle, Springfield, 15 Dec. 1952, draft, Benjamin P. Thomas Papers, Illinois State Historical Library, Springfield. Riddle eventually did publish a book making his dubious point about Lincoln's non-retirement between 1849 and 1854. Riddle, *Congressman Lincoln* (Urbana: University of Illinois Press, 1957).

173. Benjamin P. Thomas to Wendell H. Stephenson, Springfield, 16 Dec. 1952, draft, Benjamin P. Thomas Papers, Illinois State Historical Library, Springfield.

174. Benjamin P. Thomas to Alfred A. Knopf, Springfield, 22 Dec. 1952, Alfred A. Knopf Archive, University of Texas at Austin.

175. William B. Hesseltine, clipping in Benjamin P. Thomas Papers, Illinois State Historical Library, Springfield.

176. Harry Hansen, "Experts Overlook Obvious Need; Ben Thomas Fills Gap," *Chicago Tribune Magazine of Books*, 23 Nov. 1952, 13; Benjamin P. Thomas to Paul M. Angle, Springfield, 19 Nov. 1953, Paul M. Angle Papers, Chicago Historical Society. In September 1954, Thomas proposed to Knopf that he would interrupt his work on Stanton to write a biography of Adlai Stevenson. The publisher dissuaded him. Benjamin P. Thomas to Alfred A. Knopf [Springfield], 25 Sept. 1954, Alfred A. Knopf Archive, University of Texas at Austin; Knopf to Thomas, New York, 30 Sept. 1954, Benjamin P. Thomas Papers, Illinois State Historical Library, Springfield.

177. Adlai Stevenson to Benjamin P. Thomas, Chicago, 31 Oct. 1950, Springfield, 6, 22 Nov. 1950, 24 Dec. 1951, Benjamin P. Thomas Papers, Illinois State Historical Library, Springfield.

178. Lloyd Lewis to Angus Cameron, Chicago, 15 Dec. 1945, in *Letters from Lloyd Lewis: Showing Steps in the Research for His Biography of U. S. Grant*, ed. Robert Maynard Hutchins (Boston: Little, Brown, 1950), 15.

179. Benjamin P. Thomas, "A Wisconsin Newsman with Grant," *Wisconsin Magazine of History* 39 (Summer 1956): 239; Thomas, "A Book Is Born," blurb for the Civil War Book Club, Benjamin P. Thomas Papers, Illinois State Historical Library, Springfield.

180. Benjamin P. Thomas to Joe Fox, Springfield, 1 Nov. 1954, Alfred A. Knopf Archive, University of Texas at Austin.

181. Bruce Catton, clipping in Benjamin P. Thomas Papers, Illinois State Historical Library, Springfield.

182. Thomas to Fox, Springfield, 1 Nov. 1954.

183. U. S. Grant III, letter to the editor, Washington, n.d., in *American Heritage* 5 (Aug. 1956): 107; see also Grant, "Civil War: Fact and Fiction," *Civil War History* 2 (June 1956): 29–40. A less indignant but nonetheless hostile review by William B. Hesseltine criticized Thomas for "uncritically" accepting the story about Grant's drunkenness. "It makes a good yarn but it adds only one more spurious account to an intriguing but thoroughly insignificant controversy," Hesseltine observed. Unidentified clipping dated 25 Dec. 1955, Benjamin P. Thomas Papers, Illinois State Historical Library, Springfield.

184. Benjamin P. Thomas to [Alfred A. Knopf], n.p., n.d., draft, Benjamin P. Thomas Papers, Illinois State Historical Library, Springfield.

185. Kenneth P. Williams, as quoted in a press release issued as a postal card by Knopf, Oct. 1952, Benjamin P. Thomas Papers, Illinois State Historical Library, Springfield.

186. Kenneth P. Williams, letter to the editor, Bloomington, Ind., n.d., in *Amer-*

ican Heritage 5 (Aug. 1956): 107–9; see also Williams, *Lincoln Finds a General* (New York: Macmillan, 1956), 4:447–48.

187. Thomas to [Alfred A. Knopf], n.p., n.d.. Thomas, letter to the editor, Springfield, n.d., in *American Heritage* 5 (Aug. 1956): 109–11.

188. Brooks D. Simpson, introduction to the paperback reissue of *Three Years with Grant* (Lincoln: University of Nebraska Press, 1996), x.

189. Benjamin P. Thomas to Earl Schenck Miers, Springfield, 19 May 1952, Earl Schenck Miers Papers, Rutgers University, New Brunswick, N.J.

190. Sandburg to Thomas, n.p., 24 June 1953.

191. Earl Schenck Miers to Paul M. Angle, New York, 11 Feb. 1953, Paul M. Angle Papers, Chicago Historical Society.

192. Miers, *Trouble Bush*, 232–33.

193. Benjamin P. Thomas to Alfred A. Knopf, Springfield, 8 March 1953, Alfred A. Knopf Archive, University of Texas at Austin.

194. Benjamin P. Thomas to Alfred A. Knopf, Springfield, 13 June 1953, Alfred A. Knopf Archive, University of Texas at Austin.

195. Benjamin P. Thomas to David C. Mearns, Springfield, 25 Sept. 1955, David C. Mearns Papers, Library of Congress.

196. Benjamin P. Thomas to Alfred A. Knopf, Springfield, 19 March 1954, Alfred A. Knopf Archive, University of Texas at Austin.

197. Benjamin P. Thomas to Carl Sandburg, Springfield, 29 June 1953, Carl Sandburg Papers, University of Illinois at Urbana-Champaign.

198. Benjamin P. Thomas to Alfred A. Knopf, Springfield, 12 March 1953, Alfred A. Knopf Archive, University of Texas at Austin.

199. Benjamin P. Thomas to Alfred A. Knopf, Springfield, 29 Aug. 1953, Alfred A. Knopf Archive, University of Texas at Austin.

200. Robert V. Bruce to the author, [Madbury, N.H.], 16 Nov. 1996.

201. Benjamin P. Thomas to Robert V. Bruce, Springfield, 11 Jan. 1954, copy, lent by Robert V. Bruce. I am indebted to Robert Bruce for kindly providing me copies of his extensive correspondence with Thomas. On 5 April 1954, Thomas wrote a letter of recommendation in which he said, "For some six months, Dr. Bruce did research for me at the Library of Congress and in various manuscript collections elsewhere, and I am certain that I could not have found a more competent or more conscientious young man to do this sort of work. He proved to be fully reliable and unusually resourceful."

202. Robert V. Bruce, *Lincoln and the Tools of War* (Indianapolis: Bobbs Merrill, 1956), xv.

203. Benjamin P. Thomas to Alfred A. Knopf, Springfield, 2 Oct. 1953, Alfred A. Knopf Archive, University of Texas at Austin.

204. Benjamin P. Thomas to Alfred A. Knopf, Springfield, 9 Nov. 1954, Alfred A. Knopf Archive, University of Texas at Austin.

205. Benjamin P. Thomas to Alfred A. Knopf, Springfield, 15 Dec. 1955, Alfred A. Knopf Archive, University of Texas at Austin.

206. Benjamin P. Thomas to David C. Mearns, Springfield, 1 Sept. 1956, David C. Mearns Papers, Library of Congress.

207. Among other things, he worked on a script for a "Wide Wide World" show on Lincoln. Benjamin P. Thomas to Mrs. Earnest Ives, Springfield, 7 Feb. 1956, Mrs. Earnest Ives Papers, Illinois State Historical Library, Springfield.

208. Bruce to author, [Madbury, N.H.], 16 Nov. 1996.

209. Miers, *Trouble Bush*, 233–34. Some believed that "Ben's suicide was unnecessary; his cancer was minor." Richard Graebel diary, 1 Dec. 1956, Richard Graebel Papers, Illinois State Historical Library, Springfield.

210. Quoted in Earl Schenck Miers to Paul M. Angle, Edison, N.J., 10 Jan. 1957 [misdated 1956], Paul M. Angle Papers, Chicago Historical Society.

211. Clyde Walton, review of *Stanton, Springfield State Journal-Register*, clipping, Benjamin P. Thomas Papers, Illinois State Historical Library, Springfield.

212. Benjamin P. Thomas, autobiographical sketch [1953].

"LINCOLN'S HUMOR" AND OTHER ESSAYS

PART I

The Words of Lincoln

1 *Lincoln's Humor: An Analysis*

In attempting an analysis of Lincoln's humor one is immediately confronted with two difficulties. In the first place, many stories attributed to Lincoln were never told by him. A. K. McClure's *Lincoln Stories* is recognized as the most reliable collection, yet Isaac N. Arnold, an intimate friend of Lincoln's, wrote on the fly-leaf of his copy of this book that Lincoln probably told no more than half the stories with which McClure credited him.[1] To prove that Lincoln did or did not tell a particular story is often impossible, for in most cases one must rely upon hearsay evidence or reminiscences.

The second difficulty lies in the fact that the effectiveness of a joke depends in large measure upon the manner of its telling. We may not be at all amused by reading some of Lincoln's jokes or hearing them at secondhand; whereas we might have split our sides had we heard them as he told them. For Lincoln was a master of the story-telling art; and when told by a master, even a dull joke may be irresistible.

"His stories may be literally retold," wrote Henry C. Whitney, "every word, period and comma, but the real humor perished with Lincoln"; for "he provoked as much laughter by the grotesque expression of his homely face as by the abstract fun of his stories."[2]

His manner of recital, declared Judge David Davis, was "in many respects unique, if not remarkable.[3] His countenance and all his features seemed to take part in the performance. As he neared the pith or point

Abraham Lincoln Association Papers, 1935 (Springfield: Abraham Lincoln Association, 1936), 61–90.

of the joke or story every vestige of seriousness disappeared from his face. His little gray eyes sparkled; a smile seemed to gather up, curtain-like, the corners of his mouth; his frame quivered with suppressed excitement; and when the point—or 'nub' of the story, as he called it—came, no one's laugh was heartier than his."[4]

His humor had a general appeal. Not only the circuit lawyers and the Western villagers and farmers, but even urbane Easterners readily succumbed to it. In 1842, Ex-President [Martin] Van Buren, making a tour of the West, stopped one night at the village of Rochester, a few miles from Springfield. The Democratic politicians of Springfield went out "en masse" to meet and entertain him, taking Lincoln and a few other Whigs along. Van Buren related several amusing incidents of New York politics, while others told tales of early life on the frontier. But all yielded at last to Lincoln, who kept them in an uproar far into the night with a seemingly inexhaustible supply of yarns, until Van Buren insisted that "his sides were sore with laughing."[5]

In many cases the stories Lincoln told were not original, although he often embellished and improved them. He himself repeatedly disclaimed credit for authorship and described himself as merely a retail dealer. His proficiency lay rather in a retentive memory, an uncanny power of association and histrionic skill.[6] "He did not forget the good things that he heard," wrote Charles Sumner, "and was never without a familiar story to illustrate his meaning. When he spoke, the recent West seemed to vie with the ancient East in apologue and fable. His ideas moved, as the beasts entered Noah's ark, in pairs. At times his illustrations had a homely felicity, and with him they seemed to be not less important than the argument, which he always enforced with a certain intensity of manner and voice."[7]

Much of Lincoln's success as a storyteller was due to a talent for mimicry. "In the role of storyteller," said T. G. Onstot, son of the New Salem cooper, "I never knew his equal. His power of mimicry was very great. He could perfectly mimic a Dutchman, Irishman or negro."[8] F. B. Carpenter, who spent several months in the White House painting Lincoln's portrait, recalled a half-hour's entertainment given there by Stephen Massett, better known as "Jeems Pipes of Pipesville."[9] His repertoire included a series of comic imitations, one of which, a takeoff on a stammering man, was especially amusing to the President. After the "lecture" Lincoln, in congratulating "Pipes," ventured a suggestion. "I once knew a man who invariably 'whistled' with his stammering," he said—and gave an imitation. "Now if you could get in a touch of nature like that it would be irresistibly ludicrous." "Pipes" approved the idea, rehearsed the whistle until he had mastered it to Lincoln's satisfaction, and used it in subsequent performances.[10]

On one occasion—in the campaign of 1840—Lincoln used his skill as a mimic to discomfit a political antagonist. Jesse B. Thomas, in a speech at the courthouse in Springfield, made some sarcastic allusions to the "Long Nine" and particularly to Lincoln; and at the conclusion of his speech, Lincoln replied. "He felt the sting of Thomas' allusions," said [William H.] Herndon, "and for the first time on the stump or in public, resorted to mimicry for effect. In this . . . he was without a rival. He imitated Thomas in gesture and voice, at times caricaturing his walk and the very motions of his body. Thomas, like everybody else, had some peculiarities of expression and gesture, and these Lincoln succeeded in rendering more prominent than ever. The crowd yelled and cheered as he continued. Encouraged by the demonstration, the ludicrous features of the speaker's performance gave way to intense and scathing ridicule. Thomas, who was obliged to sit near by and endure the pain of the unique ordeal, was ordinarily sensitive; but the exhibition goaded him to desperation. He . . . actually gave way to tears. . . . The next day it was the talk of the town, and for years afterwards it was called the 'skinning' of Thomas. . . . I heard him [Lincoln] afterwards say that the recollection of his conduct that evening filled him with the deepest chagrin. He felt that he had gone too far and to rid his good nature of a load, hunted up Thomas and made ample apology."[11] Never again did he go to such lengths in a public address.[12]

In thinking through a proposition Lincoln's mental processes were deliberate and slow; yet he was ready with an instant witticism or retort under almost any circumstances. During the Hampton Roads conference, when he refused to enter into any agreement with persons in arms against the government, R. M. T. Hunter, one of the Confederate commissioners, tried to prove that such agreements were sanctioned by precedent by citing repeated instances of agreements between Charles I of England and those in arms against him.[13] But Lincoln waved the argument aside. "I do not profess to be posted in history," he said. "On all such matters I will turn you over to Seward. All I distinctly remember about the case of Charles I is that he lost his head."[14]

His quick wit and power of association were again evidenced when he was informed that the Cleveland Convention of dissatisfied Republicans had nominated John C. Fremont to oppose him in the election of 1864. His informant told him that instead of the thousands who were expected to attend the convention, only about four hundred had appeared. Struck by the number, Lincoln reached for a Bible on his desk, and after thumbing through a few pages, found and read these words: "And every one that was in distress, and every one that was in debt, and every one that was discontented, gathered themselves unto him; and he became a captain over them; and there were with him about four hundred men."[15]

In general, Lincoln's humor was the humor of his time. In Kentucky, Indiana and Illinois he became familiar with the gargantuan exaggeration and calm-faced falsehood—the "tall tales"—for which the West was famous, and which had their origin in the early settlers' imaginative accounts of frontier life. From this source he drew such far-fetched characterizations as that which he applied to [Stephen A.] Douglas' principle of popular sovereignty—"as thin as the homeopathic soup that was made by boiling the shadow of a pigeon that had starved to death."[16]

He appreciated the unconventional, earthy humor and homespun philosophy of the farmers and frontiersmen. He contended in later life that country people were the originators of most good stories; and it was to them and to the experiences of his own rural life that he went for many of his best yarns.

Shortly after Simon Cameron's retirement from his cabinet, for example, some gentlemen called on Lincoln, expressed gratification at the change, and suggested the advisability of further cabinet replacements. Lincoln heard them through; then slowly shook his head. Their suggestion, he said, brought to mind a certain Joe Wilson, who built a shed and raised a flock of chickens. The chickens were so bothered by skunks, however, that one night Joe went out with his shotgun to keep watch. He soon saw six or seven skunks running in and out of the hen-house. Loading his gun with a double charge, he blazed away, hoping to kill the whole "tribe" with one shot. But he hit only one, and the rest ran off across a field. Being asked why he didn't follow and kill the rest, he said: "Why, blast it, it was eleven weeks before I got over killin' one. If you want any more skirmishing in that line you can just do it yourselves."[17]

On another occasion, talking to a friend who was concerned about Salmon P. Chase's ambition for the presidency, and who thought Lincoln should ask Chase to resign, Lincoln observed that Chase's department was functioning very well, and as long as it continued to do so he would not worry about Chase's presidential aspirations. The situation reminded him of a time when he and his stepbrother were plowing a corn field in Indiana, he driving the horse and his stepbrother guiding the plow. The horse, naturally lazy and slow, suddenly rushed across the field so fast the boys could hardly keep pace with him. On reaching the end of the furrow, Lincoln discovered an enormous chin fly fastened to the horse and knocked it off. His stepbrother asked why he did that; whereupon

Lincoln explained that he didn't want the horse bitten. "But," protested his stepbrother, "that's all that made him go." "Now," said Lincoln, "if Mr. Chase has a presidential chin fly biting him, I'm not going to knock it off if it will only make his department go."[18]

Again, in the Hampton Roads conference, when Hunter raised the point that slaves, accustomed to working under overseers, would be unable to get along without them, while on the other hand, the whites, deprived of their slaves, would be unable to make a living, and both would starve, Lincoln was reminded of an old Illinois farmer who hit upon the expedient of planting potatoes and turning his hogs into the patch to root, thereby saving the labor of feeding the hogs and digging the potatoes. A neighbor, happening by, asked him what the hogs would do when the ground froze. The farmer had not thought of that; but after several moments of rumination he observed: "Well, it may come pretty hard on their snouts, but I guess it will be 'root, hog, or die!'"[19]

Lincoln's conversation was interlarded with rural analogies. "I will pitch into that like a dog at a root," he exclaimed when presented with a legal problem.[20] "Well, I have got that job husked out," he sighed with relief on completing a perplexing presidential task.[21] The sight of the diminutive Alexander H. Stephens divesting himself of voluminous wraps moved him to comment: "That is the largest shucking for so small a nubbin that I ever saw."[22] He referred to the Post Office Department's "cutting its own fodder."[23] In reviewing some court martial proceedings he came upon the case of a condemned deserter who had escaped to Mexico; and apparently relieved that the man had gotten away, he observed: "We will condemn him as they used to sell hogs in Indiana—as they run." His notion of the plan of exerting simultaneous pressure at all points of the Confederate line to prevent reinforcements being sent to the main point of attack, was that "those not skinning can hold a leg."[24] When he prevented a threatened disruption of his cabinet by securing the resignations of both Seward and Chase, he exulted: "Now I have a pumpkin in each end of my sack. Now I can ride!"[25] His exasperation at McClellan's underestimates of the number of his men in the face of repeated reinforcements vented itself in the observation that "sending men to his army is like shoveling fleas across a barnyard—not half of them get there."[26]

Lincoln's return to the "grass roots" for the gems of his wit is not without significance. For a sense of humor connotes an intimate acquaintance with human nature and life, a sense of proportion, and thus of disproportion, a realization of the petty conceits, the affectations, the foibles and weaknesses of men. It implies, in other words, the possession of the qualities of "horse sense" and discernment. And Lincoln's preference for the humor of the common people, evincing a recognition of the fact that they possessed these qualities, was an attestation of his confidence in the fundamental soundness of their judgment.

The keenness of Lincoln's own sense of humor was due in large degree to his intimate knowledge of men. Acquired in considerable measure at New Salem, where he lived on common terms with the villagers, this knowledge was broadened by his practice of the law and his experiences on the old Eighth Circuit. In no other occupation or setting would he have had a better opportunity to study life. On the circuit Lincoln not only studied human nature at first hand, but also developed to the full his story-telling art. Free from the cares and worries of home, in the company of congenial and appreciative companions, he gave full vent to his whimsicality. Although "Illinois was conspicuous for the number of its storytellers. . . ," as Joseph Gillespie said, "when Mr. Lincoln was about I never knew a man who would pretend to vie with him in entertaining a crowd."[27] Judge Davis sometimes stopped court to listen to his yarns. "O Lord, wasn't he funny," exclaimed Usher F. Linder, himself a noted humorist. "Any remark, any incident brought from him an appropriate tale."[28] "In our walks about the little towns where courts were held," said Whitney, "he saw ludicrous elements in everything, and could either narrate some story from his storehouse of jokes, or else he could improvise one. . . . In anything and everything Lincoln saw some ludicrous incident."[29] Judge Davis recalled having seen him many times, surrounded by a crowd, all deeply interested in the outcome of a story which, when finished, speedily found repetition in every grocery and lounging place within reach.[30]

Many stories which Lincoln told during his presidency originated on the circuit. In discussing the advisability of pardoning a condemned deserter, he recalled the time that Usher F. Linder saved a client who had stolen a hog by advising him to go get a drink, suggesting that the water was better in Tennessee.[31] Another time he told of John Moore, onetime State Treasurer of Illinois, who confessed that on one occasion in the early days he came to Bloomington on Saturday to get supplies, and having purchased them, filled up with liquor and started home.[32] He drove a cart drawn by two red steers. Passing through a grove, the cart struck a tree stump and the steers broke loose and ran away. Moore, who had fallen asleep, did not even waken, but slept on until morning. Opening his eyes finally, he looked about in bewilderment. "If my name is John Moore," he exclaimed, "I've lost a pair of steers; if it is not John Moore, I've found a cart."[33]

On another occasion, while discussing with Benjamin F. Butler and John W. Forney the treatment to be accorded the secession leaders, Lincoln recalled an old drunkard he had known in one of the county towns of Illinois, who had been induced several times to sign the temperance pledge.[34] At last he was told that if he broke his pledge once more he would be given up as a hopeless vagrant. Wandering into a saloon one day shortly afterward, he called for lemonade. Then drawing the bartender aside he asked: "Couldn't you put just a drop of the 'cratur' in it unbeknownst to me?" Lincoln remarked that if Jeff Davis and the other leaders could be permitted to get out of the country "unbeknownst to him," it would save him a "deal" of trouble.[35]

Lincoln's stories ran the whole gamut of humor from cheap puns to subtle aphorisms. He could perpetrate such atrocities as that recounted by Governor Saunders, whose mention of a river in Nebraska named Weeping Water provoked the President to ask: "I suppose the Indians out there call it Minneboohoo, don't they, since Laughing Water is Minnehaha in their language?"[36] Or, on the other hand, as Emerson observed, he could utter sage thoughts "so disguised as pleasantries that it is certain they had no reputation at first but as jests, and only later, by the very acceptance and adoption they find in the mouths of millions, turn out to be the wisdom of the hour."[37]

At times he liked sheer nonsense. On one of his frequent visits to the War Department Telegraph Office, he was informed that the Federal pickets still held a certain position and that no firing had been heard since sunset. Inquiring if there had been any before sunset, he was informed that there had not. "That reminds me," said he, "of the man who described a child, supposedly a freak of nature, as being black from the hips down. And upon being asked its color from the hips up, he said, 'Why, black, of course.'"[38]

McClure recalled that once when he left Lincoln's office at the conclusion of an interview during the period of Sherman's march to the sea, when for days the North had heard nothing of the position or fate of Sherman's army, the President called after him and asked: "McClure, wouldn't you like to hear something from Sherman?" Tense with eagerness, McClure replied that he surely would. "Well," said Lincoln, resuming his work, "I'll be hanged if I wouldn't myself."[39]

"Bulls" were a form of humor in which Lincoln frequently indulged.[40] Witness, for example, his unwillingness to apply the death penalty to soldiers who deserted because of cowardice for the reason that "it would frighten the poor devils to death to shoot them"; and his tale about the Irishman with the new boots who was afraid he would not be able to get them on until he had worn them a day or two to stretch them.[41]

Occasionally Lincoln's jokes had a touch of the practical. Colonel

"Dick" Taylor, one of Lincoln's earlier Democratic political opponents, could readily have vouched for this.[42] Colonel Dick was wont to denounce the aristocratic proclivities of the Whigs and to extol the Spartan simplicity of himself and his Democratic confreres. One day, when he was expatiating in his usual style, Lincoln slipped up to his side, caught hold of the bottom of his vest and suddenly pulled it open, revealing to the astonished crowd a ruffled shirtfront adorned with a massive gold watchchain, seals and other jewelry. The exponent of Democratic simplicity was dumbfounded, while the audience roared with laughter.[43]

James Shields did not see the practical humor in Lincoln's choice of weapons—"cavalry broadswords of the largest size"—when he challenged Lincoln to a duel; but we can picture, as Lincoln undoubtedly could, the ludicrous figure the diminutive Shields would have cut in a combat with such weapons with the long-armed railsplitter.[44] Nor did Clement L. Vallandigham, the Ohio Copperhead, appreciate the ironic practicality of Lincoln's order which released him from jail and deported him across the Southern lines.[45]

Mild-mannered to an unusual degree, Lincoln could nevertheless resort to scathing sarcasm and ridicule.[46] One of his earlier efforts in this line almost precipitated the duel above referred to. The cause of the challenge was an anonymous letter written by Lincoln and published in the *Sangamo Journal* of September 2, 1842. Purporting to come from Aunt 'Becca, in the "Lost Townships," and written in the colloquial idiom, it satirized James Shields, the state auditor, and other Democratic officials so effectively that it was only with difficulty that a meeting was averted. In the course of the letter Lincoln described Shields as follows: "I seed him when I was down in Springfield last winter. They had a sort of a gatherin' there one night among the grandees, they called a fair. All the gals about town was there, and all the handsome widows and married women, finickin' about trying to look like gals, tied tight in the middle, and puffed out at both ends, like bundles of fodder that hadn't been stacked yet, but wanted stackin' pretty bad. . . . I looked in at the window, and there was the same fellow Shields, floatin' about on the air, without heft or earthly substances, just like a lot of cat fur where cats had been fighting. He was paying his money to this one, and that one, and t'other one . . . his very features, in the ecstatic agony of his soul, spoke audibly and distinctly, 'Dear girls, it is distressing, but I cannot marry you all. Too well I know how much you suffer; but do, do remember, it is not my fault that I am so handsome and so interesting.'"[47]

Lincoln's speeches, prior to 1854, are replete with ridicule. In 1848, in a speech in Congress, he belittled the military record of Lewis Cass, the Democratic candidate for president, by comparing it with his own experiences in the Black Hawk War.[48] In 1852 he did the same sort of thing with reference to Franklin Pierce with a burlesque description of the old Illinois militia musters. "We remember one of the parades ourselves here," he said, "at the head of which, on horseback, figured our old friend Gordon Abrams, with a pine wood sword about nine feet long, and a pasteboard cocked hat, from front to rear about the length of an ox-yoke, and very much the same shape of one turned bottom upwards; and with spurs having rowels as large as the bottom of a teacup, and shanks a foot and a half long.[49] That was the last militia muster here. Among the rules and regulations, no man is to wear more than five pounds of codfish for epaulets, or more than thirty yards of bologna sausages for a sash; and no two men are to dress alike, and if any two should dress alike the one who dresses most alike is to be fined (I forget how much). Flags, they had too, with devices and mottoes, one of which latter was, 'We'll fight till we run, and we'll run till we die.'

"Now, in the language of Judge Douglas, 'I submit to you gentlemen,' whether there is not great cause to fear that on some occasion when Gen. [Winfield] Scott suspects no danger, suddenly Gen. Pierce will be discovered charging upon him, holding a huge roll of candy in one hand for a spyglass; with BUT labelled on some appropriate part of his person; with Abrams' long pine sword cutting the air at imaginary cannon balls, and calling out 'boys, there's a game of ball for you' and over all streaming the flag, with the motto, 'We'll fight till we faint, and I'll treat when it's over.'"[50]

Numerous other instances could be given. Indeed, prior to 1854 humor and ridicule were among Lincoln's chief reliances on the stump.

But 1854 marks a turning point. After that his speeches became intensely serious.[51] There were occasional flashes of humor, it is true, but the humor was merely incidental to the argument which it elucidated.

During his presidency Lincoln appreciated the humor that pointed out the shortcomings of the members of his cabinet, and often called their attention to comic newspaper comments on their personal idiosyncrasies and administrative acts. Sometimes he indulged in gentle thrusts at them himself. He asked a certain man if he was an Episcopalian, explaining that he thought he must be because he swore just like [Secretary of State William Henry] Seward, who was of that faith.[52] To the meticulous Stanton he sent an order to appoint a certain man colonel of a colored regiment, "regardless of whether he could tell the exact shade of Julius Caesar's hair."[53]

In fact, his sense of humor greatly facilitated his sustained relations with the testy [Secretary of War Edwin M.] Stanton and the pompous

[Secretary of the Treasury Salmon P.] Chase. For instance, when a delegation, which he had sent to Stanton with orders to grant their request, returned and reported that not only had Stanton refused to do so, but had actually called Lincoln a fool for sending such an order, Lincoln, with mock astonishment, inquired: "Did Stanton call me a fool?"—and, upon being reassured upon that point, remarked: "Well, I guess I had better go over and see Stanton about this. Stanton is usually right."[54] To have got along at all with such a cabinet would have been impossible without a sense of humor as a saving grace.

While Lincoln liked to tell a joke on others, he also had the rare faculty of being able to appreciate one on himself. He could both give and take. In fact, he made himself the butt of many of his own best jokes. He had no illusions about his personal appearance and joked about it so often that there is reason to believe that he deliberately tried to capitalize upon his homeliness. Speaking at a banquet held by Anti-Nebraska editors at Decatur, on February 22, 1856, he apologized for being present, explaining that not being an editor he felt out of place. He illustrated his feelings by telling of an extremely ugly man who, riding along a narrow road, was met by a woman. As she passed the woman looked at him intently and finally observed: "Well, you are the ugliest man I ever saw." "Perhaps so," admitted the unfortunate fellow, somewhat crestfallen, "but I can't help that, madam." "No, I suppose not," agreed the woman, "but you might stay at home."[55]

In a reply to Douglas at Springfield, on July 17, 1858, Lincoln referred to the politicians seeing in Douglas' "round, jolly, fruitful face, post-offices, land offices, marshalships and cabinet appointments, chargéships and foreign missions, bursting and sprouting out in wonderful exuberance, ready to be laid hold of by their greedy hands"; whereas in his own "poor, lean, lank face" nobody had ever seen "that any cabbages were sprouting out."[56]

Lincoln frequently told of the man who accosted him on a train, saying: "Excuse me, sir, but I have an article in my possession which rightfully belongs to you." "How is that?" asked Lincoln in amazement. Whereupon the stranger produced a jackknife and explained: "This knife was placed in my hands some years ago, with the injunction that I was to keep it until I found a man uglier than myself. Allow me now to say, sir, that I think you are fairly entitled to it."[57]

Lincoln also derived great pleasure from telling of an experience he had on his way from Springfield to Washington in 1849. He traveled as far as Indianapolis by stage, the only other passenger being a grizzled Kentuckian. In the course of the journey the Kentuckian offered Lincoln a drink, a smoke and a chew, each of which was in turn refused. As he left the stage the Kentuckian turned to Lincoln and remarked: "See here, stranger, you're a clever but strange companion. I may never see you again, and I don't want to offend you, but I want to say this: my experience has taught me that a man who has no vices has damned few virtues."[58]

Cognizant of his personal deficiencies, Lincoln was also aware of the vulnerable points of his administration. This is well illustrated by his reply to a request for a suggestion of a suitable motto to be engraved on the new greenback currency. "How would it do," he whimsically inquired, "to say silver and gold have I none, but such as I have give I thee?"[59]

The complacency of humor which manifests a willingness to laugh at one's own weaknesses and shortcomings indicates a total absence of false pride, a calm self-assurance untinctured by conceit.

There is too much evidence to the contrary to insist that Lincoln did not tell broad stories.[60] In many instances, however, his stories have been coarsened in the retelling and he has been accused of telling others which he never would have uttered. He was quite capable, however, of telling the story of the man in the theatre who placed his high hat on the adjoining seat, open side up, and becoming interested in the play, failed to note the approach of a fat dowager until she had plumped down upon it. Then gazing ruefully at the rim of his top-piece, he reproachfully observed: "Madam, I could have told you the hat wouldn't fit before you tried it on."[61] Nor is there reason to doubt the story of the cabinet member who, returning from New York, informed the President of the discouraging state of politics there. Pacing grimly back and forth across the room, Lincoln finally observed: "Well, it is the people's business,—the election is in their hands. If they turn their backs to the fire and get scorched in the rear, they'll find they have got to sit on the blister."

Leonard Swett declared that while Lincoln's stories were sometimes broad, he did not tell them for that reason. "When hunting for wit he had no ability to discriminate between the vulgar and refined substances from which he extracted it. It was the wit he was after, the pure jewel, and he would pick it up out of the mud or dirt just as readily as he would from a parlor table."[62]

Many explanations of why Lincoln indulged in humor have been offered. David Davis remembered how, on the circuit, "if the day was long and he was oppressed, the feeling was soon relieved by the narration of a story. The tavern loungers enjoyed it, and his melancholy, taking to itself wings, seemed to fly away."[63] And many others noted how he would suddenly emerge from the deepest dejection with a quick sally or a brilliant yarn.

But humor was more to Lincoln than a psychological reaction. It served many useful purposes.

For one thing it provided him with a means of getting on good terms with people. In Indiana his fun and wit lightened the toil in fields and woods and won him many friends at the social gatherings. When he came to New Salem, on election day in 1831, he established himself in the good graces of villagers by entertaining them with stories as they lounged about the polls. And many a visitor at the White House was put at his ease by the President's narration of an anecdote.

At times Lincoln found in humor a necessary safety-valve to his overburdened mind. In cabinet meetings he frequently read passages from his favorite humorists—Charles Farrar Browne, R. H. Newell and David Ross Locke, better known respectively as Artemus Ward, Orpheus C. Kerr (office-seeker) and Petroleum V. Nasby[64]—to ease his mind before tackling a difficult problem or deciding upon an important step.[65] When he read Browne's description of a "Highhanded Outrage at Utica" before opening a cabinet meeting he could not understand why the cabinet failed to appreciate the humor as he did. "Gentlemen," he is reported to have reproached them, "why don't you laugh? With the fearful strain that is upon me night and day, if I did not laugh occasionally I should die, and you need this medicine as much as I do."[66]

In the brief moments of leisure which his official duties permitted, Lincoln found his chief relaxation in reading these contemporary wits. Often they were content with the externals of humor—bad grammar, misspelling, buffoonery and impudence—and much of what they wrote has little appeal to readers of today; but to Lincoln it afforded great amusement; for his taste in humor, like the humor he purveyed—was simply that of his time. Moreover all three of these humorists were wholeheartedly loyal, and were doing all in their power to arouse public opinion to the support of the Union cause. So great was Lincoln's admiration of Locke that he invited him to the White House, and is reported to have told him that he would almost trade places with him for the ability to write as he could.[67] And when General [Montgomery C.] Meigs confessed that he was unfamiliar with Newell's *Orpheus C. Kerr Papers,* Lincoln opined that "anyone who has not read them is a heathen."[68]

Besides employing humor to ingratiate himself, to put people at ease, and to relieve his troubled mind, Lincoln often turned to it as a means of escaping from a difficult position or avoiding an embarrassing commitment. John Hay tells of a gathering at Seward's where a Captain Schultz showed very bad taste in alluding to Seward's defeat in the Chicago convention. "The President," said Hay, "told a good yarn."[69] Herndon recorded that Lincoln was most adroit in outwitting people who came to him to get information which he did not wish to divulge. In such cases Lincoln did most of the talking, "swinging around what he suspected was the vital point, but never nearing it, interlarding his answers with a seemingly endless supply of stories and jokes." The inquisitive visitor would leave in high good humor; but after walking a few blocks would realize that he had learned nothing whatsoever. "Blowing away the froth of Lincoln's humorous narratives," said Herndon, "he would find nothing left."[70]

Often the use of a story enabled him to soften a refusal or rebuke. General [John A.] Creswell once came to Lincoln to request the release of an old friend who had been captured and imprisoned.[71] "I know the man has acted like a fool," admitted Creswell, "but he is my friend, and a good fellow; let him out; give him to me, and I will be responsible that he will have nothing further to do with the rebels." Lincoln pondered the matter. The request brought to his mind a group of young people who went "Maying." In the course of their rambles they crossed a shallow stream in a flatboat, but on their return they discovered that the boat was gone. So each boy picked up a girl and carried her across, until the only ones remaining were a little short chap and a great "Gothicbuilt" old maid. "Now Creswell," complained Lincoln, "you are trying to leave me in the same predicament. You fellows are all getting your friends out of this scrape; and you will succeed in carrying off one after another, until nobody but Jeff Davis and myself will be left, and then I won't know what to do. How should I feel? How should I look, lugging him over?"[72]

"He can snake a sophism out of its hole better than all the trained logicians of all schools," wrote John Hay in admiration, during the third year of the war.[73] And this faculty, used in conjunction with his wit, enabled Lincoln to reduce an argument to absurdity with a jest directed at its flaw. When the supporters of an applicant for the position of commissioner of the Hawaiian Islands urged that their man was not only competent for the post but also needed it because the climate would benefit his health, Lincoln retorted: "Gentlemen, there are eight other applicants for that position and they are all sicker'n your man."[74] "What would you do in my position?" he asked a Southerner who complained of the hardships his policy was working upon the Southern loyalists. "Would you drop the war where it is? Or would you prosecute it in future with elder-stalk squirts charged with rose water?"[75]

But the most frequent use to which Lincoln put his wit was as an aid to clarity of meaning. His conversation was as heavily freighted with stories as were his letters with similes and metaphors. For as Herndon explained, "Mr. Lincoln was often perplexed to give expression to his ideas. . . . He was frequently at a loss for a word, and hence was compelled to resort to stories, maxims, and jokes to embody his idea."[76]

On the circuit an apt yarn frequently put across his point to the jury in a clearer manner than hours of argument could have done. And in his presidency he found his stories no less useful. "I have found in the course of a long experience," he explained to Chauncey M. Depew, "that common people—common people—take them as they run, are more easily influenced and informed through the medium of a story than in any other way."[77] Thus we see in this habit of expression another instance of his continual search for a point of meeting with the common mind. "His quaint wit," as *Punch* expressed it, "made home truth seem more true."

Yet while many of Lincoln's stories had a purpose, others were told for sheer fun. He often stopped work to enjoy fun, then, relaxed and refreshed, went back to work again. John H. Littlefield, a clerk in the Lincoln-Herndon office, testified that no matter how busy or how deeply engrossed in his work he might be, whenever anyone came in he would greet him with a pleasant or humorous remark, and before he left would inevitably tell a joke or anecdote.[78] Sometimes he told the same story to four or five different persons in the course of a day, and each time laughed as heartily as anyone. In the White House in the midst of a tense discussion he would frequently digress upon a story. "And much as his stories were enjoyed by his hearers," said McClure, "none enjoyed them more than Mr. Lincoln himself."[79]

But his was not merely an egotistical enjoyment. He loved to pass along the good things he picked up. His own pleasure was enhanced by the pleasure he gave others. Yet despite his good fellowship, Lincoln's innate reserve protected him from undue familiarity. He could unbend and still preserve a simple dignity.

Lincoln's humor, in its unrestraint, its unconventionality, its use of back-country vernacular, its willingness to see things as they were, its shrewd comments in homely, earthy phrase, its frequent contentment with externals, typified the American humor of his time. Two strains— pioneer exaggeration and Yankee laconicism—met in him. In his humor, as in his rise from obscurity to fame and in his simple, democratic faith and thought, he epitomized the American ideal.

Notes

1. Alexander K. McClure, *Lincoln's Yarns and Stories* (Chicago: John C. Winston, 1904). Far more trustworthy and scholarly is Paul M. Zall, ed., *Abe Lincoln*

Laughing: Humorous Anecdotes from Original Sources by and about Abraham Lincoln (Berkeley: University of California Press, 1982).

2. Henry C. Whitney, *Life on the Circuit with Lincoln*, ed. Paul M. Angle (Caldwell, Idaho: Caxton, 1940), 174.

3. In 1836, Maryland-born David Davis (1815–86) settled in Bloomington, Illinois. A close friend of Lincoln, he served as judge of the Eighth Circuit from 1848 to 1862, when Lincoln named him to the U.S. Supreme Court.

4. Paul M. Angle, ed., *Herndon's Life of Lincoln: The History and Personal Recollections of Abraham Lincoln as Originally Written by William H. Herndon and Jesse W. Weik* (Cleveland: World, 1942), 250. This reminiscence of Lincoln's story-telling is by Herndon, not Davis.

5. Angle, ed., *Herndon's Lincoln*, 208.

6. *Thomas's note:* Lincoln's skill as a raconteur may have been to some extent hereditary. "From his father came that knack of story-telling, which has made him so delightful among acquaintances, and so irresistible in his stump and forensic drolleries," wrote William Dean Howells in his campaign biography of Lincoln. And Lincoln, when he corrected a copy of this book for his friend Samuel C. Parks, "let the statement stand." *Editor's note:* W. D. Howells, *Life of Abraham Lincoln* (Springfield: Abraham Lincoln Association, 1938), 20. Samuel C. Parks of Springfield was a friend of Lincoln's. In 1863 he became an associate justice of the Idaho Supreme Court. His copy of Howells's biography, complete with Lincoln's penciled corrections, is reproduced in facsimile in this edition.

7. Charles Sumner, "Eulogy," in *A Memorial of Abraham Lincoln* (Boston: City Council, 1865), 134.

8. Thompson Gaines Onstot (b. 1829), author of *Pioneers of Menard and Mason Counties* (Forest City, Ill.: Onstot, 1902), was the son of Henry Onstot.

9. Francis Bicknell Carpenter (1830–1900) was in the White House from February through July 1864. Stephen C. Massett of California wrote *Drifting About; or, What James Pipes of Pipesville Saw and Did* (New York, 1863), and sent a copy to Lincoln. Abraham Lincoln to Stephen C. Massett, Washington, 4 Dec. 1863, in *The Collected Works of Abraham Lincoln*, ed. Roy P. Basler, Marion Dolores Pratt and Lloyd A. Dunlap, asst. eds., 8 vols. plus index (New Brunswick: Rutgers University Press, 1953–55), 7:34.

10. Francis B. Carpenter, *Six Months at the White House with Abraham Lincoln: The Story of a Picture* (New York: Hurd and Houghton, 1866), 160–61.

11. Angle, ed., *Herndon's Lincoln*, 159–60. Other accounts of this event can be found in reminiscences by David Davis quoted in Willard L. King, *Lincoln's Manager: David Davis* (Cambridge: Harvard University Press, 1960), 38; Alfred Taylor Bledsoe in the *Southern Review* (April 1873) quoted in *Lincoln among His Friends: A Sheaf of Intimate Memories*, ed. Rufus Rockwell Wilson (Caldwell, Idaho: Caxton, 1942), 467; Henry C. Whitney, *Lincoln the Citizen* (New York: Baker and Taylor, 1908), 144–45; *Illinois State Register*, 24 July 1840; and S. C. Parks to William H. Herndon, Lincoln, Ill., 25 March 1866, in *Herndon's Informants: Letters, Interviews, and Statements about Abraham Lincoln*, ed. Douglas L. Wilson and Rodney O. Davis (Urbana: University of Illinois Press, 1997), 238–39.

12. Lincoln continued to ridicule men on the stump after 1840. Michael Burlingame, *The Inner World of Abraham Lincoln* (Urbana: University of Illinois Press, 1994), 153–54.

13. Robert M. T. Hunter (1809–87) of Virginia had served as the Confederate secretary of state (1861–62).

14. Alexander H. Stephens, *A Constitutional View of the Late War between the States*, 2 vols. (Philadelphia: National Publishing, 1868–70), 2:613.

15. John G. Nicolay and John Hay, *Abraham Lincoln: A History*, 10 vols. (New York: Century, 1890), 9:40–41.

16. From the sixth debate with Stephen A. Douglas in *Collected Works*, ed. Basler et al., 3:278.

17. Carpenter, *Six Months at the White House*, 138–39; Titian J. Coffey quoted in *Reminiscences of Abraham Lincoln by Distinguished Men of His Time*, ed. Allen Thorndike Rice (New York: North American Publishing, 1886), 236.

18. Carpenter, *Six Months at the White House*, 129–30.

19. Henry J. Raymond, *The Life and Public Services of Abraham Lincoln* (New York: Derby and Miller, 1865), 746.

20. Lawrence Weldon quoted in *Reminiscences of Abraham Lincoln*, ed. Rice, 201.

21. Carpenter, *Six Months at the White House*, 158.

22. Cf. U. S. Grant, *Personal Memoirs of U. S. Grant*, 2 vols. (New York: C. L. Webster, 1885–86), 2:423; and Horace Porter, *Campaigning with Grant*, ed. Wayne C. Temple (Bloomington: Indiana University Press, 1961), 385.

23. Basler et al., eds., *Collected Works*, 1:175.

24. John Hay, *Inside Lincoln's White House: The Complete Civil War Diary of John Hay*, ed. Michael Burlingame and John R. Turner Ettlinger (Carbondale: Southern Illinois University Press, 1997), 64 (entry for 18 July 1863) and 194 (entry for 30 April 1864).

25. Ira Harris quoted by Frederick William Seward in *An Oral History of Abraham Lincoln: John G. Nicolay's Interviews and Essays*, ed. Michael Burlingame (Carbondale: Southern Illinois University Press, 1996), 87.

26. Whitney, *Life on the Circuit*, 184.

27. Joseph Gillespie to William H. Herndon, Edwardsville, Ill., 8 Dec. 1866, in *Herndon's Informants*, ed. Wilson and Davis, 508.

28. Usher F. Linder to Joseph Gillespie, 8 Aug. 1867, Gillespie Papers, Chicago Historical Society. In 1835 Kentucky-born Usher F. Linder (1809–76) settled in Coles County, Illinois. He was "a trifle vain, but just enough to spur him on." John M. Palmer, ed., *Bench and Bar of Illinois: Historical and Reminiscent*, 2 vols. (Chicago: Lewis, 1899), 1:181.

29. Whitney, *Life on the Circuit*, 174.

30. Angle, ed., *Herndon's Lincoln*, 249. It was Herndon, not Davis, who reported this phenomenon.

31. Burlingame and Ettlinger, eds., *Inside Lincoln's White House*, 64 (entry for 18 July 1863).

32. In 1830 Democrat John Moore (1793–1866) settled in McLean County, where he was elected to the state legislature. He became lieutenant governor of Illinois in 1840 and state treasurer in 1848.

33. Isaac N. Phillips, ed., *Abraham Lincoln by Some Men Who Knew Him* (Bloomington: Pantograph Printing, 1910), 99–100.

34. Massachusetts politician Benjamin F. Butler (1818–93) was a Democrat who had supported Jefferson Davis for the presidency in 1860. During the war he became a controversial general in the Union Army. John W. Forney (1817–81) was editor of the *Washington Chronicle* and *Philadelphia Press*.

35. There are several versions of this story. See Zall, ed., *Abe Lincoln Laughing*, 51–52.

36. Alvin Saunders (1817–99) was territorial governor of Nebraska (1861–67). "Humors of the Day," *Harper's Weekly*, 28 April 1860.

37. Ralph Waldo Emerson's eulogy on Lincoln, 19 April 1865, in *Building the Myth: Selected Speeches Memorializing Abraham Lincoln*, ed. Waldo Braden (Urbana: University of Illinois Press, 1990), 32.

38. William B. Wilson, *Glimpses of the United States Military Corps and of Abraham Lincoln* (Holmsburg, Pa.: privately printed, 1889), 20.

39. A. K. McClure, *Lincoln and Men of War-Times* (Philadelphia: Times, 1892), 216.

40. A "bull" is an absurd jest.

41. Burlingame and Ettlinger, eds., *Inside Lincoln's White House*, 64 (entry for 18 July 1863); Speech in the U.S. House of Representatives, 20 June 1848, in *Collected Works*, ed. Basler et al., 1:487.

42. Edmund D. Taylor was a merchant in Springfield who won election to the Illinois House of Representatives in 1830 and 1832 and the Senate in 1840. He was, according to Springfield residents who knew him, "a talkative, noisy fellow, with a fatal fondness for fine clothes." J. McCan Davis to Ida Tarbell, Springfield, Ill., 11 March 1895, copy, James G. Randall Papers, Library of Congress.

43. Isaac N. Arnold, *The Life of Abraham Lincoln* (Chicago: Jansen, McClurg, 1885), 50; James H. Matheny, interview with William H. Herndon, [3 May 1866], and Ninian W. Edwards, interview with Herndon, [1865–66], both in *Herndon's Informants*, ed. Wilson and Davis, 251, 447; Angle, ed., *Herndon's Lincoln*, 157; Whitney, *Lincoln the Citizen*, 143–44.

44. James Shields (1810–79) was a U.S. senator from Illinois (1849–55) and became a general in the Civil War. In 1842 he and Lincoln nearly fought a duel.

45. In 1863 Clement L. Vallandigham (1829–71) of Ohio, a leading Peace Democrat, had been exiled to the Confederacy after being arrested by Gen. Ambrose E. Burnside.

46. Robert Bray, "'The Power to Hurt': Lincoln's Early Use of Satire and Invective," *Journal of the Abraham Lincoln Association* 16 (1995): 43–51; Burlingame, *Inner World of Abraham Lincoln*, 150–55.

47. Letter of 27 Aug. 1842, in *Collected Works*, ed. Basler et al., 1:291–97 (quotation on 295–96).

48. Speech in the U.S. House of Representatives on the presidential question, 27 July 1848, in *Collected Works*, ed. Basler et al., 1:510–11. Lewis Cass (1782–1866) of Michigan served as secretary of war under President Andrew Jackson, as U.S. minister to France, as a U.S. senator, and as the Democratic presidential standard-bearer in 1848.

49. Gordon Abrams was the proprietor of a hotel in Springfield.

50. Speech in Springfield, 14, 26 Aug. 1852, in *Collected Works*, ed. Basler et al., 2:150.

51. On the dramatic difference between the pre-1854 and post-1854 Lincoln, see Burlingame, *Inner World of Abraham Lincoln*, 1–19.

52. Horatio King's speech at a Lincoln Fellowship Dinner, 11 Feb. 1911, in *Abe Lincoln Laughing*, ed. Zall, 128–29.

53. Letter of 11 Nov. 1863, in *Collected Works*, ed. Basler et al., 7:11.

54. George W. Julian in *Reminiscences of Abraham Lincoln*, ed. Rice, 57.

55. Manuscript by Benjamin F. Shaw, McLean County Historical Society, quoted in Otto R. Kyle, *Abraham Lincoln in Decatur* (New York: Vantage Press, 1957), 76.

56. Speech of 17 July 1858 in Springfield, in *Collected Works*, ed. Basler et al., 2:506.

57. Carpenter, *Six Months at the White House*, 148–49.

58. William H. Herndon to Jesse W. Weik, Springfield, 8 Jan. 1886, Herndon-Weik Papers, Library of Congress.

59. Ward Hill Lamon, *Recollections of Abraham Lincoln, 1847–1865*, ed. Dorothy Lamon Teillard (Chicago: McClurg, 1911), 221.

60. Lincoln enjoyed telling a story about a fellow "who had a great veneration for Revolutionary relics. He heard that an old lady . . . had a dress which she had worn in the Revolutionary War. He made a special visit to this lady and asked her if she could produce the dress as a satisfaction to his love of aged things. She obliged him by opening a drawer and bringing out the article in question. The enthusiastic person took up this dress and delivered an apostrophe to it. 'Were you the dress,' said he, 'that this lady once young and blooming wore in the time of Washington? No doubt when you came home from the dressmaker she kissed you as I do now!' At this the relic hunter took the old dress and kissed it heartily. The practical old lady rather resented such foolishness over an old piece of wearing apparel and she said: 'Stranger if you want to kiss something old you had better kiss my ass. It is sixteen years older than that dress.'" (Scrapbook, 45, 47, George Alfred Townsend Papers, Library of Congress.) In 1878 this was told to Townsend by John Palmer Usher, who had originally heard Lincoln tell it in Paris, Illinois, around 1844. Lincoln's fondness for smutty stories was legendary. One day in 1859, when he was asked, "Why do you not write out your stories and put them in a book," Lincoln "drew himself up—fixed his face, as if a thousand dead carcusses—and a million of privies were Shooting all their Stench into his nostrils, and Said 'Such a book would Stink like a thousand privies.'" (Henry E. Dummer, interview with Herndon, [1865–66], in *Herndon's Informants*, ed. Wilson and Davis, 442.) The Ohio journalist Donn Piatt claimed that Lincoln "interlarded all his official acts with the dirtiest stories that ever fell from human lips." (Piatt, in the *Washington Capital*, n.d., quoted in John N. Taylor to Jesse W. Weik, Crawfordsville, Ind., 25 Nov. 1923, Weik Papers, Illinois State Historical Library, Springfield.) William Herndon explained that even though "Lincoln's jokes were *vulgar—indecently so*," yet he "was not a dirty foul mouthed man by any means." He "was raised among a peculiar people—an ignorant but good people—honest ones. Hence Mr Lincoln preferred jokes to fables or maxims as they, for his people, had the pith-point and force about them to make the point luminous—clear—plain." (William H. Herndon to "Mr. Noyes," Chinkapin Hill, Ill., 4 Feb. 1874, Herndon Papers, Illinois State Historical Library, Springfield.) Leonard Swett reported that "[i]f he told a good story. . . . that [was] outrageously low and dirty, he never seemed to see that part of it. . . . Almost any man that will tell a vulgar story, has got in a degree a vulgar mind, but it was not so with him." (Leonard Swett to William H. Herndon, Chicago, 17 Jan. 1866, in *Herndon's Informants*, ed. Wilson and Davis, 165–66.)

61. David Homer Bates, *Lincoln in the Telegraph Office: Recollections of the United States Military Telegraph Corps during the Civil War* (New York: Century, 1907), 197–98.

62. Leonard Swett to William H. Herndon, Chicago, 17 Jan. 1866, in *Herndon's Informants*, ed. Wilson and Davis, 166.

63. Angle, ed., *Herndon's Lincoln*, 249.

64. Charles Farrar Browne (1834–67) created comic characters based on backwoods and Down East folk in his native Maine. He edited *Vanity Fair* briefly and was a well-known lecturer in London when tuberculosis struck him down. Robert Henry Newell (1836–1901) of New York wrote satirical pieces for newspapers, poking fun at the solemn and relying heavily on deliberate misspellings. In 1861 David Ross Locke (1833–88) of Toledo, Ohio, created "Petroleum Nasby," an ignorant, semiliterate Copperhead critic of the Lincoln administration.

65. *Thomas's note:* From his youth Lincoln enjoyed humorous articles and books. In Indiana he and other boys would retire on Sundays to the woods where he would read from a book called *Quinn's Jests*. In later life he derived much pleasure from J. G. Baldwin's *Flush Times in Alabama*. [Joseph G. Baldwin, *The Flush Times of Alabama and Mississippi: A Series of Sketches* (New York: Appleton, 1853).] Written by a frontier circuit lawyer, its characters and settings were similar in many respects to those which Lincoln knew so well in Illinois, this book had a powerful appeal. Lincoln liked especially Baldwin's characterization of Cave Burton who, far from being a liar, "had such great regard for the truth that he spent most of his time embellishing it," and who was so gluttonous that "he was not satisfied that Esau made as foolish a bargain with his brother Jacob as some think. Before committing himself, he should like to taste the pottage, and see some estimate of the net value of the birthright in the beef . . . market." Another character was Jonas Sykes, a most valiant man—"a very Samson in a fight, but who, like Samson, preferred to do his fighting with the jaw bone."

66. *Thomas's note:* In his description of the troubles of the itinerant showman, Artemus Ward Browne is at his best. Ward takes his wax "figgers" of the Lord's Supper to Utica and in the midst of his ballyhoo sees a big burly fellow seize Judas Iscariot by the feet, drag him out on the ground, and commence to pound him lustily. When Ward protests, the fellow demands to know how he had the effrontery to "bring this pussylanermus cuss here," and despite Ward's expostulations that Judas is merely a wax "figger," he continues to belabor him until he bashes in his head, declaring that "Judas Iscarrott can't show hisself in Utiky with impunerty by a darn site."

67. *Thomas's note:* David Ross Locke's character, Petroleum V. Nasby, was an indolent besotted "Dimekrat," who was a continual applicant for a postoffice. "No man," said he, "hez drunk more whiskey than I hev for the party—none hez dun it moar willingly." Through the medium of this character Locke ridiculed Northern fears of negro immigration and equality, draft dodgers, secessionists, Confederate money ("Our pay is irregular, and not jest ez good quality ez cood be wished"), and Copperheads. Nasby's brother, a Democrat, who went to sea in 1849, returns during the war and is amazed to learn that the party of Jefferson and Jackson has come to regard slavery as a blessing, favors its extension into new territories and is attempting to disrupt the Union. "Ef I hed staid at home," says he, "perhaps I mite hev took these changes down, wun at a time, but at wun dose it's to much." Nasby ridicules the dilatory tactics of McClellan whom he likens to a kicking shotgun—"dangerous only to them ez held it." On one occasion Nasby has an interview with Lincoln which he concludes: "Linkin! Goriller! Ape! I hev dun." [Lincoln asked Ohio Congressman James M. Ashley to tell Locke "that

for the ability to write the queer, quaint and good things he does, I'd give up my office tomorrow." James M. Ashley to David Ross Locke, 5 March 1865, quoted in Mrs. W. R. Hearst to Benjamin Thomas, New York, 24 Jan. 1953, Benjamin P. Thomas Papers, Illinois State Historical Library, Springfield.]

68. *Thomas's note:* Newell described his own writings as a series of "unpremeditated extravagances." Written in mock-heroic style and characterized by broad exaggerations and absurdities, his humor demands an uproarious reader such as Lincoln. Replete with parodies, quips and puns—such as the veterinarian being called to mend a Colt revolver and the quartermaster who, unable to furnish rations to his men, gave them lead pencils and let them draw their own—the *Papers* also contain some good satire on disloyalists and office-seekers. ("Though you find me in Washington now, I was born of respectable parents.") There are some well-meant jests at the administration, such as the account of Kerr and his companions catching some chickens and deciding to eat them at once lest the President administer the oath of allegiance and let them go. Lincoln was especially fond of an allegorical poem which compared McClellan to a monkey about to fight a serpent but afraid to do so until he got a longer tail. He kept calling on Jupiter for more tail until he had so much he couldn't move.

69. John Hay (1838–1905) was Lincoln's assistant private secretary. Burlingame and Ettlinger, eds., *Inside Lincoln's White House*, 26 (entry for 17 Oct. 1861).

70. Angle, ed., *Herndon's Lincoln*, 269.

71. John A. J. Creswell (1828–91) of Elkton, Md., represented his district in the U.S. House from 1863 to 1865 and represented Maryland in the Senate from 1865 to 1867.

72. Lamon, *Recollections of Abraham Lincoln, 1847–1865*, 248.

73. John Hay to John G. Nicolay, Washington, 11 Sept. 1863, in *At Lincoln's Side: John Hay's Civil War Correspondence and Selected Writings*, ed. Michael Burlingame (Carbondale: Southern Illinois University Press, 2000), 54.

74. Titian Coffey in *Reminiscences of Abraham Lincoln*, ed. Rice, 240.

75. Abraham Lincoln to Cuthbert Bullitt, Washington, 28 July 1862, in *Collected Works*, ed. Basler et al., 5:345–46; cf. Lincoln to Reverdy Johnson, Washington, 26 July 1862 (5:342–43) and entry for 26 July 1862 in Orville H. Browning, *The Diary of Orville H. Browning*, 2 vols., ed. Theodore C. Pease and James G. Randall, Collections of the Illinois State Historical Library (Springfield: Illinois State Historical Library, 1925, 1933), 1:564.

76. William H. Herndon, lecture on Lincoln, 12 Dec. 1865, in Carpenter, *Six Months at the White House*, 330.

77. Chauncey Depew in *Reminiscences of Abraham Lincoln*, ed. Rice, 427–29.

78. John H. Littlefield, in *Herndon's Lincoln*, ed. Angle, 256. In 1858, New York–born John Harrison Littlefield (1835–1902), a graduate of Oberlin College, was commended to Lincoln's attention by his older brother, Milton Smith Littlefield. He began his legal studies with Lincoln and Herndon the following year. He later forsook the law for art and painted a portrait of Lincoln.

79. McClure, *Lincoln's Yarns and Stories*, xii.

2 *Abraham Lincoln*

The United States was entering its darkest hour as Abraham Lincoln took the oath of office as president on March 4, 1861. Already seven states had renounced the Union and formed a new nation of their own. Eight more states were wavering and four of them would soon go out. Within six weeks the North and the South would be locked in bloody war.

No president ever entered office under more trying circumstances or faced more critical problems. None was so hated, so blamed, so reviled—and in the end so loved. For, despite the self-seeking politicians, the impatient abolitionists, the headstrong and unfit generals, and the venomous defeatists, whom he constantly had to deal with, Lincoln remained patient, tolerant, and forbearing, and, above all, steadfast in his determination to preserve the American Union.

To the Founding Fathers—Washington, Jefferson, Madison, John Adams—the American Revolution had meant the beginning of higher and better things for all men everywhere. And a similar vision of America had come to Lincoln very early in his life. Addressing the New Jersey Senate on his way to Washington in 1861, he said: "May I be pardoned if, on this occasion, I mention that away back in my childhood, the earliest days of my being able to read, I got hold of a small book, 'Weems' Life of Washington.' I remember all the accounts there given of the battle fields and struggles for the liberties of the country . . . and you all know, for you have all been boys, how these early impressions last longer than others. I rec-

---

Undated typescript, Benjamin P. Thomas Papers, Illinois State Historical Library.

ollect thinking then, boy even though I was, that there must have been something more than common that those men struggled for."

And the boy became a man and, about to assume office as President of the United States, went on to say: "I am exceedingly anxious that the thing which they struggled for; that something even more than National Independence; that something that held out a great promise to all people of the world to all time to come; I am exceedingly anxious that this Union, the Constitution and the liberties of the people shall be perpetuated in accordance with the original idea for which that struggle was made, and I shall be most happy indeed if I shall be an humble instrument in the hands of the Almighty, and of this His almost chosen people, for perpetuating the object of that great struggle."[1]

Throughout the war Lincoln never ceased insisting that the real issue was whether the nation, born so auspiciously in 1776, and dedicated to the proposition that all men are created equal and are alike entitled to life, liberty, and the pursuit of happiness, would live on to vindicate democracy in the sight of all mankind or end in inglorious failure.

Lincoln's faith in democracy was buttressed by the facts of his own life. He was living proof of what a man, untrammeled, can make of himself, if he will.

Born in Kentucky of poor and illiterate parents, reared in backwoods Indiana, and migrating to the Illinois prairies when he came of age, Lincoln had been molded but not mastered by the lusty, primal forces of the American frontier. Hard fare and hard toil had been his lot, until at last he broke away from family hindrances and struck out on his own.

Striving against poverty and lack of schooling, he rose from laborer and flatboatman to surveyor and village postmaster. He served as a soldier in the Black Hawk War. He failed as a storekeeper. Through hard study he equipped himself to be a lawyer. He got himself elected to the Illinois legislature.

He learned from each new experience; he learned from his contacts with people. He became familiar with a few great works of literature such as Shakespeare and the Bible. From them and from patient self-teaching, he gained skill in using words. His mind moved slowly and cautiously, as the man himself seemed to move. It was logical and tenacious; it sought and demanded proof.

Intellect and temperament often seemed at odds in Lincoln; for along with his coldly logical mind he had a warm and tender heart. Honesty became his best known attribute in politics, in the law practice, and in his personal dealings. He would break out of a chronic, haunting melancholy with droll quips and comic stories; it has been said of him that "perhaps no human clay-pot has held more laughter and more tears."

Lincoln's law partner described his ambition as "a little engine that knew no rest."[2] At last, through unwavering service to his party, he gained a seat in Congress. But there he made a serious, if conscientious, misstep by opposing the Mexican War. Renounced by the people whom he represented, he despaired of a future in politics.[3]

Reconciling himself to the life of a country lawyer, Lincoln continued his self-teaching, determined to make himself a better lawyer and an enlightened man. For five years Lincoln applied himself assiduously to the law. Then came a moral awakening and the turning point in his life, when the repeal of the Missouri Compromise, in 1854, brought slavery to the fore again as a flaming national issue.

For as long as Lincoln could remember he had reasoned "if slavery is not wrong, nothing is wrong."[4] Yet, throughout his political career he had been cautious about slavery, knowing full well the danger it held to national unity. In this issue, as in so many others, he had looked to the Founding Fathers, and if he correctly understood their attitude toward slavery, they had sought to keep it from spreading so that it would one day die for lack of growth. So their policy became Lincoln's policy too, even though toleration of human bondage violated his concept of America as the land of freedom and equality.

But the repeal of the Missouri Compromise [in 1854], by opening new areas to slavery, might grant it indefinite life. To Lincoln, such a change in policy meant rejection of the ideal of ridding America of a hypocrisy and making it a genuine democracy at the earliest practicable time. He was roused, he said, as he had never been roused before.[5] Within four months he was back in politics, moved by a moral earnestness that gave his words new power, and thrust him forward as a leader. And six years later he was president.

Only in America could such a thing have happened. And how well Lincoln knew it. "To the humblest and poorest among us are held out the highest privileges and positions," he told the men of the 148th Ohio Regiment. "The present moment finds me at the White House, yet there is as good a chance for your children as there was for my father's child."[6] It would have been well for the country, in 1860, had people known better the thought-pattern of this man, and the background of experience which fashioned it. For he would not lightly allow a Union which he held so highly to be lost; he would not surrender easily the ideals that Union stood for.

With war upon the nation, Lincoln fumbled at first. He was haphazard as an administrator. He was plagued by bungling generals. And when they failed, he sometimes interfered mistakenly in military matters. Before long, however, Lincoln showed that, notwithstanding his idealistic thinking, sound common-sense controlled his actions. In formulating policy he demonstrated an uncanny skill in harmonizing the diverse factions in his party. He demonstrated his primacy over rivals in his cabinet. He maneuvered adeptly against headstrong men in Congress. He handled the touchy slavery problem with the tact that it demanded; one misstep there and the loyal border slave states might have elected to leave the Union.

Lincoln knew that victory over the brave, determined people of the South, who were fighting for their families and their firesides and for the right as they saw it, could come only by vanquishing their armies, wasting their economic resources, and wearing down their will to win. It was not a task to his liking, nor did the Northern people like it. Lincoln's most challenging duty was to bring home to them the broader meanings of the conflict, to convince them that theirs was a cause worth dying for, and to persuade them that their sacrifices would lift themselves, their enemies, and all mankind toward a brighter, better future.

Lincoln's long schooling in politics had given him an almost perfect sense of timing. Knowing that the function of a leader in a democracy is not to impose his will but to encourage the people to choose wisely for themselves, he moved forward or waited as the nation's mood quickened or flagged. The exercise of power endowed him with new strength. Always he had shown a rare capacity to summon inner resources for whatever demands he had faced. Now, under the stress of war, his mind and spirit burgeoned. Tenderness and pity were intextured in his heart; his own soul writhed in torment as he hurled the thunderbolts of war. His face, etched deeply by the prairies years, took on new depths, new shades, new highlights, as the war years wrought upon it.

His faith in the basic goodness of the people survived the harshest trials, and as the people saw him, steady and courageous, even when the cause seemed lost, they came to trust their simple, homespun president, and to call him "Father Abraham." They accepted his decisions because he epitomized their hopes. And so, with the people behind him, he brought the nation through.

As victory became certain, Lincoln turned his thoughts to binding up the nation's wounds. Renouncing vengeance toward an enemy whom he could never hate, he besought the people's mercy for their vanquished countrymen. To help lift the Southern people from the ruin of defeat, he was willing to offer payment for the slaves whom he had freed.

At that moment an assassin struck him down. And the gentlest, and perhaps the most peace-loving of our presidents, whose ironic lot it had become to launch the nation on a brothers' war, himself became part of the sacrifice.

Perhaps he himself has best summed up the meaning of it all. For as the signs began to look better and peace seemed less distant than before, he had written, from a brimming heart: "Thanks to all. For the great Republic,—for the principle it lives by and keeps alive,—for man's vast future,—thanks to all."[7]

Notes

1. Speech of 21 Feb. 1861, in *The Collected Works of Abraham Lincoln*, ed. Roy P. Basler, Marion Dolores Pratt and Lloyd A. Dunlap, asst. eds., 8 vols. plus index (New Brunswick: Rutgers University Press, 1953–55), 4:235–36.

2. Paul M. Angle, ed., *Herndon's Life of Lincoln: The History and Personal Recollections of Abraham Lincoln as Originally Written by William H. Herndon and Jesse W. Weik* (Cleveland: World, 1942), 304.

3. Gabor Boritt has challenged this interpretation of Lincoln's "unpopularity." G. S. Boritt, "A Question of Political Suicide: Lincoln's Opposition to the Mexican War," *Journal of the Illinois State Historical Society* 68 (1974): 79–100. Lincoln claimed that he retired from the House after one term because he and other Whig leaders had agreed to rotate the candidacy for the post among themselves. In a third-person autobiography he wrote: "Mr. L. was not a candidate for re-election. This was determined upon, and declared before he went to Washington, in accordance with an understanding among whig friends, by which Col. [John J.] Hardin, and Col. [Edward D.] Baker had each previously served a single term in the same District." Autobiography written for John Locke Scripps, [ca. June 1860], in *Collected Works*, ed. Basler et al., 4:66–67.

4. Abraham Lincoln to Albert G. Hodges, Washington, 4 April 1864, in *Collected Works*, ed. Basler et al., 7:281.

5. Autobiography written for John Locke Scripps, 4:67.

6. Speech of 31 Aug. 1864, in *Collected Works*, ed. Basler et al., 7:528.

7. Abraham Lincoln to James C. Conkling, Washington, 26 Aug. 1863, in *Collected Works*, ed. Basler et al., 6:410.

3   Lincoln's Way with Words

When I was in college, one of the first acquaintances I made, and one of the enduring friendships I formed was with a boy fresh from the farm. He didn't have hayseed in his hair; but you could tell it had been there. He didn't smell of the barnyard; but you knew he was familiar with it. He was built like a teddy-bear, with a long, heavy body supported by short, thick bow-legs. His speech had a sharp twang. He was so shy he wouldn't ask a streetcar conductor for a transfer, preferring to pay two fares. He was awkward. Once, in later life, while serving as a pallbearer, he fell into the grave.

Now he is a successful surgeon, with a beguiling bedside manner; but in private, with his cronies, he loves to relapse into his old rural idiosyncrasies of speech. "My ambition," he once told me, "is to be a cultured hick, I don't ever want to lose my hickishness."

Abraham Lincoln must have felt somewhat the same way. Born and brought up in the country, living seven years in a village, and twenty-four years in a small town, he never got over it. Nor do I believe he wanted to.

Only in comparatively recent times have students realized how much Lincoln owed to his early environment. At first it was regarded solely as a handicap. More than that, early Lincoln writers depicted it as more wretched than it really was, in order to make Lincoln's achievements appear all the more remarkable. Chauncey F. Black, who was ghostwriter for Ward Hill Lamon's *Life of Lincoln*, wrote: "We must point mankind to the dia-

---

Undated manuscript, Benjamin P. Thomas Papers, Illinois State Historical Library, Springfield.

mond glowing on the dunghill and then to the same resplendent jewel in the future setting of great success and brilliant achievement."[1]

We know now that Lincoln's background, after all, was the typical frontier background of his day, and that while it posed certain handicaps, it also offered certain challenges and opportunities that were not to be found elsewhere. Nowhere else were vigor and courage so much appreciated. Nowhere else did democracy and independence flourish in a purer form. Here was rural America in its pristine vigor. And it was not a question of how much of this Lincoln could cut loose from, but how much of it he could take with him as he grew.

Lincoln's roots were in the raw, rich soil of rural America, and throughout his life that soil would nurture him. As Ida Tarbell said, his very speech took flavor from this elemental life. "The horse, the dog, the ox, the chin fly, the plow, the hog, these companions of his youth became interpreters of his meaning, solvers of his problems in his great necessity of making men understand him."[2]

Charles Sumner said that Lincoln's ideas "moved, as the beasts entered Noah's ark, in pairs."[3] Almost every thought brought to his mind an analogy with which he could illustrate it; and most of these analogies derived from his background—the people he had known, the places he had seen, the animals with which he was familiar.

In forecasting the outcome of an election, for example, Lincoln declared that the result was "as plain as the adding up of the weight of three small hogs."[4] He once said that he didn't want the Republican Party to become "a mere sucked egg, all shell and no meat, the principle all sucked out."[5]

This knack of clarifying an idea by a vivid metaphor or simile was especially helpful to Lincoln in his dealings with his generals. During the war Lincoln became, of necessity, a close student of military matters. Visiting the War Department daily, studying the telegrams from the front, following the movements of every detachment of troops, occupying his leisure with study of military textbooks, he soon acquired a grasp of military matters which sometimes proved superior to that of his generals. But the picturesque imagery with which he expressed his ideas remained peculiarly his own—and here again we see the influence of his antecedents.

To him the Navy suggested "Uncle Sam's web-feet," leaving their "tracks" on all the "watery margins."[6] For harbor defense he advocated the use of steam rams whose duty it would be to guard a particular harbor as a bulldog guards his master's door. He deplored the dilatoriness of General Meade, who, after Gettysburg, let his noble army expend "all the skill, and toil and blood, up to the ripe harvest, and then let the crop go to waste."[7] On October 4, 1863, he telegraphed to General Rosecrans that as long as he held Chattanooga he could "board at home so to speak," and menace or attack the enemy constantly.[8] To Halleck he wired that if Rosecrans "can only maintain this position, without more, the rebellion can only eke out a short and feeble existence, as an animal sometimes may with a thorn in its vitals."[9]

Lincoln continually thought of an army as an animal. In a telegram to General Hooker he warned: "In one word, I would not take any risk of being entangled upon the river, like an ox jumped half over a fence and liable to torn by dogs front and rear without a fair chance to gore one way or kick the other."[10] And again he telegraphed to Hooker: "If the head of Lee's army is at Martinsburg and the tail of it on the plank road between Fredericksburg and Chancellorsville, the animal must be very slim somewhere. Could you not break him?"[11]

After General Grant became commander-in-chief, Lincoln's military telegrams became less frequent, for Grant fought without needing to be prodded. In August 1864, however, Grant, temporarily checked at Petersburg, was tempted to weaken his army in order to send reinforcements to Phil Sheridan, who was hard-pressed in the Shenandoah Valley. But Grant finally decided to stay where he was. Lincoln approved his decision in characteristic phraseology when he wrote: "I have seen your dispatch expressing your unwillingness to break our hold where you are. Neither am I willing. Hold on with a bulldog grip and chew and choke as much as possible."[12]

With all his kindly sympathy, Lincoln was sometimes driven to distraction by the importunity of friends and office-seekers. Sometimes he became impatient.[13] But even his manifestations of displeasure were often softened by a pertinent analogy designed to take the sting out of a refusal or to show the ridiculousness of a request. He wrote, for instance, to Governor Richard Yates and William Butler, old Illinois friends and supporters: "I fully appreciate General Pope's splendid achievements with their invaluable results; but you must know that major generalships in the regular army are not as plenty as blackberries."[14] And of a Southerner who deplored the hardships that his policy was working on the loyal people of the South, he inquired: "What would you do in my position? Would you drop the war where it is? Or would you prosecute it in the future with elder-stalk squirts charged with rose-water?"[15]

Time and again some incident suggested to him—almost unconsciously—a rural analogy. "I will pitch into that like a dog at a root," he exclaimed when presented with a legal problem.[16] "Well, I have got that

job husked out," he sighed with relief upon completing a perplexing presidential task.[17] The sight of Alexander H. Stephens, a tiny wisp of a man,
divesting himself of voluminous wraps moved him to remark: "That is
the largest shucking for so small a nubbin that I ever saw." He referred
to the Post Office Department's "cutting its own fodder."[18] In reviewing
some court-martial proceedings, he came upon the case of a condemned
deserter who had escaped to Mexico. Apparently relieved that the man
had got away, he observed: "We will condemn him as they used to sell
hogs in Indiana,—as they run." His notion of the plan to exert simultaneous pressure on all points of the Confederate line to prevent reinforcements being sent to the main point of attack was that "those not skinning can hold a leg."[19]

Like his writings and his speech, Lincoln's humor was indigenous to
the soil. He appreciated the unconventional, earthy humor and the homespun philosophy of the farmers and townspeople with whom he grew up.
He always insisted that country people were the originators of most good
stories, and it was to them and to the experiences of his own rural life
that he went for most of his own best yarns. In discussing the advisability of pardoning a condemned deserter, he recalled the time that Usher
F. Linder, a fellow lawyer, had saved a client who had stolen a hog by
advising him to go get a drink, and suggesting that the water was better
in Tennessee. Another time he told of John Moore, one-time State Treasurer of Illinois, who confessed that on one occasion in the early days he
came to Bloomington on Saturday to get supplies, and also got pretty well
"liquored up." Moore drove a cart drawn by two red steers, and starting
home he fell asleep. As he passed through a grove the cart struck a tree
stump and the steers broke loose and ran away. Deep in his cups, Moore
didn't even wake up but slept blissfully on until morning. Finally he
opened his eyes and looked around him in bewilderment. "If my name
is John Moore," he exclaimed, "I've lost a pair of steers. If it is not John
Moore, I've found a cart."

Lincoln enjoyed reading the works of the contemporary humorists,
because the characters they depicted reminded him of people he had
known. One of Lincoln's favorite books was J. G. Baldwin's *Flush Times
in Alabama*, for unquestionably Lincoln had known small-town characters like Cave Burton and Jonas Sykes.[20] Burton, you remember, far from
being a liar, "had such great regard for the truth that he spent his time embellishing it." Sykes was a most valiant man, "a very Samson in a fight,"
but like Samson, "he preferred to do his fighting with the jaw bone."

Lincoln could readily understand the troubles that Charles Farrar
Brown's character, Artemus Ward, got into at Utica, for they illustrated

the perfervid religious feeling, not unmixed with ignorance, with which he was fully familiar. You remember that Artemus Ward, the itinerant showman, was exhibiting his wax figures of the Lord's Last Supper in the town of Utica. In the midst of Ward's ballyhoo, he was astonished to see a rough-looking fellow in the crowd seize the wax figure of Judas Iscariot, wrestle it to the ground, and proceed to bash in Judas's head. Ward protested that Judas was only a wax figure; but the irate spectator would not be pacified, and said: "Judas Iscariot can't show his face in Uticy with impunity, by a dern sight."

Long years in Washington change all too many of our legislators and administrators. In its artificial atmosphere they lose touch with America. Their heads get in the clouds and their feet get off the ground. Flattery often inflates them; money sometimes beguiles them; power makes them hard. Lincoln avoided these pitfalls, because, like my friend, he did not want to lose his "hickishness." He was of the people and remained one of them. While becoming a leader he never lost the common touch. He grew beyond his beginnings but not away from them.

Notes

1. Chauncey F. Black to Ward Hill Lamon, 8 March 1870, Herndon-Weik Papers, Library of Congress.

2. Ida M. Tarbell, *In the Footsteps of the Lincolns* (New York: Harper and Brothers, 1924), 137.

3. Charles Sumner, "Eulogy," in *A Memorial of Abraham Lincoln* (Boston: City Council, 1865), 134.

4. Abraham Lincoln to Fillmore Men, Springfield, 8 Sept. 1856, in *The Collected Works of Abraham Lincoln*, ed. Roy P. Basler, Marion Dolores Pratt and Lloyd A. Dunlap, asst. eds., 8 vols. plus index (New Brunswick: Rutgers University Press, 1953–55), 2:374.

5. George Sumner to John A. Andrew, Springfield, 21 Jan. 1861, in *Concerning Mr. Lincoln*, ed. Harry E. Pratt (Springfield: Abraham Lincoln Association, 1944), 42.

6. Abraham Lincoln to James C. Conkling, Washington, 26 Aug. 1863, in *Collected Works*, ed. Basler et al., 6:409.

7. Abraham Lincoln to O. O. Howard, Washington, 21 July 1863, in *Collected Works*, ed. Basler et al., 6:341.

8. Abraham Lincoln to William S. Rosecrans, Washington, 4 Oct. 1863, in *Collected Works*, ed. Basler et al., 6:498.

9. Abraham Lincoln to Henry W. Halleck, Washington, 21 Sept. 1863, in *Collected Works*, ed. Basler et al., 6:471.

10. Abraham Lincoln to Joseph Hooker, Washington, 5 June 1863, in *Collected Works*, ed. Basler et al., 6:249.

11. Abraham Lincoln to Joseph Hooker, Washington, 14 June 1863, in *Collected Works*, ed. Basler et al., 6:273.

12. Abraham Lincoln to U. S. Grant, Washington, 17 Aug. 1864, in *Collected Works*, ed. Basler et al., 7:499.

13. Michael Burlingame, *The Inner World of Abraham Lincoln* (Urbana: University of Illinois Press, 1994), 147–235.

14. Abraham Lincoln to Richard Yates and William Butler, Washington, 10 April 1862, in *Collected Works*, ed. Basler et al., 5:186.

15. Abraham Lincoln to Cuthbert Bullitt, Washington, 28 July 1862, in *Collected Works*, ed. Basler et al., 5:346.

16. Lawrence Weldon quoted in *Reminiscences of Abraham Lincoln by Distinguished Men of His Time*, ed. Allen Thorndike Rice (New York: North American Review, 1888), 201.

17. Carpenter, *Six Months at the White House*, 158.

18. Speech on the Sub-Treasury, [26] Dec. 1839, in *Collected Works*, ed. Basler et al., 1:175.

19. John Hay, *Inside Lincoln's White House: The Complete Civil War Diary of John Hay*, ed. Michael Burlingame and John R. Turner Ettlinger (Carbondale: Southern Illinois University Press, 1997), 194 (entry for 30 April 1864).

20. Joseph G. Baldwin, *The Flush Times of Alabama and Mississippi: A Series of Sketches* (New York: Appleton, 1853).

4   *The Meaning of the*
Gettysburg Address,
Then and Today

A search for the genesis of the Gettysburg Address leads to a lonely cabin in backwoods Indiana, where a gangling, rough-handed pioneer boy lay reading a life of George Washington by the blaze of a pine-knot fire. The boy thrilled to the account of the Revolutionary War—the tenacious determination of the footsore soldiers, the hard marches and fierce battles, the cruel winter at Valley Forge. And the boy, Abraham Lincoln, told himself, "There must have been something more than common that those men struggled for."[1]

What was it that inspired those men to persevere? he asked. He found the answer not merely in the desire of the colonials for independence from the mother country, but in that sentiment of the Declaration of Independence which declares that all men are created equal, that they are endowed by the Creator with certain inalienable rights, among which are life, liberty, and the pursuit of happiness. Here was not merely a touchstone for the people of America, it was a message of hope to all the world. It was a promise that "in due time the weights should be lifted from the shoulders of all men and that all should have an equal chance."[2]

As Lincoln overcame the obstacles of poverty to grow in mind and

---

Address delivered 19 Nov. 1950, at the Chicago Historical Society, reprinted in *Chicago History* 2 (Fall 1950): 264–72.

character, the story of America took on rich meaning for him. In no other country of the world was man so much the master of his destiny, nowhere else was he offered such a chance to rise through his own efforts. While Lincoln carved out his own career in law and politics, all about him, at home and on the circuit, he saw men, who starting life as farmers, clerks, mechanics, flatboat men, had become lawyers, merchants, doctors, landed farmers, and successful politicians. "There is no permanent class of hired laborers amongst us," he declared in a speech at Milwaukee. "Twenty-five years ago, I was a hired laborer. The hired laborer of yesterday works on his own account today, and will hire others to labor for him tomorrow. Advancement—improvement in condition—is the order of things in a society of equals."[3]

Lincoln's own pedigree of toil, culminating in the generous fulfillment of his highest hopes, verified his faith in democracy. During the war, in an address to an Ohio regiment, he tried to impress upon the soldiers that free government must be perpetuated. "I beg you to remember this," he said, "not merely for my sake, but for yours. I happen temporarily to occupy this big White House. I am a living witness that any one of your children may look to come here as my father's child has. It is in order that each of you may have through this free government which we have enjoyed, an open field and a fair chance for your industry, enterprise and intelligence; that you may all have equal privileges in the race of life, with all its desirable human aspirations. It is for this the struggle should be maintained, that we may not lose our birthright. . . . The nation is worth fighting for, to secure such an inestimable jewel."[4]

Lincoln did not need to develop a political philosophy of his own. He was content to base his thought and action upon the eternal truths so well affirmed by Jefferson in the nation's charter of freedom. "I have never had a feeling politically," he said, "which did not spring from the sentiments embodied in the Declaration of Independence."[5]

Lincoln liked to let his mind drift back upon that scene in Independence Hall, where Jefferson and those other earnest patriots set man's feet on a new path. How noble and far-seeing were these Founding Fathers, Lincoln thought, as they laid the cornerstone of a new nation in a belief that nothing in God's image is sent into the world to be oppressed or imbruted by its fellows; as they took into account not only the race of men then living but all men in all future time, erecting a beacon for their children and their children's children. Knowing the tendency of posterity to breed tyrants, they had proclaimed those everlasting truths, so that if, in time to come, some race or faction or interest should set up the doctrine that none but rich men, or none but white men, or none but

Anglo-Saxons were entitled to life, liberty, and the pursuit of happiness, their posterity might find in this great human document a source of faith and courage to keep up the fight for truth, justice, and mercy among men. In relation to the principle that all men are created equal, Lincoln observed, "let it be as nearly reached as it can. If we cannot give freedom to every creature, let us do nothing that will impose slavery upon any other creature."[6] "They meant," said Lincoln of the Founding Fathers, "to set up a standard maxim for free society, which should be familiar to all, constantly looked to, constantly labored for, and even though never perfectly attained, constantly approximated, and thereby constantly spreading and deepening its influence and augmenting the happiness and value of life to all people, of all colors, everywhere."[7]

In this affirmation of democracy, thought Lincoln, lay the great hope of the world. The mission of America was to demonstrate its truths; to prove that in its principles mankind would find the surest way to peace, prosperity, and happiness; to show that man's welfare rested not in the favor of some ruler of supposedly divine election, not in the grudging concessions of a privileged class, not in the notion of a master race, but in the people's right to order their own affairs.

Here we find an explanation of Lincoln's boundless human sympathy, his global outlook. Here we find the reason for his implacable hatred of slavery. For slavery mocked American ideals. Our sufferance of human bondage enabled those who scorned democracy to sneer at us as hypocrites. The plight of the Negro appealed strongly to Lincoln's sense of justice among men, but far more fundamental loomed the stark inconsistency between slavery and the doctrines of equal human rights to which he believed America stood committed. And a condition of servitude, if condoned in the case of the black man, might become the lot of the free white laborer as well.

Lincoln never professed learning in world history. Yet, from the very beginning, he sensed the world significance of our Civil War. From the time of the American Revolution, Europe had looked to America as the proving ground of democracy. Inspired by the example of that Revolution, various European peoples had tried to win freedom and self-government for themselves, only to fall back before entrenched reactionism. But America remained a source of inspiration for liberal strivings; while the privileged classes, denying man's capacity for self-government and identifying democracy with mob rule and lawlessness, predicted certain failure for the American experiment. With the United States threatened with dismemberment their forecast seemed about to be fulfilled. Lincoln knew that the conflict in America carried fateful consequences in the world-wide and eternal struggle between freedom and oppression. America faced the tragic failure of her mission. To Lincoln, the bark of Confederate guns was like the measured death dirge of democracy.

It was tragically ironic that Lincoln's own election to the presidency should threaten democracy's downfall by moving the South to secede. Lincoln might have let "the erring sisters go in peace." But to do so would be to permit the violation of a fundamental principle of democracy—the acquiescence of the minority in the mandate of an election. One need not imagine the inner torment of this man of peaceful disposition as he launched the nation on a brothers' war; successive photographs of Lincoln, taken throughout the conflict, depict the torture of his soul. But some things in life and history are worthy of bloodshed and suffering. Lincoln could not peaceably surrender what he held to be "the last, best hope of earth."[8]

One day, soon after the fall of Fort Sumter, John Hay, the President's young secretary, brought some papers to Lincoln's office. The two men discussed the meaning of the war. "For my part," the older man explained, "I consider the central idea pervading this struggle is the necessity that is upon us of proving that popular government is not an absurdity. We must settle this question now, whether in a free government the minority have the right to break up the government whenever they choose. If we fail, it will go far to prove the incapability of the people to govern themselves."[9]

In July 1861, in a message to the Congress, Lincoln defined the issue as he saw it. "This is essentially a people's contest," he declared. "On the side of the Union it is a struggle for maintaining in the world that form and substance of government whose leading object is to elevate the condition of men—to lift artificial weights from all shoulders; to clear the paths of laudable pursuit for all; to afford all an unfettered start, and a fair chance in the race of life. . . .

"Our popular government has often been called an experiment," he continued. "Two points in it our people have already settled—the successful establishing and the successful administering of it. One still remains—its successful maintenance against a formidable internal attempt to overthrow it. It is now for them to demonstrate to the world that those who can fairly carry an election can also suppress a rebellion; that ballots are the rightful and peaceful successors of bullets; and that when ballots have fairly and constitutionally decided, there can be no appeal back to bullets; that there can be no successful appeal, except to ballots themselves, at succeeding elections. Such will be a great lesson of peace; teaching men that what they cannot take by an election, neither can they take it by a war; teaching all the folly of being the beginners of a war."[10]

By reason of Lincoln's reiterated determination to save the Union, most people in his time and since have seen this as his ultimate design throughout the war, not penetrating to his deeper purpose. But why was it so essential that the Union be preserved? Because, as Lincoln analyzed the issue, upon the fate of the Union hung the fate of world democracy.

Free institutions, Lincoln told the Congress, had elevated the American people beyond any others in the world. So large an army as the government had at its command "was never before known, without a soldier in it but has taken his place there of his own free choice." And there was scarcely a regiment in that army from which a President, a Cabinet, a Congress, and perhaps a Supreme Court capable of administering the government could not be chosen. The same held true of the Confederate Army. Whoever chose to abandon such a government, warned Lincoln, had best think well of what might come in place of it.[11]

Throughout the war Lincoln strove to drive home this idea. In state papers, in private letters, in informal talks to soldiers—any time that opportunity offered—he tried to explain that the North was battling for democracy throughout the world, that in a people's government the decision of the electorate must be final, that in rejecting this principle and seeking to establish a new nation on the idea of the master race, some of America's own people had challenged the country's most cherished doctrines.

This was the reason Lincoln refused to compromise with the secessionists in the weeks before war broke out. To do so would be equivalent to buying the right to assume an office which he had fairly and constitutionally won. This explains why he would never admit that the Southern states could legally place themselves outside the Union. From this came his inflexible opposition to peace on any terms save full reestablishment of the national authority throughout the rebellious states.

When Lincoln was asked to say a few appropriate words at the dedication of the cemetery at Gettysburg the theme of democracy must have suggested itself to him at once. He pictured the setting in his mind—the blue haze softening the outline of the hills where two great armies had locked in stubborn combat for three days, the valley across which brave men, who fought for right as it was given them to see the right, had swept to death against the Union guns, the ridge where the Union boys hung on with such grim resolution, meeting those brave men with equal bravery. And Lincoln knew he would see something else—long lines of small white wooden crosses, marking the final resting place of both Southern and Northern boys. There would be no exultation in Lincoln's message; he never had it in his heart to condemn the South. What could he say? How futile were mere words to express the meaning of a holocaust like Gettysburg. What if those dead could speak? To what purpose had they died? Surely they must understand the meaning of their sacrifice. And the living, too, should understand it.

So, from the field of Gettysburg, on November 19, 1863, Lincoln, looking back to the promise of the Founding Fathers, then forward into the far reach of time, touched those chords that link America with all mankind as he brought a message to the living from the dead.

"Four score and seven years ago," he said, "our fathers brought forth on this continent, a new nation, conceived in liberty, and dedicated to the proposition that all men are created equal.

"Now we are engaged in a great civil war, testing whether that nation, or any nation so conceived and so dedicated, can long endure. We are met on a great battlefield of that war. We have come to dedicate a portion of that field, as a final resting place for those who here gave their lives that that nation might live. It is altogether fitting and proper that we should do this.

"But in a larger sense, we can not dedicate, we can not consecrate, we can not hallow, this ground. The brave men, living and dead, who struggled here, have consecrated it, far above our poor power to add or detract. The world will little note, nor long remember, what we say here, but it can never forget what they did here. It is for us the living, rather, to be dedicated here to the unfinished work which they who fought here have thus far so nobly advanced. It is rather for us to be here dedicated to the great task remaining before us—that from these honored dead we take increased devotion to that cause for which they gave the last full measure of devotion—that we here highly resolve that these dead shall not have died in vain—that this nation, under God, shall have a new birth of freedom—and that government of the people, by the people, for the people, shall not perish from the earth."

Another four score and seven years have passed. Democracy again fights for survival, not alone against a rival ideology but also against those subtle passions lurking in men's hearts which often wear a false mask of democracy. Lincoln would not be surprised to find it so. He realized that the struggle for human freedom is eternal; he cherished no illusions of its ending in his time. He understood that the antagonisms between man's better nature and his selfishness endure, that the battle for justice among men is never fully won, that every generation must guard and perhaps fight for its liberties. Out of the depths of a wisdom born of patient thought, of hard experience and mental anguish, Lincoln, like the Founding Fathers he revered, appealed to generations yet unborn, pleading that they be dedicated to the great unfinished work of making the precepts of our Declaration of Independence the great stepping stones to human advancement that they were meant to be.

In faithfulness to the principles of our democracy, Lincoln saw our best hope of peace, prosperity, and happiness at home, and of winning the trust and friendship of those in other lands.

We do not need to look abroad, where old deceptions in new guises contend with democracy for the homage of men's minds, to realize that Lincoln's is an unfinished work. In our own land our practice of democracy often falls short of our professions. Every one of us knows men and women who would be sincerely shocked to be called enemies of true democracy, yet who, through intolerance, greed, unfaithfulness to public trust, or mental reservations in their adherence to American ideals, subscribe, unwittingly perhaps, to sophistries and rationalizations which profane our democratic principles and paralyze their appeal.

Yet where is our hope in the great worldwide struggle of today, except in rededication to the ideals to which our country stands committed? This is an all-out fight in which lip service and hollow reverence are not enough. In renewed devotion to those ideals for which so many Americans have given, and are giving, the last full measure of devotion lies our strength.

"Let us have faith that right makes might, and in that faith, let us, to the end, dare to do our duty, as we understand it."[12] "The fiery trial through which we pass will light us down in honor or dishonor to the latest generation."[13] These are imperishable words. And just so, "It is for us the living" is a strong, clear call to us, today.

Notes

1. Address to the New Jersey Senate, Trenton, 21 February 1861, in *The Collected Works of Abraham Lincoln*, ed. Roy P. Basler, Marion Dolores Pratt and Lloyd A. Dunlap, asst. eds., 8 vols. plus index (New Brunswick: Rutgers University Press, 1953–55), 4:236.

2. Speech at Philadelphia, 22 Feb. 1861, in *Collected Works*, ed. Basler et al., 4:240.

3. Fragment of Speech on Free Labor, [17 Sept. 1859?], in *Collected Works*, ed. Basler et al., 3:462.

4. Speech to the 166th Ohio Regiment, 22 Aug. 1864, in *Collected Works*, ed. Basler et al., 7:512.

5. Speech at Philadelphia, 22 Feb. 1861, in *Collected Works*, ed. Basler et al., 4:240.

6. Speech at Chicago, 10 July 1858, in *Collected Works*, ed. Basler et al., 2:501.

7. Speech at Springfield, 26 June 1857, in *Collected Works*, ed. Basler et al., 2:406.

8. Message to Congress, 1 Dec. 1862, in *Collected Works*, ed. Basler et al., 5:537.

9. John Hay, *Inside Lincoln's White House: The Complete Civil War Diary of John Hay*, ed. Michael Burlingame and John R. Turner Ettlinger (Carbondale: Southern Illinois University Press, 1997), 20 (entry for 7 May 1861).

10. Message to Congress, 4 July 1861, in *Collected Works*, ed. Basler et al., 4:439.

11. Ibid.

12. Speech at Cooper Union, New York, 27 Feb. 1860, in *Collected Works*, ed. Basler et al., 3:550.

13. Message to Congress, 1 Dec. 1862, in *Collected Works*, ed. Basler et al., 5:537.

PART 2

The Life of Lincoln

5 Lincoln and Democracy

To make possible the establishment of democratic government, the people of America waged a bitter eight-years' war. Eighty-five
years later they fought for four years to preserve the form of government
they had established. In 1917 they entered a great European conflict when
called upon "to make the world safe" for it.

The truth of the first and last statements will be generally admitted,
but the accuracy of the second may not be so readily apparent. For the
Civil War is usually regarded as a struggle for the Union. And in the narrow sense, of course, it was. But in its broader aspect, and aside from the
slavery question, democracy was just as much the issue then as in our
other two great struggles.

This was not generally realized at the time, nor have American historians since appreciated it. But Lincoln saw it clearly from the first. And
while he tried repeatedly to make it plain to all, tried, in fact, to make it
the vital issue and rallying cry of the war, narrower but more tangible issues superseded it in the minds of most of his American contemporaries.

Lincoln and the cause of democracy are inseparably associated in the
minds of men. In the first place, because Lincoln, in his rise from poverty and obscurity to the presidency of the United States, was the vindica-
tor of democracy, the living proof of the feasibility of the democratic ideal
of equal and unlimited opportunity. "With him as President," said
Charles Sumner, "the idea of Republican Institutions, where no place is

Undated essay, Abraham Lincoln Association research files, Illinois State Historical Library,
Springfield.

too high for the humblest, was perpetually manifested, so that his simple presence was like a Proclamation of the Equality of all Men." His
career epitomized "the drama of Democracy."[1]

Moreover, Lincoln, by consistently advocating political equality and
justice, and by freeing four million slaves and thus forcing the South to
accept the philosophy of freedom, was the outstanding leader in the
march of democracy during the nineteenth century.

Yet many of those who see in Lincoln the embodiment and foremost
champion of democracy fail to appreciate the extent to which his life was
dedicated to the democratic ideal, and the extent to which devotion to
that ideal conditioned his policies and acts. His emancipation of the
Negro has overshadowed and diverted attention from other less obvious
but more important contributions to the democratic cause. As a matter
of fact, not only his opposition to the extension of slavery, but also his
refusal to compromise with the secessionists even to avert a war, and his
determination to save the Union even at the cost of war, were all based
upon his conviction of the desirability of perfecting, perpetuating, and
extending the ideal of popular government.

From an early point in his political career, Lincoln conceived of the
people of the United States as being the inheritors of a sacred trust, the
benefits of which they must conserve for their posterity. In a speech before the Young Men's Lyceum of Springfield on January 27, 1838, he said,
"We find ourselves under the government of a system of political institutions conducing more essentially to the ends of civil and religious liberty than any of which the history of former times tells us. We, when
mounting the stage of existence, found ourselves the legal inheritors of
these fundamental blessings. We toiled not in the acquirement or establishment of them; they are a legacy bequeathed us by a once hardy, brave,
and patriotic, but now lamented and departed race of ancestors. Theirs
was the task . . . to possess themselves, and through themselves us, of this
goodly land, and to up-rear upon its hills and valleys a political edifice of
liberty and equal rights; 'tis ours only to transmit these—the former
unprofaned by the foot of an invader, the latter undecayed by the lapse
of time and untorn by usurpation."[2]

In subsequent addresses Lincoln expanded this philosophical concept to make all mankind potential beneficiaries. In an address to the
Springfield Washingtonian Society on February 22, 1842, he said, "Of
our political revolution of '76 we are justly proud. It has given us a degree of political freedom far exceeding that of any other nation of the
earth. In it the world has found a solution of the long-mooted problem
as to the capability of man to govern himself. In it was the germ which

has vegetated, and still is to grow and expand into the universal liberty of mankind."[3]

Lincoln's opposition to the spread of slavery was based only partially on moral grounds. Equally fundamental was the inconsistency of slavery and democracy. In his famous address at Peoria on October 16, 1854, he stated his position clearly. "This declared indifference, but as I must think, covert zeal, for the spread of slavery, I cannot but hate," said he. "I hate it because of the monstrous injustice of slavery itself. I hate it because it deprives our republican example of its just influence in the world; enables the enemies of free institutions with plausibility to taunt us as hypocrites; causes the real friends of freedom to doubt our sincerity; and especially because it forces so many good men among ourselves into an open war with the very fundamental principles of civil liberty, criticizing the Declaration of Independence, and insisting that there is no right principle of action but self-interest."[4]

Although deploring Negro slavery, Lincoln was willing to tolerate it as a temporary contradiction. The important thing was not to lose sight of the ideal. Speaking at Chicago on December 10, 1856, he said, "Our government rests on public opinion. Whoever can change public opinion can change the government practically just so much. Public opinion, on any subject, always has a 'central idea,' from which all its minor thoughts radiate. That 'central idea' in our political public opinion at the beginning was, and until recently has continued to be, the 'equality of men.' And although it has always submitted patiently to whatever inequality there seemed to be as a matter of actual necessity its constant working has been a steady progress toward the practical equality of all men."[5]

Lincoln has been frequently criticized for refusing to consider any compromise with the seceding states on the question of slavery in the territories. George Fort Milton, in his recent book, *The Eve of Conflict*, ascribes his refusal to partisanship, and because of his intransigence blames him in considerable degree for precipitating war.[6] But Lincoln justified his attitude on grounds far higher than those of partisan politics. Here again it was solicitude for democracy which determined his position. To him the basic principle of popular government was the acquiescence of a minority in the result of an election. To be forced to make concessions to a defeated party as a condition to being permitted to assume control of the government was to him a denial of "the vital principles of a free government." He explained his position in a letter of January 11, 1861 to J. T. Hale. "We have just carried an election, on principles fairly stated to the people," he wrote. "Now we are told in advance the government shall be broken up unless we surrender to those we have beaten, before we take the offices. In this they are either attempting to play upon us or they are in dead earnest. Either way, if we surrender, it is the end of us and of the government. They will repeat the experiment upon us *ad libitem.*"[7]

In an interview with a reporter for the *New York Tribune,* he elaborated this belief. "I will suffer death," said he, "before I will consent or advise my friends to consent to any concession or compromise which looks like buying the privilege of taking possession of the government to which we have a constitutional right; because, whatever I might think of the merit of the various propositions before Congress, I should regard any concession in the face of menace as the destruction of the Government itself, and a consent on all hands that our system shall be brought down to a level with the existing disorganized state of affairs in Mexico."[8] He was willing, however, to submit the matter to the people. If they wished to call a convention to placate the grievances of the South or to guarantee the South in the possession of its vested rights, he would acquiesce. But the people had spoken, and until they reversed or modified their decision as expressed in the election, he, as their servant, refused to give way on the leading plank of the platform on which they had elected him.

By the time Lincoln set out for Washington to assume the duties of the presidency, the conviction that the crisis involved the fate of democracy had become firmly fixed in his mind. If any group, chagrined by electoral defeat, could withdraw from the Union at will, democratic government would be a farce. It therefore became imperative to compel the disaffected element to accede, to prevent their secession, even by force if necessary.

This necessity was by no means generally understood. In fact, there was considerable diversity of opinion, both north and south, as to just what the crisis involved. Nathaniel Hawthorne, writing to a friend in London three months after the fall of Fort Sumter, observed, "We also have gone to war, and we seem to have little, or at least a very misty idea of what we are fighting for. It depends upon the speaker; and that, again, depends upon the section of country in which his sympathies are enlisted. The Southern man will say, 'We fight for States' rights, liberty, and independence.' The Middle-Western man will avow he fights for the Union; while our Northern and Eastern man will swear that from the beginning his only idea was liberty to the blacks and the annihilation of slavery."[9] To Lincoln, however, all of these were incidental issues. To him the crisis presented the vital test of man's ability to govern himself.

Looked at from this viewpoint, the issue in America assumed a world significance, for in 1861 democratic government was still in the experimental stage. It had worked in the United States for seventy years, but tried in other countries it had failed. The people of France had twice attained it, only to see monarchy shortly restored again. In Spain, Portugal, Poland, the German and Italian States, attempts to obtain it had proved abortive. England had made progress towards it by the enfranchisement of the upper middle class in 1832. But of all the countries of Europe only Switzerland had a degree of self-government comparable to that in the United States. If the republican experiment failed in the latter country, little hope remained, so Lincoln thought, for the remainder of mankind.

Furthermore, as has been pointed out by Andrew C. McLaughlin, Lincoln believed that America's most noble possession was an idea—the equality of man.[10] The American people, racially dissimilar, with a comparatively short history, and few historical or cultural traditions, with no distinctive national literature or speech, were bound together as a nation principally by this idea. "Without the idea the nation was lost; and without the nation the idea was lost. . . . Its acceptance by the nation made the nation a reality; its rejection deprived the nation of its vitality." The fate of the nation would determine the fate of the idea.

At Independence Hall, Philadelphia, on February 22, 1861, Lincoln said, "I have often inquired of myself what great principle or idea it was that kept this Confederacy so long together. It was not the mere matter of separation of the colonies from the motherland, but that sentiment in the Declaration of Independence which gave liberty not alone to the people of this country, but hope to all the world, for all future time. It was that which gave promise that in due time the weights would be lifted from the shoulders of all men, and that all should have an equal chance. This is the sentiment embodied in the Declaration of Independence. . . . If this country cannot be saved without giving up that principle, I was about to say I would rather be assassinated on the spot than surrender it."[11]

In his first inaugural address Lincoln gave public expression to his conviction of the incompatibility of secession and democracy. "Plainly, the central idea of secession is the essence of anarchy," he declared. "A majority held in restraint by constitutional checks and limitations, and always changing easily with deliberate changes of popular opinions and sentiments, is the only true sovereign of a free people. Whoever rejects it, does, of necessity, fly to anarchy or to despotism. Unanimity is impossible; the rule of a minority, as a permanent arrangement, is wholly inadmissible; so that, rejecting the majority principle, anarchy or despotism in some form is all that is left."[12]

During the early months of his administration, as Lincoln pondered deeply over the situation, more and more he became convinced that the future of democracy hung in the balance. On May 7, in a conversation with John Hay, his young secretary, he observed, "For my own part, I consider the central idea pervading this struggle is the necessity that is upon us of proving that popular government is not an absurdity. We must settle this question now, whether, in a free government, the minority have the right to break up the government whenever they choose. If we fail, it will go far to prove the incapability of people to govern themselves."[13]

This same thought was the theme of a large part of Lincoln's first message to Congress. "And this idea embraces more than the fate of these United States," he said. "It presents to the whole family of man the question whether a constitutional republic or democracy—a government of the people by the same people—can or cannot maintain its territorial integrity against its own domestic foes. It presents the question whether discontented individuals, too few in numbers to control administration according to organic law in any case, can . . . break up their government, and thus practically put an end to free government upon the earth. It forces us to ask: 'Is there, in all republics, this inherent and fatal weakness?' 'Must a government, of necessity, be too strong for the liberties of its own people, or too weak to maintain its own existence?' . . . A right result at this time will be worth more to the world than ten times the men and ten times the money."[14] He then proceeded to demonstrate how democratic government made possible a greater development of individual ability than any other type of government known to man. There was scarcely a single regiment, North or South, he declared, from which there could not be drawn a group of men sufficiently intelligent to fill all the important offices of the government. Those who would abandon a government capable of developing such a generally high level of intelligence and ability should consider long and well. "This is essentially a people's contest," he asserted. "On the side of the Union it is a struggle for maintaining in the world that form and substance of government whose leading object is to elevate the condition of men—to lift artificial weights from all shoulders; to clear the paths of laudable pursuit for all; to afford all an unfettered start, and a fair chance in the race of life. Yielding to partial and temporary departures from necessity, this is the leading object of the government for whose existence we contend.

"Our popular government has often been called an experiment," he continued. "Two points in it our people have already settled—the successful establishing and the successful administering of it. One still remains—its successful maintenance against a formidable internal attempt to overthrow it. It is now for them to demonstrate to the world that those who can fairly carry an election can also suppress a rebellion; that ballots are the rightful and peaceful successors of bullets; and that when ballots have fairly and constitutionally decided, there can be no successful appeal back to bullets; that there can be no successful appeal, except to ballots themselves, at succeeding elections. Such will be a great lesson of peace: teaching men that what they cannot take by an election, neither can they take it by a war; teaching all the folly of being the beginners of a war."

This message contains the fullest explanation ever given of Lincoln's conception of the issue. But it is by no means the last exposition of it. In a second message to Congress on December 3, 1861, he declared that "It continues to develop that the insurrection is largely, if not exclusively, a war upon the first principle of popular government."[15] In addressing regiments going to or from the front, in replies to serenades, in private letters, he strove to put this point across. In addressing the 166th Ohio Regiment, he gave the thought a personal application. "I happen, temporarily, to occupy this White House," he declared. "I am a living witness that any one of your children may look to come here as my father's child has. It is in order that each one of you may have, through this free government which we have enjoyed, an open field and a fair chance for your industry, enterprise and intelligence; that you may all have equal privileges in the race of life, with all its desirable human aspirations. It is for this the struggle should be maintained, that we may not lose our birthright. . . . The nation is worth fighting for, to secure such an inestimable jewel."[16]

"As you would perpetuate popular government," began Lincoln's plea to the representatives of the border states to agree to compensated emancipation of their slaves.[17] In urging compensated emancipation upon Congress he explained that "in giving freedom to the slave, we assure freedom to the free"—by assuring the successful outcome of the war, and thus upholding the basic principle of popular government.[18] When a delegation of clergymen urged him to issue an emancipation proclamation and thus make the war a clear-cut issue between slavery and freedom, he replied, "I think you should admit that we already have an important principle to rally and unite the people, in the fact that constitutional government is at stake. This is a fundamental issue going down about as deep as anything."[19]

Throughout the war he voiced this idea publicly at every opportunity, and from it he drew the inspiration of his greatest and most beautiful address. For the sentiment "that we here highly resolve that these dead shall not have died in vain, that this nation, under God, shall have a new birth of freedom; and that government of the people, by the people, for the people, shall not perish from the earth" was simply the lyric re-statement of a thought of times previously expressed.[20]

Yet this idea, despite his reiteration of it, apparently lacked popular appeal. Perhaps it was too intangible for the popular grasp. Perhaps others were incapable of Lincoln's breadth of view. At any rate, to the end of the war "the Union," not "democracy," remained the Northern watchword. Lincoln evidently realized that in this matter, at least, he had failed to make the people understand him, because on August 18, 1864, addressing an Ohio regiment he said, "I wish it might be more generally and universally understood what the country is now engaged in." And he then proceeded to explain once more his idea of the war.[21]

But if Americans generally failed to see the war as Lincoln saw it, the European reaction verified his perspicacity. For within a year of the outbreak of war, in England, France, Spain, Switzerland, Germany, and, to a lesser degree, in other counties, public opinion split squarely along the lines of liberalism and conservatism. Those elements favorable to democracy and liberalism were sympathetic towards the North, while the aristocracy and other vested interest were outspoken for the South. The cleavage of opinion was influenced to some extent, of course, by factors such as diplomatic policy, slavery, war profits, wheat and cotton; but the primary determinant was, on the one hand, the desire of the liberals to see a popular government demonstrate its ability to surmount a crisis, and, on the other, the hope of the conservatives that the collapse of the Union would prove the impracticability of a form of government whose continued success was a menace to privilege everywhere.

In England, for example, the conservative element had been looking askance for years at the American experiment. In 1847 Alexander MacKay, in his *The Western World; or, Travels in the United States*, observed that "Englishmen are too prone to mingle severity with their judgments whenever the Republic is concerned. It is the interest of aristocracy to exhibit republicanism, where ever it is found, in the worst possible light. . . . They recognize America as the stronghold of republicanism. If they can bring it into disrepute here they know that they inflict upon it the deadliest blow in Europe."[22]

In 1861 the reactionaries seemed to have their opportunity. With liberalism in England already at low ebb, and with many leaders in both parties inclined to regard the Reform Act of 1832 as a finality so far as the extension of the franchise was concerned, failure of republicanism in America might well give the final blow to proponents of "mobocracy." The conservative press, convinced from the outset that the Union faced its doom, immediately made democracy the issue. "I see in America," the Earl of Shrewsbury proclaimed, "the trial of Democracy and its failure."[23] "Democratic institutions," observed the *Times*, "are now on their trial in America." "It is precisely because we do not share the admiration of America for her own institutions and political tendencies that we do not now see in the impending change an event altogether to be deplored," gloated *Blackwood's Magazine*.[24] If England after such an example should permit herself to be led into democracy she "will have perished by that willful infatuation which no warning can dispel," warned the *Quarterly Review*.[25] "In that reconstruction of political philosophy which the American calamities are likely to inaugurate," predicted the *Saturday Review*, "the value of the popular element will be reduced to its due proportions. . . . The true guarantee of freedom will be looked for more in the equilibrium of classes than in the equality of individuals. . . . We may hope, at last, that the delusive confusion between freedom and democracy is finally banished from the minds of Englishmen."[26]

As the war progressed, conservative papers exulted over Northern embarrassments. When the President and Congress moved cautiously, they were weak and vacillating; when arbitrary arrests and censorship of the press were resorted to, they were tyrannical. But most persistent was conservative scorn of a nation unable to settle its differences except "in accordance with the will of an inflamed and exasperated population."

So outspokenly hostile to the North was the conservative press at times that W. H. Russell, the famous British war correspondent, felt called upon to explain to Charles Sumner, "I do not approve of the tone of many papers in Britain in reference to American matters. But do not forget I pray you that in reality it is Brightism and republicanism at home which most of these remarks are meant to smite—America is the shield under which the blow is dealt."[27] John Lothrop Motley, American Minister to Austria, confirmed this when he wrote, "The real secret of the exultation which manifests itself in the *Times* and other organs over our troubles and disasters, is their hatred not to America, so much as to democracy in England."[28]

John Bright and other liberals, realizing the possible effect of events in America upon their own fortunes, and handicapped by repeated Northern disasters, were hard put to it to reply. A Scotch Whig wrote in 1861, "Liberals like ourselves who had long looked with pride and hope to the splendid fabric of free government and national and commercial greatness, built up by our kinsmen across the sea . . . felt as if their own principles had exhibited failure, and as if the capacity of mankind for self-government had been half refuted."

Liberal newspapers and individuals, fearful of the outcome, denied at first that democracy was on trial. The *Daily News* protested that up to the election of Lincoln it was paradoxical to say that popular institutions had failed, and it was no less absurd to say so now. Had similar crises never befallen any other forms of government? How about England's loss of her American colonies, Spain's loss of Mexico, Austria's loss of Italy? Were these deemed failures of that type of government?

But such protests were ineffectual against the roar of the reactionary barrage. Finally, in December 1861, John Bright in desperation resolved to meet the conservatives on their own ground. Accepting the challenge, he worked throughout the remainder of the war to convince the working class that the Northern cause was their own. Frequent meetings to express sympathy for the North were held in working-class districts, and at one of these—a huge Trades Union meeting in London on March 26, 1863—one speaker went so far as to declare that the success of free institutions in America was a political question of such deep consequence in England that the working classes would tolerate no interference unfavorable to the North.

So clear-cut and bitter did the issue become in English politics that on April 2, 1863, Charles Francis Adams, the American Minister in London, warned, "I am not sure that some parties here would not now be willing even to take the risk of a war in order more effectively to turn the scale against us, and thus, as they think, to crush the rising spirit of their own population."[29]

The rise and fall of British liberalism closely follow the course of events in America. The first two years of the war saw a swing to conservatism which defeated two reform bills and a proposal to abolish compulsory church rates, and culminated in a feeling among conservatives, openly expressed by *Blackwood's*, that "every sensible man in this country now acknowledges that we have already gone as far toward democracy as it is safe to go. . . . This is the great moral benefit which we have derived from the events in America."[30]

But with Lee's retreat from Pennsylvania after Gettysburg, and with the fall of Vicksburg, the tide began to turn. With continued Northern success the conservative papers began to fear that they had thrown a boomerang. They no longer presented the war as a trial of democracy. "The existence of the United States as a prosperous republic has been the example against which all reasoning contrary to the popular feeling has been steadily losing strength," wrote Adams to Seward on April 15, 1864. "It was the outbreak of war that in an instant gave such revived hopes to all the privileged classes in Europe. For three years they have been making every possible use of the advantage. But it is now manifestly on the wane once more."[31]

But as the Conservatives tried to soft-pedal the democratic issue, the Liberal press and speakers, realizing that their turn had come, dinned it into them. In May 1864 Gladstone asserted every man's right to vote; and by the end of the war conservatism was in slow but sure retreat. Watchfully following the trend of events in England, Adams predicted to Seward, "The very moment the war comes to an end and a restoration of the Union follows, it will be the signal for a reaction that will make Mr. Bright perhaps the most formidable public man in England."[32]

In France, Louis Napoleon's Mexican venture and the slavery issue presented extraneous factors, but here, as in England, the press and the political leaders reacted to the American war according to their inclinations in domestic politics. Court circles, higher banking circles, army officers, high churchmen, and the official press were pro-Southern; republicans, liberal monarchists and Catholics, and the progressive press were for the North.[33] "Sympathy for the North," wrote John Stuart Mill from Avignon, "animated all *liberal-minded* Frenchmen from the start."[34] Liberal papers and periodicals like *L'opinion nationale, Le temps, Le courrier du Dimanche, La revue des deux mondes,* and *Le journal des debates* were vigorous defenders of the North, as were most of the provincial newspapers. [Eugene] Forcade, editor of *La revue des deux mondes,* made a special study of the election of 1864, the orderly outcome of which seemed to him "a stupendous moral victory for liberty."[35] [Antoine Auguste] Laugel, a collaborator of Forcade, regarded secession as "a coup d'etat by a minority."[36] The liberal historians [Louis] Thiers and [Edouard] Laboulaye struck at Louis Napoleon and French imperialism by extolling democracy in America.[37]

The chairman of a student meeting in Paris presented [John] Bigelow, the American Consul General, with an address stating that "we young people, to whom the future belongs, must have the courage to found a true democracy, and we will have to look beyond the ocean to learn how a people who have made themselves free can preserve their freedom."[38]

"My country, France, was then governed by Napoleon III," said Jean Jules Jusserand before the Abraham Lincoln Association on February 12, 1909; "all liberals had their eyes fixed on America. Your example was the great example which gave heart to our most progressive men. You had proved that republican government was possible by having one. If it broke to pieces, so would the hopes of all those among us who expected one day we would have the same. And the partisans of autocracy were loud in their assertion that a republic was well and good for a country without enemies or neighbors but that, if a storm arose, it would be shattered."[39]

As the war wore on, the importance of its outcome in French politics became clearer day by day. On February 6, 1863, Bigelow wrote to Seward, "After all, this struggle of ours both at home and abroad is but a struggle between the principle of popular government and government by a privileged class. The people therefore all the world over are in a species of solidarity which it is our duty and interest to cultivate to the utmost."[40]

In other countries of Europe extraneous considerations complicated the division of opinion to a greater degree than in England and France. In Austria, the dominant state of the heterogeneous German Confederation, for example, court circles favored the North, not because of concern for democracy, but because of aversion to revolution and secession. The Spanish reaction was influenced by Spain's participation in Napoleon's Mexican scheme. The House of Savoy, eager for the unification of Italy, saw only unfavorable consequences to that movement in the dismemberment of a sister state. The Czar of Russia and his entourage were openly friendly to the North because Russian foreign policy had always favored the maintenance of a strong, united American state as a maritime counterpoise to England in the "universal" balance of power.

Yet despite these complicating factors, opinion in these and other countries divided fairly generally along the lines of progress and reaction. In Spain, for example, the official press interpreted the Civil War as an inevitable result of the baneful influence of democracy, while republican papers combated this view with the assertion that, on the contrary, not democracy but slavery, the negation of democracy, was its real cause. The American Minister in Berne reported that sympathy in republican Switzerland was practically unanimous for the North, and that "the war is everywhere understood to be a struggle between freedom and despotism." In Prussia, court and army circles favored the South, but among the people of German Confederation generally, and especially in the South-German States, opinion was overwhelmingly pro-Northern. Concerned with their own struggle for unification, the Italians were for the most part apathetic, yet even here [Giuseppe] Mazzini, the famous liberal and unificationist, wrote to a friend in America, "You have done more for us in four years than fifty years of teaching, preaching, and writing from all your European brothers have been able to do."[41]

Pratt and Jordan, co-authors of Europe and the American Civil War, to whom I am indebted for many of the quotations given above, are convinced from their study of European opinion that "the North won an earlier and more decisive victory in the contest of opinion abroad than it did in the war of arms at home," that by 1863 the liberal element was so fortified and increased that no European government dared defy it, and that the liberal element in England, France, and Spain thus helped considerably to prevent European intervention or recognition of the Confederacy.[42]

While American historians have depicted the Civil War as a struggle between opposing constitutional theories, or between incompatible political or economic philosophies, few of them have sensed its significance with relation to the progress of democracy. Andrew C. McLaughlin and Nathaniel W. Stephenson have done so, and there are some working in the field of foreign relations whose contact with European opinion has brought it home to them. But by historians generally this aspect of the war has been overlooked, inadequately treated, or ignored.

Yet the events of history prove that Lincoln's conception was correct, and that once again he had demonstrated his ability to probe to the fundamentals of an issue. For it was not by mere coincidence that two years after the war England extended the franchise to the lower middle class, and in 1888 granted what was practically equivalent to manhood suffrage; that the rule of Louis Napoleon became increasingly liberal in the later sixties, and finally gave place to a republic in 1871; that serfdom was abolished in Russia in 1866; that new constitutions and reforms were granted in Austria-Hungary; and that the Bourbons were driven from Spain in 1868 and a constitutional monarchy established.

Some of these reforms, particularly those in England, would have been deferred for years but for the successful demonstration of democracy in America, while all of them were abetted in some degree by the liberal impetus from that direction. In the United States the outcome of an election, legally conducted, has never since been questioned, while in Europe, Lincoln, in the language of Lord Charnwood, is regarded "as the greatest among those associated with the cause of popular government."[43]

Notes

1. Charles Sumner, eulogy for Abraham Lincoln delivered in Boston on 1 June 1865, in *The Works of Charles Sumner*, 15 vols. (Boston: Lee and Shepard, 1870–83), 9:410.

2. Address before the Young Men's Lyceum of Springfield, 27 Jan. 1838, in *The Collected Works of Abraham Lincoln*, ed. Roy P. Basler, Marion Dolores Pratt and Lloyd A. Dunlap, asst. eds., 8 vols. plus index (New Brunswick: Rutgers University Press, 1953–55), 1:108.

3. Address to the Springfield Washingtonian Society, 22 Feb. 1842, in *Collected Works*, ed. Basler et al., 1:278.

4. Speech at Peoria, 16 Oct. 1854, in *Collected Works*, ed. Basler et al., 2:255.

5. Speech at Chicago, 10 Dec. 1856, in *Collected Works*, ed. Basler et al., 2:385.

6. George Fort Milton, *The Eve of Conflict: Stephen A. Douglas and the Needless War* (Boston: Houghton Mifflin, 1934).

7. Abraham Lincoln to J. T. Hale, Springfield, 11 Jan. 1861, in *Collected Works*, ed. Basler et al., 4:172. Republican James T. Hale (1810–65) of Bellefonte, Pa., represented his district in the U.S. House (1859–65).

8. Remarks Concerning Secession, [ca. Jan. 19–21, 1861], in *Collected Works*, ed. Basler et al., 4:176.

9. Nathaniel Hawthorne to Francis Bennoch, Concord, Mass., [ca. July 1861], in *Nathaniel Hawthorne: The Letters, 1857–1864*, ed. Thomas Woodson et al. (Columbus: Ohio State University Press, 1987), 387.

10. Andrew C. McLaughlin, "Lincoln, the Constitution, and Democracy," *International Journal of Ethics* 47 (1936): 1–24. McLaughlin was a constitutional historian at the University of Chicago.

11. Address at Independence Hall, 22 Feb. 1861, in *Collected Works*, ed. Basler et al., 4:240.

12. First Inaugural Address, 4 March 1861, in *Collected Works*, ed. Basler et al., 4:268.

13. John Hay, *Inside Lincoln's White House: The Complete Civil War Diary of John Hay*, ed. Michael Burlingame and John R. Turner Ettlinger (Carbondale: Southern Illinois University Press, 1997), 20.

14. Message to Congress, 4 July 1861, in *Complete Works*, ed. Basler et al., 4:421–41.

15. Message to Congress, 3 Dec. 1861, in *Complete Works*, ed. Basler et al., 5:51.

16. Speech to the 166th Ohio Regiment, 22 Aug. 1864, in *Collected Works*, ed. Basler et al., 7:512.

17. Appeal to Border State Representatives, 12 July 1862, in *Collected Works*, ed. Basler et al., 5:318–19.

18. Message to Congress, 1 Dec. 1862, in *Collected Works*, ed. Basler et al., 5:537.

19. Reply to Emancipation Memorial, 13 Sept. 1862, in *Collected Works*, ed. Basler et al., 5:423–24.

20. Gettysburg Address, 19 Nov. 1863, in *Collected Works*, ed. Basler et al., 7:23.

21. Speech to the 164th Ohio Regiment, 18 Aug. 1864, in *Collected Works*, ed. Basler et al., 7:504–5.

22. Alexander MacKay, *The Western World; or, Travels in the United States in 1846–47*, 2 vols. (Philadelphia: Lea and Blanchard, 1849).

23. Ephraim D. Adams, *Great Britain and the American Civil War*, 2 vols. (New York: Longmans, Green, 1925), 2:282.

24. *Blackwood's Magazine*, July 1861, in Adams, *Great Britain and the American Civil War*, 2:278–79.

25. "Democracy on Its Trial," *Quarterly Review*, July 1861, in Adams, *Great Britain and the American Civil War*, 2:279.

26. *Saturday Review*, 14 Sept. 1861, in Adams, *Great Britain and the American Civil War*, 2:280.

27. Donaldson Jordan and Edwin J. Pratt, *Europe and the American Civil War* (Boston: Houghton Mifflin, 1931), 59. William Howard Russell (1820–1907) was a special correspondent for the *Times of London*.

28. Adams, *Great Britain and the American Civil War*, 2:280–81.

29. Charles Francis Adams to William H. Seward, London, 2 April 1863, State Department Records, National Archives.

30. *Blackwood's Magazine*, Feb. 1863, in Adams, *Great Britain and the American Civil War*, 2:289.

31. Charles Francis Adams to William H. Seward, London, 15 April 1864, State Department Records, National Archives.

32. Charles Francis Adams to William Henry Seward, 29 Jan. 1864, in Adams, *Great Britain and the American Civil War*, 2:298.

33. Serge Gavronsky, *The French Liberal Opposition and the American Civil War* (New York: Humanities Press, 1968).

34. In 1862 Mill told John Lothrop Motley, the U.S. minister to Austria that "all Liberal Frenchmen seem to have been with you, from the first." Mill to Motley, Avignon, 31 Oct. 1862, in *The Later Letters of John Stuart Mill, 1849–1873*, ed. Francis E. Mineka and Dwight N. Lindley (Toronto: University of Toronto Press, 1972), 802.

35. The influential journalist Eugene Forcade (1820–69) was well known for his political commentary. His consistent espousal of the Union cause in *La revue des deux mondes* is examined in Louis Martin Sears, "A Neglected Critic of Our Civil War," *Mississippi Valley Historical Review* 1 (1915): 532–45. Jordan and Pratt, *Europe and the American Civil War*, 235.

36. Trained as a geologist, Antoine Auguste Laugel (1830–1914) wrote scientific books and contributed frequently to contemporary journals of opinion, most notably *La revue des deux mondes* and *The Nation*. In 1864–65 he traveled extensively throughout the United States and described his experiences in *The United States during the War* (1866). He married Marian Chapman, daughter of the prominent antislavery leader Maria Weston Chapman. Jordan and Pratt, *Europe and the American Civil War*, 235.

37. Louis Adolphe Thiers (1797–1877), author of the ten-volume *Histoire de la revolution francaise* (1823–27) and the twenty-volume *Histoire du consulat et de l'empire* (1845–61), was a leading champion of efforts to reform France under Louis Napoleon. He served in different governmental posts between 1830 and 1848. A professor of general and philosophical history and comparative legislation, Edouard René Lefebvre de Laboulaye (1811–83) of the College of France lectured on American constitutional law, among other things, and wrote for publications such as the *Journal des debats*.

38. In 1861 Secretary of State Seward appointed the journalist John Bigelow (1817–1911) as consul general to France, where he served as a propagandist for the Union cause. In 1865 he became U.S. minister to France.

39. Lincoln Centennial Association, *Addresses Delivered at the Memorial Exercises Held at Springfield, February 12, 1909* (Springfield: Illinois Centennial Commission, 1909), 18–19.

40. John Bigelow, *Retrospections of an Active Life*, 5 vols. (New York: Baker and Taylor, 1909–13), 1:600.

41. Giuseppe Mazzini (1805–72) founded the "Young Italy" movement, which sought to establish a united, democratic Italy. Pratt and Jordan, *Europe and the American Civil War*, 266.

42. Ibid., 265.

43. Godfrey R. Benson, Lord Charnwood, *Abraham Lincoln* (New York: Garden City Publishing, 1938), 455.

6 *Some Popular Misconceptions about Lincoln*

No man in American history looms larger today than Abraham Lincoln. Each year the circle of his admirers grows. Both in this country and abroad there is an ever-increasing interest in him. Thousands of books and articles have been written about him. Many of these are mere rehashing of facts or legends already known. A few of them have given us new information or have corrected errors made in earlier books. But many of these errors and misconceptions still survive.

For instance, most people think that Lincoln sprang from poverty-stricken, illiterate, ignorant parents who were more or less of the dregs of society or at least far below the average level of the people of the various communities in which they lived. William H. Herndon, Lincoln's law partner, upon whose *Life of Lincoln* most subsequent lives have been based, characterized Thomas Lincoln, the father, as roving and shiftless; but his opinions were based on statements of a few old men who had known Thomas Lincoln, and are not in accord with recent findings. Patient search in the public records of the Kentucky and Indiana counties where the Lincoln lived has brought to light evidence that proves that while Thomas Lincoln could not be called a leader in any sense, he was sober, industrious—at least in his earlier life—honest, and at one time or another owned considerable land and some personal property. He held

Undated manuscript, Abraham Lincoln Association research files, Illinois State Historical Society, Springfield.

minor political offices and served on juries. He was a respected church member in every community in which he lived. He could write his name long before he was married, in spite of the tradition that his wife taught him to do so, and he probably learned to read, although he could never do it without a struggle. He did change his residence frequently; and this has been taken as an indication of shiftlessness; but we must remember that the whole population of the frontier was migratory.[1] Nancy Hanks Lincoln, Abraham's mother, was the counterpart of the mothers of hundreds of other western pioneers. Sarah Bush Lincoln, Abraham's stepmother could not write but she could read. In other words, while the Lincoln family was poor, and in some respects crude, it was a typical farming family of the early West, below the average of that region in no respect.[2]

The environment of Lincoln's youth was a difficult one, and he deserves credit for resisting its retarding influences. He saw the value of education, whereas most of his associates scoffed at it or didn't care. He had ambition for betterment, while most of the youths with whom he associated were content to go on as their fathers had done. He deserves admiration for overcoming the handicaps imposed by the frontier; yet he also owes something to that frontier environment.

Take his life at New Salem, for example. While New Salem was new, small, and in some respects raw, and while living there handicapped Lincoln in some ways, yet he had advantages there that he could not have had in an older, settled community—an Eastern town, for instance. Humble origin and lack of schooling were no drawbacks, for they were common deficiencies. As a newcomer in a Western town he found no difficulty in establishing himself, for no one had been there long, no propertied class had emerged, and social castes had not solidified. Equality of opportunity was in large degree a fact.

Courage, honesty, self-reliance, democracy, and nationalism were the ideals of the frontier. Lincoln absorbed these qualities to the full, and benefited by the opportunities that the frontier afforded. But at the same time he avoided the weaknesses of the frontier, or at least outgrew them in time. He became self-reliant without becoming boastful—boastfulness was a common weakness of our frontier—and without overestimating himself; analytical and conservative rather than impulsive and opportunistic; respectful for law and traditions in a region where people often took the law into their own hands and where most men were concerned about the future and more or less indifferent about the past.

As you know, Lincoln made his living first as a common laborer or farmhand. Then, at New Salem, he tried to run a store and failed. He became postmaster at New Salem and a surveyor and finally entered politics. He was elected to the State Legislature. Meanwhile he studied law and came to Springfield to practice.

There are a variety of opinions about his legal ability. Some think that he was simply a mediocre lawyer, traveling around the circuit, trying unimportant cases in little country towns. This is probably correct so far as his early legal career is concerned. Others would have him the greatest lawyer in the state, head and shoulders above his colleagues. This he certainly was not. No one has yet done the research necessary to a final estimate of Lincoln as a lawyer; but such an estimate can be made for the last six years of his legal career. During that period there is no doubt that he was one of the outstanding lawyers of central Illinois. During those years he was riding the circuit as he had done before, trying many small, unimportant cases; but he was also getting a good share of the business in the Supreme Court of Illinois and the federal courts here in Springfield. In the federal courts he was well up among the leaders in volume of business, he and Herndon ranked about fourth or fifth, and, after all, volume of business is one of the best tests of a lawyer's ability. His reputation was such that he was frequently called to Chicago to handle cases in the federal courts there. In the Supreme Court, from 1854 to 1860, the firm of Lincoln and Herndon ranked third in number of cases and got much more than their proportionate share of business coming up to the Supreme Court from those counties where they were best known.

But Lincoln was not a great student of the law. His knowledge of legal theory was small. His ability lay in his sincerity, his power of expression, his logic and sound common-sense, rather than in knowledge of precedents and authorities. Stephen T. Logan, Lincoln's second partner, to whom Lincoln probably owed more than anyone else so far as his early legal development was concerned, said: "Lincoln's knowledge of law was very small when I took him in. I don't think he studied very much. I think he learned his law more in the study of cases. He would work hard and learn all there was in a case he had in hand. He got to be a pretty good lawyer though his general knowledge of law was never very formidable. But he would study out his case and make about as much of it as anybody. After awhile he began to pick up a considerable ambition in the law. He didn't have confidence enough at first. . . .

"Both he and [Edward D.] Baker were exceedingly useful to me in getting the good will of juries. Lincoln seemed to put himself at once on an equality with everybody—never of course while they were outrageous, never while they were drunk or noisy or anything of the kind. . . .

"Lincoln was growing all the time, from the time I first knew him. He was not much of a reader. Lincoln was never what might be called a very industrious reader. But he would get a case and try to know all there was connected with it; and in that way before he left this country he got to be quite a formidable lawyer.

"But he had this one peculiarity: he couldn't fight in a bad case.

"So far as his reading knowledge of law went he had a quite unusual grasp of the principles involved. When he was with me, I have seen him get a case and seem to be bewildered at first, but he would go at it and after a while he would master it. He was very tenacious in his grasp of a thing he once got hold of."[3]

Lincoln had an unquenchable fondness for politics. He was five times elected to the Illinois Legislature, served one term in Congress, was twice a candidate for the United States Senate, and, of course, was finally elected to the presidency. Some folks think that he was not at all ambitious, that he simply sat back and let political honors come to him. Nothing could be farther from the truth. He was undoubtedly ambitious and worked hard for every political office that he got—and for some that he didn't get. In his first campaign for the Legislature he said: "Every man is said to have his peculiar ambition. Whether it be true or not, I can say, for one, that I have no other so great as that of being truly esteemed of my fellow-men, by rendering myself worthy of their esteem."[4]

In 1846, when he wanted to go to Congress, he was afraid that John J. Hardin of Jacksonville would get the Whig nomination instead of himself. There had been a sort of unwritten understanding between Hardin, E. D. Baker, and Lincoln that they should take turns and go to Congress in that order. Hardin and Baker had gone, Baker had refused to run again so that Lincoln could have his chance; but Lincoln was afraid that Hardin was going to ruin his chances by opposing him for the nomination. Faced with this situation Lincoln wrote a long letter to Hardin in which he practically demanded that he withdraw and give Lincoln his chance. And Hardin did.

Here are extracts from letters written by Lincoln during his campaign for the United States Senate in 1854. The State Legislature elected the Senators at that time. On November 10, he wrote to Charles Hoyt of Aurora: "Some friends here are really for me, for the U.S. Senate, and I should be grateful if you could make a mark for me among your members. Please write me at all events giving me the name, post offices, and political position of members [of the Legislature] round about you."[5] Lincoln evidently intended to write to all of them. On November 27, he wrote to T. J. Henderson of Stark County, "think it over, and see whether you can do better than go for me."[6] A little later he wrote to Joseph Gillespie of Edwardsville: "I have really got it into my head to try to be United States Senator, and, if I could have your support, my chances would be reasonably good. But I know, and acknowledge, that you have as just claims to the place as I have; and therefore I cannot ask you to yield to me, if you are thinking of becoming a candidate, yourself. If, however, you are not, then I should like to be remembered affectionately by you; and also to have you make a mark for me with the Anti-Nebraska members down your way."[7] On December 11, he wrote to Elihu B. Washburne of Galena: "I have not ventured to write all the members in your district, lest some of them should be offended by the indelicacy of the thing—that is, coming from a total stranger. Could you not drop some of them a line?"[8]

Similar quotations from letters written in 1860 show that Lincoln wanted the presidency and was working hard for it. In early February he was afraid that a factional fight in Illinois would cost him the presidential nomination in the Republican State Convention, and he wrote to Norman B. Judd, a Chicago friend, "Your enemies are most bitter against me, and for revenge upon you will lay to the Bates egg in the South, and to the Seward egg in the north, and go far toward squeezing me out in the middle with nothing. Can you not help me a little in this matter in your end of the vineyard?"[9] To Samuel Galloway he wrote concerning the strategy to be used in the Republican National Convention at Chicago: "My name is new in the field and I suppose I am not the first choice of a very great many. Our policy, then, is to give no offense to others—leave them in a mood to come to us if they shall be compelled to give up their first love."[10]

In his early political life Lincoln was frankly and perhaps selfishly ambitious.[11] He continued to be ambitious throughout life; but after 1854, when the question of the extension of slavery was reinjected into politics his ambition was tempered and restrained by devotion to a cause, and its selfish aspect is distinctly subordinated. In 1855, after he had given up his own chance of becoming U.S. Senator in order to prevent a pro-slavery man from being elected, he wrote: "I could not, however, let the whole political result go to smash, on a point merely personal to myself."[12] After his defeat by Douglas in 1858, he wrote: "I think we have fairly entered upon a durable struggle as to whether this nation is to ultimately become all slave or all free, and though I fall early in the contest, it is nothing if I shall have contributed, in the least degree, to the final rightful result."[13] To his friend Dr. A. G. Henry he wrote: "I am glad I made the late race. It gave me a hearing on the great and durable ques-

tion of the age, which I could have had in no other way; and though I now
sink out of view, and shall be forgotten, I believe I have made some marks
which will tell for the cause of civil liberty long after I am gone."[14]

The change in Lincoln is evident in his speeches. Prior to 1854 they
often tended to the "spread-eagle" type, and were marked by broad humor and floridity. After 1854, they were direct, simple, appealing, [and]
sincere.

Lincoln's attitude on slavery is very commonly misunderstood. Many
people think that from his youth he detested slavery and that his whole
life was a crusade for its abolishment. You all know the story of his having seen a slave auction on his second trip to New Orleans on a flatboat
and of his vowing that if he ever got a chance to hit that thing he would
hit it hard. This story appears in Herndon's *Life of Lincoln.*[15] Herndon
got it from John Hanks, who supposedly was present when Lincoln made
the statement.[16] But in one of the short autobiographical sketches that
he wrote in later life Lincoln said that John Hanks went only as far as St.
Louis on this trip.[17]

In considering Lincoln's position on slavery you must distinguish
between his personal views and his political position, and between his
attitude on slavery in the states where it already existed and the extension of it into new territory.

Personally, Lincoln detested slavery. On April 4, 1864, he wrote: "I
am naturally anti-slavery. If slavery is not wrong, nothing is wrong. I
cannot remember when I did not so think and feel."[18]

Yet politically he took a conservative position upon it. He was never
an Abolitionist; the Abolitionists stood for destroying slavery everywhere. He was not even one of the founders of the Republican Party, as
some think. He did not join that party for two years after its formation,
primarily because he feared that it would take too radical a stand on
slavery.

He did not condemn the Southerners for holding slaves or for seeking to preserve slavery, nor did he have a ready solution for the slavery
question. In his speech at Peoria on October 16, 1854, he said: "I have no
prejudice against the Southern people. They are just what we would be
in their situation. . . . When Southern people tell us they are no more
responsible for the origin of slavery than we are, I acknowledge the fact.
When it is said the institution exists, and that it is very difficult to get
rid of it in any satisfactory way, I can understand and appreciate the saying. I surely will not blame them for not doing what I should not know
how to do myself. If all earthly power were given me, I should not know
what to do as to the existing institution."[19]

Prior to the Civil War, the farthest that Lincoln ever went was to oppose the extension of slavery into new territories. He took the view that the national government had no right to disturb it in the states where it already existed. But he believed that if it was kept from spreading into new territory it would eventually die a natural and peaceable death.

Lincoln was elected President on a platform which opposed the extension of slavery in the territories, and while he repeatedly disavowed any intention of interfering with slavery in the states he wouldn't give way an inch on the matter of its extension. But his determination not to give way was due not to hatred of slavery primarily, but to belief that the principle of democratic government was at stake. By electing him the people had shown that they opposed the extension of slavery. The Southern states, by seceding, refused to acquiesce in the will of the people by accepting the result of the election. But in a Democracy the result of an election must be accepted if Democracy is to mean anything. If a state or a group of states were to secede every time they disliked the result of an election or every time a law was passed to which they were opposed, popular government just wouldn't work. Lincoln took this view and believed that the South must be forced to stay in the Union and accept the result of the election.

He told John Hay, his young secretary, "For my own part, I consider the central idea pervading this struggle is the necessity that is upon us of proving that popular government is not an absurdity. We must settle the question now, whether, in a free government, the minority have the right to break up the government whenever they choose. If we fail, it will go far to prove the incapability of people to govern themselves."[20]

In his first message to Congress, Lincoln said: "Our popular government has often been called an experiment. Two points in it our people have already settled—the successful establishing and the successful administering of it. One still remains—its successful maintenance against a formidable internal attempt to overthrow it. It is now for them to demonstrate to the world that those who can fairly carry an election can also suppress a rebellion; that ballots are the rightful and peaceful successors of bullets; and that when ballots have fairly and constitutionally decided, there can be no successful appeal back to bullets; that there can be no successful appeal, except to ballots themselves, at succeeding elections. Such will be a great lesson of peace: teaching men that what they cannot take by an election, neither can they take it by a war; teaching all the folly of being the beginners of a war."[21]

Both of these statements were forerunners of the Gettysburg Address, and makes more clear the meaning of Lincoln's famous statement at

Gettysburg "that we here highly resolve that these dead shall not have died in vain; that this nation, under God, shall have a new birth of freedom; and that government of the people, by the people, for the people, shall not perish from the earth."[22]

So you see to Lincoln the fate of slavery was simply incidental to the fate of the Union which to him was synonymous with the fate of Democracy. If any further proof is needed of this listen to Lincoln's famous letter to Horace Greeley:

"I would save the Union. I would save it the shortest way under the Constitution. The sooner the national authority can be restored the nearer the union will be 'the Union as it was.' If there be those who would not save the Union unless they could at the same time save slavery, I do not agree with them. If there be those who would not save the Union unless they could at the same time destroy slavery, I do not agree with them. My paramount object in this struggle is to save the Union, and is not either to save or to destroy slavery. If I could save the Union without freeing any slave, I would do it; and if I could save it by freeing all the slaves, I would do it; and if I could save it by freeing some and leaving others alone, I would also do that. What I do about slavery and the colored race, I do because I believe it helps to save the Union; and what I forbear, I forbear because I do not believe it would help to save the Union. I shall do less whenever I shall believe what I am doing hurts the cause, and I shall do more whenever I shall believe doing more will help the cause. I shall try to correct errors when shown to be errors, and I shall adopt new views so fast as they shall appear to be true views. I have here stated my purpose according to my view of official duty; and I intend no modification of my oft-expressed personal wish that all men everywhere could be free."[23]

Lincoln realized that to win the war he must keep the border slave states—Maryland, Delaware, Kentucky, and Missouri—from seceding. If they joined the Confederacy all hope of subduing the South was lost. On the other hand, if the South could be shown that there was no possibility of their joining the Confederacy, the people of the South would be more apt to become discouraged and give up the fight. Lincoln's policy then was to do nothing to antagonize the border states, and at the same time try to get them to give up slavery voluntarily, by allowing the federal government to buy their slaves—compensated emancipation. He even went so far as to write a bill with his own hand providing for the federal government's buying all the slaves in Delaware and setting them free.[24] This was introduced in the Delaware legislature, but failed to pass; and efforts to secure similar legislation in the other border slave states were futile.

When Lincoln finally issued the Emancipation Proclamation he did it not on moral grounds, but as a military measure, because he believed he was weakening the South and permitting the North to use Negroes as soldiers. The proclamation freed only the slaves in the states that were in rebellion. It did not free those in Delaware, Maryland, Kentucky, Missouri, Tennessee and West Virginia. In other words Lincoln did not act from personal motives; while he was glad to be able to free the slaves, he would have respected what he considered the rights of the South had they not forced emancipation upon him.

Another misconception about Lincoln is belief that he was always a poor man. Moreover, because he failed in business at New Salem and because of his careless bookkeeping as a lawyer it has been assumed that he was naive or incompetent in the management of business affairs. He was not. Whenever he accumulated any surplus funds he invested them wisely and conservatively in mortgages and land. At the time of his nomination to the presidency he was worth about $10,000. During his presidency he invested most of his salary in government bonds. At the time of his death he owned about $60,000 worth of government bonds. Besides these he had about $8,000 worth of unpaid salary warrants, he had about $9,000 on deposit in the Springfield Marine Bank, about $1,400 on deposit in Washington, and enough real estate and mortgages to bring the total value of his estate to $85,000 or $90,000.[25]

All of this raises the question of what constitutes Lincoln's greatness. I wish that I could go into this in more detail, but time will not permit. Is he great because he freed the slaves? Evidently not; for this was part of a larger purpose. Was it the fact that he rose from humble environment to the presidency, in other words is it because he is the embodiment of the American ideal of equal opportunity for even the humblest men? I have shown that his environment was not as bad as has been claimed, and that in some respects it actually offered advantages. To say this is not to detract from Lincoln as an example of what it is possible for one to do in a democracy like ours. Nor does it take credit from Lincoln. It simply shows that the American environment does, or did, offer advantages and opportunities to those who like Lincoln have the capacity and good sense to take advantage of them.

Notes

1. More recent scholarship suggests that Thomas's portrait of Lincoln's father is far too defensive. See John Y. Simon, *House Divided: Lincoln and His Father*, pamphlet (Fort Wayne: Louis A. Warren Lincoln Library and Museum, 1987).

2. Abundant evidence suggests that the Lincolns were unusually poor, even by frontier standards.

3. Stephen T. Logan interview by John G. Nicolay, Springfield, 6 July 1875, in *An Oral History of Abraham Lincoln: John G. Nicolay's Interviews and Essays*, ed. Michael Burlingame (Carbondale: Southern Illinois University Press, 1996), 34–39.

4. Communication to the People of Sangamon County, 9 March 1832, in *The Collected Works of Abraham Lincoln*, ed. Roy P. Basler, Marion Dolores Pratt and Lloyd A. Dunlap, asst. eds., 8 vols. plus index (New Brunswick: Rutgers University Press, 1953–55), 1:8.

5. Abraham Lincoln to Charles Hoyt, Clinton, 10 Nov. 1854, in *Collected Works*, ed. Basler et al., 2:286.

6. Abraham Lincoln to Thomas J. Henderson, Springfield, 27 Nov. 1854, in *Collected Works*, ed. Basler et al., 2:288.

7. Abraham Lincoln to Joseph Gillespie, Springfield, 1 Dec. 1854, in *Collected Works*, ed. Basler et al., 2:290.

8. Abraham Lincoln to Elihu B. Washburne, Springfield, 11 Dec. 1854, in *Collected Works*, ed. Basler et al., 2:293.

9. Abraham Lincoln to Norman B. Judd, Springfield, 9 Feb. 1860, in *Collected Works*, ed. Basler et al., 3:517.

10. Abraham Lincoln to Samuel Galloway, Chicago, 24 March 1860, in *Collected Works*, ed. Basler et al., 4:34.

11. On Lincoln's ambition, see Michael Burlingame, *The Inner World of Abraham Lincoln* (Urbana: University of Illinois Press, 1994), 236–67.

12. Abraham Lincoln to William H. Henderson, Springfield, 21 Feb. 1855, in *Collected Works*, ed. Basler et al., 2:307.

13. Abraham Lincoln to H. D. Sharpe, Springfield, 8 Dec. 1858, in *Collected Works*, ed. Basler et al., 3:344.

14. Abraham Lincoln to A. G. Henry, Springfield, 9 Nov. 1858, in *Collected Works*, ed. Basler et al., 2:339.

15. Paul M. Angle, ed., *Herndon's Life of Lincoln: The History and Personal Recollections of Abraham Lincoln as Originally Written by William H. Herndon and Jesse W. Weik* (Cleveland: World, 1942), 64.

16. John Hanks's statement to Wiliam H. Herndon [1865–66], in *Herndon's Informants: Letters, Interviews, and Statements about Abraham Lincoln*, ed. Douglas L. Wilson and Rodney O. Davis (Urbana: University of Illinois Press, 1997), 457.

17. Autobiography written for John Locke Scripps, [June 1860], in *Collected Works*, ed. Basler et al., 4:64.

18. Abraham Lincoln to A. G. Hodges, Washington, 4 April 1864, in *Collected Works*, ed. Basler et al., 7:281.

19. Speech at Peoria, 16 Oct. 1854, in *Collected Works*, ed. Basler et al., 2:255.

20. John Hay, *Inside Lincoln's White House: The Complete Civil War Diary of John Hay*, ed. Michael Burlingame and John R. Turner Ettlinger (Carbondale: Southern Illinois University Press, 1997), 20 (entry for 7 may 1861).

21. First Message to Congress, in *Collected Works*, ed. Basler et al., 4:439.

22. Gettysburg Address, 19 Nov. 1863, in *Collected Works*, ed. Basler et al., 7:23.

23. Abraham Lincoln to Horace Greeley, Washington, 22 Aug. 1862, in *Collected Works*, ed. Basler et al., 5:388–89.

24. Drafts of a bill, in *Collected Works*, ed. Basler et al., 5:29–31.

25. When Lincoln died, his estate was worth $83,343.70. When it was distributed in 1868, it had grown to $110,974.70. Harry E. Pratt, *The Personal Finances of Abraham Lincoln* (Springfield: Abraham Lincoln Association, 1943), 141.

7 Lincoln and New Salem

The outstanding feature of Lincoln's life was his capacity for development. He was neither a born genius, nor a man of mediocre talents suddenly endowed with wisdom to guide the nation through the trials of civil war. Rather, he developed gradually, absorbing from his environment that which was useful and good, growing in character and mind. That growth began here at New Salem [where this talk was given].

Recent historical studies have given us a better understanding of the influence of the frontier in shaping American institutions, characteristics, and life. With this comes a better appreciation of the part the frontier played in shaping Lincoln. We are beginning to realize that while Lincoln's early frontier environment was hard and crude in some respects, it was also a powerful developer of self-reliance, independence, and energy.

Lincoln had less than a year of formal schooling. For the rest, he was self-made. He learned; he was not taught. What he read he mastered; but he did not read widely. He learned principally by mingling with people and discussing things with them, by observation of their ways and their reactions—in short, from his environment. Carl Sandburg in his *Abraham Lincoln: The Prairie Years* says that Lincoln was "keenly sensitive to the words and ways of people around him. Therefore those people, their homes, occupations, songs, proverbs, schools, churches, politics, should

Typescript in the reference files of the Abraham Lincoln Association, Illinois State Historical Library, Springfield. A slightly different version of this essay, "Lincoln and New Salem: A Study in Environment," appeared in *The Transactions of the Illinois State Historical Society* 41 (1934): 61–75.

be set forth with the incessant suggestion of change that went always with pioneer life. They are the backgrounds on which the life of Lincoln moved, had its rise and flow and was moulder and moulded."[1]

With this conception New Salem assumes a new importance as a factor in Lincoln's development. No other period of his life lends itself so readily to intensive study as do his six years here. His physical surroundings have been recreated. The names and occupations and something of the character of most of the inhabitants of the village are known, and information on the village life is available in letters, newspapers, and reminiscences of residents or their descendants.

In villages such as this, economic problems, social life, and political thought were reduced to elemental terms. It was in such places that American ideals were nurtured and defined. Here indeed were the "grassroots" of the nation.

New Salem was founded in 1829. Its beginnings were a mill, a store and a saloon. At first its growth was slow. Then, in 1832, expectation of the Sangamon River's being made navigable for light-draft steamboats and anticipation of New Salem's becoming a thriving river town caused a boom in it and the surrounding country. But navigation of the river proved impracticable, and in two or three years New Salem's growth had stopped. By 1836 it had begun to decline. Its inaccessibility, a conviction that it had no future as a river town, and restrictions of its trading area by the growth of other towns induced its residents to try their luck again somewhere else. Year by year the inhabitants drifted away, until by 1840, three years after Lincoln left the town, New Salem did not exist.

At the height of its prosperity it contained about twenty-five families, and was the center of a prosperous agricultural region. Within a radius of ten or fifteen miles were scattered farms and smaller settlements, from all of which the village drew trade and visitors. In August 1834, Charles Clarke, one of the residents of the village, described conditions to his friends in the East.[2] "I should judge," he wrote, "that nine tenths of the people live in log houses and cabins; the other tenth either in brick or framed houses. The people generally have large farms and have not thought so much of fine buildings as they have of adding land to land, they are now however beginning to build better houses. Many a rich farmer lives in a house not half so good as your old hogs pen and not any larger. We live generally on bacon, eggs, bread, coffee. Sweet potatoes are raised here very easily. The wheat crop is very good, corn is very promising. There is a considerable quantity of cotton raised here, but none for exportation. Tobacco grows well."[3]

The pioneer women worked harder than the men. They prepared the food, bore and cared for the children, spun thread, made clothes, churned the butter, made soap and candles, and performed most of the humble, hum-drum necessary tasks. An English traveler noted that Central Illinois was a "hard country for women and cattle."

Marriageable girls did not stay single long. One of the New Salem settlers told of one who arrived from the West in June, and by August had "had no less than four suitors, three widowers and one old bachelor." A man often outlived two wives, and sometimes three. Families were large, and babies came in annual crops. "When weaned, usually by the almanac, youngsters began to eat corn bread, biscuits and potlikker like grown-ups. The fittest survived and the rest, as they said, 'the Lord seen fitten to take away.'"

Most of New Salem's inhabitants were young, enthusiastic, full of hope and confidence. They were of the third wave of migration, having been preceded by the roving hunters and trappers and the restless squatters. They were homebuilders, most of them with some stock and capital, who bought land or hoped to do so soon. They too were restless, however, and many of them moved on in search of something better. Courage, persistence, [and] ingenuity were the requisites of success. Wealth, "kin and kin-in-law," as one of the old settlers said, "didn't count a cuss." Government was of, by and for the people, with public opinion as its principal sanction.

There were two elements in the place. One was a rough and roistering, happy-go-lucky crowd known as the Clary's Grove boys.[4] They lived in and around the community of that name, but came to New Salem to drink, gossip, trade and play. Physical strength and courage were their ideals. In individual and free-for-all fights they had demonstrated their superiority over the boys from other settlements, and they ruled the town when they chose to.

Less picturesque but more important in the life of the village were men of a more serious turn like Dr. Allen; Dr. Regnier[;] James Rutledge, the tavernkeeper[;] Mentor Graham, the schoolmaster[;] Henry Onstot, the cooper[; and] Joshua Miller, the blacksmith.[5]

But the fact that we can distinguish two types of inhabitants does not mean that social lines were drawn or social distinctions made. Doctor and laborer, preacher and ne'er-do-well took part together in the village life. Saloonkeeper and temperance advocate, Yankee and Southerner, rubbed elbows with each other. Diverse types were represented in the groups that idled at the stores. Discussion in such groups brought out differences of opinion and divergent points of view. Men learned what other men were thinking.

The majority of the settlers in and around New Salem were Southerners; so that here, as well as in his former homes in Kentucky and Indiana, and later in Springfield, Lincoln lived in a Southern pioneer atmosphere. His contact with these people helped him understand the Southern temperament and point of view.

Interspersed with the predominant Southern element were some Yankees and a few settlers from the Middle States. Doctor Allen, for example, was a native of Vermont and had some of the characteristics of the New England reformer. He organized a temperance society and Sunday School in the village. He was a strict Sabbatarian, giving all Sunday fees to the church, and having all his Sunday food cooked on Saturday. The Southerners usually came by families; the Easterners were individuals who had separated from their families and had come West to seek health, wealth or adventure.

Most of the people in the community made their living from the soil, or with their hands; but the place was not devoid of intellectuality. James Rutledge is said to have owned twenty-five or thirty books. He was organizer and president of the New Salem Debating Society. Jack Kelso, a lazy, dreamy man, an expert fisherman and marksman, could quote long passages of Shakespeare and Burns.[6] Doctor Allen was a graduate of Dartmouth College Medical School. Four boys from New Salem attended Illinois College at Jacksonville, thirty miles from here.[7] According to an old settler, that institution "did more for this country than any eastern man could expect," and its students "astonished the old folks when they came home."

New Salem had no church, but services were held in the school-house and in the homes of the inhabitants. The strongest religious sects were the "Hardshell" Baptists, Cumberland Presbyterians and Methodists. Strange new sects were continually forming, however, as the self-reliant pioneer—usually with untrained mind and faulty logic—exercised the cherished prerogative of interpreting the Scriptures for himself.

Deeply concerned with creeds and the externals of religion, church members despaired not only of unbelievers and skeptics but of those of different faiths as well. Methodists and Baptists argued endlessly "about the way to heaven, whether it was by water or dry land," while both scorned what they called the "high toned doctrines of Calvinism" and the "muddy waters of Campbellism."[8]

Yet religion was a potent force for good, and in some respects an intellectual stimulus. Sermons, poor as they often were, gave many people their only examples of creative mental work, while discussions of salvation, baptism, morals and faith provided a sort of intellectual free-for-all.

Lincoln came to New Salem in late July 1831. Long, lean, awkward, with big frame and coarsened hands, he was a typical youth of the American frontier. His total schooling did not amount to a year; but principally by his own efforts he had learned to write a clear, distinctive hand, and to read and cypher "to the rule of three." He had made his living as a laborer and river man. He came to New Salem to work as a clerk in Denton Offut's store.[9] His first contacts were with the rougher element, with whom he speedily established himself. His courage and physical prowess commanded their respect, while his honesty and truthfulness soon won their confidence. The Clary's Grove boys became his staunch admirers, and followed and supported him in anything he did. As time passed he won the respect and admiration of the better element as well.

In the spring of 1832, when he had been in New Salem less than a year, the Black Hawk War broke out, and Lincoln immediately volunteered. He saw no fighting, but from this, his only military experience, he learned something of soldiers and the soldier's life, the value of leadership, discipline, morale. He met men whose friendship was valuable to him—John Calhoun, who later appointed him deputy surveyor; John T. Stuart, who became his law partner; and several rising young Illinois politicians.[10] Returning from the war, Lincoln found himself out of a job, for Offut's store had failed. Before enlisting he had announced himself as a candidate for the state legislature, and he now plunged into his campaign. But he was not elected. He had lived in New Salem only a year, and was still relatively unknown outside that community.

Lincoln pondered over what he should do. He thought of becoming a blacksmith, but decided against it; thought of studying law, but was afraid that with his deficient education it was useless to attempt it. Eventually he bought a half-interest in a store on credit. But neither Lincoln nor Berry, his partner, was cut out for a business career.[11] The store failed, Berry died, and Lincoln was left with a burden of debt from which he was not free for fifteen years.

He was greatly discouraged. The easy way out would have been to move away and make a fresh start somewhere else, leaving his debts unpaid. But Lincoln remained. He did not blame the town for his failure, as many men would have done. He believed that if he could succeed anywhere he could do it at New Salem. He had no intention of evading his obligations, and he wished to remain with his friends.

Lincoln could make a living, but he was not content to remain a laborer. He was looking for a chance to better himself. In his spare time he took advantage of the opportunity to improve his education. During his last months in Offut's store, he studied grammar and mastered it. He studied history and literature at New Salem, and during the winter of 1832 became a regular attendant at the meetings of the New Salem Debating Society. The members of the society, who had expected only humorous remarks from him, were amazed at his ability.

In May 1833, Lincoln's ambition was gratified to some extent when he was appointed postmaster at New Salem, and in the autumn of that year he was appointed a deputy to the county surveyor, John Calhoun.

His positions as clerk, storekeeper, postmaster and surveyor gave him a wide acquaintance in the community, and in 1834, when he ran for the legislature a second time, he was elected easily. He was reelected in 1836. During his second term his Whig colleagues made him the minority floor leader. At Vandalia, the state capital, his ambition was further stimulated. There he saw wealth, education, breeding, [and] charm, things relatively unknown to him. He met skillful politicians, able lawyers, [and] distinguished men from all parts of the state. His experience there was a liberal education, of the type he could not get from books. Small wonder that at the end of his first legislative session he returned to New Salem with his ambition fired, and renewed his studies with such determination that his friends were concerned for his health.

During the legislative campaign of 1834 John T. Stuart, a young lawyer in Springfield, had encouraged him to study law and make it his profession. After the campaign he decided to do so. At an auction in Springfield he bought a copy of Blackstone's *Commentaries*. Other books he borrowed from Stuart, walking or riding to Springfield to get them. Finally he applied for a license and was admitted to practice.

When Lincoln returned to New Salem from the legislative session of 1837 the decline of the village was well underway. He realized that there was no chance here for a legal or a larger political career. But Springfield, twenty miles southeast of New Salem, which had just been chosen as the new state capital, offered great political and legal opportunities. Lincoln had many friends there. He had taken a leading part in having Springfield made the capital, and this action had increased his popularity. John T. Stuart was willing to take him as his law partner. On April 15, 1837, astride a borrowed horse, and with all his personal possessions in his saddlebags, Lincoln moved to Springfield.

In his six years in this place, Lincoln had gone far. He could justly take pride in his progress. He came here at twenty-two, an aimless pioneer youth. When he left at twenty-eight he was a recognized political leader not only in the village, but in the state. He had made valuable friendships in the county and the state at large. He had learned to think for himself, and to express himself with force, clarity and individuality. He had equipped himself to make a living with his brain instead of his hands.

At New Salem Lincoln found himself. His coming here freed him from the retarding influence of his family. The community was more diversified, more complex, more stimulating than those places where he spent his boyhood and youth. The activities and contacts of his New Salem years revealed the possibility of betterment and gave him some conception of his own capacity.

Lincoln's success as politician and President was largely due to the fact that he knew how the common man would think. This he learned in no small measure at New Salem, where, during part of his residence at least, he worked on common terms with the humblest of the villagers. He learned how and what the blacksmith thought, how the storekeeper, the saloonkeeper, the farmhand, the cobbler viewed things. At no other period of his mature life did he have such intimate contact with the common people. And he took away with him an abiding understanding of them.

The New Salem environment, typical of that of the West in general, offered opportunities which Lincoln would not have had in an older community. Humble origin and lack of schooling were no handicaps, for they were common deficiencies. A newcomer had no difficulty in establishing himself, for no one had been here long, no propertied class had emerged, and social castes were unknown. Equality of opportunity was in large degree a fact, and democracy and nationalism were the political ideals.

Lincoln accepted these ideals, and benefited by the opportunities that the frontier afforded. But at the same time he avoided the frontier's weaknesses or at least outgrew them with time. He became self-reliant without becoming boastful and without overestimating himself, analytical and conservative rather than opportunistic and impulsive. In a region where men sometimes made their own law, where informality prevailed, and where people were concerned with the present and the future rather than the past, he realized the value of law, and was respectful of form and traditions. At New Salem as in his later life his individuality stands out. Yet while becoming a leader of his fellows Lincoln never lost touch with them. He grew beyond his associates, but not away from them.

Notes

1. Carl Sandburg, *Abraham Lincoln: The Prairie Years*, 2 vols. (New York: Harcourt, Brace and World, 1926), 1:viii.
2. In 1833 Charles James Fox Clarke (1806–70) moved from his native New Hampshire to New Salem, where he became a judge of the Menard County Commissioners Court.

3. Charles James Fox Clarke to his mother, New Salem, 3 Aug. 1834, in Charles R. Clarke, "Sketch of Charles James Fox Clarke with Letters to His Mother," *Journal of the Illinois State Historical Society* 22 (1929–30): 563.

4. The Clary's Grove boys were "emphatically wild and rough, and were the terror of all those who did not belong to the company." James Short to William Henry Herndon, Petersburg, Ill., 7 July 1865, in *Herndon's Informants: Letters, Interviews, and Statements about Abraham Lincoln*, ed. Douglas L. Wilson and Rodney O. Davis (Urbana: University of Illinois Press, 1997), 73; John Todd Stuart, interview with James Q. Howard, [May 1860], copy in John G. Nicolay's hand in John Hay Papers, John Hay Library, Brown University.

5. John Allen moved to New Salem by 1831 and then to Petersburg around 1839. Francis Regnier lived briefly in New Salem before moving to Clary's Grove. Born in South Carolina, James Rutledge (d. 1835) moved to the neighborhood of New Salem around 1825. He and his nephew, John M. Camron, founded New Salem. Kentucky-born William Mentor Graham (1800–86) helped Lincoln master grammar. Around 1826, Henry Onstot moved to Illinois from Kentucky, settling in New Salem four years later. In addition to making barrels and kegs, he owned a tavern. In 1831 Virginia-born Joshua Miller (1805–94) settled in New Salem with his family. A decade later he moved to Iowa.

6. An autodidact of broad culture, John A. Kelso performed odd jobs in the village and spent much time hunting and fishing.

7. The young men attending Illinois College were David Rutledge, William F. Berry, Lynn McNulty Greene, and William G. Greene.

8. Campbellites, followers of Alexander Campbell, were also known as Reformed Baptists and later as Disciples of Christ.

9. Offutt was remembered in Illinois as a garrulous, bibulous, and "short, rather stockily built man, of good natured, amiable disposition, free handed and of great sociability—a trader and speculator who always had his eyes open to the main chance." Lincoln's friends thought him "wild," "reckless," "unsteady," "noisy," "fussy," "rattle brained," "unprovidential," "gassy," "windy," and "careless." Thomas P. Reep, *Lincoln at New Salem* (Chicago: Old Salem Lincoln League, 1927), 98. The following are in *Herndon's Informants:* James Short to William H. Herndon, Petersburg, Ill., 7 July 1865 (73); Mentor Graham to Herndon (interview), Petersburg, Ill., 29 May 1865 (9); Hardin Bale to Herndon (interview), Petersburg, Ill., 29 May 1865 (13); and William G. Greene to Herndon (interview), Elm Wood, Ill., 30 May 1865, (18).

10. In 1830 Massachusetts-born John Calhoun (1808–59) settled in New Salem, where he became county surveyor. Kentucky-born John Todd Stuart (1807–85) of Springfield was also Lincoln's mentor. The men were law partners from 1837 to 1841.

11. William F. Berry (1811–35), son of the stern Presbyterian minister John M. Berry, had met Lincoln in the Black Hawk War. His greatest drawback as a businessman was his fondness for liquor.

8   Lincoln and the South

In a speech at Cincinnati on September 17, 1859, Abraham Lincoln directed his remarks across the Ohio River to the people of the South. They were disturbed by the prospect of a Republican victory in the election to be held the next year. He sought to reassure them. He said that if his party won, "We mean to treat you, as nearly as we can, as Washington, Jefferson and Madison treated you. We mean to leave you alone. . . . We mean to remember that you are as good as we; that there is no difference between us other than the difference of circumstances. We mean to recognize and bear in mind always that you have as good hearts in your bosoms as other people, or as we claim to have, and to treat you accordingly. We marry your girls when we have a chance—the white ones, I mean, and I have the honor to inform you that I once did have a chance in that way."[1]

Although there was a long period of time during which the South had little disposition to claim Abraham Lincoln as her own, he rightfully belongs to the South. By ancestry and birth, by marriage, by numerous friendships, by the cultural influences of his formative years, and by his early political associations he was attached to and drawn toward the South. For fifty-two of his fifty-six years he was steeped in Southern influences. One of his favorite songs was "Dixie."

The first Lincoln in the direct line to come to America from England settled in Massachusetts. Migrations took the family to Pennsylvania and then to Virginia. Both of Lincoln's parents were Virginians. He himself

---

Undated typescript, Benjamin P. Thomas Papers, Illinois State Historical Library, Springfield.

was born in Kentucky, as you know. As a toddling boy he knew the warmth of the Southern sun. It was Kentucky earth that he first trod. It was Kentucky speech that he first heard and learned to imitate.

The Lincolns moved to Indiana when Abe was only seven, and he grew to manhood there. Living in southern Indiana for fourteen years, he was molded in the Hoosier pattern. And the Hoosier pattern was Southern. Though there was an intermingling of human ingredients in the region where Lincoln grew up, most of the inhabitants had come there from the South. They spoke and thought and lived like Southerners. Their humor, their culture, and their political thinking all had a Southern flavor.

Rivers were the only dependable arteries of commerce where Lincoln spent his youth and young manhood. And the rivers led South. At nineteen, and again at twenty-two, Lincoln helped to take a flatboat loaded with hogs and other local produce to New Orleans. These trips provided his only first hand contacts with the *deep* South. One of them also gave him his first personal contact with Negroes. One night when he and his companions had tied up their boat along the shore and gone to sleep, they were attacked by a band of thieving black men. In the short, hard fight that followed Lincoln received a scar which he took through life.

It was the practice to sell both boat and cargo at New Orleans and return home by steamboat, earning the passage money by helping to load wood. Frances Trollope encountered a group of these flatboatmen when she took a steamboat up the Mississippi in 1828 and described them in her *Domestic Manners of the Americans.* "We had about two hundred of these men on board," she wrote, "but the part of the vessel occupied by them is so distinct from the cabins, that we never saw them, except when we stopped to take on wood; and then they ran, or rather sprung and vaulted over each other's heads to the shore, whence they all assisted in carrying wood to supply the steam engine."[2] It is easy to imagine the agile, angular, tatterdemalion young Lincoln as a member of just such a group.

These two trips to New Orleans gave young Lincoln his first glimpse of urban life. He saw wealth such as he had never imagined piled along the waterfront. He heard foreign tongues, probably for the first time. He saw a commingling of people betokening what he would one day call "the whole great family of man." And this great family of man would come to have a warm place in his heart.

The story of Lincoln's attending a slave auction at New Orleans and saying "if I ever get a chance to hit that thing, I'll hit it hard" has been rejected by Lincoln students.[3] But Lincoln did see human bondage at New Orleans, and he was repelled by it.

When Lincoln returned from his second trip to New Orleans, he threw off the encumbrance of his family and struck out on his own. He started his own life at the little village of New Salem in central Illinois. The evidence indicates that it was at New Salem that Lincoln gained his great faith in humankind, for the people there showed him friendliness of an uncommon sort, and aided him in his efforts to make something of himself. Lincoln said years afterward that he arrived at New Salem like a piece of floating driftwood, and he remained a drifter for some time, earning his living first as a store clerk and millhand, and then failing as a storekeeper. He worked at odd jobs. He learned surveying and got himself appointed postmaster. He had his only experience as a soldier in the Black Hawk War. Somehow his ambition was awakened, and he determined to equip himself to make a living with his brain instead of his hands. He studied mathematics and literature. He made his first formal efforts at speechmaking and debate. He was elected to the Illinois legislature. He gained admission to the bar. When he moved to Springfield after six years at New Salem, he had found his place in life.

He had been able to do it because of the encouragement and help of his neighbors; and he would never afterward believe otherwise than that people, just ordinary people, are trustworthy and good. It was a faith that would one day be momentous for men the whole world over. As a matter of fact, was there ever anything more significant in Lincoln's life than his trust in the common people? He gained that faith from Southern people.

When Lincoln first moved to Springfield, which had just become the capital of Illinois, he felt out of place. "This business of living in Springfield is rather a dull business after all," he wrote to a friend, "at least it is so to me. I am quite as lonesome here as I ever was anywhere in my life. I have been spoken to by but one woman since I've been here, and should not have been by her, if she could have avoided it. I've never been to church yet, and probably shall not be soon."[4] He was still pretty much of a backwoodsman, and he stood in awe of Springfield "society."

But Springfield was predominantly Southern in population, culture, and thought pattern, and Southern hospitality and cordiality soon brought him out of himself. His middle years, those spent in Springfield, were a time of happiness mixed with sorrows, of triumphs and defeats. And yet, looking back, when he left Springfield for the last time, to go to Washington as president, he said: "To this place, and the kindness of these people, I owe everything."[5] And they were Southern people.

The majority of the men whom Lincoln met in the Illinois legislature, where he served four terms, came from the South. When he traveled the Eighth Judicial Circuit he associated mostly with former Southerners. All three of his law partners—John T. Stuart, Stephen T. Logan, and William H. Herndon—were born in Kentucky. He married a Bluegrass belle.

For twenty-three years he lived in marriage, not always easily, with a cultured Southern woman who was proud of her Southern lineage and sympathetic toward the Southern way of life. Lincoln's marriage to Mary Todd brought him admission to Springfield society, which was Kentucky-dominated. And strangely enough, in some quarters, it marked him as an aristocrat. Soon after his wedding he wrote to a friend back in the New Salem neighborhood: "It would astonish, if not amuse, the older citizens of your County who twelve years ago knew me as a strange, friendless, uneducated, penniless boy, working on a flatboat at ten dollars per month to learn that I have been put down here as the candidate of pride, wealth, and aristocratic family distinction."[6]

By marriage Lincoln allied himself with a prominent family of the Old South. On the numerous visits that he and Mrs. Lincoln made to her relatives in Lexington he came to know the ease, the grace, the stateliness of upper-class Southern life. In the home of his father-in-law, Robert S. Todd, he saw liveried household slaves well treated and seemingly satisfied. But just a few strides from his wife's grandmother's house were the cramped and filthy slave pens of Lexington's wealthiest Negro trader. Not much farther off were an auction block and whipping post. Slaves were sold at auction almost every day. Lincoln's visits to Lexington enabled him to see slavery at its best and its worst. More significant than that, perhaps, these visits also acquainted him with the problems of the slave owner. He understood the distress the South must suffer in getting rid of slavery.[7]

From the time that Lincoln entered politics until the demise of the Whig Party in the 1850s, he was a Whig, which meant that he was a loyal member of a party which appealed strongly to the aristocratic element in the South, which regularly looked to that section for its presidential candidates and which could never hope to win the presidency without wide Southern support. In every presidential election from 1836 to 1852, Lincoln regularly worked for and voted for a Southern man for president: Hugh L. White of Tennessee, William Henry Harrison of Virginia, Henry Clay of Kentucky, Zachary Taylor of Louisiana, and Winfield Scott of Virginia.[8] It is noteworthy that he worked especially hard for Taylor in 1848, when many antislavery Whigs bolted to vote the Free-Soil ticket.

During the early years of Lincoln's political career his political idol was Henry Clay. Looking to Clay for the solution to practical political

problems and for effective political strategy, he turned to another Southerner, Thomas Jefferson, for his political philosophy. Lincoln once said:
"I never had a feeling politically that did not spring from the sentiments
embodied in the Declaration of Independence." He looked upon Jefferson as "the most distinguished politician in our history."⁹

Lincoln's introduction to the Declaration of Independence came at
an early age and is a charming little story in itself. It goes back to what
Lincoln called the earliest years of his "being able to read," the Indiana
years, when, as a boy, he lay stretched out on the dirt floor of the family
cabin in the wilderness, reading Mason Weems's Life of George Washington by the light of a pine-knot fire. The boy Lincoln thrilled to the account of the Revolutionary War—the tenacious determination of the
colonial soldiers, the hard marches and fierce battles, the cruel winter at
Valley Forge. And in after years he said: "I recollect thinking then, boy
even though I was, that there must have been something more than common that those men struggled for."¹⁰

And as he overcame the obstacles of poverty and grew in mind and
character, the story of America took on rich meaning for him. In no other country of the world, he thought, were ordinary people so much the
masters of their destiny. Nowhere else were they offered such a chance
to rise by their own efforts. As he carved out his own career in law and
politics, all about him, at home and on the circuit, he saw men who, starting life as laborers, mechanics, millhands, and flatboatmen, or in other
lowly walks of life, had become lawyers, merchants, doctors, farmers,
editors, successful politicians. And he saw these people come together
in equality and mutual respect, not only in the state legislature and in
Congress, where he served a single term, but also at the grass-roots level, in private homes and crossroads meeting-houses, to make their own
decisions and work out their own problems under a political system "conducing more essentially to civil and religious liberty," he thought, "than
any of which the history of former times tells us."¹¹

So, as the years passed, he arrived at the conviction that the Founding Fathers of the new republic, and he looked particularly to Jefferson,
had embodied the true meaning of that republic in the document that gave
it birth, and that in the assertions of the Declaration of Independence that
all men are created equal and are alike entitled to life, liberty, and the
pursuit of happiness was a promise "not only to the people of this country, but hope for the world to all future time."¹²

Lincoln thought that free government—government of the people,
by the people, for the people—was the greatest boon ever granted to
mankind, and it was to prove that free government could function suc-

cessfully that he was willing to fight a brothers' war. To him the surviv-al of free government was the big issue in 1861.

A supreme realist in politics, Lincoln was also a man of vision. He saw the American Union as an experiment in government holding forth the promise that in due time the weight would be lifted from the shoul-ders of all men. If the experiment resulted in failure, through the sever-ance of the Union, the light of hope would dim all over the world. The Negro was incidental. The Union was all important—but not merely in itself. It was important because it symbolized and embodied man's aspi-ration to determine his own destiny. Lincoln saw the future of humani-ty as the true issue of the war.

It was not lost on Lincoln that the South, to its way of thinking, was fighting for much the same thing. No matter what part slavery may have played in bringing on the war, after hostilities began, the South, too, was fighting for freedom, according to its lights, and for the right to shape its own destiny. Could the realization of this have accounted for Lincoln's magnanimity toward the South?

Lincoln once said: "If slavery is not wrong, nothing is wrong."[13] And he also said that if all earthly power were given to him, he would not know what to do with slavery as an established institution. He was nev-er an abolitionist. He never claimed that Southern people were wicked for tolerating slavery. "They are just what we would be in their situation," he said. "If slavery did not exist amongst them, they would not introduce it. If it did now exist amongst us, we should not instantly give it up. This I believe of the masses north and south."[14]

In dealing with slavery Lincoln favored the gradual approach. He thought it best that liberation should come slowly and by the action of the Southern people or the Southern states themselves. He thought that the North and the South were equally guilty of bringing the curse upon the nation, and that both had profited from it.

If the South had not seceded, Lincoln would never have freed a sin-gle slave. He would have opposed the extension of slavery to new terri-tory, and there is no doubt that he hoped and believed that such a policy would eventually strangle slavery in the states where it existed. But that would have been a slow process, and perhaps a relatively painless one, especially if it could have been accompanied by colonization of the Ne-groes in some foreign land and with compensation to the slave owner, both of which measures Lincoln favored.

In his first inaugural address Lincoln declared his intention to leave slavery undisturbed. "I have no purpose, directly or indirectly, to interfere with the institution of slavery in the states where it exists," he said. "I believe I have no lawful right to do so, and I have no inclination to do so."[15]

As the war went on he believed that he had acquired the right to strike down slavery as a measure of war; it was the economic mainstay of the South. And yet the war went on for fifteen months before he felt inclined to strike it. After he decided to do so, he stayed his hand for three more months. When he acted, it was not to free a single slave, but merely to give warning that he intended to free them in those states which were still resisting the federal government at the end of one hundred days. Return to the Union, he said in effect, and I shall not disturb your slaves. Having issued the Emancipation Proclamation, he said that he had not controlled events, events had controlled him. It is a far different picture from the traditional one of an antislavery zealot—"the Great Emancipator"—eagerly striking the shackles from all black men with one sweeping pen-stroke. As a matter of fact, as you all know, Lincoln's Emancipation Proclamation had little effect, except psychologically. It exempted the slaves in those states which had not left the Union—Maryland, Delaware, Kentucky, and Missouri—and in other areas controlled by Union arms and applied only to the slaves it could not reach.

Alexander Stephens, vice president of the Confederacy, has left us an account of the celebrated peace conference at Hampton Roads which gives striking proof of Lincoln's kindly feeling toward the South. "He said it was not his intention in the beginning to interfere with slavery in the States," wrote Stephens, "and that he never would have done it, if he had not been compelled by necessity to do it, to maintain the Union; that the subject presented many difficulties and perplexing questions to him, that he had hesitated for some time, and had resorted to this measure, only when driven to it by public necessity, that he had been in favor of the General Government prohibiting the extension of slavery into the Territories, but did not think that Government possessed power over the subject in the States, except as a war measure; and that he had always himself been in favor of emancipation, but not immediate emancipation, even by the States.

"He went on to say that he would be willing to be taxed to remunerate the Southern people for their slaves. He believed that the people of the North were as responsible for slavery as the people of the South, and if the war should then cease, with the voluntary abolition of slavery by the States, he should be in favor, individually, of the Government paying a fair indemnity for the loss to the owners. He said he believed this feeling had an extensive existence at the North. He knew some who would be in favor of an appropriation as high as four hundred millions of dollars for this purpose."[16]

In thinking that many people at the North would be so generous, Lincoln was probably wrong. Passions were too hot, and the outcome of the struggle was no longer in doubt. In February 1865, when Lincoln suggested to the cabinet that he should ask Congress to appropriate $400,000,000 as compensation to slave owners if hostilities soon ceased, he got not a single favorable response.

But the proposal was in keeping with Lincoln's attitude throughout the war. He had always been mindful of the future harmony of the whole nation. He wished to bring the Southern states back into the Union without humiliation. He wanted to help the impoverished Southern people to rebuild their ravaged economy, and he hoped by this act of sweeping generosity to assuage the hatreds born of war.

As a man of Southern origins, Lincoln understood that slavery in itself was not the great problem confronting the nation. Far more perplexing was the race problem which would result from emancipation. This was primarily a Southern problem, and Lincoln preferred to have Southerners solve it for themselves. He did not want the matter of race relations in the South to fall into the hands of intolerant Northern partisans wearing the humanitarian cloak. As J. G. Randall has said in his book *Lincoln and the South:* "To take a thing so complex and so potentially uplifting as emancipation and to associate it with the hateful spirit of party and sectional abuse would be the worst disservice to the Negro. To enlist for him the helping hands of those nearest to him, those with whom he would have to live, to make freedom one with normal Southern rebuilding, would be the part of statesmanship."[17]

But Lincoln also knew that a crucial sectional problem can become a national problem demanding settlement at the national level. And it can become peremptory when, as Lincoln put it, "it deprives our republican example of its just influence in the world," and "enables the enemies of free institutions . . . to taunt us as hypocrites."[18]

Lincoln tried to be realistic about the race problem. But his thinking changed over the years. In one of the great debates with Stephen A. Douglas in 1858, he said: "I am not, nor ever have been in favor of bringing about in any way the social and political equality of the white and black races . . . I am not nor ever have been in favor of making voters or jurors of negroes, nor of qualifying them to hold office, nor to intermarry with white people; and I will say in addition to this that there is a physical difference between the white and black races which I believe will forever forbid the two races living together on terms of social and political equality. And inasmuch as they cannot so live, while they remain together there must be the position of superior and inferior, and I as much as any other man am in favor of having the superior position assigned to the white race."[19]

It was while holding to this opinion that Lincoln favored gradual, compensated emancipation with colonization of freed Negroes abroad. As president he tried to work out a scheme of colonization, but finally gave it up. It could not be done on a large scale. More than that, the Negroes themselves opposed it. They had come to look on America as their country, too, and they did not wish to leave it. If they would not depart voluntarily, Lincoln did not propose to make them go.

When Lincoln was driven by the pressure of events to issue his Emancipation Proclamation, he realized that it might encourage the Southern Negroes to revolt. He did not want this to happen, and so, in one paragraph of the edict he addressed himself to the Negro. "And I hereby enjoin upon the people so declared to be free to abstain from all violence," he said, "unless in necessary self-defense; and I recommend to them that, in all cases when allowed, they labor faithfully for reasonable wages."[20]

With emancipation proclaimed, many Northern antislavery leaders urged Lincoln to arm Negroes and allow them to fight for their own freedom. He was extremely reluctant to do it. He shrank from permitting black men to kill white men. When he finally approved of the enlistment of Negro troops, it was under the compulsion of defeat. By the end of the war some 180,000 Negro troops were serving in the Union armies. By and large they proved to be brave and intelligent.

By the autumn of 1863, Lincoln had concluded that the only solution for the race problem in America was for whites and blacks to learn to live together as free men. Efforts were underway to establish a restored state government in Louisiana, and Lincoln wrote to General [Nathaniel P.] Banks, the Union commander there, that he hoped the people, in framing a new constitution, would adopt some practical system whereby whites and blacks "could gradually live themselves out of their old relation to each other, and both come out better prepared for the new." Education for young blacks should be included in the plan, he said.[21]

At the same time, Lincoln realized that racial adjustments would take time and careful planning. Inherited and deep-seated opinions must be recognized as realities to be dealt with, because, as he once said, "a universal feeling, whether well- or ill-founded, cannot be safely disregarded."[22] The important thing was to make a start. If a new state government would recognize the permanent freedom of the Negroes and take measures to prepare them for their new status, Lincoln declared that he would not object to temporary restrictions made necessary by "their present condition as a laboring, landless, and homeless class." Provided certain overriding principles were respected, he was willing to allow the Southern people to solve their own race problem.

In March 1864, when Louisiana prepared to draw up a new state constitution along the lines that Lincoln had suggested, Lincoln wrote to Michael Hahn, the newly elected governor: "I congratulate you on having fixed your name in history as the first free-state governor of Louisiana. Now you are about to have a Convention, which among other things, will probably define the elective franchise. I barely suggest for your private consideration, whether some of the colored people may not be let in—as, for instance, the very intelligent, and especially those who have fought gallantly in our ranks. They will probably help in some trying time to come, to keep the jewel of liberty within the family of freedom. But this is only a suggestion, not to the public, but to you alone."[23]

Lincoln was already under terrific pressure from the radicals of his own party to deal sternly with the South. He knew that resistance to racial adjustment on the part of the South would play into the hands of the radicals. Here we find him dealing confidentially, and in utter friendliness, with Southern leaders, urging them to meet their problems in the enlightened spirit of the times.

The question is often asked whether Lincoln, had he lived, could have put through his lenient plan of restoration for the South and spared her the torment of reconstruction. It is one of those big "ifs" of history which cannot be answered with certainty. Lincoln would probably have had trouble with the vindictive element in the North, just as Andrew Johnson did.[24] But Lincoln was a far subtler and more far-seeing man than Johnson was; and few politicians have known so well how to appeal to public opinion. Moreover, at the close of the war, Lincoln had reached the pinnacle of personal popularity. He had brought the nation safely through its trial, and the Northern people were in a mood to listen to him. He would have encountered enormous difficulties, but it seems likely that, for the most part, he would have had his way. It was the South's tragedy that he died.

Notes

1. Speech at Cincinnati, 17 Sept. 1859, in *The Collected Works of Abraham Lincoln*, ed. Roy P. Basler, Marion Dolores Pratt and Lloyd A. Dunlap, asst. eds., 8 vols. plus index (New Brunswick: Rutgers University Press, 1953–55), 3:453.

2. Frances Trollope, *Domestic Manners of the Americans* (1832, repr. New York: Dodd, Mead, 1927), 13.

3. Paul M. Angle, ed., *Herndon's Life of Lincoln: The History and Personal Recollections of Abraham Lincoln as Originally Written by William H. Herndon and Jesse W. Weik* (Cleveland: World, 1942), 64.

4. Abraham Lincoln to Mary Owens, Springfield, 7 May 1837, in *Collected Works*, ed. Basler et al., 1:78.

5. Farewell Address to Springfield, 11 Feb. 1861, in *Collected Works*, ed. Basler et al., 4:190–91.

6. Abraham Lincoln to Martin S. Morris, Springfield, 26 March 1843, in *Collected Works*, ed. Basler et al., 1:320.

7. William H. Townsend, *Lincoln and the Bluegrass: Slavery and Civil War in Kentucky* (Lexington: University Press of Kentucky, 1955).

8. Hugh Lawson White (1773–1840), who represented Tennessee in the U.S. Senate (1825–40), ran for the presidency in 1836.

9. Speech at Peoria, 16 Oct. 1854, in *Collected Works*, ed. Basler et al., 2:240, 2:249.

10. Address to the New Jersey Senate, 21 Feb. 1861, in *Collected Works*, ed. Basler et al., 4:236.

11. Speech of 27 Jan. 1838, in *Collected Works*, ed. Basler et al., 1:108.

12. Speech in Philadelphia, 22 Feb. 1861, in *Collected Works*, ed. Basler et al., 4:240.

13. Abraham Lincoln to Albert G. Hodges, Washington, 4 April 1864, in *Collected Works*, ed. Basler et al., 7:281.

14. Speech at Peoria, 2:255.

15. Ibid., 4:249.

16. Alexander H. Stephens, *A Constitutional View of the Late War between the States*, 2 vols. (Philadelphia: National Publishing, 1868–70), 2:613–14, 617.

17. James G. Randall, *Lincoln and the South* (Baton Rouge: Louisiana State University Press, 1946), 110–11.

18. Speech at Peoria, 2:255.

19. Speech of 18 Sept. 1858, in *Collected Works*, ed. Basler et al., 3:145–46.

20. Emancipation Proclamation, 1 Jan. 1863, in *Collected Works*, ed. Basler et al., 6:30.

21. Abraham Lincoln to N. P. Banks, Washington, 5 Aug. 1863, in *Collected Works*, ed. Basler et al., 6:365.

22. Speech at Peoria, 2:256.

23. Abraham Lincoln to Michael Hahn, Washington, 13 March 1864, in *Collected Works*, ed. Basler et al., 7:243.

24. It is highly unlikely that Lincoln would have alienated Congress and public opinion as Andrew Johnson did. Hans L. Trefousse, *Andrew Johnson* (New York: W. W. Norton, 1989), 196–97.

9 · *Lincoln from 1847 to 1853*

At the beginning of the year 1847 Abraham Lincoln had attained an ambition upon which he had set his heart five years before. He was congressman-elect from the Seventh Congressional District of Illinois. Although his term would not begin until December, he could have gone to Congress immediately had he chosen to do so, for E. D. Baker, the incumbent representative from his district, had just resigned his seat to serve in the Mexican War.[1] Lincoln declined to be a candidate to fill Baker's unexpired term, however, preferring to await the convening of the Thirtieth Congress to which he had been regularly elected.[2]

In the interim he followed his usual routine. During January and February he attended the sessions of the State Supreme Court and the Federal Courts and during the spring months followed the Eighth Judicial Circuit for at least part of the time. In addition he delivered two speeches under the auspices of the Sangamon County Temperance Union, and in his leisure moments wrote and exchanged poetry with a friend who also had poetic inclinations.[3] During the summer months he kept in touch with the proceedings of the convention which was sitting in Springfield to frame a new state constitution, watching with particular interest the changes which it effected in the organization of the courts.[4]

In July he made what was probably his first trip to the rapidly growing city of Chicago, where he attended the great River and Harbor Con-

---

Benjamin P. Thomas, ed., *Lincoln, 1847–1853, Being the Day-by-Day Activities of Abraham Lincoln from January 1, 1847 to December 31, 1853* (Springfield: Abraham Lincoln Association, 1936), v–lx.

vention.[5] Called upon to reply to David Dudley Field, an administration spokesman who irritated the convention by taking a strict construction view of internal improvement questions, he acquitted himself in such a manner as to elicit a favorable comment from Horace Greeley, who covered the convention for the *New York Tribune*.[6] He heard speeches by such men as Thomas Corwin, Greeley, Edward Bates, Nathaniel P. Tallmadge of New York, Andrew Stewart, congressman from Pennsylvania, and one of the promoters of the Chesapeake and Ohio Canal, and undoubtedly became personally acquainted with a number of them.[7]

Returning to Springfield, he participated in county politics and took a leading part in promoting a railroad from Springfield to Alton.

In the autumn he again set out upon the circuit. In October he took part in the Matson slave trial, a case which evoked considerable local interest and which gives us some insight into his attitude on the slavery question. Early in his political career Lincoln had voiced his moral opposition to slavery, and by the time of the annexation of Texas he had taken the political position to which he was to adhere throughout his life: "To let the slavery of the other States alone . . . [but] never lend ourselves, directly or indirectly, to prevent that slavery from dying a natural death— to find new places for it to live in, when it can no longer exist in the old."[8] Nevertheless, in the Matson trial he was on the side of the master against the slaves, a fact which indicates that the slavery issue had not yet seared itself into his conscience to the point of inducing him to place the plight of a few hapless negroes above the abstract legal aspects of the slavery question.[9]

In mid-October Lincoln left the circuit and returned to Springfield to prepare for his departure for Kentucky, where he and his family spent three weeks before continuing on to Washington.

During all this time he followed carefully the progress of the Mexican War and the drift and complicated cross-currents of national politics.

A long accumulation of grievances and claims, the annexation of Texas by the United States, and finally an attack on a detachment of United States troops commanded by General Zachary Taylor, who had been sent to occupy disputed territory between the Nueces and Rio Grande Rivers, culminated in a declaration of war by the United States on May 13, 1846. Events then moved rapidly. General Taylor, advancing from the north, won the battles of Palo Alto (May 8), Resaca de la Palma (May 9), Monterey (September 24) and Buena Vista (February 22 and 23, 1847). In March 1847, General [Winfield] Scott landed at Vera Cruz, captured Cerro Gordo (April 18), Churubusco (August 20), Chapultepec (September 12 and 13) and entered the city of Mexico on September 14. Meanwhile American detachments invaded California and New Mexico and speedily conquered them.

In September 1846, Mexico rejected Polk's first overtures for peace. The following April Nicholas P. Trist was sent to Mexico in a second attempt to end the war. He was authorized to offer $20,000,000 and the assumption by the United States of the claims of its citizens against Mexico in return for the cession of Upper California and New Mexico, and also to obtain a right of transit across the isthmus of Tehauntepec, if possible. Trist was unable to make headway against the obstinacy of Mexico and in September negotiations were abandoned. For some time Polk had been dissatisfied with Trist's conduct, and his displeasure had been heightened by Trist's forwarding to Washington a proposal of Santa Anna's that the territory between the Nueces and the Rio Grande be made a neutral zone, for the fact that Trist would even consider such a proposition gave plausibility to the Whig contention that the United States had only a doubtful claim to the territory on which the first blood of the war had been shed. Polk finally decided to recall Trist and on October 5 the order of recall was dispatched. By the time it reached Mexico, however, negotiations had been resumed; and Trist, believing that a treaty could now be obtained, resolved to risk Polk's displeasure and to continue negotiations in the face of his recall. This, in brief, was the military and diplomatic situation when Lincoln arrived in Washington.

At the beginning of the war many Whigs, Lincoln among them, had doubted its justness and necessity. But only two in the Senate and fourteen in the House had dared risk the accusation of lack of patriotism by voting against the bill authorizing the President to call volunteers, appropriated $10,000,000 for the conduct of the war, and declaring in its preamble that war existed "by the Act of the Republic of Mexico." Not a Democratic vote was cast against the bill, although many Van Buren Democrats criticized it privately, and John Calhoun refused to vote because of the preamble.

With the subsidence of the first surge of enthusiasm, however, the opposition to the war became more vocal. Many Whigs sincerely believed that the United States had not had sufficient reason to go to war, while few of them could resist the political opportunities in a situation where they could criticize the Democrats for starting hostilities and for their manner of conducting the war, and at the same time show their own patriotism by voting supplies.

Public opinion deterred the Whigs from placing any real impediments in the way of the prosecution of the war, but did not prevent them from plaguing the administration ceaselessly. Resolutions were introduced in

Congress calculated to publicize the troubles and mistakes of the administration, to make the war appear to be one of conquest, and generally to put the Democrats in an unwholesome light.

Added to the Whig opposition was that of Abolitionists and Liberty men, who envisioned the war as a conspiracy to extend slavery, and were resolved to resist this at all cost. This idea was most prevalent in New England, where the Abolitionists were joined in their resistance by those traditionally opposed to acquisition of any territory, slave or free, because of their belief that it would diminish the relative influence of New England in the national government.

Although the war was represented in some quarters as a slaveholders' conspiracy, as a matter of fact many Southern Whigs and some Southern Democrats opposed it as vehemently as their Northern colleagues. One of its most bitter and consistent opponents was John C. Calhoun, who believed that Mexican territory was unsuited to slavery and feared that the acquisition of territory would intensify the slavery issue, with disastrous consequences to the Democratic party and perhaps to the South as well.

Many Democrats who would not oppose the war publicly, criticized the administration in private. President Polk was unpopular, even in his own party, and the party itself had been rent into factions by personal rivalries and disagreements over policy. The strongest support of the administration came from the Democrats of the Northwest and Southwest, where nationalism and the idea of "manifest destiny" were rampant, and where the abandonment of our claim to 54° 40' and the compromising of the Oregon dispute had simply served to whet the appetite for expansion elsewhere.

As Calhoun foresaw, the probability of the annexation of Mexican territory soon raised the slavery issue. Within two months of the outbreak of war Polk had decided that the United States must have Upper California and New Mexico as an indemnity and in settlement of the claims of our citizens. With the rejection of our offers of peace and the prolongation of the war, public opinion began to demand more territory to defray the costs. Even in New England, and especially in the West, this demand was expressed. The *Illinois State Register*, in Springfield, was one of the earliest advocates of the complete absorption of Mexico. In the Twenty-ninth Congress the justness or unjustness of the war, the amount of indemnity to be demanded and the status of slavery in the territory to be acquired were almost the sole topics of debate. During the first session of this Congress, an effort was made to add the Wilmot Proviso, prohibiting slavery in all territory which might be acquired from Mexico, to an appropriation bill. The Proviso passed the House, but the session ended before it came to a vote in the Senate. In the second session the House again added the Proviso to an appropriation bill; but on the last day of the session it was stricken out, and the bill was passed without it. But the debates upon it aroused both the North and South to fever pitch, widened the rifts within the Democratic party and threatened to split the Whigs as well.

With the approach of the presidential election efforts were made to close the breaches in the rival parties. Some Democrats were persuaded to renounce the Wilmot Proviso by the argument that Mexican territory was economically unsuited to slavery and that no legal prohibition was necessary to prevent its spread. The extension of the Missouri Compromise line to the Pacific was also urged as a solution, while Vice-President Dallas advanced the idea of popular sovereignty which was later taken up by Cass and Douglas.[10]

By the time Lincoln entered Congress most of the Whigs, having succumbed to the force of popular opinion, were willing to take California and New Mexico. But on the slavery question they were divided, with Southern Whigs opposed to extensive annexations, yet determined to oppose on principle the Wilmot Proviso or any other measure denying the South equal rights in any territory which might be acquired. The Democrats were fairly well united in support of the war and on the annexation of California and New Mexico, but as to further annexations and slavery they were split wide open. Many Eastern Democrats insisted that any new territory must be free, but those from the Northwest were so anxious for expansion that they were willing to leave the slavery question in abeyance until territory was actually acquired. In the South the Calhoun faction still opposed extensive annexations, but some Southerners were not only in favor of taking all of Mexico they could get, but were already arguing that neither Congress, a territorial legislature, nor the people of a territory could exclude slavery until a territory's admission as a state. On the whole, expansionist sentiment was on the rise, although it was still retarded by the sectional controversy over slavery. The task of both the Democratic and Whig leaders was to find some policy with regard to slavery upon which the Northern and Southern factions could unite.

Lincoln and his family arrived in Washington on the evening of December 2, and took temporary lodgings at Brown's Hotel. A few days later they rented quarters at Mrs. Sprigg's boardinghouse on the present site of the Library of Congress.[11]

Several other legislators roomed at Mrs. Sprigg's—Elisha Embree of Indiana, Patrick W. Tompkins of Mississippi, Joshua R. Giddings of Ohio, and John Blanchard, John Dickey, John Strohm, James Pollack and Abraham R. McIlvaine of Pennsylvania.[12] All of them were Whigs. Duff Green and his family, who lived a few doors away, and Nathan Sargent, sergeant-at-arms of the House, took their meals there.[13] Another of Mrs. Sprigg's boarders was a young doctor, Samuel C. Busey, who was later President of the Medical Society of the District of Columbia, and who told in his *Reminiscences* of his acquaintance with Lincoln, whom he "soon learned to know and admire for his simple and unostentatious manners, kind-heartedness, and amusing jokes, anecdotes and witticisms."

"When about to tell an anecdote during a meal," Busey recalled, "he would lay down his knife and fork, place his elbows on the table, rest his face between his hands, and begin with the words, 'that reminds me,' and proceed. Everybody prepared for the explosions sure to follow. I recall with vivid pleasure the scene of merriment at the dinner after his first speech in the House of Representatives, occasioned by the descriptions, by himself and others of the Congressional mess, of the uproar in the House during its delivery."[14]

The conversation at Mrs. Sprigg's table turned often to slavery and the Wilmot Proviso. Dickey, who was positive and aggressive in his views, frequently antagonized Tompkins and other Southerners by his outspoken comments on these questions. Lincoln, according to Busey, "was so discreet in giving expression to his convictions on the slavery question as to avoid giving offense to anybody, and was so conciliatory as to create the impression, even among the proslavery advocates, that he did not wish to introduce or discuss subjects that would provoke a controversy. When such conversation would threaten angry or even unpleasant contention he would interrupt it by interposing some anecdote, thus diverting it into a hearty and general laugh, and so completely disarrange the tenor of the discussion that the parties engaged would either separate in good humor or continue conversation free from discord. This amicable disposition made him very popular with the household."[15]

As Lincoln first saw it, Washington was a dirty, sprawling town of forty thousand, often cold in winter and humid and malarial in summer. Three-fourths of the population were whites, while eight thousand free negroes and two thousand slaves made up the balance. Georgetown, close by, had an additional 8,500 inhabitants.

So far as improvements and conveniences were concerned, the town was little better than Springfield. Privies, pigsties, and cowsheds cluttered the back yards; while streets and alleys were littered with garbage. Chickens, geese and pigs roamed at will, feasting on the refuse. Water was supplied by wells, while produce was brought in from Maryland and Virginia farms in carts driven by slaves, and sold at the market, which was just off Pennsylvania Avenue midway between the Capitol and the White House.

Few streets were paved, and sidewalks consisted of gravel or ashes. The north side of Pennsylvania Avenue, where bricks had been laid from the Capitol to the White House, was the city's promenade. The only street lights were along a part of Pennsylvania Avenue, where oil lamps shed a smoky glow; but even these were dispensed with when Congress was not in session. The four hotels provided omnibus service to and from the depot, and other buses connected the depot and the Capitol with the wharves at Georgetown; but the only other street conveyances were antiquated hackney carriages. Almost everyone got about on "Shank's mare"; while a colored maid or nurse could not get a ride at any price unless she had a white child with her.

Fifteen policemen were on duty at night; and when fires broke out not only the volunteer companies, but "men, women, children, dogs, and every living and creeping beast . . . ran pell-mell to the scene of the conflagration."

The White House was essentially as it is today; but neither wing of the capitol had been built and an old wooden dome still surmounted its central portion. Only the front part of the Treasury Building had been completed, and the foundation of the Smithsonian Institution had just been laid. The State Department occupied a two-story house on the site of the north front of the Treasury, while the War and Navy departments were housed in two-story dwellings on the site of the present State, War and Navy Building.

A disgrace to the capital in the eyes of many Northerners was the domestic slave trade of which it was a center. Lincoln was deeply impressed by seeing gangs of slaves shuffling through the streets in chains and in his Peoria address, six years later, recalled the "sort of negro livery-stable," plainly visible from the capitol, "where droves of negroes were collected, temporarily kept, and finally taken to Southern market, precisely like droves of horses."[16]

Two quasi-official newspapers with national circulation—the *Union,* [a] Democratic organ, and the *National Intelligencer,* the mouthpiece of the Whigs—were published in the capital; and the *National Era,* an abolition sheet, was also printed there.

The influence of the thirty-seven churches, of eight denominations, was offset by the numerous saloons and gambling houses which lined Pennsylvania Avenue. There were some shops along this thoroughfare; but most ladies and gentlemen of fashion shopped in Baltimore.

Balls, receptions and dinners provided most of the formal social life.

Cabinet members, the speaker of the House, and local business and social leaders entertained; but the fact that only five senators and four representatives had houses and the austerity of the presidential levees during Polk's occupancy of the White House were deterrents to social life.
Social position depended on manners, family and official position rather
than wealth. Mrs. John Sherwood summed up Washington life at this time
as "a strange jumble of magnificence and squalor. Dinners were handsome
and very social, the talk delightful, but the balls were sparsely furnished
with light and chair. The illumination was of wax and stearine candles,
which used to send down showers of spermaceti on our shoulders. Brilliant conversation was the order of the day, and what Washington lacked
of the upholsterer it made up in the manners and wit of its great men . . .
[but] some of the Southwestern members got fearfully drunk at dinners."

In such life a western small-town lawyer hardly had a place, and Lincoln's social activities were limited to an occasional dinner or public
ceremony, and the concerts given by the Marine band on Wednesday and
Sunday evenings on the White House lawn.

Favorite recreations of congressmen were whist and bowling. Lincoln
and other members of Mrs. Sprigg's "mess" met frequently at the bowling alley of John Casparis, near the boardinghouse. Although enthusiastic, Lincoln was awkward and unskilled, and excelled at repartee rather
than as a player. Busey asserts that when it was learned that he was in
the alley a crowd usually collected to watch and listen to him.[17]

In intelligence and ability the Thirtieth Congress ranked with the
best. In the Senate were John J. Crittenden, Hannibal Hamlin, Daniel
Webster, Lewis Cass, Jefferson Davis, John M. Clayton, Reverdy Johnson,
Thomas H. Benton, David R. Atchison, John P. Hale, John A. Dix, Willie
P. Mangum, Simon Cameron, John C. Calhoun, John Bell, Sam Houston,
James M. Mason, R. M. T. Hunter, William L. Dayton and other outstand-
ing figures.[18] Howell Cobb, Alexander H. Stephens, Robert Toombs, Caleb
B. Smith, Robert C. Winthrop, John G. Palfrey, George Ashmun, John
Quincy Adams, Horace Mann, Jacob Thompson, Amos Tuck, David
Wilmot, Robert C. Schenck, R. Barnwell Rhett, Andrew Johnson and John
Minor Botts were members of the House.[19] Horace Greeley also sat as a
member from December 1848, until the end of the term. The Illinois
delegation consisted of Stephen A. Douglas, serving his first term as a
Senator, and his Senate colleague Sidney Breese, and in the House, be-
sides Lincoln, Robert M. Smith, John A. McClernand, Orlando B. Fick-
lin, John Wentworth, William A. Richardson and Thomas J. Turner, all
Democrats.[20] The Senate was predominately Democratic, while the
Whigs controlled the House.

With the opening of Congress Lincoln had to decide what position he would take on the questions of the day. He had had no particular interest in the annexation of Texas—he could "not very clearly see how the annexation would augment the evil of slavery," he had said.[21] Nor had he openly opposed the war. In fact, before the outbreak of hostilities, the *Illinois State Journal*, whose editorials usually reflected his views, had denounced Polk for his conciliatory attitude towards Mexico. Moreover, on May 30, 1846, Lincoln, together with Governor [Thomas] Ford, and other political leaders, had addressed a patriotic mass meeting held in Springfield to encourage enlistment. All of the speeches were reported to be "warm, thrilling, effective," and some seventy men had volunteered.

Nevertheless, Lincoln had some doubts from the first as to the justness and necessity of the war. "When the war began," he later explained on the floor of Congress, "it was my opinion that all those who because of knowing too little, or because of knowing too much, could not conscientiously approve the conduct of the President in the beginning of it should nevertheless as good citizens and patriots, remain silent on that point, at least till the war should be ended. Some leading Democrats, including ex-President Van Buren, have taken this same view, as I understand them; and I adhered to it and acted upon it, until since I took my seat here."[22]

While in Lexington [Kentucky] on his way to Washington, however, Lincoln had listened to a rousing speech by Henry Clay which undoubtedly influenced his thinking on this subject. "This is no war of defense," declared Clay, "but one of unnecessary and of offensive aggression. It is Mexico that is defending her firesides, her castles and her altars, not we." Clay then proceeded to denounce the administration for not defining the purposes of the war and to protest against annexation of Mexican territory. Towards the close of his address he presented a series of resolutions which were "almost unanimously" adopted and one of which pledged unalterable opposition to the acquisition of any foreign territory "for the purpose of propagating slavery or introducing slaves from the United States."[23]

Upon taking his seat in Congress Lincoln found that he could not remain passively acquiescent even if he so desired. On the second day of the session the President in his message reasserted that Mexico had struck the first blow and had shed the blood of American citizens on American soil. Two weeks later, Richardson of Illinois, one of the administration's most aggressive supporters, introduced a resolution declaring the war to be just and necessary, and that the amount of indemnity must depend on Mexico's obstinacy in protracting it. On this resolution Lincoln and practically all the other Whigs unhesitatingly voted no. Lincoln was a practical politician; and as such would probably have gone along with the Whig majority in any event. But by this time he had come to the conclusion that the President was in the wrong. A few days after Richardson's resolution was defeated Lincoln entered the Whig lists by introducing a series of resolutions calculated to embarrass the President by forcing him to admit that Mexico and not the United States had jurisdiction over the "spot" where the first blood of the war was shed.[24] About three weeks later he clarified his position in his first important speech.

Accepting Polk's contention that the Rio Grande had been the western boundary of the Louisiana purchase, he contended that this was immaterial, because by our treaty of 1819 we had sold all the territory between the Rio Grande and the Sabine to Spain. He admitted that Texas, after obtaining independence from Mexico, claimed the Rio Grande as her boundary; but pointed out that Mexico had never recognized this claim. True, Santa Anna, after his capture by the Texans, had recognized it; but he had done so under duress, in a document having "none of the distinguishing features of a treaty," and his action had been repudiated by the Mexican government. Furthermore, the document had stipulated that the Texan army should not go within five leagues of the Rio Grande, a singular feature if it intended to make that river the boundary. He admitted that Texas had exercised jurisdiction beyond the Nueces, but denied that her jurisdiction had extended as far as the Rio Grande. And this, the exercise of jurisdiction, was the real test. "The extent of our territory in that region depended not on any treaty—fixed boundary (for no treaty had attempted it), but on revolution. Any people anywhere being inclined and having the power have the right to rise up and shake off the existing government, and form a new one that suits them better. This is a most valuable, a most sacred right—a right which we hope and believe is to liberate the world. . . . All Mexico, including Texas, revolutionized against Spain; still later Texas revolutionized against Mexico. In my view, just so far as she carried her revolution by obtaining the actual, willing or unwilling, submission of the people, so far the country was hers, and no farther. Now, sir, for the purpose of obtaining the very best evidence as to whether Texas had actually carried her revolution to the place where the hostilities of the present war commenced, let the President answer the interrogatories I proposed."[25] The reasoning here advanced shows the influence of Lincoln's study of Jeffersonian philosophy; and it is worthy of note that some recent writers on the subject are of the opinion that the United States' claim to the territory in question was at least of doubtful validity. Polk, however, completely ignored the interrogatories.

Throughout the session, until the treaty of peace was ratified, Lincoln voted with the Whigs on all resolutions designed to put the administration in the wrong on the origin of the war, and to capitalize on its mistakes in waging it. On January 3, 1848, he voted for Ashmun's amendment which added the phrase "in a war unconstitutionally and unnecessarily begun by the President" to a resolution of thanks to General Taylor for his victory at Buena Vista. On the fourth he voted aye on a resolution requesting information regarding instructions sent to our naval officers to permit Santa Anna to return to Mexico—a most embarrassing subject, since Santa Anna, once within the country, had immediately put himself at the head of the Mexican army instead of suing for peace as the administration had supposed he would do. On the thirty-first Lincoln supported a resolution requesting information as to why Scott had been removed from his command, and again voted for a similar resolution on April 17. This also was a delicate subject for the administration, because Scott's victories had made him extremely popular, and many persons suspected that he was the victim of political jealousy. Lincoln voted to print copies of a memorial from Quakers of New England praying for a speedy termination of the war, and also for the printing of ten thousand copies of an abstract of war contracts—always inflammable political material—which had been let by the administration. But whenever supply bills were presented, he, like most other Whigs, voted for them rather than risk popular disfavor. Furthermore, he took a practical view regarding annexation of territory, and refused to vote for a resolution sponsored by the extreme anti-expansionist group which demanded that our army be withdrawn to a defensive line on the east bank of the Rio Grande, and that peace be made without indemnity.

Lincoln's "spot" resolutions, his anti-administration speech, and his attitude on the war in general created surprise and resentment in his district. At first criticism was relatively mild. The *Register* warned that the obstructionists in Congress "will find that the masses—the honest and patriotic citizens of Illinois—will mark their course and condemn them to an infamy as deep as that which rests upon the opposers of the last war. . . . Thank Heaven, Illinois has eight representatives who will stand by the honor of the nation. Would that we could find Mr. Lincoln in their ranks doing battle on the side of his country as valiantly as did the Illinois volunteers on the battle fields of Buena Vista and Cerro Gordo. He will have a fearful account to settle with them, should he lend his aid in an effort to neutralize their achievements and blast their fame."[26]

The Whig press attempted to defend Lincoln, but its support merely goaded the opposition. Warnings and regrets were followed by denunciation. The Ottawa *Free Trader* expressed its shame that an Illinois representative had broken the state's united and patriotic front. A mass meeting in Pinckneyville passed resolutions declaring that those who tried to render their own government odious "deserved to be regarded as little better than traitors to their country." Another meeting in Clark County denounced Lincoln for the stain he had placed on the "patriotism and glory" of his state. Never before had such "black odium and infamy" been heaped upon the "living brave and illustrious dead." A Morgan County meeting resolved that "this Benedict Arnold of our district be known here only as the Ranchero Spotty of one term."[27] Other Democratic meetings passed similar resolutions.

The Sangamon County Democratic Convention, in congratulating Illinois on the patriotism of its citizens and representatives, felt "compelled to recognize one unfortunate exception, in the person of the Hon. Abraham Lincoln, present whig representative from this congressional district; who, contrary to the expectations and wishes of his constituents, and in contempt of the two gallant regiments which they furnished for the war, has lent himself to the schemes of such men as Corwin, Giddings, Hale and others, apologists and defenders of Mexico, and revilers of their own country."[28]

"Out Damned Spot!" screamed the *Register*, which duly reprinted every denunciation and also added comments of its own. To an article on a peculiar disease called "spotted fever," which was prevalent in Michigan, it appended the observation: "This fever does not prevail to any very alarming extent in Illinois. The only case we have heard of that is likely to prove fatal, is that of 'spotty Lincoln,' of this state. This 'spotty' gentleman had a severe attack of 'spotted fever' in Washington city not long since, and fears were entertained that the disease would 'strike in,' and carry him off. We have not heard of any other person in Washington being on the 'spotted' list—and it is probable that the disease died with the patient.—What an epitaph: 'Died of Spotted Fever.' Poor Lincoln!"

The defense of the *Journal* and other Whig papers was weak and unavailing in the face of the overwhelming opinion in favor of the war. The appellation "Spotty Lincoln" stuck, with devastating effect on Lincoln's future political aspirations.[29] Even in the presidential campaign of 1860, it was occasionally applied to him.

Herndon, frightened by the indignation which Lincoln's course had aroused, and disagreeing with his attitude, warned him of the consequences. In reply Lincoln wrote a confidential letter explaining and defending his position. "I will stake my life that if you had been in my place you would have voted just as I did," he declared. "Would you have voted what you felt and knew to be a lie? I know you would not. Would you have gone out of the House—skulked the vote? I expect not. If you had skulked one vote, you would have had to skulk many more before the end of the session. Richardson's resolutions, introduced before I made any move or gave any vote upon the subject, make the direct question of the justice of the war; so that no man can be silent if he would. You are compelled to speak; and your only alternative is to tell the truth or a lie. I cannot doubt which you would do. . . . The Locos [Democrats] are untiring in their efforts to make the impression that all who vote supplies or take part in the war do of necessity approve the President's conduct in the beginning of it; but the Whigs have from the beginning made and kept the distinction between the two."[30]

Still fearful and unconvinced, Herndon attempted to defend Polk's action as a defensive measure to repel a threatened invasion. Lincoln replied that the President himself had never gone this far; and even so, "Allow the President to invade a neighboring nation whenever he shall deem it necessary to repel an invasion . . . and you allow him to make war at pleasure. . . . Your view . . . places our President where kings have always stood."[31]

Lincoln further attempted to justify himself in letters to Usher F. Linder and J. M. Peck; but for the most part his defense consisted in sending copies of Whig speeches on the war to the Whig newspapers of his district.[32] Most of these never saw the light; because the editors, realizing the strength of local sentiment, foresaw the disastrous political consequences which would result from further publicizing the attitude of the Whig representatives in Congress.

During the early weeks of his term Lincoln, informed by Herndon that some of his constituents favored his renomination, had expressed a willingness to run again if no one else desired the nomination.[33] But his hopes for a second term were speedily withered by the Democratic blasts.

On the other major issues before Congress Lincoln reflected more accurately the sentiments of his constituents. He voted consistently for bills and resolutions looking to the prevention of the spread of slavery into any new territories. On February 28, 1848, he expressed his attitude on the Wilmot Proviso when he voted against a motion to table a resolution, practically identical with the Proviso, which would have prohibited slavery in any territory which might be acquired from Mexico. On July 28, he voted against a Senate bill to establish territorial governments in Oregon, California and New Mexico. This bill would have continued in effect the antislavery laws of Oregon; but would have enjoined the legislatures of the other territories from passing any law relating to slavery, thus leaving the question to be settled by appeal to the Supreme Court. It was tabled, 105–93, on a vote which split both parties. Having rejected this bill, the House then formulated one of its own, giving territorial government to Oregon alone, and providing that the Ordinance of 1787 should be extended over it. Lincoln voted against an amendment striking out this provision, and for the passage of the bill with the provision included. It passed in this form; but the Senate struck out the provision and substituted a section extending the Missouri Compromise line to the Pacific. The House likewise rejected this, again on a sectional vote. The House bill was finally accepted by the Senate and signed by President Polk, although he preferred the Missouri Compromise provision.

Early in the second session, on December 13, 1848, Lincoln voted for a resolution which instructed the Committee on Territories to report a bill establishing territorial governments in California and New Mexico, and excluding slavery. Toward the close of the session such a bill was introduced, and passed; but the Senate rejected it, and in its place attached a rider, the so-called Walker amendment, to the general appropriations bill. This provided temporary governments for the two territories and extended over them the Constitution and laws of the United States. As the Constitution recognized the right of property in slaves, this would have been a tacit victory for the South. The antislavery majority in the House, including Lincoln, voted the amendment down; and on the last day of the session debated an amendment continuing in effect the laws of Mexico, one of which excluded slavery. Throughout the night Polk waited with a veto message, resolved to kill the whole appropriation bill if this amendment was included. But in the early morning the House receded, and the appropriations bill was passed with both the Walker and the House amendments deleted. With this dramatic finale the stage was set for the great struggle in the next Congress which ended in the Compromise of 1850.

Despite his stand on slavery in the territories, Lincoln was obviously opposed to unnecessary agitation of the slavery question. He took no part in the debates on the subject and maintained a conciliatory attitude whenever possible. He voted against a resolution to inquire into the expediency of raising $5,000,000 annually until the extinction of the public debt, by taxes on personal property, stocks, and money at interest, a measure which many congressmen regarded as an attempt to make the Southern slaveowners and the Northern capitalists bear a disproportionate share of the burden of the war. He likewise voted against a preamble, stating that "no despotism is more effective than that which exists under the semblance of popular institutions," which the Abolitionists proposed to affix to a resolution congratulating the people of France on their establishment of a republican government. In April 1848, when a mob threat to dismantle the press of the *National Era* led to a bitter debate on slavery, Lincoln with other moderates, both North and South, voted to end the discussion to prevent the matter's going "to the country to a greater extent than it had already gone out."

Lincoln's vote for a petition for a law appropriating the proceeds of the sale of public lands for the extinction of slavery indicates that already he believed compensated and gradual emancipation to be the best solution of the problem. And this is confirmed by his position on slavery and the slave trade in the District of Columbia, although his votes on these subjects were at times confusing. On December 21, 1847, he voted against a motion to table a memorial of eighteen citizens of the District requesting that all laws sanctioning the slave trade be repealed. A week later he voted against a motion to table a petition from citizens of Indiana looking to the same purpose. On January 17, 1848, he voted against tabling a resolution to inquire into the advisability of abolishing the slave trade or moving the capital to a free state. But on May 29, he voted with the proslavery men against a motion to suspend the rules to permit Amos Tuck, of New Hampshire, to introduce a resolution directing the various committees, to which petitions for the abolition of the slave trade had been referred, to report a bill. All strong antislavery men voted aye; while Southerners of both parties, regular Northern Democrats and a few moderate Northern Whigs, like Lincoln, voted no.

Early in the second session the question came up again, when Palfrey of Massachusetts asked permission to introduce a resolution directing the Committee on the District of Columbia to report a bill abolishing the slave trade in the District. Lincoln voted against giving leave to introduce, although most Northern members favored it. Five days later, Lincoln voted to table a resolution, offered by Giddings of Ohio, which would have authorized a referendum by the people of the District on the further toleration of slavery. This vote can be explained by the fact that he already had in mind a similar plan of his own, with more moderate features.

Again, on December 21, Lincoln voted against a resolution directing the Committee on the District to report a bill abolishing slavery. The resolution passed, but on January 10, 1849, before the committee had had time to draw a bill, Lincoln gave notice of an amendment which he proposed to add to the resolution of instruction. His plan would direct the committee to bring in a bill confining slavery in the District to such slaves as were already there and such as might be brought in temporarily by government officials. Children born of slave mothers after January 1, 1850, should be free, but should serve as apprentices to their masters until they reached a certain age. If any master wished to free a slave already in the District he should be paid the fair value of the slave, such value to be determined by a slave-valuation board consisting of the President, the Secretary of State and the Secretary of the Treasury. His plan also contemplated that the municipal authorities would provide efficient means for apprehending and delivering to their owners all fugitive slaves escaping into the District—a provision which aroused the ire of the Abolitionists and later caused Wendell Phillips to denounce him as "that slave hound from Illinois."[34] The final and most significant stipulation was that all white male citizens, twenty-one years old or over, who had lived in the District for one year, should vote for or against the project, which, if accepted, should be put into effect at once.

Lincoln stated that his plan had the approval of fifteen leading citizens of the District; but when called upon to give their names he made no answer. Three days after his presentation of the plan, he gave notice that he would introduce it as a bill; but he never did so.[35]

On January 31, 1849, the committee reported its bill—a disappointment to the radicals since it merely prohibited the slave trade. A motion to table was defeated, 72–117, Lincoln voting with the majority. Bitter debate followed and the Southern members became so alarmed that they held a conference at which they determined to appeal to their constituents to resist the "aggressions" of the North. Throughout the remainder of the session the debate flared up at intervals; but nothing further had been done when the Congress adjourned on March 4.

With the ratification of the peace treaty the Whig fulminations against the war lost much of their effectiveness. Consequently they shifted their attack to other administration policies. Among the most vulnerable of these was the administration's attitude on internal improvements and the tariff. Both of these issues, but particularly the former, cut across party lines to some extent. In fact, opposition to internal improvements was almost as dangerous to a Western representative as opposition to the war; while Polk, by his veto of a river and harbor bill passed by the Twenty-ninth Congress, had not only aroused the hostility of the Whigs, but had antagonized many Democrats as well. The tariff of 1846, which effected a general reduction in duties, had also elicited both Whig and Democratic criticism. As for Lincoln, he had been an early convert to Henry Clay's "American System" of high tariff and internal improvements at government expense, and his attendance at the Chicago River and Harbor Convention had strengthened his convictions.

In the Thirtieth Congress these matters first came to a test on December 21, 1847, when a resolution was introduced declaring that the general government had the right to construct such rivers and improve such harbors as were essential to commerce and national defense. The resolution passed by a large majority, Lincoln voting aye. On June 19, 1848, Lincoln again voted with the majority in favor of a motion to refer the memorial drawn up by the Chicago River and Harbor Convention to the Committee on Commerce. The following day he delivered a speech on internal improvements in which he criticized Polk's veto of the river and harbor bill and attempted to show that while internal improvements at government expense necessarily entailed difficulties and objections, nevertheless, the advantages outweighed the disadvantages.[36]

On July 5 the matter came to a direct issue when a resolution was introduced declaring that Polk's reasons for vetoing the river and harbor bill were "insufficient and unsatisfactory." A motion to table resulted in a stinging rebuke to the President when it was defeated, 65–108. Lincoln voted against it.

When the general appropriations bill for the year 1848 came up for consideration in the House, it contained a provision making an appropriation for the removal of obstructions to navigation in the Savannah River. The opponents of internal improvements objected to this on principle, and an amendment was introduced to strike it out. The amendment was defeated by the negative vote of the speaker, 85–85, Lincoln voting against it. This was on July 18. Two days later, however, the Democratic leaders whipped the party into line and the appropriation bill was defeated because of the inclusion of this grant. A lively partisan debate on internal improvements followed. The bill came up again on the 22d. This time the Democratic recalcitrants could not be controlled, and the bill was passed with the item included.

In the Senate, however, it was stricken out; and when the bill was returned to the House it finally acquiesced in the Senate's action. The vote was very close, 95–92, with Lincoln supporting the appropriation to the end. On August 11, he voted for the passage of a river and harbor bill.

Related to the general question of internal improvements was the policy of granting lands to various states to aid in the construction of railroads. In this matter Lincoln did what he could to obtain lands for Illinois. He presented eight petitions or memorials of Illinois citizens for grants of this type, most of them to facilitate the construction of a railroad to connect "the upper and lower Mississippi with Chicago." He likewise presented a joint resolution of the state legislature having the same object. On December 28, 1848, he voted against a motion to table a bill giving Illinois and other western states the same amount of land to aid in railroad construction, as had been given to Ohio. Thus, while Sidney Breese and Stephen A. Douglas were primarily responsible for obtaining the grant which made possible the building of the Illinois Central Railroad, Lincoln did what he could to keep the matter of a land grant before Congress.

On May 11, 1848, Lincoln spoke on the policy of granting alternate sections of land to states to aid in internal improvements, and then increasing the prices of the reserved sections. He favored grants in any event but thought it better not to raise the price of the government's remaining sections. On February 13, 1849, he made a brief speech in reply to an argument that the increasing number of representatives from states containing public lands would soon wrest control of these lands from the general government. This was erroneous, he claimed, since the new states were continually selling their lands and thus coming gradually to view the question from the point of view of the older states whose lands had already been disposed of. "We can never outnumber you," he said, ". . . those that are opposed to that interest must always hold a vast majority here, and they will never surrender the whole or any part of the public lands unless they themselves shall choose to do so."[37]

In the routine work of Congress Lincoln was diligent and faithful. He was regular in attendance, and did his full share of the work of the two standing committees—that on the Post Office and Post Roads and that on Expenditures in the War Department—to which he was appointed. In the business of the former committee, he was particularly active, frequently reporting bills or resolutions and explaining their provisions.

During the entire term of the Congress the main concern of the Whigs was the presidential election of 1848. No sooner had General Taylor's victories begun to bring him popularity than the Whig leaders began to consider his availability. He had never taken an active part in politics, had never announced any views, was an exponent of the military spirit which they denounced, a slaveowner, and an advocate of annexation of Mexican territory. In fact, his prominence rested altogether on his success in the "illegal, unrighteous and damnable war." But his vote-getting potentialities were great.

Early in 1846 the Taylor boom got under way, and gathered momentum as election year approached. The Whigs were mindful that the only presidential election they had won was that of 1840, when they passed over Henry Clay, their recognized leader, and rode to victory on the military reputation of William Henry Harrison. Now, with their opponents divided, and victory once more within their reach, they again relegated

Clay to the background to take advantage of the popularity of a "military chieftain."

Since Lincoln's entry into politics, Henry Clay had been his idol. Keenly sensitive to the feelings of the people, however, and practical, as ever, in his views, he recognized Taylor's pulling powers and was not slow to clamber on the Taylor bandwagon. On February 9, 1848, he declined an invitation to attend a Taylor meeting at Philadelphia; but announced himself as "decidedly in favor of General Taylor as the Whig candidate for the next Presidency." He also stated that during the previous summer the Whig representatives at the Illinois State Constitutional Convention had gone on record overwhelmingly for Taylor and that this, "together with other facts falling within my observation, leave no doubt in my mind that the preference of the Whigs of the State is the same."[38]

On February 17, he explained his position in a letter to T. S. Flournoy. "In answer to your inquiries," he wrote, "I have to say I am in favor of Gen. Taylor as the Whig candidate for the Presidency because I am satisfied we can elect him, that he will give us a Whig administration, and that we cannot elect any other Whig. In Illinois his being our candidate, would certainly give us one additional member of Congress, if not more; and probably would give us the electoral vote of the state. That with him, we can, in that state, make great inroads among the rank and file of the Democrats, to my mind is certain; but the majority against us there, is so great, that I can do no more than express my belief that we can carry the state."[39]

Through the early months of 1848, Lincoln kept in close touch with the trend of opinion, particularly in Illinois, and did what he could to swing the Clay men over to Taylor; "not," as he explained to Jesse Lynch of Magnolia, "because I think he would make a better president than Clay, but because I think he would make a better one than Polk, or Cass, or Buchanan, or any such creatures, one of whom is sure to be elected, if he is not."[40] To E. B. Washburne, Archibald Williams and other influential Whigs in Illinois he sent letters urging them to send Taylor delegates to the Whig National Convention.[41] In his letter to Williams, dated April 30, he analyzed the situation. "Mr. Clay's chance for an election is just no chance at all," he urged. "He might get New York, and that would have elected him in 1844, but it will not now, because he must now, at the least, lose Tennessee, which he had then, and in addition the fifteen new votes of Florida, Texas, Iowa, and Wisconsin. I know our good friend [Orville H.] Browning is a great admirer of Mr. Clay, and I therefore fear he is favoring his nomination. If he is, ask him to discard feeling, and try if he can possibly, as a matter of judgment, count the votes necessary to elect him."[42]

Early in June Lincoln left Washington to attend the Whig National Convention at Philadelphia. Here he had the pleasure of witnessing Taylor's nomination, and of seeing Illinois contribute to it. On the first ballot the Illinois votes were cast: three for Clay, one for Scott, and four for Taylor (one district was not represented); on the second and third ballots there was no change; but on the fourth and final ballot the whole delegation voted for the General.

From June until election day Lincoln labored hard. In another letter to Williams on June 12, he portrayed the situation as he saw it. "By many, and often," he wrote, "it had been said they would not abide the nomination of Taylor; but since the deed has been done, they are fast falling in, and in my opinion we shall have a most overwhelming, glorious triumph. One unmistakable sign is that all the odds and ends are with us— Barnburners [antislavery Democrats], Native Americans [xenophobes], [John] Tyler men, disappointed Locofocos [Democrats], and the Lord knows what. This is important, if in nothing else, in showing which way the wind blows. Some of the sanguine men have set down all the States as certain for Taylor but Illinois, and it is doubtful. Cannot something be done even in Illinois?"[43]

Illinois gave him his greatest anxiety; and much of his time was devoted to it. Of friends in various counties he requested the names of both Whigs and Democrats who might be persuaded to switch their votes. Their replies enabled him further to analyze the situation and to send campaign literature to those whose minds were not made up. Upon Herndon, who was pessimistic about the outcome in Sangamon County, he urged the necessity of getting the young men together in a "Rough and Ready Club." "Take in everybody you can get . . . as you go along gather up all the shrewd, wild boys about town, whether just of age or a little under age. . . . Let everyone play the part he can play best,—some speak, some sing, and all 'holler.'" He was impatient with Herndon for asking for Whig speeches when he had been regularly sending him the *Congressional Globe.* This he had also sent to the Whig papers; "yet, with the exception of my own little speech, which was published in two only of the then five, now four, Whig papers, I do not remember having seen a single speech, or even abstract from one, in any single one of those papers. With equal and full means on both sides, I will venture that the 'State Register' has thrown before its readers more of Locofoco speeches in a month than all of the Whig papers of the district has done of Whig speeches during the session."[44]

But Herndon "was not easily warmed up." He knew of the defections from the party which Lincoln's course had caused, of the discouragement which prevailed among the Whigs in Springfield, and of the dissatisfaction of the young men "at the stubbornness and bad judgment of the old fossils in the party, who were constantly holding the young men back." These sentiments, together with newspaper clippings, he forwarded to Lincoln. Under date of July 10, Lincoln wrote a fatherly reply, disclaiming any intention on the part of the "old men" to act ungenerously, and advising that the "way for a young man to rise is to improve himself every way he can, never suspecting that anybody wishes to hinder him. Allow me to assure you that suspicion and jealousy never did help any man in any situation."[45]

Herndon was mollified; and he and others set to work; but with discouraging results. The congressional election on August 6, seemed to indicate the outcome. Stephen T. Logan, Whig candidate to succeed Lincoln, was defeated by Thomas L. Harris, of Jacksonville, 7,095 to 7,201.[46]

Lincoln tried to explain the result on the ground that Logan was unpopular with many Whigs, while Harris was looked on as a hero by reason of his war record. "That there is any political change against us in the district I cannot believe," he said.[47]

Yet the *Register* probably had a more accurate explanation. "The whigs about Springfield are attributing their defeat to Judge Logan solely," it observed, "alleging that the Judge's unpopularity brought about the result. This will not do, gentlemen, you must put the saddle on the right horse. It was the crushing load Logan had to carry in the shape of whig principles, and the course of the whig party for the past two years. Besides his own dead weight, Logan had to carry the votes of the whig party, including Lincoln, that the war was unconstitutional and unnecessary. If this whig reasoning will apply to Logan, why not to Stuart and Edwards? The former received but twenty-two and the latter but sixteen more votes than the Judge in Sangamon. 'Acknowledge the corn,' whiggery is getting in bad odor."[48]

Meanwhile Lincoln labored on. He sent copies of the *Battery*, a Whig campaign paper, to constituents, and flooded his district with government documents. On July 27, he made a speech in Congress ridiculing the efforts of the Democrats to extol the military qualities of Lewis Cass, their presidential candidate, by comparing Cass' military record to his own experiences in the Black Hawk War. In the more serious part of his speech he defended Taylor's attitude on the exercise of the veto power, and his failure to announce his position on the questions of the day.[49]

At the end of the first session of Congress Lincoln remained in Washington, franking documents and writing letters to such men as William Schouler and Thaddeus Stevens, in order to keep in touch with the political trend.[50] In this he was probably acting in close cooperation with the National Committee, although not a member of it.

In the latter part of August and the first week of September he made a few speeches in and around Washington and on September 9, began a speaking tour in New England. Here his efforts were directed to proving that the Whigs and Freesoilers occupied the same ground with respect to the extension of slavery, that a Democratic victory would facilitate extension, and that the Freesoilers, by voting for Van Buren, would split the anti-extension vote and conduce to the election of Cass. Lincoln closed his tour at a huge meeting at Tremont Temple [in Boston], where he and William H. Seward spoke from the same platform.[51] He was deeply impressed with Seward's remarks, and upon taking leave of him next day expressed the opinion that politicians of all parties must give more attention to the slavery problem in the future. In fact, his contact with New England leaders and sentiment and his experiences in Congress were major factors in awakening him to the immediacy of the slavery problem and to the necessity of uniting the various antislavery factions upon a definite and practicable program.

His New England tour ended, Lincoln headed for home. Traveling leisurely to Chicago, he spoke there at a Whig rally.[52] On August 23, he had been selected as an assistant Taylor elector, with the understanding that he would assist in the campaign in Illinois. On October 21, he opened his campaign at Jacksonville and proceeded from there through the northern part of the Congressional district. Here, as in New England, he tried to unite the Whigs and Freesoilers, but whenever an opposition speaker appeared on the same platform he diverted Lincoln and put him on the defensive by bringing up his record on the war.[53] A correspondent of the *Register* claimed that "Lincoln has made nothing by coming to this part of the country to make speeches. He had better have stayed away." Nevertheless, on election day, Taylor carried the district by 1500 votes, a result for which Lincoln, in his autobiography, assumed a large measure of credit.[54]

The election over, Lincoln evidently took a much-needed rest, for there is no record of his activities until December, when he returned to Washington for the second session of Congress. In this he continued his diligent but unimpressive role, attending regularly, voting on almost every roll call, participating in the work of his committees, presenting numerous petitions from his constituents, and continuing to do what favors he could for them. As the only Whig congressman from Illinois, he recommended several candidates for office under the incoming Whig administration and tried unsuccessfully to secure a cabinet appointment for his friend E. D. Baker.

While in Washington Lincoln tried one of the two cases which he had before the United States Supreme Court, the only one in which he appeared personally before that tribunal. This case, William Lewis, for use of Nicholas Longworth v. Thomas Lewis, administrator of Moses Broadwell, involved the construction of the Illinois statute of limitations as applied to non-residents. As the case was appealed from the United States Circuit Court for the District of Illinois, Lincoln had probably tried it in the lower court also, although lack of records makes it impossible to determine this with certainty. Lincoln lost the case when the Supreme Court decided for the defendant.[55]

Having had a taste of national politics and life in the Federal capital, Lincoln was reluctant to return to the less eventful life of Springfield. Moreover, with his own party in power, he hoped with E. D. Baker, the only Whig who had been elected to Congress from Illinois in the last election, to control the Federal patronage in his state. On March 9 he wrote to William M. Meredith, Secretary of the Treasury, requesting that he and Baker be consulted when any appointments were to be made for Illinois, as the Whigs of that state were holding them responsible to some extent for appointments. But an indication of the extent of his influence was given in the conclusion of his letter. "We do not know you personally," he wrote, "and our efforts to see you have, so far, been unavailing."[56]

For almost three weeks after Taylor's inauguration, Lincoln lingered in Washington. Finally he set out for Springfield, where he arrived on March 31. For the next six weeks he devoted most of his time to patronage.

His most important and perplexing problem concerned the Commissionership of the General Land Office at Washington. This office had been virtually promised to Illinois, and on February 14, Lincoln had received a letter from Cyrus Edwards of Edwardsville soliciting his aid in securing the position. Lincoln promised Edwards his support, but instead of presenting Edwards' credentials to the Secretary of the Interior he left them with Gen. Duff Green to be used as Lincoln or Edwards might direct. On his way home Lincoln wrote to Edwards from Alton, on March 27, explaining that he had done this because while he was willing to support Edwards, Baker was for Don Morrison, and unless one of them would withdraw so that Lincoln and Baker could unite in recommending the other, some other state would probably obtain the prize.[57]

Shortly after Lincoln arrived home, friends in Jacksonville and Springfield urged him to apply for the commissionership himself as the only means of saving it to Illinois. On April 7, however, Lincoln replied to these friends, explaining that he had promised to support either Edwards or Morrison and would become an applicant himself only as a final means of obtaining the office for Illinois. "In relation to these pledges," he said, "I must not only be chaste, but above suspicion. If the office shall be tendered to me, I must be permitted to say: 'Give it to Mr. Edwards, or, if so agreed by them, to Colonel Morrison, and I decline it; if not, I accept.' With this understanding you are at liberty to procure me the appointment if you can; and I shall feel complimented by your effort, and still more by its success."[58]

On April 15, Edwards wrote Lincoln that he was convinced Morrison would not withdraw and that he had written to Duff Green to "lay in my application with all the papers in his possession."[59] Lincoln replied on the nineteenth, reiterating his helplessness until either Morrison or Edwards should give way. He informed Edwards that he had been urged to try for the office himself, and restated his position as set forth in his letter to his friends in Jacksonville. "This letter," he said, "they have sent to the Department and I suppose it is the strongest recommendation I could possibly give you."[60] Evidently this satisfied Edwards, for he now wrote Lincoln that he wished him to "feel himself entirely untrammeled and take such course as he might think best . . . if I could not obtain the appointment for myself."[61] Lincoln, in reply, urged Edwards to continue as a candidate.[62]

Meanwhile, the contest was intensified by the entry of a "dark horse" in the person of Justin Butterfield of Chicago.[63] Lincoln learned of his candidacy from J. M. Lucas, a friend from Jacksonville, who was a clerk in the land office at Washington.[64] Immediately on receipt of Lucas' letter, on April 25, he sent a hasty reply. He admitted that Butterfield was qualified for the office, but protested that "of the quite one hundred Illinoisans equally well qualified, I do not know one with less claims to it." For Butterfield, said Lincoln, had not only done nothing in the campaign of 1840, but in the recent campaign he had supported Clay for the presidential nomination against Taylor "to the bitter end." "It will now mortify me deeply," he said, "if General Taylor's administration shall trample all my wishes in the dust merely to gratify these men."[65]

According to the available records, Lincoln did nothing of consequence for the next two weeks. But on May 15 he was alarmed by the receipt of letters from Washington which informed him that Butterfield would probably be given the position. Immediately he bent every effort to prevent this. To cabinet members and congressmen went letters of protest.[66] At Lincoln's request, friends of his also wrote to the Department. In desperation Lincoln grasped at every straw. To Duff Green, on May 18, he wrote: "Some kind friends think I ought to be an applicant, but I am for Mr. Edwards. Try to defeat Butterfield, and in doing so use

Mr. Edwards, J. L. D. Morrison, or myself, whichever you can to best advantage."[67]

But while Lincoln still kept faith with Edwards, some of his friends were not so circumspect. Indeed, Dr. Anson G. Henry committed the indiscretion of writing to Edwards himself urging him to send a letter to President Taylor in behalf of Lincoln.[68]

The zeal of Lincoln's supporters had already provoked Edwards' suspicion. Convinced now that Lincoln was guilty of double-dealing, Edwards not only refused to comply with Henry's request but wrote a long letter to Butterfield in which he disclosed everything that had taken place between him and Lincoln. He had refused to recommend Lincoln, he said, "as it is not necessary in order to save it to the State—yourself being a citizen of the State as well as Mr. Lincoln, and because I retained a little too much self-respect to be used as a cats-paw to promote the success of one on whom I relied to procure the appointment for myself. . . . I have not considered my application withdrawn—nor would I, under the circumstances, raise a finger to ensure it."[69]

By June 1, the contest had narrowed down to Butterfield and Lincoln. Ewing, Secretary of the Interior, favored Butterfield; but Taylor, at the request of Lincoln's friends, who insisted that he was the choice of the overwhelming majority of the Whigs of Illinois, agreed to delay the appointment for three weeks.[70] Secretary Preston, who was evidently favorably disposed to Lincoln, informed the latter's supporters of this decision and wrote that Lincoln was the only man in Illinois who stood a chance of beating Butterfield, but that he could do so if he came on to Washington and his friends supported him.[71] Upon receipt of this news Lincoln cast aside all reservations. From June 3 to 10 he worked frantically, requesting influential persons to recommend him at Washington, where he intended to go as soon as possible. Even Mrs. Lincoln was pressed into service to write letters in his name.[72]

On June 6, Butterfield, who was working as assiduously as Lincoln, came to Springfield. Both candidates now busied themselves in circulating petitions and attempting to get as many signatures as possible affixed to them. Lincoln's political standing in his own district was indicated by the fact that the clerks of the circuit and county courts, the sheriff, the probate judge and other Whig county officials signed Butterfield's petition, while twenty-eight Whig mechanics of Springfield, "dissatisfied with the course of Abraham Lincoln as a member of Congress from this Congressional district," petitioned the Department of the Interior in behalf of Butterfield.[73] Judge Pope of the Federal District Court, Benjamin Bond, the United States Marshal, and Don Morrison, upon whose support Lincoln had been counting, merely wrote the Department that the selection of either Lincoln or Butterfield would be equally satisfactory.[74]

Having investigated the situation in Springfield, Butterfield wrote to a friend complaining that "a little cabal" composed of Logan, N. W. Edwards and three or four others was attempting to deceive the cabinet as to the relative popularity of Lincoln and himself.[75] He accused Logan and Lincoln of calling on those who had signed his petition, and of beseeching them "in the most pathetic manner to retract, but I am informed they have all refused with the exception of one or two against whom they prevailed by threats and menaces." Butterfield was further incensed by the fact that Lincoln's petitions were being circulated among the farmers, many of whom signed without even knowing what the papers concerned. "The attempt to obtain an office by virtue of petitions thus circulated," he wrote, "is as ridiculous as it is undignified, and the Cabinet will know how to appreciate them. I have circulated petitions only among professional men and leading and intelligent whigs who are presumed to know something about the nature of the office and the qualifications requisite to fill it."[76]

To Butterfield, Lincoln said nothing; but he informed one of Butterfield's friends that while he was not yet a candidate for the office, he might be. Butterfield interpreted this as an attempt to lull him while Lincoln's petitions were being passed around.

Butterfield was further angered by the fact that certain persons, friends of Lincoln's he supposed, had informed the cabinet that Butterfield had had a stroke of apoplexy which had impaired his mind and health. To disprove this Butterfield secured testimonials from two doctors, a druggist and the mayor of Chicago. He also submitted a petition signed by the members of the Chicago, Galena, Joliet and Ottawa bar, as well as recommendations from Judge [John] McLean of the United States Supreme Court, E. B. Washburne, and George Meeker.[77] In Washington, Henry Clay and Daniel Webster were both backing him.

Knowing that he had the inside track, Butterfield tried to persuade Lincoln to agree to remain in Illinois pending the administration's decision. This Lincoln refused to do, and on June 10 the rival candidates both set off posthaste for the capital.

But all of Lincoln's efforts were unavailing. On June 21, Butterfield received the prize.

The next day, suspecting that some of his papers had been withheld from the President, Lincoln requested Secretary Ewing to send him all his letters of recommendation which were on file. His suspicions were later confirmed by a letter from a friend in Washington; but while he was keenly sensitive over his defeat he made no public protest. "My great devotion to General Taylor personally; and, above all, my fidelity to the great Whig cause," he wrote to John Addison, his informant, on August 9, 1850, "have induced me to be silent. . . . A public expose, however, though it might confound the guilty, I fear might also injure some who are innocent; to some extent, disparage a good cause; reflect no credit upon me, and result in no advantage to you."[78]

One result of the matter, Edwards' belief that he had been duped, caused Lincoln sincere regret; and through a mutual friend he tried to convince Edwards that he had not deceived him.[79] According to Edwards' granddaughter he was finally successful and a reconciliation was effected.

An important factor in Butterfield's success was the growing importance of his part of the state. During the struggle for the office, he argued: "You know that there is more intelligence and enterprise, more Whigs and more of the materials for making Whigs in the North part of the State than there is in all the rest of the State besides—it contains as I have stated before the only Whig Congressional District; and Chicago containing now (about) twenty thousand inhabitants (more than twice the size of any other town in the State) gave at the Congressional election last fall a large whig majority."[80] The growing importance of Chicago and northern Illinois was a factor which could not be ignored by the national administration.

Lincoln returned to Springfield much disheartened. He continued to send recommendations to the administration, but as his lack of influence became increasingly evident his political enthusiasm cooled. Throughout the summer of 1849 he did little of importance, and by the time the August session of the Sangamon Circuit Court arrived he had turned his back on politics in favor of the law.

During the next four years he evinced no desire for political preferment and took slight interest in political happenings. In June 1850, when two or three newspapers brought him forward as a possible Whig nominee for Congress, he showed no desire to enter the contest. In November of that year, when it was rumored that Butterfield intended to resign and that Lincoln might succeed him, the *Journal* came out with a disclaimer—probably inspired by him—of any wish to do so. When the Whig administration attempted to placate him with an offer of an appointment in Oregon, he (at Mrs. Lincoln's insistence, it is said) refused to accept it.[81] With the country alarmed and anxious over the fate of the Compromise of 1850, the only public expression from him was a casual remark in favor of the Compromise in a eulogy of President Taylor.[82] In October 1852, when his name was presented to a county convention as a prospective nominee for the State Legislature, Herndon, undoubtedly acting under instructions, informed the Convention that his partner could not accept, because business demanded all his time. Mention of Lincoln as a possible candidate for Governor evoked no interest on his part.

The presidential campaign of 1852 aroused him only mildly. His name headed a call for a Whig State Convention to meet on December 22, 1851, to organize for the coming election; and in the convention he served on a committee to nominate delegates to the Whig National Convention and on a committee to choose a State Central Committee. He was also selected as Whig National Committeeman from Illinois. In the campaign which followed, he spoke at Pekin, Peoria, four times at Springfield, and perhaps at other places; but in comparison with his activity in other campaigns his efforts were perfunctory.[83]

In the social reforms of the 1850s he took little part. While he favored the temperance movement and encouraged the dissemination of temperance propaganda, he did not actively participate in the campaign against liquor which swept the state and country. With free soil and abolition movements rapidly gaining adherents in the North, his only public attempt to contribute to a solution of the slavery problem was an address on "Colonization" which he delivered in Springfield on August 30, 1853.

While several of his fellow lawyers and other professional men were laying the bases of fortunes by speculation in farm land and city real estate, which were rapidly enhancing in value with the influx of immigration, he was content to confine his investments to conservative commitments in mortgages and town lots. As he said in his autobiography, by 1854 the practice of his profession had practically superseded politics in his mind.[84]

When Lincoln resumed the practice of law, the Eighth Judicial Circuit comprised fourteen counties in central and eastern Illinois. As he made his first trip around the circuit in the fall of 1849, he found it not much different from what it had been before. Population was increasing rapidly; log cabins were giving place to frame dwellings; some farmers were wearing boots, and clothes of manufactured cloth, instead of brogans and homespun. But farm implements were still crude and inefficient, although the more progressive farmers were replacing scythes, cradles and wooden plows with reapers, mowers and steel-shod plows, and were using horses in place of oxen. While buggies, carryalls and stage coach lines were gradually supplanting or supplementing saddle horses as a means of conveyance, travel was still hazardous and slow, for little or no improvement had been made in the roads, which were muddy and often impassable in winter, dusty in summer and fall, and rutted all year round.

The rate of speed depended on the roads. Under favorable conditions an average of four to five and a half miles an hour was good time; when roads were bad a mile an hour was about all a struggling team could make. Thirty-five miles was a good day's drive. Frequently Judge [David] Davis and the lawyers had to rise before dawn and drive all day and into the night to reach the next court on time. Often in early spring and late autumn the weather was uncomfortably cold, with occasional flurries of snow. Sometimes lawyers arrived in town drenched to the skin by a shower which had overtaken them on the open prairie. Again, it was necessary to drive all day in the rain. Wooden bridges were often carried away by freshets, in which case swollen streams must be forded or swum. Runaways and breakdowns were frequent. Houses were sometimes miles apart; inns were small, cold and cheerless; villages unkempt, crude and at certain seasons almost isolated.

Little change had taken place in social life. Men still gathered at the stores or groceries to discuss crops, weather, roads, politics, letters from friends who had gone to California in the gold rush, and the latest news and local gossip. Around the stove in winter and on the porch in summer one could always find a group whittling, smoking, bespattering the surrounding terrain with tobacco juice, as they talked, joked and ruminated. Here was the forum of the people, where Lincoln, as he traveled from town to town, could learn the workings of their minds, how their ideas changed from one court term to the next, how they reacted to certain conditions and circumstances.

Old recreations and social festivities like hunting, house raisings, corn huskings and quilting bees were being supplemented by sewing societies, charivaries, spirit rappings and lyceums and debating societies. But books and newspapers were few; and intellectual indeed was the home which boasted more than a five-foot bookshelf.

Under such conditions court week was a gala time for villagers and farmers. The latter flocked to town by scores to purchase supplies, renew friendships and enjoy the court proceedings. Judge and lawyers were looked on as celebrities, and a popular lawyer with political ambitions could build up a large potential following from acquaintances and admirers.

When the circuit lawyers arrived in town they were met by the local lawyers who wished to obtain their assistance. These associations were usually not permanent, but merely for the trial of a particular case. Lincoln's only permanent connection on the circuit was made with Ward Hill Lamon of Danville in 1853.[85]

The Supreme Court Library at Springfield was the only collection of legal books on the circuit, and after leaving Springfield, lawyers were dependent on their memories or such books as they carried with them. For the most part, however, cases were simple and were decided on principle rather than by legal precedent. With little time for preparation, common sense and sound reasoning were the principal requisites of success.

The need for volume, accentuated by the prevailing low fees, prevented lawyers from specializing to any extent. Most of them took whatever cases they could get. Lincoln, for example, handled partition suits, foreclosures, appeals from justices' courts, actions in debt, trespass, replevin, [and] suits over dower rights. Most of his cases were of the dull, humdrum sort, typical of farming communities, with an occasional slander suit or divorce case providing some sensation.

Although civil suits made up the bulk of Lincoln's practice, he did some criminal work. He defended a man who was accused of keeping a disorderly house, an adulterer, three persons charged with gambling and one charged with keeping a gambling house. He defended two larceny suits, two perjury suits, four indictments for illegal sales of liquor, three assault cases and two murder cases. As attorney for the plaintiff he secured a verdict of guilty in a bastardy case. His reputation as a prosecutor is attested by his being appointed special prosecuting attorney at Pekin in May, 1853, in order to insure a conviction in a vicious rape case.

One might assume that the local lawyers wrote the pleadings and did the preparatory work, leaving the court work to the circuit lawyers who assisted them; but this was not the case, at least so far as Lincoln was concerned. Hundreds of pleadings in Lincoln's handwriting have been found in the various courthouses of the circuit, and hundreds more have disappeared from the files. Always neatly and carefully drawn, and usually signed by Lincoln with his own last name and that of his associate, they prove that besides conducting the trials, Lincoln also did his full share of the laborious formal work.

So far as the firm of Lincoln and Herndon was concerned, Lincoln did most of the circuit work. The firm had a large practice in Menard County, and after that county was transferred from the circuit Herndon handled practically all the firm's business there. When the circuit was reorganized in 1853 he also finished the pending cases in some of the counties which were transferred to other circuits and which Lincoln could no longer visit because of conflict in court dates. Most of the time, however, he remained in Springfield.

While the Illinois to which Lincoln returned in 1849 was not essentially different from the state he left in 1847, nevertheless important changes were impending; for the next five years marked Illinois' emergence from the pioneer stage, while the years which followed witnessed a development in some respects unparalleled.

Of fundamental importance was the constantly accelerating immigration. From 1845 to 1850 the population of the state increased from 662,150 to 851,470 and by 1860 it had reached 1,711,951. Most of the larger towns were in the center of grain growing areas or on rivers, strategically located with respect to the interior agricultural regions.

The counties and towns of the Eighth Circuit shared the general growth. Sangamon County increased its population from 19,224 in 1850 to 25,604 in 1855. Champaign grew from 2,649 to 6,565; Christian from 3,203 to 7,041; Logan from 5,128 to 8,324; McLean from 10,163 to 19,285; [and] Tazewell from 12,052 to 17,371. Growth of the other counties was commensurate.

Several of the county seats doubled in size. Bloomington, with about four hundred houses and two thousand inhabitants in 1850, had 1,500 houses and five thousand people by 1855. The population of Clinton increased from 760 to 1,400, [and] that of Urbana from five hundred to 1,100. Springfield grew from 5,106 to 7,250. Pekin, which became the county town of Tazewell County in 1850, derived great benefit from the opening of the Illinois and Michigan Canal [in 1848] which connected Lake Michigan with the Illinois River and brought about a huge increase in the steamboat traffic on that stream. In 1852, 1,800 boats passed the Peoria bridge above Pekin, and the trade of the latter place, which served as the chief distributing point for the back country as far as Bloomington, was enormously augmented.

In other towns, however, growth was slow. Mt. Pulaski, in Logan County, contained 360 people in 1850, and grew but slightly in the next five years. Metamora, in Woodford County, Sullivan in Moultrie, [and] Monticello in Piatt remained small villages.

By 1853, the growth of population had brought such an increase in the volume of litigation that it was necessary to decrease the circuit's size from fourteen counties to eight; and Shelby, Macon, Christian, Moultrie, Edgar and Piatt were transferred to other circuits.

An important factor in the development of Illinois was the coming of the railroads. As early as 1837 the state embarked on a grandiose program of railroad construction which was abruptly stopped by the panic which occurred that year. The sole result of this "internal improvement scheme" was the construction of the Northern Cross railroad from Meredosia to Springfield. Later this road was transferred to private hands and became known as the Springfield and Meredosia or Sangamon and Morgan. In 1853 its name was changed to the Great Western.

From 1837 to 1848, with the state slowly liquidating the havoc of the panic, railroad building was impossible. By the latter year, however, the railroad fever was again rampant. That year the Galena and Chicago Union laid tracks from Chicago to Harlem, and the next year the Sangamon and Morgan built a spur from Naples to Bluffs. When Lincoln returned from Congress this was the extent of the railroad mileage of the state.

The real impetus came in 1850, when Stephen A. Douglas and Sidney Breese secured from Congress a grant of 2,595,000 acres of land to the state to aid in the construction of a road from the junction of the Illinois River and the Illinois and Michigan Canal to the confluence of the Ohio and Mississippi rivers. A group of Eastern capitalists, headed by Robert Rantoul of Massachusetts, agreed to construct the road and turn over 7 percent of the gross revenue to the state in return for the Federal land grant.[86] The state accepted their proposition, and the road was incorporated on February 10, 1851. Construction began at once and by 1854 the main line from Mendota to Bloomington and a branch line from Chicago to Kankakee were completed and in operation.

The present Chicago and Alton Railroad was built under two charters, one granted February 27, 1847 to the Alton and Sangamon Railroad Company to build from Alton to Springfield, and the other granted June 19, 1852, to the Chicago and Mississippi to build from Springfield to Joliet. The former road was finished in 1852, and by 1853 the latter road had laid tracks from Springfield to Bloomington.

By the end of the decade of the 1850s the increase in population, with the resulting volume of business, and the building of a railroad net, which made travel quick and easy, were destined to bring an end to circuit life; but the influence of these factors, especially the latter, was little felt as yet. While a few of the more successful lawyers were giving up circuit practice, and some were confining themselves to counties contiguous to their homes, most of them, like Lincoln, still found it necessary to travel the whole circuit.

The railroads brought to the lawyers of the circuit a new type of business, in which Lincoln and Herndon participated. In 1851 Lincoln was retained by the Sangamon and Alton in two suits to compel stockholders to pay their assessments. Two years later he was again retained by this company in two appeals to the Supreme Court. In the latter year Lincoln and Herndon also tried two appeals from assessments for damages for right of way for the Chicago and Mississippi. Indeed, from the *Illinois State Register* of that year it appears that Lincoln was in the regular retainer of this company.

The Illinois Central also employed him frequently and later made a permanent arrangement with him. In August 1853, he handled a case involving an assessment for right of way in Champaign County, and at the fall term was given charge of several cases in DeWitt and McLean. When McLean County started proceedings to force the Illinois Central to pay taxes on the property it owned within the county, Lincoln was once more engaged by the company. And in October 1853, he was asked to act as arbiter in a crossing dispute between it and the Northern Indiana Railroad.

For six months in spring and fall Lincoln traveled the circuit; but during the winter months he remained in Springfield to practice in the Supreme and Federal Courts. Although Springfield was still important in the political, legal and social life of the state, it was losing the preeminent position it once held. From 1837 to 1848, the Supreme Court had met only in Springfield; but the new constitution divided the state into three grand divisions and provided that an annual session of the court should be held in each of them. The Second Grand Division, which held its sessions at Springfield, included Sangamon, Champaign, Vermilion, DeWitt, Logan, Edgar, Coles, Moultrie, Shelby, Montgomery, Macoupin, Greene, Pike, Adams, Highland, Hancock, McDonough, Schuyler, Brown, Fulton, Mason, Cass, Morgan, Scott, Christian, Macon, Piatt, Menard, Cumberland and Clark counties. The counties to the south constituted the First Grand Division, while those to the north made up the Third Grand Division. Court for the First Grand Division sat at Mt. Vernon, while the Third Grand Division held its sessions at Ottawa. By consent of the parties a case appealed from a county in one grand division could be tried in an adjoining one. Thus cases from any county in the state might be adjudicated in Springfield. During this period all except two of Lincoln's cases were tried in Springfield; those were tried in Ottawa.

The Supreme Court was composed of three judges, one from each grand division. They served for nine years, one being elected every three years and the one with the oldest commission presiding as chief justice. Judges must be thirty-five years old, and received salaries of $1,200 a year. The judges during this period were Samuel H. Treat, John D. Caton and Lyman Trumbull, whose average age in 1849 was only thirty-seven.[87]

With cases relatively few, rules of procedure were simple. Arguments were usually oral, and until 1853 there was no limit to the time allowed the litigants. In that year, however, the court adopted a rule which limited arguments to two hours with the right to extend the opening argument to three hours by special permission of the court. The court kept no minutes, and the only memoranda of arguments and citations were such notes as the individual judges chose to jot down.

Usually cases were considered and opinions rendered immediately after hearing, with the concurrence of two judges necessary to a decision. Sometimes, however, decision was deferred until the judges had considered the case individually. After a decision was reached the Chief Justice delegated himself or one of his associates to write the opinion. Usually several decisions which had demanded special consideration were handed down together at the end of a term.

The volume of Lincoln's business before the Supreme Court is indicative of his increasing competence. From 1849 to 1853 he participated in thirty cases, winning eighteen and losing twelve. Despite the fact that he had to rebuild his practice after returning from Washington, only three or four firms tried more cases before the Central Grand Division than he and Herndon; and of the cases appealed from the counties of the Eighth Circuit, where they were best known, they handled more than any other firm or individual with the exception of Stephen T. Logan.

In the Supreme Court, as well as on the circuit, there was considerable differentiation in their work. The printed court reports often give the firm name in cases in which either of them appeared; but the original written records show that they seldom appeared together in the same case. Lincoln attended to most of the cases coming up from Sangamon and the other counties of the circuit; while Herndon tried all cases from Menard, where he also attended to circuit work, several from Morgan and some from miscellaneous counties. Each partner not only argued his own cases but drew his own pleadings and did his own preparatory work.

In the Supreme Court, as well as in the lower courts, their practice was heterogeneous. Lincoln represented the Sangamon and Alton Railroad in four cases (and incidentally won every one of them); tried cases involving the constitutionality of a legislative act which merged two counties without the consent of their inhabitants, the liability of sureties on a collector's bond, the admissibility of oral evidence to change the terms of a written contract, the right of an individual partner to collect the assets of an insolvent partnership, and the right of the governor to reject bids submitted after the time set for their presentation. One of his cases involved the question whether the maker of a note payable in State of Illinois indebtedness was liable for the face value of his note or for the market value of the nominal amount of state indebtedness due. He tried two cases—*Adams et al. v. Logan County* and *Harris v. Shaw et al.*—which involved the right of persons who had given property to a county on condition of the county seat being located at a particular place to compensation by reason of the removal of the county seat. In the former case he was on the side of the county and won; while in the latter he argued the other side of the question and lost.

Like the Supreme Court, the Federal Courts met only in Springfield from the time the town became the capital until 1848. But with the

growth of Chicago and the rapid settlement of northern Illinois, it became increasingly inconvenient for lawyers from that section to try their
cases downstate. Consequently, in 1848, Congress provided that two annual terms should be held in Chicago in addition to the two sessions at
Springfield.

The United States Judge for the District of Illinois was Nathaniel
Pope, who died in 1850 and was succeeded by Thomas Drummond.[88] The
Federal Circuit Courts were presided over by the chief justice or one of
the associate justices of the United States Supreme Court, the judge for
the Seventh Circuit, which included Illinois, Michigan, Ohio and Indiana, being Associate Justice John McLean.

The records of the Federal Courts for this period are incomplete; but
enough are available to show that here, as in the Supreme Court, Lincoln
was rapidly gaining recognition as a leader of the bar. Most of his Federal cases involved the collection of debts; but he was also counsel in a
number of patent suits and in one mail robbery case. His widening reputation is attested by his being called to Chicago in 1850 to participate in
an important patent case.

At the December term, 1851, he had a case of extraordinary interest
because of its similarity to *Hurd et al. v. Railroad Bridge Company*—the
famous "Effie Afton" case—which he tried at Chicago in 1857. This
case—*Columbus Insurance Company v. Curtenius et al.*—was an action
for damages sustained by the plaintiff as insurer of a canal boat and cargo of wheat which were sunk by striking a pier of a bridge across the Illinois River at Peoria. The defendants pleaded an act of the legislature
authorizing the construction of the bridge, but Lincoln and [William]
Chumasaro for the plaintiff demurred on the ground that the legislature
had no right to authorize the obstruction of a navigable stream. The court
upheld the demurrer and the case then turned on the question whether
the bridge was in fact an obstruction. The jury, unable to agree, was discharged, and the suit was finally compromised. Thus four years before
the "Effie Afton" case Lincoln was engaged in a case in which the facts
and the question at issue were practically identical with those in the more
famous suit. In this case, however, he opposed the bridge interests, whereas in the latter case he defended them. No doubt the experience gained
in this suit was of material assistance to him in the later, more important case.

Practically all of the business of Lincoln and Herndon in the Federal
Courts was managed by the senior partner; although here, as in the Supreme Court, it was sometimes transacted in the firm name. More of-

ten, however, Lincoln was associated with other lawyers—Logan or Browning, especially—and Herndon's name does not appear at all.

If Springfield was becoming relatively less important as a political, legal and social center as the tide of immigration shifted to the north, this fact was hardly apparent from mid-December to mid-March, when the Supreme and Federal Courts were in session. At that time—and particularly in the years when the legislature was also sitting—the town was crowded with visitors. From all parts of the state, but especially from the central tier of counties, in stage coaches, buggies and on horseback, came judges, lawyers and legislators. With the coming of the railroads those from counties along the Illinois River or the Mississippi often took steamboats to the railroad termini at Alton or Naples and came from there by train.

Travel during December and January was frequently uncertain and dangerous. Crossing rivers was usually an adventure, accomplished sometimes on solid ice and again by ferry amid floating ice cakes; and snow storms often added to the hazards. Even summer travel was not without vicissitudes. On July 7, 1853, Orville H. Browning on his way to attend the Federal Courts at Springfield recorded that en route to Naples to board the train "the horses became unruly—kicked furiously and came near running away. . . . Half mile East of Kingston one of the hind wheels of the omnibus gave way—the spokes all crushed out and let us down in the road. Procured a two horse lumber wagon, piled in the mail bags & our trunks, mounted on the top of the trunks, and thus exposed to the dust and burning sun pursued our journey." Even after reaching Naples and boarding the train their troubles were not over. "Reached Jacksonville at 3 & Springfield at 8 P.M.," Browning continued, "having been eleven hours on the way. Boiler was burnt out—leaked & put out fire so we could not raise steam."[89]

Arriving in Springfield the visitors found a straggling prairie town, its appearance distorted by the growing pains of adolescence. Log cabins and mansions could both be seen in the residential sections, while many of the business houses around the public square were ramshackle and antiquated. The groves of maple, locust, elm and oak trees which beautified the town in summer were bare and sere in wintertime. On warmer days, when ice thawed, wagons and horses soon churned the streets to muddy sloughs. "Pleasant, and beautiful and flourishing will I term it," wrote a summer visitor from Alton, "though very opposite adjectives have been prefixed to Springfield by many of those editors and politicians who have seen it during the winter's cold mud, and cloudy sky and foggy air—when an unusual and ill-assorted and turbulent crowd of visitors are here from the highways and by-ways of 'Suckerdom,' when bird and bee, and blossom have given place to pelting rain, and driving wind and general gloom."[90] As late as 1850 the town did not possess a single good hotel, and experienced visitors preferred to lodge at boardinghouses or private homes whenever possible.

At times dissatisfaction with Springfield brought proposals to move the capital elsewhere; but the citizens were staunch in their resistance to such movements. In their minds the city's future greatness was a certainty. And, as a matter of fact, many signs of progress were in evidence. Already lots on the public square sold for $100 a front foot and neighboring farms brought as much as $100 an acre. On a Saturday afternoon the editor of the *Journal* counted 150 double teams and as many saddle horses at the hitching posts around the square besides those scattered in side streets and alleys. From his observations he calculated a fair Saturday's trade at $15,000, and considered $250,000 a conservative estimate of the city's annual business.

In July 1849, the rehabilitated Sangamon and Morgan Railroad ran its first train into the city from Jacksonville; and by 1853 the Alton road had given Springfield rail connections with Alton and Bloomington. By 1851, the first local bank, the Springfield Marine and Fire Insurance Company, was doing business, with Lincoln as one of its depositors, and the next year N. H. Ridgely established Clark's Exchange Bank.[91] A new governor's mansion was begun in 1853. Two newspapers, the *Sangamon Journal* and the *Illinois State Register,* served the community. The former, edited by Simeon Francis, a close friend of Lincoln, was ardently Whig; the latter, under the editorial guidance of Charles H. Lanphier and George Walker, was just as staunchly Democratic.[92]

The most beautiful and imposing structure in Springfield was the state capitol, situated in the center of the public square. Here the governor and other executive officers had their offices, and here every two years—and oftener in case of an extra session—the legislature sat. Here also the Supreme Court held its annual sessions.

Across from the state house, on the southeast corner of Sixth and Washington streets, was the Sangamon County Courthouse, an oblong, two-story brick building "with a lofty doric portico, finished in imitation stone." Across the street to the north the Federal Courts met in rented quarters on the second floor of a building owned by Stephen T. Logan.

The unattractiveness of Springfield was compensated to some extent by the hospitality of its citizens. "Dined at Jno Cooks in company with Judge Drummond, B. Bond, Wm. Pope, N. Edwards & R. S. Blackwell Esqrs," wrote Browning on December 16, 1851.[93] "Spent the evening at

Ridgely's with Drummond, Pope, Bushnell & Lawrence"; "went to Wm. Popes to supper"; "after supper called on Mrs. Johnson"; "dined with Rev. Mr. Dodge"; "in the afternoon I walked out to Ridgely's Green House, and went to his house to tea"; "to exhibition of Deaf & Dumb at State House" are other typical entries in his *Diary* during the days he spent in Springfield.[94] Yet despite the friendliness of the townsfolk, Springfield was often dull and the lawyers were usually glad when they could leave for home. "No festivities of any kind in this dull Town," complained Browning in December, 1851, and two years later he wrote: "Taking care of my health & amusing myself as well as I can."[95]

During the day, when they were not busy in court, and in the evenings, lawyers repaired to the Supreme Court library in the capitol building to prepare their cases. Often, when a crowd had gathered, work was laid aside, news and gossip were exchanged and political plans were formulated. The more serious topics exhausted, the group relaxed in lighter vein with Lincoln or some other wit as the center of attraction. When jokes and repartee were liveliest the crowd stayed on long after midnight. To Lincoln, however, these sessions meant more than mere conviviality; for in them he exchanged ideas, kept in touch with political happenings and developments and made friendships with influential men from all parts of the state, whose help was later of inestimable value.

When the legislature was in session some of the more influential lawyers found employment in lobbying. Always in evidence since the earliest days of the state, this type of activity was stimulated to a degree hitherto unknown by the development of corporations. Largely dependent upon political favors not only for success but for actual existence in many cases, plank road companies, canal companies, coal mining companies and especially railroads found it essential to employ men with political connections and influence to look after their interests in the legislature. With his numerous friends and wide experience in state politics, Lincoln was well fitted for this work, and was solicited both for small gratuitous favors and professional services. A typical example of activity of this sort is revealed in his letter of February 15, 1853 to John A. Rockwell. "I have failed to get your Coal Mining Charter," he wrote. "A little more than a week before the close of the Session, I got a Bill for the Charter howsoever into the Senate, which Body passed it in about five days—It then went to the H.R. and was lost for want of time.... If you continue to desire it, I will get it passed at the next session."[96]

Many conjectures have been offered as to whether Lincoln was retained by the Illinois Central Railroad to help secure its charter. Years after the charter was obtained, Judge Anthony Thornton of Shelby County made affidavit that he was the only living member of the legislature which granted the charter and that he had "a distinct recollection that Mr. Lincoln and several members of the legislature were engaged by the Illinois Central."[97]

While there is no available data which will prove this statement, there is considerable evidence to support it. In the first place, Lincoln was following the proceedings of the legislature with great interest during the session of 1851, for at the end of the session he wrote to William Martin: "The Legislature having got out of the way, I at last find time to attend to the business you left with me."[98]

In the second place, letters written by James F. Joy, agent for the company, to William P. Burrall, its president, show that at the time the charter was granted the company was employing a lobbyist, and that he was later placed in the permanent retainer of the company.[99] On January 16, 1854, Joy wrote to Burrall: "I do not know whether it is contemplated by the committee that I shall employ aid at the Legislature if I deem it expedient. There is one man, however, whom it is for the interest of the company to have with us in every way and whom hitherto I have always had with me and whom for no consideration should I want against me at the Legislature. I would recommend that he be interested permanently for the company, as it is apparent that you will need more or less legislation frequently. A retainer or a salary of $1,000 a year will command him, and he is a valuable ally and a dangerous opponent in any matter before the Legislature. I would also recommend that this be a matter entirely confidential and that nothing ever be said about his being employed. I would recommend an understanding with him for two or three years. Of course, I mean that this shall be decided by the committee but that it shall be deemed confidential by each of them."

On February 2, Joy wrote: "It might be necessary for me to engage more influence at Springfield. A single man to whom I alluded in a postscript to my last letter to you was sufficient last winter. I shall probably have to strengthen him this winter to accomplish the purpose I deemed last winter of sufficient importance to induce me to give such instructions as defeated B's bill."[100]

"B's bill," to which Joy referred, was a bill to incorporate the Mississippi and Atlantic Railroad, under the leadership of John Brough.[101] It is significant that Lincoln was a vigorous and consistent opponent of Brough's road and that on February 24, 1854, he, John T. Stuart and Benjamin S. Edwards wrote an opinion denying the validity of the organization of the Mississippi and Atlantic road under the terms of the railroad incorporation act.[102]

Coincidental with this is the fact that Lincoln was in the regular retainer of the Illinois Central for a number of years. On February 12, 1857, he wrote to a firm of attorneys in Paris, Illinois: "I have been in the regular retainer of the Co. for two or three years, but I expect they do not wish to retain me any longer."[103] If he had been in the company's retainer for three years, his connection would have begun just about the time Joy made his recommendation that the company make "an understanding" for two or three years with the man whom he had previously found indispensable.

A relationship such as this is extremely difficult to prove, but the congruity of evidence points to Lincoln as the man referred to. On the other hand we have the statement of Robert Rantoul, son of one of the promoters of the road, before the Massachusetts Historical Society in 1909 to the effect that Lincoln in a conversation with his father at the White House in 1863 said that "he did all he could to stop it, but was not successful."[104]

All in all, the period from 1847 to 1853 was for Lincoln a time of great development. During his term in Congress he broadened his outlook and political education and made valuable acquaintances. Having come in contact with the views of representative men of various sections, and especially those from New England, on the problems of the day, he came to realize the importance of the slavery issue. During the latter part of this period he gave it much of his thought and by 1854, when it again became acute, he had definitely determined his own attitude upon it. From the reaction to his attitude on the Mexican War he learned that in a democratic government a politician who hopes to be successful and to continue in public life can go no farther in any direction than public opinion will permit. In 1849 when he was forced to give up politics, with its chances of relatively easy and rapid preferment, he turned to the more arduous business of the law. Gradually he regained the practice and prestige which he had lost while in Washington, and by 1854 was recognized as one of the leading lawyers of central Illinois.

While his legal ability grew, and his political thought matured, his general education was not neglected. In his leisure time at home and on the circuit, he read all the newspapers which came to hand. Although not a wide reader of books, he read with thoughtfulness and care in those fields in which he had an interest. Possessing an analytical and mathematical bent, he began at this time the mastery of the six books of Euclid.

That the period was one of mental discipline and growth is clearly evident when the speeches which he made before 1849 are compared with those delivered after 1853. Those of the earlier period tended to grandiloquence and were replete with boisterous humor. After 1853 they are characterized by a burning seriousness, keen analysis, close-knit reasoning, and plain, well-chosen words.

Not only did Lincoln develop mentally, but as he traveled the circuit he kept in constant contact with the common people, gauged the currents of popular opinion, got the people's viewpoints on the political, economic and social problems of the day, and unconsciously prepared himself to be their spokesman. Honest, friendly, a skillful spinner of yarns, he made a host of friends.

The Lincoln who reentered politics in 1854, when the repeal of the Missouri Compromise "aroused him as he had never been before," was a different man from the ambitious politician of seven years before.[105] He was still ambitious, it is true, but his ambition was restrained now by devotion to a cause. Always a clear thinker and a clever man before a crowd, he demonstrated in 1854 that he had become a political analyst of the first rank, with conviction in his reasoning and power in his words.

Such development is difficult to trace, but the record of his daily life which follows may illuminate to some extent the process of the change.[106]

Notes

1. Edward D. Baker (1811–61), a close friend of Lincoln, served in Congress in the mid–1840s and was killed at the battle of Ball's Bluff on 21 October 1861.
2. Wishing to avoid conflict with fellow Whigs, Lincoln had refused to fill the unexpired term of his friend Edward D. Baker, who in January 1847 quit his seat to participate in the Mexican War (*Sangamo Journal* [Springfield], 7 Jan. 1847). According to John Henry, the candidate who eventually received the nomination, "It was . . . supposed that Mr. Lincoln would be a candidate for the nomination.— Mr. Lincoln, however, at the meeting [of the legislators on 30 December], declined being considered a candidate. . . . When the matter was first spoken of, I supposed, as a matter of course, that Mr. Lincoln would receive the nomination." (John Henry to the Voters of the Seventh Congressional District, 7 Jan. 1847, *Sangamo Journal*, 14 Jan. 1847.) Henry told Richard Yates that those legislators attending the meeting "mostly thought that as Lincoln had to go the next session that we had better send him to fill the vacancy when we met Linco[l]n declined coming in contact with any friend concequently friend [William] Brown was nominated with out op[p]osition in fact there was not time to make anny arrangements." (John Henry to Richard Yates, Springfield, 2 Jan. 1847, Richard Yates Papers, Illinois State Historical Library, Springfield.) To serve out Baker's term, the Whig legislators were inclined to choose William Brown, who said that friends pressured him to withdraw because "they looked upon the present election, as a race for dollars and cents—and that, feeling under obligations to [John] Henry for favors, heretofore conferred, and as he was poor, and I was not, and the money would be of great service to him,—they should vote for him on that ground." (William Brown to the Voters of the Seventh Congressional District, 9 Jan. 1847, *Sangamo*

Journal, 14 Jan. 1847; cf. Paul Findley, *A. Lincoln: The Crucible of Congress* [New York: Crown, 1979], 54–57.) Findley called Lincoln's decision "one of the great mysteries of his life." The Sangamon County Whigs may have wanted to appease their party colleagues in Morgan County by nominating either Brown or Henry. (*Illinois State Register* [Springfield], 8 Jan. 1847).

3. Lincoln spoke to the Temperance Union on 31 August and 17 September 1846 and 30 August 1847. He wrote to Andrew Johnston, a Quincy lawyer, about his poetry on 24–25 February and 18 April 1846 and 25 February 1847.

4. The Constitutional Convention met in Springfield from June 7 to August 31.

5. The convention took place between July 5 and 7.

6. Horace Greeley (1811–72) edited the *New York Tribune*. For convention coverage, see the *New York Weekly Tribune*, 17 July 1848. One delegate recalled that Field's auditors, not sympathizing with his argument, tried to silence him with shouts of derision. Lincoln then rose "and in a few well chosen words, to the effect that full and free discussion had been invited and must be favorable to the cause they had at heart, ended the disturbance, and Mr. Field was permitted to proceed." Reminiscences of E. B. McCagg, *Chicago Tribune*, 12 Feb. 1900, 14.

7. Thomas Corwin (1794–1865) represented an Ohio district in the U.S. House from 1831 to 1840 and 1859 to 1861, served as governor of Ohio (1840–42), represented his state in the U.S. Senate from 1845 to 1850, and served as secretary of the treasury (1850–53). In 1861 Lincoln appointed him minister to Mexico. Edward Bates (1793–1869) represented a Missouri district in the U.S. House of Representatives (1827–29) and served as Lincoln's attorney general (1861–64). Nathaniel Pitcher Tallmadge (1795–1864) represented New York in the U.S. Senate (1833–44). Andrew Stewart (1791–1872) of Uniontown represented his district in the U.S. House (1821–29, 1831–35, 1843–49).

8. Abraham Lincoln to Williamson Durley, Springfield, 3 Oct. 1845, in *The Collected Works of Abraham Lincoln*, ed. Roy P. Basler, Marion Dolores Pratt and Lloyd A. Dunlap, asst. eds., 8 vols. plus index (New Brunswick: Rutgers University Press, 1953–55), 1:348.

9. Duncan T. McIntyre, "Lincoln and the Matson Slave Case," *Illinois Law Review* 1 (1906–7): 386–91; John J. Duff, *A. Lincoln Prairie Lawyer* (New York: Holt, Rinehart and Winston, 1960), 130–47; Jesse W. Weik, "Lincoln and the Matson Negroes: A Vista into the Fugitive-Slave Days," *Arena* 17 (April 1897): 752–58; Charles H. Coleman, *Abraham Lincoln and Coles County, Illinois* (New Brunswick: Scarecrow Press, 1955), 104–11; Albert A. Woldman, *Lawyer Lincoln* (Boston: Houghton, Mifflin, 1937), 56–66.

10. George M. Dallas (1792–1864) of Pennsylvania served as vice president from 1845 to 1849. Lewis Cass (1782–1866) of Michigan represented his state in the U.S. Senate (1845–48, 1849–57) and ran as the Democratic presidential nominee in 1848. Stephen A. Douglas (1813–61) represented his Illinois district in the U.S. House (1843–47) and served in the U.S. Senate (1848–61). In 1860 he ran against Lincoln for the presidency.

11. As Theodore Dwight Weld described Mrs. Sprigg's boardinghouse, "Mrs. Spriggs is directly in front of the Capitol. . . . The iron railing around the Capitol Park comes within fifty feet of our door. Our dining room overlooks the whole Capitol Park which is one mile around and filled with shade trees and shrubbery. I have a pleasant room on the second floor with a good bed, plenty of covering, a bureau, table, chairs, closets and clothes press, a good fire place, and plenty of dry

wood to burn in it. We have about twenty boarders, mostly members of Congress, eight of them from Pennsylvania and the rest from the free states. Only Gates and Giddings [are] abolitionists, but *all* the others are *favorable.*" Theodore Dwight Weld to Angelina G. Weld, Washington, 1 Jan. 1842, in *Letters of Theodore Dwight Weld, Angelina Grimké Weld, and Sarah Grimké, 1822–1844,* ed. Gilbert H. Barnes and Dwight L. Dumond (Washington, D.C.: American Historical Association, 1934), 883. In a 2 January 1842 letter to Angelina Weld, he reported that "Mrs. Sprigg, our landlady, is a Virginian *not* a slaveholder, but hires slaves. She has eight servants all colored, three men, one boy and four women. All are free but three which she hires and these are buying themselves" (885).

12. Elisha Embree (1801–63) of Princeton represented his district in the U.S. House (1847–49). Patrick Watson Tompkins (1804–53) of Vicksburg represented his district in the U.S. House (1847–49). Joshua Reed Giddings (1795–1864) of Jefferson represented his district in the U.S. House (1842–59). In 1861 Lincoln appointed him consul-general to the British North American Provinces. John Blanchard (1787–1849) of Bellefonte represented his district in the U.S. House (1845–49). John Dickey (1794–1853) of Old Brighton represented his district in the U.S. House (1843–45, 1847–49). John Strohm (1793–1884) of Providence represented his district in the U.S. House (1845–49). James Pollock (1810–90) of Milton represented his district in the U.S. House (1844–49). As director of the mint from 1861–66 and 1869–73, he originated the motto "In God we trust." Abraham Robinson McIlvaine (1804–63) represented his district in the U.S. House (1843–49).

13. Duff Green (1791–1875) was a leading Democratic journalist and politician. Nathan Sargent (1794–1875), a successful journalist, served as sergeant-at-arms of the U.S. House (1847–51).

14. Samuel C. Busey, *Personal Reminiscences and Recollections of Forty-Six Years' Membership in the Medical Society of the District of Columbia, and Residence in This City* (Washington: Dornan, 1895), 25.

15. Busey, *Personal Reminiscences,* 28.

16. Speech in Peoria, 16 Oct. 1854, in *Collected Works,* ed. Basler et al., 2:253.

17. "Congressman Lincoln was very fond of bowling, and would frequently join others of the mess, or meet other members in a match game, at the alley of James Casparis, which was near the boarding house. He was a very awkward bowler, but played the game with great zest and spirit, solely for exercise and amusement, and greatly to the enjoyment and entertainment of the other players and bystanders by his criticisms and funny illustrations. He accepted success and defeat with like good nature and humor, and left the alley at the conclusion of the game without a sorrow or disappointment. When it was known that he was in the alley there would assemble numbers of people to witness the fun which was anticipated by those who knew of his fund of anecdotes and jokes. When in the alley, surrounded by a crowd of eager listeners, he indulged with great freedom in the sport of narrative, some of which were very broad. His witticisms seemed for the most part to be impromptu, but he always told the anecdotes and jokes as if he wished to convey the impression that he had heard them from some one; but they appeared very many times as if they had been made for the immediate occasion." Busey, *Personal Reminiscences,* 28.

18. John Jordan Crittenden (1786–1863) represented Kentucky in the U.S. Senate (1842–48, 1855–61). Hannibal Hamlin (1809–91) represented Maine in the U.S.

Senate (1848–61). Daniel Webster (1782–1852) represented Massachusetts in the U.S. Senate (1827–41, 1845–50). Jefferson Davis (1808–89) represented Mississippi in the U.S. Senate (1847–51, 1857–61). John Middleton Clayton (1796–1856) represented Delaware in the U.S. Senate (1829–36, 1845–49). Reverdy Johnson (1796–1876) represented Maryland in the U.S. Senate (1845–49, 1863–68). Thomas Hart Benton (1782–1858) represented Missouri in the U.S. Senate (1821–51). David Rice Atchinson (1807–86) represented Missouri in the U.S. Senate (1843–55). John Parker Hale (1806–73) represented New Hampshire in the U.S. Senate (1847–53, 1855–65). John Adams Dix (1798–1879) represented New York in the U.S. Senate (1845–49). Willie Person Mangum (1792–1861) represented North Carolina in the U.S. Senate (1831–36, 1840–53). Simon Cameron (1799–1889) represented Pennsylvania in the U.S. Senate (1845–49, 1857–61). John Bell (1797–1869) represented Tennessee in the U.S. Senate (1847–59). Samuel Houston (1793–1863) represented Texas in the U.S. Senate (1846–59). James Murray Mason (1798–1871) represented Virginia in the U.S. Senate (1847–61). Robert Mercer Taliaferro Hunter (1809–87) represented Virginia in the U.S. Senate (1847–61). William Lewis Dayton (1807–64) represented New Jersey in the U.S. Senate (1842–51).

19. Howell Cobb (1815–68) of Athens, Georgia, represented his district in the U.S. House (1843–51, 1855–57). Alexander Hamilton Stephens (1812–83) of Crawfordsville, Georgia, represented his district in the U.S. House (1843–59). Robert Toombs (1810–85) of Washington, Georgia, represented his district in the U.S. House (1845–53). Caleb Blood Smith (1808–64) of Connersville, Indiana, represented his district in the U.S. House (1843–49). Robert Charles Winthrop (1809–94) of Boston represented his district in the U.S. House (1842–50). John Gorham Palfrey (1796–1881) of Boston represented his district in the U.S. House (1847–49). George Ashmun (1804–70) of Springfield, Massachusetts, represented his district in the U.S. House (1845–51). John Quincy Adams (1767–1848) of Quincy, Massachusetts, represented his district in the U.S. House (1831–48). Horace Mann (1796–1859) of Dedham, Massachusetts, represented his district in the U.S. House (1848–53). Jacob Thompson (1810–85) of Pontotoc, Mississippi, represented his district in the U.S. House (1839–51). Amos Tuck (1810–79) of Exeter, New Hampshire, represented his district in the U.S. House (1847–53). David Wilmot (1814–68) of Towanda, Pennsylvania, represented his district in the U.S. House (1845–51). Robert Cumming Schenck (1809–90) of Dayton, Ohio, represented his district in the U.S. House (1843–51, 1863–71). Robert Barnwell Rhett (1800–76) of Beaufort, South Carolina, represented his district in the U.S. House (1837–49). Andrew Johnson (1808–75) of Greenville, Tennessee, represented his district in the U.S. House (1843–53). John Minor Botts (1802–69) of Richmond, Virginia, represented his district in the U.S. House (1839–43, 1847–49).

20. Sidney Breese (1800–78) of Kaskaskia represented Illinois in the U.S. Senate (1843–49). Robert Smith (1802–67) of Alton represented his district in the U.S. House (1843–49, 1857–59). John Alexander McClernand (1812–1900) of Shawneetown represented his district in the U.S. House (1843–51). Orlando Bell Ficklin (1808–86) of Charleston represented his district in the U.S. House (1843–49, 1851–53). John Wentworth (1815–88) of Chicago represented his district in the U.S. House (1843–51, 1865–67). William Alexander Richardson (1811–75) of Shelbyville represented his district in the U.S. House (1847–56, 1861–63). Thomas Johnston Turner (1815–74) of Freeport represented his district in the U.S. House (1847–49).

21. Abraham Lincoln to Williamson Durley, Springfield, 3 Oct. 1845, in *Collected Works*, ed. Basler et al., 1:348.

22. Speech of 12 Jan. 1848, in *Collected Works*, ed. Basler et al., 1:432.

23. Henry Clay, speech in Lexington, 13 Nov. 1847, in *The Papers of Henry Clay*, ed. Robert Seager and James F. Hopkins, 10 vols. (Lexington: University Press of Kentucky, 1959–91), 10:364–72.

24. "Spot Resolutions," 22 Dec. 1847, in *Collected Works*, ed. Basler et al., 1:420–22.

25. Speech in the U.S. House, 12 Jan. 1848, in *Collected Works*, ed. Basler et al., 1:438–39.

26. *Illinois State Register*, 14 Jan. 1848.

27. *Illinois State Register*, 10 March 1848.

28. *Illinois State Register*, 14 April 1848.

29. More recent scholarship suggests that Lincoln did not suffer such repercussions. See Gabor S. Boritt, "A Question of Political Suicide? Lincoln's Opposition to the Mexican War," *Journal of the Illinois State Historical Society* 67 (1974): 79–100.

30. Abraham Lincoln to William H. Herndon, Washington, 1 Feb. 1848, in *Collected Works*, ed. Basler et al., 1:446–47.

31. Abraham Lincoln to William H. Herndon, Washington, 13 Feb. 1848, in *Collected Works*, ed. Basler et al., 1:451–52.

32. Kentucky-born Usher F. Linder (1809–76) was at the time a leading Whig who later became a Democrat. The Rev. Dr. John Mason Peck (1789–1858) was a leading Baptist educator who founded Shurtleff College in Rock Spring, Illinois.

33. Abraham Lincoln to William H. Herndon, Washington, 8 Jan. 1848, in *Collected Works*, ed. Basler et al., 1:430–31.

34. Wendell Phillips in *The Liberator* (Boston), 30 June 1860.

35. Basler et al., eds., *Collected Works*, 2:20–22.

36. Speech in the U.S. House, 20 June 1848, in *Collected Works*, ed. Basler et al., 1:480–90.

37. Basler et al., eds., *Collected Works*, 2:26–27.

38. Ibid., 1:449.

39. Thomas S. Flournoy (1811–83) of Halifax, Virginia, represented his district in the U.S. House (1847–49). Abraham Lincoln to Thomas S. Flournoy, Washington, 17 Feb. 1848, in *Collected Works*, ed. Basler et al., 1:452.

40. Abraham Lincoln to Jesse Lynch, Washington, 10 April 1848, in *Collected Works*, ed. Basler et al., 1:463–64.

41. Elihu B. Washburne (1816–87) of Galena was a Whig leader.

42. Abraham Lincoln to Archibald Williams, Washington, 30 April 1848, in *Collected Works*, ed. Basler et al., 1:467–68.

43. Abraham Lincoln to Archibald Williams, Washington, 12 June 1848, in *Collected Works*, ed. Basler et al., 1:476–77.

44. Abraham Lincoln to William H. Herndon, Washington, 22 June 1848, in *Collected Works*, ed. Basler et al., 1:490–92.

45. Angle, ed., *Herndon's Life of Lincoln*, 227; Abraham Lincoln to William H. Herndon, Washington, 10 July 1848, in *Collected Works*, ed. Basler et al., 1:497–98.

46. Thomas L. Harris (1816–58) of Petersburg (not Jacksonville), who had served as a major in the Mexican War, won election to Congress in 1854, 1856, and 1858 as well as 1848.

47. Abraham Lincoln to William Schouler, Washington, 28 Aug. 1848, in *Collected Works*, ed. Basler et al., 1:518–19.

48. *Illinois State Register*, 11 Aug. 1848.

49. Speech of 27 July 1848, in *Collected Works*, ed. Basler et al., 1:501–16.

50. William Schouler (1814–72), a leading Massachusetts Whig, edited the *Boston Atlas*. Thaddeus Stevens (1792–1868) of Lancaster, Pennsylvania, represented his district in the U.S. House (1849–53, 1859–68).

51. William Henry Seward (1801–72) served as governor of New York (1838–42), U.S. senator (1849–61), and U.S. secretary of state (1861–69).

52. Speech of 6 Oct. 1848, in *Collected Works*, ed. Basler et al., 2:11.

53. Basler et al., eds., *Collected Works*, 2:11–13.

54. Autobiography written for John L. Scripps, [June 1860], in *Collected Works*, Basler et al., eds., 4:67.

55. The other case, *Forsyth v. Reynolds*, was a chancery case involving title to certain real estate in Peoria. It was appealed from the U.S. Circuit Court for the District of Illinois, docketed on 9 December 1852, tried on 31 January and 1 February 1854, and decided on 13 February 1854.

56. Abraham Lincoln to William M. Meredith, Washington, 9 March 1849, in *Collected Works*, ed. Basler et al., 2:32.

57. Attorney James Lowrey Donaldson Morrison (1816–88) of Belleville, Illinois, was a Whig leader who became a Democrat after the Whig party collapsed. Abraham Lincoln to Cyrus Edwards, Alton, 27 March 1849 in *Collected Works*, ed. Basler et al., 2:41.

58. Abraham Lincoln to William B. Warren and others, Springfield, 7 April 1849, in *Collected Works*, ed. Basler et al., 2:41.

59. The correspondence between Edwards and Lincoln is not extant but is summarized in Cyrus Edwards to Justin Butterfield, Woodlawn, Ill., 11 June 1849, Records of the Department of the Interior, Appointments Division, Central Office Appointment Papers, 1849–1907, box 32, Record Group 48, National Archives.

60. Ibid.

61. Ibid.

62. Lincoln to Edwards, 30 April 1849, summarized in Records of the Department of the Interior, Appointments Division, Central Office Appointment Papers, 1849–1907, box 32, Record Group 48, National Archives (summarized).

63. New Hampshire-born Justin Butterfield (1790–1855) was a Chicago attorney known as "a man of rare wit and humor." From 1841 to 1844 he served as the U.S. district attorney in Chicago. In 1849 he initially lobbied the Taylor administration for the post of treasury department solicitor.

64. Josiah M. Lucas had edited the *Jacksonville Illinoian*.

65. Abraham Lincoln to Josiah M. Lucas, Springfield, 25 April 1849, in *Collected Works*, ed. Basler et al., 2:43–44.

66. Abraham Lincoln to Thomas Ewing, Caleb B. Smith, John M. Clayton, William B. Preston, Elisha Embree, Richard W. Thompson, Robert C. Schenck, and Willie P. Magnum, in *Collected Works*, ed. Basler et al., 2:44–53.

67. Abraham Lincoln to Duff Green, Washington, 18 May 1849, in *Collected Works*, ed. Basler et al., 2:49–50.

68. Cyrus Edwards to Justin Butterfield, Woodlawn, Ill., 11 June 1849, Records of the Department of the Interior, Appointments Division, Central Office Appointment Papers, 1849–1907, box 32, Record Group 48, National Archives.

69. Cyrus Edwards to Justin Butterfield, Woodlawn, Ill., 11 June 1849, Records of the Department of the Interior, Appointments Division, Central Office Appointment Papers, 1849–1907, box 32, Record Group 48, National Archives.

70. Thomas Ewing (1789–1871) of Ohio served as secretary of the interior (1849–50).

71. William Preston (1805–62) of Virginia served as secretary of the navy (1849–50). He had served with Lincoln in Congress (1847–49).

72. Abraham Lincoln to Thomas Ewig (3 June), Josiah Butterick (3 June), Robert C. Schenck (3 June), Willie P. Magnum (4 June), and Nathaniel Pope (8 June), all in *Collected Works*, ed. Basler et al., 2:52–54.

73. One petition was undated, the other dated 6 June 1849, Records of the Department of the Interior, Appointments Division, Central Office Appointment Papers, 1849–1907, box 32, Record Group 48, National Archives.

74. As a delegate in Congress, Nathaniel Pope (1784–1850) had been instrumental in securing statehood for Illinois in 1818, when he became judge of the district court. Benjamin Bond (1807–66), the son of the first governor of Illinois, Shadrach Bond, served in the Illinois State Senate in the 1830s and was a delegate to the 1847 Constitutional Convention. He became a Democrat in the 1850s and was arrested in 1862 for opposition to the Civil War.

75. Ninian W. Edwards (1809–89) of Springfield, husband of Lincoln's sister-in-law Elizabeth Todd, was a leading Whig politician who turned Democrat in 1850.

76. Justin Butterfield to J. J. Brown, Springfield, 7 June 1849, Records of the Department of the Interior, Appointments Division, Central Office Appointment Papers, 1849–1907, box 32, Record Group 48, National Archives.

77. In 1837 New-Jersey-born George W. Meeker (1817–56) settled in Chicago, where he was admitted to the bar two years later. He formed a partnership with George Manierre and served as clerk of the U.S. court and as court commissioner.

78. Abraham Lincoln to John Addison, Washington, 9 Aug. 1850, in *Collected Works*, ed. Basler et al., 2:91–92. Addison was a clerk in the Interior Department.

79. Abraham Lincoln to Joseph Gillespie, Springfield, 13 July 1849, in *Collected Works*, ed. Basler et al., 2:57–59.

80. Justin Butterfield to David Hunter, Chicago, 4 June 1849, Records of the Department of the Interior, Appointments Division, Central Office Appointment Papers, 1849–1907, box 32, Record Group 48, National Archives.

81. John Todd Stuart recalled that he and Lincoln "were at Bloomington attending Court together, when a special messenger came up there who had been sent from here with the information that this appointment had been tendered him. On our way down from Bloomington he talked the matter over with me, and asked my opinion about it. I told him I thought it was a good thing: that he could go out there and in all likelihood come back from there as a Senator when the State was admitted. Mr. Lincoln finally made up his mind that he would accept the place if Mary would consent to go. But Mary would not consent to go out there. [Joshua] Speed told me that Lincoln wrote to him that if he would go along, he would give him any appointment out there which he might be able to control. Lincoln evidently thought that if Speed and Speed's wife were to go along, it would be an inducement for Mary to change her mind and consent to go. But Speed thought he could not go, and so the matter didn't come to anything." Michael Burlingame,

ed., *An Oral History of Abraham Lincoln: John G. Nicolay's Interviews and Essays* (Carbondale: Southern Illinois University Press, 1998), 15.

82. Eulogy on Taylor, 25 July 1850, in *Collected Works*, ed. Basler et al., 2:89.

83. Speech to the Springfield Scott Club, 14, 26 Aug. 1850, in *Collected Works*, ed. Basler et al., 2:135–57.

84. Autobiography written for John L. Scripps, [June 1860], in *Collected Works*, ed. Basler et al., 4:67.

85. Ward Hill Lamon (1828–93) was a close friend of Lincoln, who in 1861 named him marshal of the District of Columbia.

86. Robert Rantoul, Jr. (1805–52) was a leading antislavery Democrat as well as a champion of railroad construction.

87. Samuel Hubbel Treat (1811–87) served on the state supreme court from 1841 until 1855, when he became judge of the U.S. district court. John Dean Caton (1812–95) sat on the state supreme court (1842–64). Lyman Trumbull (1813–96) served several years on the supreme court (1841–43, 1848–53) before becoming U.S. senator (1855–73)

88. Thomas Drummond (1809–90) served as a district judge from 1850 to 1869, when he became a U.S. circuit court judge.

89. Orville H. Browning, *The Diary of Orville Hickman Browning*, 2 vols., ed. Theodore Calvin Pease and James G. Randall (Springfield: Illinois State Historical Library, 1925, 1933), 1:109 (entries for 7 and 8 July 1853).

90. Springfield correspondence, *Democratic Press*, n.d., copied in the *Illinois State Register*, 12 May 1854.

91. Nicholas H. Ridgely (1800–88) had an autocratic manner that earned him the sobriquet "Czar Nicholas." His Springfield home was "the center of musical culture in town" and "the centre of Springfield social life for the younger set—a center where music and jollity reigned, tempered by the Czar's rather rigorous ruling, where there were earnest if rather youthful efforts at improving the mind, and where foreign languages were the fashion."

92. Simeon Francis (1796–1872) founded the *Journal* in 1831 and served as its editor until 1856, when he sold it. Charles H. Lanphier (1820–1903) was publisher of the *Illinois State Register* from 1846 to 1863, and George Walker edited that publication (1847–58).

93. John Cook (1825–1910), son of Illinois Daniel P. Cook, a member of Congress from Illinois, served as colonel of the Seventh Illinois Volunteers in the Civil War. Robert S. Blackwell (1823–63), a law student of Browning's and an authority on tax titles, died prematurely of alcoholism.

94. Pease and Randall, eds., *The Diary of Orville Hickman Browning*, 1:31, 1:32, 1:34, 1:35, 1:36, 1:92, 1:93 (entries for 16 and 25 Dec. 1851, 10, 15, 20 Jan. 1852, and 28 and 31 Jan. 1853). Nehemiah Bushnell (1813–73), Browning's law partner until he died, served as president of the Northern Cross Railroad. Charles B. Lawrence (1820–83) of Quincy served on the Illinois State Supreme Court (1864–73). The Rev. Richard V. Dodge married Nicholas Ridgely's daughter Sarah.

95. Ibid., 1:32 (entry for 25 Dec. 1851) and 1:122 (entry for 30–31 Jan. 1854).

96. Abraham Lincoln to John A. Rockwell, Springfield, 15 Feb. 1853, in *Collected Works*, ed. Basler et al., 2:190–91.

97. Anthony Thornton (1814–1904) of Shelbyville served as a judge on the Illinois supreme court (1870–73) and as a member of Congress from 1865 to 1867.

98. Abraham Lincoln to William Martin, Springfield, 19 Feb. 1851, in *Collected Works*, ed. Basler et al., 2:98.

99. James F. Joy became general counsel for the Illinois Central in 1854. The Connecticut-born attorney William P. Burrall (b. 1807) was president of the Illinois Central (1853–54).

100. James F. Joy to William P. Burrall, 16 Jan. 1854 and 2 Feb. 1854, in Harry E. Pratt, *The Personal Finances of Abraham Lincoln* (Springfield: Abraham Lincoln Association, 1943), 48–49.

101. John Brough (1811–65), who actively promoted railroads between 1848 and 1863, was governor of Ohio (1863–65).

102. Benjamin Stevenson Edwards (1818–86) was a leading Whig and the law partner of John Todd Stuart (1843–85).

103. Abraham Lincoln to James Steele and Charles Summers, Springfield, 12 Feb. 1857, in *Collected Works*, ed. Basler et al., 2:389.

104. Robert S. Rantoul, "Reminiscences of Abraham Lincoln," *Proceedings of the Massachusetts Historical Society* (1908): 84.

105. Autobiography written for John Locke Scripps, [June 1860], in *Collected Works*, ed. Basler et al., 4:67.

106. Cf. Albert J. Beveridge, *Abraham Lincoln, 1809–1858*, 2 vols. (Boston: Houghton, Mifflin, 1928), 1:493, 2:244, and Michael Burlingame, *The Inner World of Abraham Lincoln* (Urbana: University of Illinois Press, 1994), 1–19.

10 Abe Lincoln, Country Lawyer

The Illinois prairies were thrusting forth new life in early April 1854 as Abraham Lincoln hitched "Old Buck" to his buggy and prepared to set forth on his customary round of the Eighth Judicial Circuit. Bidding good-bye to his wife and their three boys—Robert, aged ten; Willie, three; and "Tad," the baby, born just a year before—Lincoln tossed a threadbare carpetbag containing shirts, underwear, a homemade yellow flannel nightgown, and other necessities into the buggy, swung his long body after it, "cluck-clucked" to his horse, and turned northward through Springfield's more prosperous residential section toward the open country. Ahead of him lay a journey of some four hundred miles that would keep him away from home almost ten weeks, with stops for court sessions at seven county towns.

Lincoln loved the life of the circuit—the excitement of court week in the small country towns, the camaraderie of judge and lawyers, the speechmaking and sociability in the evenings, and the esteem in which the simple country people held the members of the bar. He had not expected to follow the circuit this long, however, and if his thoughts turned inward on this first leg of his journey, he could look back on a quick rise in life followed by a disillusionment that held him to circuit practice. For Lincoln, pulling himself loose from the poverty and aimlessness that marked his background, had learned to use his brain instead of brawn as a means of livelihood; then, employing the law as a springboard, he had rapidly advanced in politics. After serving four terms in the state legis-

The Atlantic Monthly, Feb. 1954, 57–61.

lature, he had aspired to go to Congress. Whig party rivalries stood in his way at first; but after he had waited for two other zealous young Whigs to satisfy a similar ambition, his turn had come at last. In December 1847, he had stepped forth on the national stage.

Thus, in Lincoln's early manhood, while the law provided bread and butter, politics became his life. For fifteen years he had spent hour after hour attending caucuses, conventions, and legislative sessions, writing party circulars and delivering party speeches, formulating party policy and directing party strategy. Then, during his term in Congress, had come discomfiture: he lost step with the people of his district by opposing the Mexican War.[1]

When war with Mexico began, during Lincoln's campaign for Congress, a fervid martial spirit swept the prairies; and if he harbored any feelings that his country might be wrong, he had kept them to himself. By the time he reached Washington, the fighting had stopped. But peace terms were yet to be agreed on, and he found that his fellow Whigs in Congress, looking to the election of 1848, were intent upon making political capital by accusing President Polk of bringing on an unjust war against a feeble neighbor.

Lincoln fell in with this policy and joined the clamor against Polk. Soon after the opening of the congressional session he introduced a series of resolutions designed to convict Polk of falsehood in his claim that Mexico had started hostilities by "invading our territory and shedding American blood on American soil." This was not so, Lincoln asserted; Mexico, not the United States, exercised jurisdiction over the "spot" where the first blood had been shed.[2] Three weeks later Lincoln took the floor to amplify his charges and challenge Polk to answer them.[3] Throughout the session he voted consistently with the Whig minority on all matters designed to put the President in the wrong. And when the Democrats introduced a resolution of thanks to General Zachary Taylor for his victory at Buena Vista, Lincoln joined with other Whigs in amending it to read, "in a war unconstitutionally and [unnecessarily] begun by the President."[4]

The letters in which Lincoln tried to justify his actions to his law partner, William H. Herndon, are forthright with conviction, notwithstanding Lincoln's silence on the subject before he left for Washington.[5] But Lincoln the young Whig politician had been reared to party discipline, and, thrown among the national stalwarts of his party as a freshman Congressman, he may have been convinced with undue ease.

In any event the outcome proved ruinous for Lincoln. Back home, where people's patriotism and land-hunger overrode any moral qualms they may have felt about the war, he was blasted throughout his district as a disgrace to his state. Democratic newspapers dubbed him "Spotty" Lincoln, and one even labeled him "a modern Benedict Arnold."

Heretofore Lincoln's district had been accounted such a Whig strong-hold that the Whig nomination was tantamount to election. By reason of an understanding among certain Whig leaders of the district that they would take a "turn about" in Congress, he did not stand for re-election. But his course had so discredited the party that Stephen T. Logan, the Whig candidate to succeed him, lost to Thomas L. Harris, Democrat.

The powerful Whig organization managed to keep the vote extremely close—7,201 for Harris to 7,095 for Logan—and Lincoln tried to explain the defeat on the ground of Logan's unpopularity and Harris's excellent war record.[6] But the *Illinois State Register* came nearer to the truth when it complained: "This will not do, gentlemen, you must put the saddle on the right horse. . . . Besides his own dead weight, Logan had to carry the votes of the Whig party, including Lincoln, that the war was unconstitu-tional and unnecessary."[7]

This congressional election took place in August 1848 and by the time of the Presidential election in November, the Whigs, with General Zachary Taylor, a military hero, as their candidate, succeeded in bring-ing the district right-side-up again. Lincoln, intent on proving that his course had caused no change of sentiment in the district, worked harder in this contest than he had ever worked before, and claimed the chief credit for the victory. He had also labored zealously for Taylor's nomina-tion, even at the cost of abandoning his political idol, Henry Clay. So now, with the Whigs in control of the Federal government, Lincoln, jobless and reluctant to return to the less eventful life of Springfield, sought the pol-itician's reward.

He asked for the commissionership of the General Land Office in Washington, but it went to a Chicagoan, an indication of the increasing political importance of the booming city on the lake; and the most that the administration would offer him was the governorship or secretary-ship of the far-off Oregon Territory. Lincoln had also thought that he and Edward D. Baker, who would be the sole Illinois Whig in the next Con-gress, should control the Federal patronage in Illinois. But their recom-mendations for office were consistently ignored. It was as though the door to a political future had been slammed shut in Lincoln's face. By the sum-mer of 1849 he had no choice but to return to Springfield and settle once again into the routine of a country lawyer.

So every spring and fall for the past four years, he had started out on the circuit, as he was doing now, leaving home and family for nine or ten weeks at a time, driving over muddy or dusty roads, now under a hot sun and again through pelting showers or all-day rain, putting up with the scanty comforts and monotonous fare of cheap hotels and boardinghouses where the lawyers slept two in a bed and six or eight in a room, and spending long hours in court for the ten, twenty, or fifty dollar fees, occasionally supplemented by larger ones, which, along with the more substantial fees he earned in the State Supreme Court and the federal Courts in Springfield and the interest he received from a few notes and mortgages, added up to an annual income of some $2,500.

Many lawyers settled down into contented mediocrity in such a way of life, but Lincoln, with the avenue of political advancement seemingly closed to him, resolved to make himself a better lawyer and a more enlightened man. So, as "Old Buck" plodded on from one town to another along the familiar prairie roads, Lincoln often lolled back in his buggy, his long legs over the dashboard, with an open book in hand: Robert Burns or Shakespeare, those favorites of his young manhood, or perhaps some scientific textbook. Having learned the value of mathematics as a mental discipline, he mastered the first six books of Euclid; and he also studied astronomy.

Thus Lincoln's ambition, which Herndon, without fully comprehending, compared to a little engine that knew no rest, and which Lincoln, in his first campaign for public office, described as a desire "of being truly esteemed of my fellow men by rendering myself worthy of their esteem," carried over into these years of political retirement and induced him to continue that process of self-teaching which had distinguished his earlier years.[8]

Though Lincoln appreciated the knowledge to be gained from books, observation and experience remained his chief instructors, as they had always been. A fellow lawyer remembered how, when Lincoln encountered a new piece of farm machinery on his circuit travels, he would examine it in all its parts, first closely, then at a distance, and finally, coming back to it, he would shake it, lift it, push it, "sight" it to see whether it was straight or warped, and stoop, or even lie down if necessary, to look under it in order to ascertain its every quality and utility. In the lawyers' evening discussions, which "ranged though the universe of thought and experience," he learned to apply the same careful process to propositions and ideas.[9]

A man of deep emotions, Lincoln craved the power to put his feelings into words. Of a commonplace poem ["Mortality" by William Knox] he had once declared: "I would give all I am worth and go in debt, to be able to write so fine a piece as I think that is"; and, unsatisfied with the clarity and fluency that are the lawyer's tools, he had attempted to write poems of his own.[10] A view of Niagara Falls impressed him with the power of that natural wonder "to excite reflection and emotion," and he prepared a lecture on it.[11] But he never delivered it and a sense of inadequacy induced him to reply with feigned flippancy to Herndon's query about his reaction to the falls: "the thing that struck me most forcibly . . . was, where in the world did all that water come from?"[12]

Some notes for a law lecture, which Lincoln drew up at this season of his life but never used, reveal not only his attitude toward his profession but also something of the man himself. "I am not an accomplished lawyer," he wrote. "I find quite as much material for a lecture in those points wherein I have failed, as in those wherein I have been moderately successful. The leading rule for the lawyer, as for the man in every other calling, is diligence. Leaving nothing for tomorrow which can be done today. Never let your correspondence fall behind. Whatever piece of business you have in hand, before stopping, do all the labor pertaining to it which can then be done. . . . Extemporaneous speaking should be practiced and cultivated. It is the lawyer's avenue to the public. . . . And yet there is not a more fatal error to young lawyers than relying too much on speech-making. If anyone, upon his rare powers of speaking, shall claim an exemption from the drudgery of the law, his case is a failure in advance. . . .

"There is a vague popular belief that lawyers are necessarily dishonest. I say vague, because when we consider to what extent confidence and honors are reposed in and conferred upon lawyers by the people, it appears improbable that their impression of dishonesty is very distinct and vivid. Yet the impression is common, almost universal. Let no young man choosing the law for a calling for a moment yield to the popular belief— resolve to be honest at all events; and if in your own judgment you cannot be an honest lawyer, resolve to be honest without being a lawyer. Choose some other occupation, rather than one in the choosing of which you do, in advance, consent to be a knave."[13]

Honesty became Lincoln's best-known attribute around the circuit, and next to that his gift of storytelling. "Lord, wasn't he funny," one friend later wrote; while another, with the freewheeling exaggeration of the frontiersman, recalled: "In the role of story teller I never knew his equal. His power of mimicry was very great. He could perfectly mimic a Dutchman, Irishman or Negro. . . . I have heard men say that they had laughed at his stories until they had almost shaken their ribs loose. I heard cases where men had been suffering for years from some bodily ailment and could get no relief but who have gone a couple of evenings and listened to Lincoln and laughed their ailments away, and become hale and hearty men, giving Lincoln credit of being their healer."[14]

Though Lincoln's humor scarcely qualified as such a nostrum, often it did serve a useful purpose. Abstruse points became clear to the slowest minds on a jury when Lincoln explained them with a story; and his quick perception of the ludicrous and the ridiculous enabled him to unmask pretense and vanity and hold things in true perspective.

Notwithstanding Lincoln's geniality he was a lonely man; for there was a remoteness and innate dignity about him that kept acquaintances at arm's length. Most people addressed him as "Mr. Lincoln" or "Lincoln." Not even stout, jovial Judge David Davis or any of his other intimates felt sufficiently free and easy with him to call him "Abe."

He neither smoked nor drank and seldom swore; yet he never moralized about those who did, and he had jokingly applied to himself the saying that a man with no vices is likely also to lack virtues.

Something of Lincoln's life struggle might be discerned in his face. The early death of his mother in the Indiana wilderness, a rude upbringing verging on the uncouth, the batterings of rough and tumble frontier politics, a mental breakdown resulting from uncertainty about love, the hurt of a not altogether happy marriage, the loss of an infant son, all these had added their tracings to the toil marks that seamed his features. Yet his face was kindly for all that; for the buffeting of life had sensitized instead of hardening him, and patience, tolerance, forbearance, and forgiveness were becoming the very texture of his heart.

Also a part of Lincoln's very being was a faith in the worth and fundamental goodness of plain people, like those whom he grew up with, those at the little village of New Salem who helped him get a start in life, and those he knew now on the circuit. Still vivid in his memory was a time when, as a boy in backwoods Indiana, he had lain at full length on the cabin floor before the open fire, reading Parson Weems's life of George Washington. But what moved him, even more than the deeds and character of Washington, was the heroism of the Revolutionary soldiers, and he could remember thinking, "boy even though I was, that there must have been something more than common that those men struggled for."[15]

And as he overcame the obstacles of poverty and grew in mind and character, the story of America took on rich meaning for him. In no other country of the world, he thought, were ordinary people so much the masters of their destiny. Nowhere else were they offered such a chance to rise through their own efforts. As he carved out his own career in law and politics, all about him, at home and on the circuit, he saw men who, starting life as laborers, mechanics, millhands, and flatboatmen, or in other lowly walks of like, had become lawyers, merchants, doctors, farmers, editors, successful politicians. And he saw these people come together in equality and mutual respect, not only in the state legislature and in Congress, but also at the grass-roots level, in private homes and crossroads meetinghouses, to make their own decisions and work out their own problems under a political system "conducing more essentially to civil and religious liberty," he thought, "than any of which the history of former times tells us."[16]

So, as the years passed, he had arrived at the conviction that the Founding Fathers of the new republic had embodied its true meaning in the document that gave it birth, and that in the assertion of the Declaration of Independence that all men are created equal and are alike entitled to life, liberty, and the pursuit of happiness was a promise "not only to the people of this country, but hope for the world to all future time."[17]

Religion and the Bible had been important in Lincoln's upbringing; but he had known skepticism too. During his campaign for Congress, when pressed to define his faith, he had declared: "That I am not a member of any Christian church is true; but I have never denied the truth of the Scriptures."[18] This is not the same as saying that he accepted the Scriptures fully; and, having trained his mind to demand proof, he had not yet gained that broader understanding of how the incomprehensible may still be true. Yet his very goodness bespoke a latent spirituality, which, if awakened and motivated, might widen his horizon and make his life more purposeful.

Few people realized the mental and moral growth that was taking place in Lincoln, however, or the broader outlook he was gaining since drawing off from party politics. Outwardly he remained unchanged, and those who failed to penetrate his surface qualities saw only the old melancholy that could change so quickly to boisterous laughter, the rustic mannerisms that had clung to him since boyhood, and the shambling gait of the man whose feet have been accustomed to plowed ground. The tall hat with the well-rubbed nap, the long coat bulging at the elbows, the ill-fitting trousers, and unblacked boots might have passed for the same toggery he first wore around the circuit.

Though Lincoln's complex and sometimes contradictory personality made him difficult to understand, his warm human qualities drew people to him, and he could count a host of friends. In fact, his first stop on this trip around the circuit would be at Lincoln—the newly founded county seat of Logan County, a town named in his honor.

These friends could muster an impressive tally if he cared to have another try at politics; and his experience, his enlarged humanitarianism, and his maturing wisdom all qualified him for a larger field of usefulness in public service. But his once compelling political ambition seemed to have simmered down. Two years before, when friends tried to induce him to run again for the state legislature, he had declared that his profession demanded all his time. A move to make him governor died from his own lack of interest. During the Presidential campaign of 1852, when the Whigs again nominated a military hero, General Winfield Scott, he had served as a national committeeman and delivered a few speeches. But they flashed little of the old fire. Looking back later on this period of his life, he stated that "by 1854 his profession had almost superseded the thought of politics in his mind."[19]

He might have lost interest entirely except for what was taking place in Washington. But the news from the nation's capital carried portentous overtones as Stephen A. Douglas, Lincoln's rival of bygone political contests, now a United States Senator and chairman of the powerful committee on territories, fostered a policy, which, as Lincoln saw it, threatened the very ideals the nation stood for.

Early in January, Douglas had reported out of his committee a bill to organize the territory of Nebraska with the stipulation that the people living there might admit or exclude slavery as they chose, a provision contrary to that clause of the Missouri Compromise which prohibited slavery in all the area of the Louisiana Purchase north of Missouri and the western extension of its southern boundary. Political maneuvering sent the bill back to committee; but Douglas speedily reported it out again, this time in a form which divided the affected area into two territories, Kansas and Nebraska, and expressly repealed the slavery interdiction of the Missouri Compromise. The storm of protest that broke in Congress spread rapidly through the North. Douglas was able to make his principle of "popular sovereignty" the new Democratic faith, however, and on March 3, after weeks of heated argument, he had jammed the measure through the Senate.

With that the battle shifted to the House of Representatives, and now, as Lincoln made his way from one county town to another, he conned the newspapers with more than his usual thoroughness. By the time he reached the town of Lincoln he could read of protest meetings all over northern Illinois. At Bloomington he learned that Richard Yates, Whig Congressman from his district, had spoken out against "the opening of this dangerous agitation, fraught with such imminent peril to the existence of the Union itself."[20] His hometown Whig paper, the *Illinois State Journal*, which came to Bloomington by train, was condemning "the violation of the plighted faith and compacts of the nation."

Newspapers available to Lincoln at Metamora predicted that Douglas's policy would "lead to interminable broils." At Pekin, papers from nearby Peoria told of Illinois Congressmen Jesse Norton and Elihu Washburne joining Yates in denouncing "this great wrong," of Chicago and New England clergymen petitioning Congress to defeat the measure, and of veteran Senator Thomas Hart Benton of Missouri lashing out at popular sovereignty as "a bone given to the people to quarrel and fight over at every election and at every meeting of the legislature until they become a state government."[21] The Missouri Compromise was intended to be perpetual, Benton had declared; it was as sacred and inviolable as a human instrument can be. He recalled Douglas's own assertion of less than four years before that the Missouri Compromise had "become canonized in the hearts of the American people as a sacred thing, which no ruthless hand would ever be reckless enough to disturb."[22]

By the time Lincoln reached Clinton, the administration organs, rallying behind Douglas's bill, were pursuing Benton in full cry. Fist swinging had been narrowly averted in the House of Representatives. Papers throughout central Illinois were condemning Douglas as a more dangerous fomenter of national strife and hatred than the detested Abolitionists.

As sectional feeling mounted to this frenzied pitch, Lincoln's fellow lawyers noticed that he kept more and more to himself. Often he was still awake when all the others went to bed. Rising early in the morning, they sometimes found him sitting hunched in thought, staring at the dead embers in the bedroom fireplace.

For as long as Lincoln could remember he had reasoned, "if slavery is not wrong, nothing is wrong."[23] Yet, recognizing the virulence of slavery as a political issue, he had been loath to touch it, believing, as he had declared in the state legislature, that the promulgation of Abolition doctrine tended to increase rather than abate the evil of it.[24] In this issue, as in so many others, he had looked for wisdom to the Founding Fathers, and if he correctly understood their attitude toward slavery, they had sought to restrict it to the area where it had become engrafted, in the belief that, if so restricted, it would die for lack of growth. So their policy became Lincoln's policy, too, even though toleration of human bondage did violence to that concept of America as the land of freedom and equality that he had cherished since boyhood. But Douglas would risk opening new areas where slavery might feed anew and thus prolong its life. To Lincoln's mind this constituted a rejection of the policy of ridding the nation of a hypocrisy at the earliest practicable time.

It is not our concern here that Douglas looked at the matter from a drastically different point of view, and regarded his policy as an application of the principle of self-government which, by reason of climatic and economic factors, would restrict slavery no less effectively than would a geographical line. The important fact for us, and for history, is the energizing impact on Lincoln of what seemed to him a repudiation of a national ideal. As he drove into Urbana, far over toward the eastern border of Illinois, he felt oppressed and troubled; for the struggle in the House of Representatives had reached the crisis stage.

That week the *Urbana Union* announced that the volume of business discharged by the Champaign Circuit Court exceeded that of any other term of recent date. Records are lacking to determine Lincoln's share of it, but May 23, the second day of the court term, became a fateful day for him. For sometime during that day, at just what time we do not know, the telegraph chattered out the news he had hoped would never come: the House had passed the Kansas-Nebraska Bill by a majority of thirteen votes. Where and when Lincoln received the news we likewise have no means of knowing; but we have his own assertion that "it aroused him as he had never been before."[25]

Three months later he was back in politics, and his real career had begun. Unknowingly, he had set his feet in the path to the presidency. For Lincoln will emerge now as a man of vision; and when he speaks again it will be with a new authority and a new eloquence born of moral earnestness. That little engine of ambition will throb more urgently than ever, but hereafter its energy will be directed to the advancement of a cause. And Lincoln's desire "of being truly esteemed of my fellow men" will find fulfillment in the revitalization of the ideals of human freedom and equality in the hearts of his countrymen.[26]

No less compelling than the sunburst which appeared to Saul of Tarsus on the Damascus road was the seeming renunciation of the national aspiration to genuine democracy in bringing Abraham Lincoln back into political life, and in transforming an honest, capable, but essentially self-centered small-town politician of self-developed but largely unsuspected talents into democracy's foremost spokesman.

In Lincoln's first major speech after re-entering politics, he pleaded: "Let us re-adopt the Declaration of Independence, and with it the practices, and policy, which harmonize with it. . . . If we do this, we shall not only have saved the Union; but we shall have so saved it as to make it, and to keep it, forever worthy of the saving. We shall have so saved it, that the succeeding millions of free happy people, the world over, shall rise up, and call us blessed, to the latest generations."[27]

This was the theme that Lincoln stressed in his great debates with

Douglas [in 1858], and in his speech at Cooper Union [in 1860]. And when war came, and he found himself in the very vortex of it, he explained in his first message to Congress: "This is essentially a people's contest. On the side of the Union it is a struggle for maintaining in the world that form and substance of government whose leading object is to elevate the condition of men—to lift artificial weights from all shoulders; to clear the paths of laudable pursuit for all; to afford all an unfettered start, and a fair chance in the race of life."[28]

Throughout the war, in state papers, in conversations, in private letters, [and] in informal talks to soldiers, he restated this idea in variant words. Identifying the fate of the Union with the fate of world democracy, he defined the cause of the nation in terms of human betterment throughout the world.

At last the catalyst of spiritual conviction had set Lincoln's soul on fire. Feeling himself caught up in a tempest of mighty happenings, he wrote, out of deep pondering. "The will of God prevails," and into his writings and utterances there came the spirit of prayer.[29] Touched by the magic stimulant of new-born nobility of purpose, the springs of emotion deep within him welled forth in lyric prose.

In his exercise of power he demonstrated that democratic virtues are Christian virtues too. His human sympathy and self-developed talents all rendered mighty service in the cause he had espoused. Never again did Lincoln lose touch with public opinion. He sought to lead it and restrain it, but he had learned never to defy it. From defeat and disappointment he had gained the inner stamina to discipline his aims to the attainable. Out of his faith in people came patience quietly to put himself in what he held to be the right position, and wait, confident that they would one day find him there.

When Lincoln was asked to make "a few appropriate remarks" at the dedication of the soldiers' cemetery on the battlefield at Gettysburg, it was inevitable that his thought should go back to the Founding Fathers, then forward, into the far reach of time, and that he should plead for increased devotion to the ideals the nation's sons were dying for, so that government of the people, by the people, for the people might not perish from the earth.

Yet, notwithstanding Lincoln's reiteration of this tenet and his power to express it in imperishable words, his democratic vision was so vast that few people of his day could fully comprehend it. And even today the supreme meaning of his life has not come clear by any means to all of his countrymen. Lincoln called Americans "God's almost chosen people," because he believed they have a mission in the world; the responsibility of demonstrating, by example, that human freedom and equality, far from being empty concepts, are "the last, best hope of earth."[30]

A nearer realization of the American dream became the aim of Lincoln's life. Yet he was no mere dreamer. He realized that the struggle for human freedom is eternal; he had no illusions of its ending in his lifetime or in ours. He understood that the antagonisms between man's better nature and his selfishness endure, and that it would be the fate of every generation of Americans to defend democracy from its besetting enemies of greed, intolerance, and despotism.

Walt Whitman, recognizing the seeming futility of this struggle, asked himself a question which Lincoln, too, must have asked: "Often comes the query, as one sees the shallowness and miserable selfishness of these crowds of men, with all their minds so blank of high humanity and aspiration—then comes the terrible query, and will not be denied, Is Democracy of human rights humbug after all—Are these flippant people with hearts of rags and souls of chalk, are these worthy of preaching for and dying for upon the cross? Maybe not—maybe it is indeed a dream."

But Whitman answered: "To him who, believing preaches, and to the people who work it out—this is not a dream—to work for Democracy is good, the exercise is good—strength it makes and lessons it teaches." And Lincoln answered similarly, when he said of the Founding Fathers: "They meant to set up a standard maxim for free society, which should be familiar to all and revered by all: constantly looked to, constantly labored for, and even though never perfectly attained, constantly approximated, and thereby constantly spreading and deepening its influence and augmenting the happiness and value of life to all people of all colors everywhere."[31]

So, because human freedom and equality are such lofty concepts that democracy is destined, by its very nature, always to be elusive and always to be endangered, we are still engaged in the same struggle in which Lincoln made himself a leader. That is why his life still holds so many lessons for us. That is why his words are living words.

Notes

1. Gabor Boritt has challenged this interpretation of Lincoln's alleged unpopularity. See G. S. Boritt, "A Question of Political Suicide: Lincoln's Opposition to the Mexican War," *Journal of the Illinois State Historical Society* 68 (1974): 79–100. Lincoln claimed that he retired from the House after one term because he and other Whig leaders had agreed to rotate the candidacy for the post among themselves. In a third-person autobiography he wrote: "Mr. L. was not a candi-

date for re-election. This was determined upon, and declared before he went to Washington, in accordance with an understanding among whig friends, by which Col. [John J.] Hardin, and Col. [Edward D.] Baker had each previously served a single term in the same District." Autobiography written for John Locke Scripps, [ca. June 1860], in *The Collected Works of Abraham Lincoln,* ed. Roy P. Basler, Marion Dolores Pratt and Lloyd A. Dunlap, asst. eds., 8 vols. plus index (New Brunswick: Rutgers University Press, 1953–55), 4:66–67.

2. Resolutions, 22 Dec. 1847, in *Collected Works,* ed. Basler et al., 1:420–22.

3. Speech of 12 Jan. 1848, in *Collected Works,* ed. Basler et al., 1:431–42.

4. *Congressional Globe,* 30th Cong., 1st sess., 3 Jan. 1848. The amendment carried by a vote of 85–81.

5. Abraham Lincoln to William H. Herndon, Washington, 1 and 15 Feb. 1848, in *Collected Works,* ed. Basler et al., 1:446–48, 451–52.

6. Abraham Lincoln to William Schouler, Washington, 28 Aug. 1848, in *Collected Works,* ed. Basler et al., 1:518–19

7. *Illinois State Register* (Springfield), 11 Aug. 1848.

8. Paul M. Angle, ed., *Herndon's Life of Lincoln: The History and Personal Recollections of Abraham Lincoln as Originally Written by William H. Herndon and Jesse W. Weik* (Cleveland: World, 1942), 304; Communication to the people of Sangamon County, 9 March 1832, published in the *Sangamo Journal* (Springfield) on 15 March, in *Collected Works,* ed. Basler et al., 1:5.

9. Henry C. Whitney, *Life on the Circuit with Lincoln,* ed. Paul M. Angle (Caldwell, Idaho: Caxton, 1940), 121, 66.

10. Abraham Lincoln to Andrew Johnston, Tremont, 18 April 1846, in *Collected Works,* ed. Basler et al., 1:378.

11. "Fragment on Niagara Falls," [ca. 25–30 Sept. 1848], in *Collected Works,* ed. Basler et al., 2:10.

12. Angle, ed., *Herndon's Lincoln,* 238–39.

13. Notes for a Law Lecture, [1 July 1850?], in *Collected Works,* ed. Basler et al., 2:81–82.

14. Usher F. Linder to Joseph Gillespie, 8 Aug. 1867, Gillespie Papers, Chicago Historical Society; cf. Angle, ed., *Herndon's Lincoln,* 251.

15. Speech of 21 Feb. 1861, in *Collected Works,* ed. Basler et al., 4:235–36.

16. Address to the Young Men's Lyceum of Springfield, 27 Jan. 1838, in *Collected Works,* ed. Basler et al., 1:108.

17. Speech in Philadelphia, 22 Feb. 1861, in *Collected Works,* ed. Basler et al., 4:240.

18. Statement to the voters of the Seventh Congressional District, 31 July 1846, in *Collected Works,* ed. Basler et al., 1:382.

19. Autobiography written for John L. Scripps, 4:67.

20. Richard Yates (1815–73) represented Lincoln's district in the U.S. House (1851–55), served as governor of Illinois (1861–65), and was a U.S. senator (1865–71).

21. Jesse Olds Norton (1812–75) of Joliet represented his district in the U.S. House (1853–57, 1863–65). Elihu B. Washburne (1816–87) of Galena represented his district in the U.S. House (1853–69). Thomas Hart Benton (1782–1858) represented Missouri in the U.S. Senate (1821–51).

22. Douglas's remarks, made in 1849, were quoted by Lincoln in his Peoria speech (16 Oct. 1854), in *Collected Works,* ed. Basler et al., 2:251.

23. Abraham Lincoln to A. G. Hodges, Washington, 4 April 1864, in *Collected Works*, ed. Basler et al., 7:281.

24. Protest in the Illinois legislature on slavery, 3 March 1837, in *Collected Works*, ed. Basler et al., 1:75.

25. *Collected Works*, ed. Basler et al., 4:67.

26. Communication to the people of Sangamon County, 1:8.

27. Speech delivered in Peoria, 16 Oct. 1854, in *Collected Works*, ed. Basler et al., 2:276.

28. Message to Congress, 4 July 1861, in *Collected Works*, ed. Basler et al., 4:438.

29. Meditation on the Divine Will, [2 Sept. 1862?], in *Collected Works*, ed. Basler et al., 5:403–4.

30. Address to the New Jersey Senate, 21 Feb. 1861, and Message to Congress, 1 Dec. 1862, both in *Collected Works*, ed. Basler et al., 4:236 and 5:537.

31. Speech at Springfield, 26 June 1857, in *Collected Works*, ed. Basler et al., 2:406.

11   *Lincoln and the Courts, 1854–61*

The years from 1854 to 1861 mark a distinct period in Lincoln's life. At the beginning of the former year the practice of law had almost superseded politics in his mind. But the repeal of the Missouri Compromise re-awakened his interest in politics and drew him back into political life. He was in turn a successful candidate for the State Legislature and twice an unsuccessful aspirant to the United States Senate, and by 1861 was President-elect of the United States. Meanwhile he did not abandon the law, but, as he said, "gave his attention by turns to that and politics."[1]

In the introduction to *Lincoln 1854–1861*, published last year by the Abraham Lincoln Association, Paul M. Angle described Lincoln's political activities during those years and gave some account of his legal work.[2] Here we shall consider that work in more detail, and with particular reference to the conditions under which it was carried on—the organization, procedure and terms of the various courts in which Lincoln practiced, his legal associates, and the changes that took place in legal practice from 1854 to 1861.[3]

During that time the bulk of Lincoln's practice was in the Sangamon Circuit Court and the other courts of the Eighth Judicial Circuit. He also had a substantial practice in the United States District and Circuit Courts and the State Supreme Court.

Abraham Lincoln Association Papers, 1933 (Springfield: Abraham Lincoln Association, 1934), 47–103.

Sangamon County, of which Springfield was the county seat, had been part of the Eighth Circuit since the formation of that circuit in 1839. At one time the circuit had embraced fifteen counties; but as population grew the increasing amount of legal business compelled the Legislature to decrease its size. In 1854 it was composed of Sangamon, Logan, McLean, Woodford, Tazewell, DeWitt, Champaign and Vermilion counties. The most populous county was Sangamon with 25,604 inhabitants in 1855. McLean came next with 19,285, Tazewell next with 17,371, followed by Vermilion with 15,893. DeWitt, Woodford and Logan each contained about 8,000 people. In Champaign County, whose population was 6,565, settlements were still confined almost exclusively to the groves and timber belts. Scarcely any of the streams in that county were bridged, and the roads were little more than traces.

Although the decade of the fifties brought great changes in the social, economic and political life of Illinois, these changes were hardly apparent in the sleepy county towns of the Eighth Circuit in 1854. True, all of them were increasing in size and some now had railroad connections with neighboring towns; but in economic life, social habits and political thought they differed little from what they had been ten or fifteen years before. Houses were usually small and crude, and in some places hogs ran at large in the muddy streets. Next to Springfield, Bloomington, the county seat of McLean County, with a population of 2,200 in 1850, was the largest town in the circuit. Clinton, the county seat of DeWitt County, had 760 inhabitants; Urbana, in Champaign County, had 500. Pekin, county town of Tazewell County, while small, was situated on the Illinois River and served as a distributing center for the interior country as far as Bloomington. Metamora and Danville, county seats of Woodford and Vermilion counties respectively, were straggling villages of no particular importance. Lincoln, newly established county town of Logan County, was only one year old in 1854.

Under an act of February 3, 1853—which continued in force until 1857—the spring term of the Eighth Circuit opened on the third Monday in March in Springfield, where court sat for two weeks. Then the judge and such lawyers as chose to accompany him traveled around through Logan, McLean, Woodford, Tazewell, DeWitt, Champaign and Vermilion counties in the order named. In McLean and Tazewell counties court sat for two weeks; in Logan, Woodford and DeWitt for one week. In Champaign the session lasted only from Monday to Thursday, the Vermilion court meeting on Friday and continuing into the next week. The term ended early in June.

The fall term opened in Lincoln on the first Monday in September.

Then the court sat successively at Bloomington, Metamora, Pekin, Clinton, Urbana and Danville. The fall sessions were the same length as those in the spring, and the court closed its Danville session early in November. Then, after a brief respite, it sat at Springfield on the third Monday in November to conclude the fall term. The Sangamon Court held a third session on the second Monday in June.[4]

Before the coming of the railroads bench and bar traveled from one county seat to another on horseback, or in buggies or carryalls. The *Diary* of Orville H. Browning shows that lawyers practicing in the counties west of the Illinois River often traveled by stage; but in the Eighth Circuit they do not seem to have done so.[5] At least there is no record of Lincoln's having used the stage. The rate of speed depended on the roads. Under favorable conditions an average of four to five and a half miles an hour was good time; when roads were bad a mile an hour was sometimes all that a struggling team could make. Thirty-five miles was a good day's drive. Frequently one must start before dawn, and drive all day and into the night to reach the next court on time. Sometimes in the early spring and late autumn the weather was uncomfortably cold, perhaps with an occasional flurry of snow. Now and then water froze in the pitchers in the chilly tavern bedrooms. Occasionally lawyers arrived in town thoroughly drenched by a shower that had overtaken them on the open prairie. Again it was necessary to drive all day in the rain. Bridges were sometimes submerged by freshets or washed away; in which event streams had to be forded or swum. Runaways and breakdowns were not uncommon.

On some stretches houses were miles apart. [Henry C.] Whitney tells of one occasion when he, Lincoln and Leonard Swett, traveling in a two-seated buggy from Urbana to Danville, were overtaken by darkness on a narrow road through a heavily timbered riverbottom with deep ditches on each side. The driver stopped, and insisted that someone should go ahead to guide him, whereupon Whitney and Lincoln, rolling up their pantaloons, walked ahead, hallooing and singing to show him the way.[6] Often, however, these trips were joyous and exhilarating. One lawyer remembered with pleasure the "good company, the exhilaration of great speed, over an elastic road, much of it a turf of grass, often crushing under our wheels the most beautiful wild flowers, every grove fragrant with blossoms, framed in the richest green, our roads not fenced in by narrow lanes. . . . The lusty farmer digging his fortune out of the rich earth. Everything fresh and new, full of young life and enthusiasm."

Everyone was hospitable along the way. The inmates of lonely farmhouses were glad to provide lunch or lodgings for such distinguished visitors. In the towns, hotel accommodations, although still humble, were much better than in years gone by. During court week it was often impossible to get individual rooms; and sometimes as many as eight lawyers slept in one room together, some of them upon the floor. Lincoln was fortunate in being one of Judge [David] Davis' favorites; for the best room was reserved for the judge and such lawyers as he chose to invite to put up with him. In Danville the ladies' parlor of the McCormack House was converted into a bedroom during court week, and reserved for Davis and his companions. This parlor was situated in an annex to the main building, with a door opening directly on the sidewalk. Meals were usually served at a long table, graced at the head by Davis, flanked on either side by the members of the bar. Below them sat the jurymen, witnesses, prisoners out on bail and parties litigant. The McCormack sent its overflow to the Pennsylvania House. Although more pretentious than the McCormack, with a ballroom and a dinner bell mounted on a pole on the edge of the sidewalk, the Pennsylvania lacked the prestige of the older hostelry. In Urbana, the first courthouse, moved and clapboarded, and added to from time to time, eventually became the best hotel in town.

Although the original log courthouses had given way to better structures, these were still modest and small. Most of them were built of wood and brick, two stories high, with one floor devoted to offices and the other to court and jury rooms. That at Urbana had stone floors and window sills and a bell tower on the center of the roof; while the Lincoln courthouse, built in 1857, was embellished with a ten-foot portico with six stone columns. That at Springfield had a "lofty doric portico, finished in imitation stone." The Danville courthouse dated back to 1833; and that at Bloomington was built in 1836. Most of the courthouses were situated in the center of public squares, some of which were fenced, while others served as pastures for cows.

When bench and bar arrived in town, they were met by the local lawyers who would employ the circuit riders to assist them with their cases. These associations were not usually permanent; a circuit lawyer might be associated with a particular local lawyer in one case and opposed to him in the next. Lincoln's only permanent association was his partnership with Ward Hill Lamon of Danville, which lasted from 1852 until Lamon was elected state's attorney in 1857. Whitney says that the offices of the traveling lawyers were "ambulatory, being located now on the sunny side of the Court House, then under the shade of a friendly tree, and anon, on the edge of a sidewalk."[7]

Relations between bench and bar were free and easy; and arguments were frequently enlivened by good-natured banter and flashing repartee. The judge sat at a raised table, with the clerk at a small table at one side.

At a larger table, perhaps covered with green baize, sat the lawyers, often with their feet on top of it. Tobacco juice stained floors and walls and splashed into cuspidors as court progressed. Often jury and spectators whittled as they listened, and the amount of business transacted could be gauged by the pile of shavings in the court room next morning.

The Supreme Court Library at Springfield was the only public collection of legal books in the circuit. At Clinton, Clifton H. Moore had an excellent private law library, and at Pekin, Benjamin S. Prettyman had a sizable collection; but after leaving Springfield the circuit lawyers had to depend primarily on their memories and such few books as they carried with them. For the most part, however, cases were simple and were decided on principle rather than by citation of authorities. There was little time for preparation; and common sense, sound reasoning and ready speech were the most essential qualifications for success. There was no specialization; lawyers handled any type of case that came their way. At Pekin at the May term, 1854, for example, we find Lincoln handling an ejectment suit, an action in debt, a trespass case, an indictment for forgery, one for cheating and fraud, a replevin suit, an action in trover and other cases. The great majority of actions were at common law and in chancery. Lincoln had two murder cases on the circuit during this period and occasionally he defended on charges such as manslaughter, forgery, larceny, riot and keeping a disorderly house. But compared with the number of his other cases his criminal practice was very small. The work of other lawyers was similar, in general, to his.

One might think that the local lawyers prepared the pleadings and other necessary papers, leaving the court work to the circuit lawyer who assisted them. This, however, was not the case, at least with respect to those suits in which Lincoln was retained. The researches of the Abraham Lincoln Association have brought to light in various courthouse files hundreds of bills, pleas, replications and other documents in Lincoln's handwriting; and there were hundreds more that have disappeared from the files. Always neat and carefully written, and usually signed by Lincoln with his own last name and that of the local lawyer with whom he was associated, these documents show that Lincoln did much of the laborious formal work.

Fees of lawyers were in keeping with prices and salaries, which were low. Charges at taverns were trifling; supper, lodging and breakfast for two, together with feed and stabling for two horses, could be had for seventy-five cents to a dollar. Attorneys' fees ranged ordinarily from ten to fifty dollars—with an occasional larger or smaller one. For two cases which he conducted for Benjamin Kellogg, Jr. in the Tazewell Court, one a damage suit and the other an indictment for forgery, Lincoln gave a receipt for fifty dollars, "in full balance of all fees up to this date, and also one dollar and a quarter, to be applied on the next fee."[8] To an attorney with whom he had been associated in the collection of a note he wrote: "As to the amount of my fee, take ten dollars, which you and I will divide equally." June 2, 1857, he charged ten dollars for work in connection with a land entry. September 14, 1855, he drew on the Illinois Central Railroad for $150—ten dollars apiece for fifteen cases in DeWitt and McLean counties. February 21, 1856, upon receipt of twenty-five dollars for drawing papers in connection with the easing of a hotel in Quincy, he wrote to his client: "You are too liberal with your money. Fifteen dollars is enough for the job. I send you a receipt for fifteen dollars, and return to you a ten dollar bill."[9] Clients usually made a small cash payment and gave notes for the balance. These could be sold at a discount to merchant and innkeepers, and constituted a sort of medium of exchange. Sometimes the makers defaulted and lawyers were forced to sue to collect their fees.

Court week was a great event for the inhabitants of county towns and the farmers of the back country. The latter flocked to town by the hundreds to purchase supplies, form new acquaintances, renew old friendships and enjoy the court proceedings. The court room was usually crowded with an appreciative audience, eager to appease its starved craving for entertainment. The *Urbana Clarion* of October 29, 1854, observed that "during the past week, nearly every resident of the county has been in our beautiful city—Courting." Judge and lawyers were celebrities in the eyes of the villagers. "The leading advocates had their partizans, personal and political," said Isaac N. Arnold, "and the merits of each were canvassed in every cabin, school-house, and at every horse-race, bee, and raising."[10] A popular lawyer like Lincoln, bent upon a political career, could soon develop a formidable body of supporters from acquaintances and admirers around the circuit.

Evenings on the circuit were given over to social life. Frequently the lawyers met in the room of Judge Davis, and sat talking, singing, telling stories or playing cards far into the night. David B. Campbell, the state's attorney, was the proud owner of a superb violin which he took with him on the circuit.[11] Lamon excelled in singing negro melodies. Lincoln told jokes and anecdotes. Politics often afforded subjects for discussion. The court at Danville attracted several Indiana lawyers who came principally for a "lark." Daniel W. Vorhees came from Covington, Daniel Mace, James Wilson and John Pettit from Lafayette, and John P. Usher and Richard Thompson from Terre Haute.[12] Usher F. Linder sometimes came up from Coles County, and lawyers from Iroquois County were often on hand.[13] Frequently at Danville the company repaired to Lamon's office where a pitcher of whiskey sat upon the table.

During political campaigns there were harangues by the lawyers in the afternoon or "at candle lighting," with an occasional joint debate by partisans of opposing candidates. Thus, in the fall of 1854, Lincoln spoke at Bloomington and Urbana. In 1856, he spoke at Lincoln and Urbana, he and T. Lyle Dickey spoke one night at Bloomington, and he, J. M. Scott, Dickey, Swett, Weldon and John Rosette all spoke at Clinton on the opening night of the fall term.

Such, in brief, was circuit life, which meant so much to Lincoln during the years of his mental development and growth. For as he worked, traveled, talked and ate he was constantly in contact with the common people, learning how and what they thought, how they reacted to the happenings of the day, how their ideas changed from one court term to the next. Unconsciously, perhaps, but in the best of schools, he was learning to read the public mind, and preparing himself to be the spokesman of the common man in years to come.

From 1854 to 1861 two factors were producing fundamental changes in circuit life. The first was the development of railroads, the effect of which was already evident in 1854. By that date the Chicago and Mississippi Railroad (part of the present Alton system) had been completed from Springfield to Bloomington and Lincoln could now reach both that town and Lincoln by rail. From Bloomington he could go directly to Metamora by horse and buggy as had been his custom, or he might take the Illinois Central to El Paso and drive to Metamora from there.[14] If he had occasion to go directly from Springfield to Pekin he might go by way of Bloomington, or he could take the Great Western Railroad to Naples, where he could get a steamboat going up the river. The trip from Springfield to Clinton could be shortened by taking a train to Lincoln, and driving from there. The towns in the eastern part of the circuit had no rail connections and must be reached as in the past.

Formerly, when Lincoln started out on the circuit he had usually traveled it continuously from one end to the other, being away from home for nine or ten weeks at a time. Now he found it possible to run back to Springfield for a day or two—at least from the western counties—without seriously interfering with work. Thus, on September 17 or 18, 1854, he returned to Springfield from Bloomington to attend to some business, and was back in Bloomington on the 19. From Metamora he returned to Springfield to attend the State Fair on October 3 and 4, picking up his court work again in Pekin on the 6. By 1855, Clinton had a rail connection with Springfield, and in the spring of that year we find Lincoln stopping over in Springfield for a week-end on his way from Pekin to DeWitt court.

By 1857, every county town had rail communication with Springfield; and Lincoln could follow the circuit from beginning to end by rail. For instance, he could take the Great Western from Springfield to Decatur, change to the Illinois Central and be in Clinton for the opening of the spring term. From there he could take the Illinois Central to Bloomington, where he took the Chicago and Alton to Lincoln. He returned to Bloomington on the latter road. To get from Bloomington to Urbana he would take the Illinois Central to Decatur, the Great Western from there to Tolono, and there change back to the Illinois Central. From Champaign he returned to Tolono and there boarded the Great Western for Danville. With such connections it was no longer necessary to follow the circuit uninterruptedly. With increasing frequency we find him returning to Springfield for weekends—or at least we find him in Springfield on Monday with his whereabouts on Sunday and perhaps Saturday unknown. During the fall term at Urbana in 1859 he returned to Springfield on Thursday to attend a wedding and was back at work early in the following week.

The second factor in changing circuit life was increase of population, which, by 1857, necessitated a decrease in the circuit's size. Between 1855 and 1860 the population of Champaign County more than doubled; that of Logan increased by three-fourths; that of Woodford became half as large again. In Sangamon and McLean counties the increase, while not as great in proportion to former population, was even larger numerically. Growth of the other counties was commensurate. From a little village of half a dozen small dwellings, three or four stores, a blacksmith shop, a depot and a warehouse, in 1854, Lincoln grew in six years to a town of 1,679, with a steam saw and grist mill, a fireproof courthouse (the first one was destroyed by fire in 1857), a school, three "halls," a bank, a large grain elevator, five churches and several hundred houses. The growth of other towns, while less phenomenal, was large.

Increased population meant more litigation. On the last day of the fall term in 1855, the Urbana court sat until midnight to clear the docket; and the next year a special term had to be held at Urbana to dispose of unfinished business. December 27, 1855, Judge Davis wrote to Julius Rockwell: "Ten days ago I finished my fall courts. The last court at Springfield occupied a month, and three quarters of the time from 9 in the morning to 10 o'clock at night. Courts were crowded with business everywhere in the State, and the increase through the circuit within the past two years is at least 50 per cent. The Judicial force of the state must be increased to satisfy the demands of justice."[15]

At its next session, in 1857, the Legislature granted the desired relief. By an act of February 11, Sangamon, Tazewell and Woodford counties were transferred from the Eighth to other circuits. Logan, McLean, DeWitt, Champaign and Vermilion counties now constituted the Eighth Circuit, with Bloomington as the principal town. The spring term now began in Clinton on the first Monday in March; and the court then moved progressively to Lincoln, Bloomington, Urbana and Danville. All terms were two weeks long, and court terminated early in May. In the fall, court opened in Bloomington on the first Monday in September, sat for two weeks, moved to Lincoln for two weeks, then to Clinton for a similar length of time. The fall term at Urbana, following that at Clinton, was only one week long. Court concluded at Danville, as in the spring. There was a third term of the McLean court on the second Monday in December. By 1859, one week was insufficient for the fall term at Champaign, and to lengthen it the Vermilion court was moved back to the first Monday in November.[16]

Tazewell and Woodford counties were placed in the Twenty-first circuit. Their terms now conflicted with those of the Eighth Circuit, and Lincoln was forced to give up the substantial practice that he had built up in them. He did not attend either court after 1856.

Sangamon County was placed in the Eighteenth Circuit, with Montgomery, Macoupin and Christian counties. Its spring and fall terms conflicted with those of the Champaign and Vermilion courts.[17] But by utilizing the railroads to get back and forth between Springfield and Urbana and Danville, Lincoln found it possible, when other matters did not interfere, to attend part of the terms of all three courts. For example, during the spring term, 1857, he was in Urbana from April 13 to 21. He arrived in Springfield on the evening of the 22, attended the Sangamon court through the 25, and was in Danville for the opening of the Vermilion court on the 27. Similarly, in the spring of 1859, he attended the Champaign court for several days, left for Springfield three days before court adjourned, spent three or four days in the Sangamon court, and arrived in Danville the day after court convened there.

So far as Lincoln personally was concerned, politics was a third factor interfering with circuit work. In the fall of 1854, although his attendance at the courts was sporadic, he managed to be present for at least a day or two at Bloomington, Pekin, Clinton, Urbana and Metamora. One day of the Woodford term he spent in Bloomington, listening to and replying to Douglas. From Pekin he returned to Springfield for a few days to participate in the political events occurring in connection with the State Fair. He skipped the Vermilion term to speak in Chicago and Quincy. The available evidence does not indicate whether he attended the Logan court or not. For at least three days of the Logan term he was in Springfield, and on one of those days he debated the Nebraska question at the courthouse with John Calhoun.

During the fall term in 1856, Lincoln was working much harder at politics than law. He missed the Metamora and Danville courts, and evidently attended the others only when he could do so without inter-ference with his speaking engagements. While campaigning against Doug-las, in the autumn of 1858, he missed the circuit entirely. A year later a speaking trip to Milwaukee, Janesville and Beloit cut in seriously upon his work. Preparation for the state and national Republican conventions and a speaking tour through New England took him from the circuit in the spring of 1860.

The same factors which were breaking the regularity of Lincoln's circuit life—with the exception of politics in some cases—were affect-ing the other lawyers. As volume of business increased they tended to limit their practice to their own counties, occasionally traveling to a neighboring county for a particular case, but no longer attempting to cover the whole circuit. By the end of the fifties circuit life was a thing of the past. In 1860, Leonard Swett wrote that "perhaps for five years Lincoln and myself have been the only ones who have passed habitually over the circuit"; and as we have seen, Lincoln's attendance had become increas-ingly irregular.[18] In 1861, Lawrence Weldon wrote regretfully from Ur-bana: "The Judge and I are now attending court at this place, the only wreck of that troupe that once was the life and soul of professional life in this county."

David Davis, of Bloomington, was judge of the Eighth Circuit from 1848 to 1862. Year after year he traveled the circuit from one end to the other, paying his own expenses on a salary of $1,000 a year. During the June term of the Sangamon court in 1855, Judge Charles Emmerson, of the Seventeenth Circuit, presided in his place, and on two occasions— on December 1, 1856, at Springfield and April 22 to 24, 1858, at Urbana— when Davis had business elsewhere, Lincoln took his place on the bench; but Davis' absences were rare.[19] Born in Maryland, in 1815, he was a grad-uate of Kenyon College in Ohio. For two years he studied law in the office of a Massachusetts judge, and completed his legal education at the Yale Law School. He came to Illinois in 1835, settling at Pekin. The next year he moved to Bloomington. He served one term in the State Legislature and was a member of the Constitutional Convention of 1847. Domineer-ing on the bench and at times prejudiced, it was said that he "did not know or care for, the philosophy of the law, but he was the incarnation of common sense."[20] "Brushing aside all technicalities and sometimes even the law, he seldom failed to do equity," said Gustave Koerner.[21] He was particularly fond of Lincoln, whose anecdotes amused him greatly. After Lincoln's death he was executor of his estate. The life of the circuit centered around him.

After 1856, Edward Y. Rice presided over the Sangamon court as judge of the Eighteenth Circuit. He was a Kentuckian. Securing his general education in the district schools of Illinois and at Shurtleff College, he studied law in the office of John M. Palmer. He was judge of the Eighteenth Circuit until 1870, and a lifelong Democrat.[22]

The bar of the Eighth Circuit, if the Springfield lawyers are included, was probably superior to any other group of legal talent in the state. In Springfield, Stephen T. Logan and John T. Stuart, both former partners of Lincoln's, were the leading legal practitioners. Logan was born in Kentucky in 1800, and prepared for the law in the office of an uncle. In 1854 he had already been circuit judge, four times a member of the State Legislature, a member of the Constitutional Convention of 1847 and an unsuccessful candidate for Congress. Small, careless in dress, with nervous temperament and a thin but ringing voice, he was recognized as the best all-round lawyer in Sangamon County, if not in the state.[23] Stuart, also a Kentuckian, was not far behind him in ability. A graduate of Center College, he had served two terms in Congress and one in the State Senate. Six feet tall, dignified, "with as fine and gallant a bow for his laundress as for a duchess," Stuart was considered by many to be the best jury lawyer in Illinois.[24] In 1843 he formed a partnership with Benjamin S. Edwards which continued until his death in 1885.[25] Edwards, like Stuart, was handsome and courtly, but was also vain. A graduate of Yale, he was a prodigious worker and always kept abreast of the latest legal developments and decisions.

Other Springfield lawyers were James C. Conkling, Shelby M. Cullom, John A. McClernand, Milton Hay, T. G. Taylor, Antrim Campbell, Charles S. Zane, Norman Broadwell and John E. Rosette.[26]

Conkling was born in New York City and educated at Princeton. He was not only a good lawyer, but an eloquent speaker, and a prominent businessman and extensive property owner. He was elected mayor of Springfield in 1845 and to the State Legislature in 1851.[27] Cullom was born in Kentucky in 1829, his parents moving to Illinois the next year. After teaching school for awhile, he came to Springfield in 1853 and studied law in the office of Stuart and Edwards. He was admitted to the bar in 1855, and was immediately elected city attorney. He served in the Legislature in 1856 and 1860. Later he was Governor of the state, member of the national House of Representatives and the United States Senate.[28]

McClernand, also a Kentuckian, was born in 1812, and moved to Shawneetown with his parents in 1816. He started out as a journalist, was elected to the State Legislature, then to Congress, and became one of the leading Democratic politicians in the state. He moved to Jacksonville, and then, in 1856, to Springfield. During the Civil War he became a major-general of volunteers, and was subsequently a circuit judge.[29] Hay also came from Kentucky. He studied law in the office of Stuart and Lincoln, was admitted to the bar in 1840 and began practice at Pittsfield. In 1857 he returned to Springfield and for awhile was Logan's partner.

Elliott B. Herndon, a native of Madison County, was a Democrat "of the strictest sect of our religion." From 1857 to 1860 he edited the *Illinois State Democrat,* a Buchanan organ "pure and undefiled" by Douglas heresies. Sometimes jolly, but more often morose, he was bitterly hostile to Lincoln.[30]

William H. Herndon, who had been Lincoln's partner since 1844, was another Kentuckian. Born in 1818, he was educated at private schools and at Illinois College, where he became a convert to abolitionism. He voted the Whig ticket until 1854, when he was one of the first to join the Republican Party. He was a man of violent likes and dislikes, impetuous, sometimes bibulous. From the early fifties he corresponded with Theodore Parker, William Lloyd Garrison, Wendell Phillips, Joshua R. Giddings and other abolitionists. An omnivorous reader, he collected an imposing library. He was especially interested in science and nature, and must have been a stimulating associate.[31]

Leading lawyers in McLean County were Asahel Gridley, Leonard Swett, John M. Scott and William Ward Orme. Gridley was a native of New York, and was educated at Pompey Academy in that state. He set up in Bloomington as a merchant; but was wiped out in the panic of 1837. About 1841 he commenced to study law. Able and eloquent, he soon had a good practice. He was impulsive and critical, however, and made many enemies.[32] Swett was born in Maine in 1825, and attended Waterville College, the present Colby. He studied law in Portland. From there he went to Indiana, traveling by way of New Orleans. Apparently unable to get started, he enlisted in the Mexican War, and served under Scott on his campaign to Mexico City. Prostrated by fever, he suffered terribly on shipboard on the way home. Many of his companions died. Eventually he was landed at New Orleans and sent to Jefferson Barracks in St. Louis to recuperate. Upon being discharged he started back overland to Maine;

but at Peoria suffered a relapse, and went to Bloomington to recover. This was in 1848. The next year he was admitted to the bar, and started to practice at Clinton, returning later to Bloomington. Originally a Whig, he became a Republican and was elected to the Legislature in 1858. In 1865 he moved to Chicago, where he became a leader of the bar.[33]

John M. Scott, who succeeded Davis as circuit judge in 1862, was born near Belleville in 1823. He was educated in the common schools and by a private tutor, and taught school and studied law in Belleville. He settled in McLean County in 1848 and was elected county judge in 1852. He was another Whig who became a Republican.[34] Orme was born in Washington, D.C., in 1832, educated at Mt. St. Mary's College in Maryland and was admitted to the bar in Bloomington in 1852. During the war he became a brigadier general of volunteers; but ill health forced him to retire, and he died soon after at the age of thirty-four.[35] Jesse Birch, William H. Hanna, Amzi McWilliams, J. C. Walker, J. H. Wickizer and J. C. Wright were other Bloomington lawyers.[36]

In Logan County much of the legal business was handled by Springfield and Bloomington men; but in the period under consideration there were three local lawyers of ability—L. P. Lacey, W. H. Young and Samuel C. Parks. The former, a native of St. Clair County, was known particularly as a good office man. Later he became an extremely competent judge. Highly conservative, he was a strong antebellum Democrat.[37] Young was a Know-Nothing.[38] Parks was a Republican and a friend of Lincoln's. He came from Vermont, was educated at Indiana University and read law with Stuart and Edwards in Springfield. He located in Logan County in 1846.[39]

In DeWitt County, E. H. Palmer, Clifton H. Moore and Lawrence Weldon were the leading advocates. All three were from Ohio. Palmer graduated from Wittenberg College; then went to Mississippi to take charge of a small college, reading law while there. Through the persuasion of Weldon he came to Springfield in 1855, moving to Clinton the following year.[40] Moore was educated in the common schools in Ohio, at Paynesville Academy and at Western Reserve Teachers' Seminary. He taught school while completing his education. Coming to Illinois he studied law at Pekin. In 1841 he was admitted to the bar and opened an office in Clinton. He became the local attorney for the Illinois Central Railroad, and as such often worked with Lincoln. During the Civil War he paid the taxes on land in Iowa which Lincoln owned. A lover of art, he accumulated a fine art collection. He was a Whig and Republican.[41] Weldon, like Palmer, attended Wittenberg College, but left before graduation. Coming to DeWitt County in 1854, he was admitted to the bar the same year. In 1860 he was elected to the Legislature on the ticket.[42]

In Tazewell County the greater part of the business was handled by lawyers from Peoria. Norman H. Purple and his partner, Ezra G. Sanger, Edward Jones, Lincoln B. Knowlton, Amos L. Merriman, Julius Manning and others from Peoria practiced there.[43] Up to the time of his death in 1857, Edward Jones had more business in Pekin than any other lawyer. He was born in Georgetown, D.C., in 1811, and studied at a classical academy in Georgetown and a military school in Washington. He got his legal education at the Virginia Law School in Winchester, and was admitted to the bar in 1830 at the age of nineteen. The next year he settled in Springfield, where he became the partner of George Forquer. He raised and led one of the companies of E. D. Baker's regiment in the Mexican War.[44] Norman H. Purple, who was born in Oswego County, New York, in 1803, and came to Peoria in 1837, was one of the most talented men on the circuit. A former justice of the State Supreme Court, he was the compiler of Purple's Statutes, a collection of the general acts of the Legislature in force in 1856.[45] Manning, a Canadian, and Knowlton, from Massachusetts, were both college graduates, the former from Middlebury College, Vermont, and the latter from Union College, New York.

Of the Pekin lawyers, Benjamin S. Prettyman, Samuel W. Fuller, William B. Parker, James Roberts and A. L. Davidson did the most business.[46] After Jones' death Prettyman had the largest practice in Tazewell County. He was a native of Delaware, born in 1819, and a self-made man. A leader of the Democratic Party in Tazewell County, he was a delegate to the Charleston Convention in 1860.[47]

The legal business of Woodford County was also largely in the hands of Peoria men. Several Bloomington lawyers had good practice there, as well as at Pekin. Local lawyers were S. P. Shope, Henry L. Haskell, J. A. Briggs and John B. Holland.[48]

From 1854 to 1856, William D. Somers was far ahead of all other lawyers in volume of business in Champaign County. He was originally a physician in North Carolina, and moving to Urbana in 1840, he and his brother Winston continued to practice there. In 1846 he commenced to study law under David Davis; and was admitted to the bar the same year. In 1855 he became local attorney for the Illinois Central. By that time his practice was so extensive that he took J. D. Jaquith as a partner.[49] This partnership was dissolved about a year later; and J. W. Somers, the son of Dr. Winston Somers, became his uncle's partner. W. D. Somers was originally a Whig, but turned Democrat in 1859.[50]

Another prominent lawyer in Champaign County was William N. Coler. A native of Ohio, he studied law in Mt. Vernon, and in the office of Amzi McWilliams of Bloomington. He came to Urbana in 1852, orga-

nized the Grand Prairie Bank, and for a while edited the *Urbana Union*.
By 1856 his legal practice was almost as extensive as Somers'. In 1872
he moved to New York, where he founded a brokerage business. He died
in 1914.[51] Other Champaign lawyers were J. W. Sim, another Ohioan, who
studied under Coler and was his partner from 1856 to 1858; James B.
McKinley, who practiced first in Petersburg, then for a time at Clinton
as Weldon's partner; and James S. Jones, McKinley's partner.[52] Henry C.
Whitney was the first resident lawyer of West Urbana (Champaign).[53]
Swett had a good practice in Champaign County, and Oliver L. Davis, of
Danville, often attended court there.

Whitney considered Oliver L. Davis and Clifton Moore of Clinton to
be the two best lawyers in the circuit outside of Springfield.[54] Davis' practice was by far the largest in Vermilion County. Lincoln and Lamon usually ranked second to him in amount of business there, and opposed him
in many cases. Davis was born in New York City in 1819, and was educated in the New York schools, at Hamilton Academy and in an academy at Canandaigua, New York. After completing his schooling he entered
the employ of the American Fur Company. In 1841 he came to Danville,
and was admitted to the bar the following year. He served in the Legislature in 1851 and again in 1857. Subsequently he served as circuit judge,
and as judge of the Appellate Court. Originally a Democrat, he became a
Republican in 1856.[55] Lamon was a hard-drinking, somewhat swashbuck-
ling type of Virginian; powerfully built, afraid of nothing, a practical joker
and a singer of sentimental and comic songs. He and Lincoln were strongly attracted to each other. Isaac H. Sconce, John H. Murphy, Joseph Peters, Oscar F. Harnzoll and Samuel McRoberts also practiced at Danville.[56]

These were the men with whom Lincoln worked on the circuit. Of
the fifty most prominent of them, at least a dozen, possibly a dozen and
a half, had graduated from or attended college. Many of them had tried
other occupations before turning to law; for in those days admission to
the legal profession was not difficult. Some of them, like Moore, Davis,
Logan and Prettyman, had good business judgment, and made fortunes
by shrewd investments in real estate. Practically all of them were young.
In 1854, Davis was only thirty-nine, Logan was fifty-four, Stuart forty-
seven, Edwards thirty-six, O. L. Davis thirty-five, Prettyman thirty-five,
Purple fifty-one, Edward Jones forty-three. Scott was thirty-one; Swett
was twenty-nine; Weldon twenty-five; W. H. Herndon thirty-six. Orme
was only twenty-two. Lincoln was forty-five; but was already calling
himself "an old man."[57]

Politically Lincoln owed much to these men. Logan cooperated with
him in the organization of the Republican Party in Sangamon County.

J. W. Somers was a Republican organizer in Champaign; O. L. Davis did similar service in Vermilion. Cullom, Scott and Weldon spoke frequently at Republican rallies. Conkling was a delegate to the Bloomington Convention in 1856, a member of the State Central Committee that year, and a presidential elector in 1860. Whitney and Lamon were political confidants of Lincoln's. W. H. Herndon did much of the hard but inconspicuous work necessary to success. During the campaign of 1858 he wrote: "I am all the time at the schoolhouses and village churches, where good can be done and where the 'big bugs' do not go." Jesse Fell, of Bloomington, who practically gave up law for real estate, persuaded Lincoln to write an autobiographical sketch which was the basis of several campaign biographies.[58] John Rosette edited the *Springfield Republican.*[59]

In 1862, when Swett went to Washington to consult with Lincoln about appointments, he reminded Lincoln that he owed his nomination to the presidency largely to the efforts of the lawyers of the Eighth Circuit headed by Davis; and Lincoln admitted that it was so. David Davis, Logan and O. L. Davis were delegates to the Chicago Convention in 1860. Swett was Davis' chief lieutenant in consulting delegates and lining up votes. Herndon, Parks, Lamon, Weldon and others worked assiduously backstage.

After Lincoln's election several former associates received their reward. David Davis was appointed to the Supreme Court. Parks was made Associate Justice of the Supreme Court of Idaho. Weldon became United States District Attorney for the Southern District of Illinois. Lamon was made Marshal of the District of Columbia. Cullom was given a place on the War Claims Commission at Cairo. Whitney was made a paymaster of volunteers. When Orme was forced by ill health to retire as brigadier-general of volunteers, a place was found for him as a supervising agent of the Treasury Department. And when the legal career of J. W. Somers was cut short by deafness, Lincoln appointed him to the Board of Review of the Pension Office.

For six months, in spring and fall, Lincoln was busy in the circuit courts. The winter months he spent in Springfield, working in the United States courts and the State Supreme Court. Here his cases, while less numerous, were in general more important than those on the circuit.

The Federal courts had been meeting in Springfield from the time that it became the capital of the state. With the growth of Chicago, however, it had become increasingly inconvenient to try cases originating there downstate, and beginning in 1848, two terms of the United States District and Circuit Courts were held in Chicago each year. Under an act of March 3, 1851, those courts convened in Chicago on the first Tuesday in

October and the third Tuesday in April. They met in Springfield on the first Monday in July and the third Monday in December.

In 1855, the continued growth of the northern part of the state induced Congress to divide Illinois into two Federal districts. By an act of February 13, the counties of Hancock, McDonough, Peoria, Woodford, Livingston, Iroquois and those north of them were to constitute the Northern District, the remaining counties the Southern District. Thus all counties of the Eighth Circuit, except Woodford, were in the Southern District. The courts of the Northern District met in Chicago on the first Monday in July and the third Monday in December; those of the Southern District convened in Springfield on the first Monday in March and the first Monday in October.[60] All cases pending were to be completed in the Northern District, subject to the right of either party to request completion of a suit in the Southern District. All records and files up to 1855 were moved to Chicago, where they were subsequently destroyed in the great fire.

[On] April 23, 1856, Congress changed the terms of the courts of the Southern District to the first Monday in January and the first Monday in June. It also authorized the clerk of that district to prepare, under the direction of the judge, transcripts of those records taken to Chicago which related to titles to real estate in the Southern District. These transcripts, and the records of cases begun in Springfield before 1855 and subsequently completed there, are the only remaining records of the Illinois Federal courts prior to 1855.

When the state was divided into two districts, Thomas Drummond, who had been United States District Judge for the entire state, was assigned to the Northern District, and Samuel H. Treat was appointed judge for the Southern District. Drummond presided over the Northern District for fourteen years. The same age as Lincoln, he was a native of Maine, and was educated in the common schools and academies of that state. He graduated from Bowdoin College in 1830, and studied law under William F. Dwight of Philadelphia, a son of President Dwight of Yale.[61] Treat was born in New York State in 1811, and got his education in the neighboring schools and the office of a local judge. Coming to Springfield in 1834, he was appointed circuit judge in 1838. In 1841 the Legislature elected him a judge of the Supreme Court. In those days the Supreme Court judges held the circuit courts, Treat presiding over the Eighth Circuit until this arrangement was changed in 1848. He served on the Supreme Court until his appointment to the Federal bench on which he sat for thirty-two years. A great reader, he accumulated a library of more than 2,400 volumes. He was a confirmed Democrat and a rigid Episcopalian.[62] Associate Justice John McLean, of the United States Supreme Court, presided over the Federal Circuit Courts in Illinois.[63]

Besides appearing regularly in the Federal courts in Springfield, Lincoln found it feasible, with the completion of the railroad to Chicago, in 1855, to participate in trials in the Northern District.[64] He could now get to Chicago in ten hours, as compared with three days formerly required to make the trip by stage. In July 1855, December 1856, and July 1857, we find him in Chicago, in court. In September 1857, he left the circuit to participate in the "Effie Afton" case, and in March 1860, he again missed part of the circuit to assist in the "Sand Bar" case. Doubtless he was there in connection with other cases, the records of which were burned.

Chicago was already giving ample promise of the great city it was to become. With 29,963 inhabitants in 1850, it grew to 80,028 in 1855, and by 1860 had a population of 109,260. Lincoln's trips there broadened his outlook, brought him into contact with aggressive, ambitious lawyers of a type new to him, and strengthened his acquaintance with influential upstate lawyer-politicians like Isaac N. Arnold and Norman B. Judd.[65] The amount and importance of his Chicago practice are indicative of his increasing prominence in his profession.

Equally indicative of his legal rank is his work in the Supreme Court of Illinois. For judicial purposes the Constitution of 1847 divided the state into three grand divisions, in each of which the Supreme Court held an annual session. The Second Grand Division, which sat at Springfield, consisted of Sangamon, Champaign, Vermilion, DeWitt, Logan, Edgar, Coles, Moultrie, Shelby, Montgomery, Macoupin, Greene, Pike, Adams, Highland, Hancock, McDonough, Schuyler, Brown, Fulton, Mason, Cass, Morgan, Scott, Christian, Macon, Piatt, Menard, Cumberland and Clark counties. The counties to the south constituted the First Grand Division, those to the north the Third Grand Division. The former sat at Mt. Vernon, the latter at Ottawa. Three counties of the Eighth Circuit—Tazewell, Woodford and McLean—were in the Third Grand Division, the remainder in the Second. By consent of all parties a cause appealed from a county in one grand division could be taken to the adjoining grand division. Thus, cases from any county in the state might be adjudicated in Springfield. During the period under consideration there is no evidence of Lincoln's having attended the sessions of either the First or Third Grand Divisions.

The Supreme Court was composed of three judges, one from each grand division. They served for nine years, one being elected every three years. The one with the oldest commission was chief justice. They must be thirty-five years old, and received $1,200 a year. From 1854 to 1861 the following men sat on the Supreme Bench at one time or another:

Samuel H. Treat, J. Dean Caton, Walter B. Scates, Ozias C. Skinner, Sidney Breese and Pinckney H. Walker.[66] Of these men, at least three worked their way up from humble beginnings. Handicapped by poverty in youth, Caton made a fortune as "telegraph king" of Illinois.[67] Scates gave up the printing trade to study law; Walker had clerked in a store.[68] Breese, who graduated from Union College, was the only one who was college trained.[69] Treat, Caton, Skinner and Breese were natives of New York; Scates was a Virginian; Walker from Kentucky. The average age of the six in 1854 was not quite forty-four.

Although there was no change in the organization of the Supreme Court from 1854 to 1861, the growing volume of lawsuits caused changes in the rules of procedure. In 1853 the court had adopted a rule limiting arguments of counsel to two hours, with the right to extend the opening argument to three hours by special permission. In 1858, the time allowed for each argument was reduced to one hour unless otherwise specially permitted. Counsel might, however, supplement their oral arguments by filing additional ones in writing.

The court kept no minutes, and the only notes taken were those that the individual judges chose to jot down regarding the authorities cited. In 1855, the court ruled that written abstracts must be filed by appellants or plaintiffs in error; and in 1858, printed briefs, giving the principal points of the argument and the authorities cited, were required.

Usually, cases were considered by the justices immediately after argument, the chief justice presiding in the council room, where discussion was extremely informal. The judges discussed the whole case; and whenever possible decided it immediately and announced their decision forthwith. The concurrence of two judges was necessary to decision. Frequently decision was deferred until each judge had examined the case individually, when it was discussed again in council and decided. If a decision could not be reached during the term the case was laid over for further separate examination by the judges during vacation. After a decision was reached one of the judges was delegated to write the opinion. Often several decisions that had demanded special consideration were handed down together at the end of a term. In 1855, Chief Justice Caton introduced the practice of keeping an agenda in the conference room. This was a small book in which was entered the name of the case, the points to be considered, the decision on each point, the reasons therefor and the name of the judge who was to write the opinion. A copy of the agenda was kept by each judge.

Under an act of January 1, 1849, court for the Second Grand Division was scheduled to convene in Springfield on the second Monday in December. As a matter of fact, however, the session rarely began until early in January. This occasions some confusion in referring to court terms. For example, the 1853 term met in January 1854, the 1854 term in January 1855, and so on. February 10, 1857, the time of meeting was changed to the first Tuesday after the first Monday in January.[70] Thus during most of the period we find the Supreme Court and the Federal courts for the Southern District getting under way within a week or two of each other and sitting concurrently for at least part of their terms.[71]

From all parts of the Second Grand Division and the Southern District lawyers came to Springfield to attend these courts. Those from the counties along the Mississippi could go by steamboat to Alton, and then come up to Springfield on the Alton Railroad; or they might go by stage or carriage to Naples, where they could take the Great Western to the capital. Crossing the Illinois River at Naples in December or January was often an adventure, accomplished now on solid ice and again by ferry amid floating ice cakes. Browning tells of one crossing when coach and horses had to be taken across the thin ice separately. Lawyers from counties along the Illinois frequently took a boat to Naples. Until the completion of the Illinois Central from Cairo to Decatur in 1856 and the Great Western to Danville in 1857, those from "Egypt" [southern Illinois] and the eastern counties had to drive or come by stage most of the way.

Frequently, in December and January, travel was delayed by snow; and sleighs were brought into use. In January 1855, for instance, Springfield was snowbound for several days, and Browning records instances of his having been held up by snow storms. The completion of the Burlington from Quincy to Galesburg in 1857 and the Peoria and Oquawka from Galesburg to El Paso in 1858 enabled lawyers from west of the Illinois River to use that route. The Terre Haute and Alton, finished in 1857, with connections with the Illinois Central at Pana and Mattoon, and with the Alton at Alton, facilitated travel from the southern counties of the Second Grand Division. In the odd-numbered years, and in 1854 when there was a special session, the Legislature, sitting at the same time as the Supreme and Federal courts, brought politicians—many of them lawyers—from all parts of the state. Among these men Lincoln made acquaintances of professional and political value.[72] With judges, lawyers and legislators in town, January, February and March were the social season in Springfield. Citizens dispensed quiet hospitality, with occasional larger and more formal entertainments. Balls, parties, concerts, and lectures were the chief amusements. "At night went to the Presbyterian church & heard a very good lecture from the Rev Mr. Mears of Griggsville.[73] Subject, Milton and Bunyan," recorded Browning in his *Diary* on Janu-

ary 17, 1854.[74] Other excerpts from the *Diary* give an idea of life in Springfield during court terms. For instance, January 5, 1854, "By invitation
spent the evening at S. Francis."[75] January 24, "After supper went to Mr.
Edwards & spent an hour or two." January 3, 1855, "At night attended
donation party at Mr Dodge's."[76] January 5th a hypnotist made volunteers
from the audience "exhibit any class of emotions or sensations—joy or
grief, mirth or sadness—tear off their boots in search of fleas and scratch
furiously—fight mosquitoes." January 16, "At night went to hear Yeatman of St. Louis deliver an address on the Maine law."[77] January 17, "attended the discussion of the Maine law in the house. Went again at night
with Mrs. Brown."[78] January 26, 1858, "At night went to Representative
Hall and heard a lecture from George D Prentice on the tendency of
American politics. After the lecture went to a small party at Mr Ridge-
leys."[79] February 3, "At night attended a party here in the house, being a
social gathering of the members of the third church." February 5, "At
B S Edward's to supper with the Judges & lawyers."[80] January 26, 1859,
"Went to Judge Treats to supper with the Supreme Judges, and Grimshaw
& [Joseph H.] McChesney."[81] February 2, "At large party at Lincoln's at
night." February 10, "a levee at Gov. Bissells."[82]

The social season of 1857 was gala as the Republicans celebrated the
election of William H. Bissell as Governor. The inauguration took place
on January 12, and was followed by a celebration in the evening. Then
came a round of parties and entertainments. The Lincolns gave a party
to which five hundred guests were invited on February 5. On the 13 there
was a dance at the Governor's Mansion. On the 16 Mrs. Lincoln wrote
to her sister: "Within the last three weeks there has been a party almost
every night and some two or three grand fetes are coming off this week."[83]

Yet there was much dissatisfaction with Springfield as a capital.
"Pleasant, and beautiful and flourishing will I term it," wrote a visitor
in 1854, "though very opposite adjectives have been prefixed to Springfield by many of those editors and politicians who have seen it during
winter's cold mud and cloudy sky and foggy air . . . when an unusual and
ill-assorted and turbulent crowd of visitors are here from the highways
and byways of 'Suckerdom,' when bird and bee, and blossom have given
place to pelting rain, and driving wind and general gloom."[84]

One of the chief grievances was the terrible condition of streets and
sidewalks. In 1857, Lincoln and Herndon secured damages of $700 from
the city for a client whose leg was broken by a fall on an unrepaired street.
The water supply was bad and the sewerage system defective. Another
abomination was "that miserable abortion of a Market House . . . contemptible to the eye and contemptible in itself," with its offensive odors

and clouds of green-back flies. Although it had been the state capital since 1837, Springfield did not have a single good hotel in the early fifties. Browning usually boarded at Mrs. Enos', and other lawyers stayed there or at other private homes or boardinghouses if they could. Often local attorneys shared their offices with the visitors. Otherwise the lawyers from out of town prepared their cases in the Supreme Court Library on the first floor of the State House. Browning's *Diary* has many references to his working there. This, in fact, was the rendezvous of the bar. After completion of the day's work, lawyers, Lincoln among them, and frequently judges, would sit there sometimes until midnight, swapping yarns, discussing cases or planning political campaigns.

Springfield was progressing in the fifties; and by the end of the decade dissatisfaction had been largely allayed. In 1854 the streets around the public square were planked, and it was estimated that twenty-five miles of sidewalk had been laid by 1858. In the middle of the decade several dilapidated buildings on the square burned down, and were replaced by "most substantial appearing edifices of brick, with iron fronts, and which would do honor to a more northern or eastern city." The Governor's Mansion was completed and many fine residences were erected.

Hotel accommodations were no longer inadequate. In 1854, the City Hotel built an addition which gave it a total of 130 rooms. The American House, under new management, became an excellent hostelry, "neat and tidy," said a guest, "the beds have no bugs, are always clean." Browning and other lawyers now put up there. In 1856 the St. Nicholas Hotel was built, four stories high with accommodations for 150 guests. From a town of about 6,000 in 1854, Springfield grew to 9,392 in 1860.

The men who came to Springfield for the sessions of the Supreme and Federal courts were a different group, for the most part, from that with which Lincoln was associated on the circuit. Naturally the Springfield lawyers practiced in the higher courts, but the other lawyers of the circuit did so very rarely.[85] Most business coming up to the Supreme Court from the Eighth Circuit was entrusted to Springfield lawyers—usually to Lincoln and Herndon, Stuart and Edwards, or Logan. After Milton Hay became Logan's partner in 1857, he had a number of cases from the circuit. From 1854 to 1860, thirty-one cases from counties in the Eighth Circuit were tried before the Second Grand Division of the Supreme Court, and Lincoln and Herndon were retained on one side or the other in nineteen of them. Of the twenty cases that came up from Sangamon County, either Lincoln or Herndon participated in nine.

Taking the Second Grand Division as a whole, from 1854 to 1861,

David A. Smith of Jacksonville, formerly a partner of John J. Hardin, led all the lawyers in number of cases before the Supreme Court.[86] Jackson Grimshaw of Pittsfield came second; with Lincoln and Herndon third. Murray McConnel of Jacksonville was fourth.[87] Archibald Williams of Quincy, who was "as angular and ungainly in his form as Mr. Lincoln himself; and for homeliness of face and feature surpassed Mr. Lincoln," Stuart and Edwards, and Logan and Hay had extensive practice in the Supreme Court. Chauncey L. Higbee of Pike County, Orville H. Browning of the Quincy firm of Browning and Bushnell, A. Wheat of Quincy and William N. Grover of Warsaw, William C. Goudy of Lewistown and his partner and brother-in-law S. Corning Judd, and Joseph Gillespie of Edwardsville all had numerous cases.[88] Sometimes Gustave Koerner of Belleville and John M. Palmer of Carlinville came to Springfield to argue a suit.[89] Many other attorneys appeared before the court with more or less regularity.

Essentially the same group that appeared before the Supreme Court handled the greater part of the litigation in the Federal courts in Springfield. In the latter courts, however, Stuart and Edwards outranked all others in volume of business. Conkling came second. Following him were Williams, Jackson Grimshaw and William A. Grimshaw, Logan and Hay, and Lincoln and Herndon, with little difference in the number of their cases.[90] Campbell and Cullom, McClernand, Browning and Bushnell, and Goudy and Judd had good practice in the Federal courts.

As might be expected, the average age of these men was somewhat higher than that of the lawyers of the Eighth Circuit; yet they, too, were young. Browning, for example, was forty-eight in 1854; Williams was fifty-three, McConnell fifty-six, Smith forty-five; McClernand forty-two, Gillespie forty-five. Jackson Grimshaw was only thirty-four, Higbee was thirty-three, Goudy thirty, Judd twenty-seven. Eight of the twenty-five mentioned were college men—Jackson Grimshaw, who attended Bristol College, Pennsylvania, Goudy, of Illinois College, Browning, who attended Augusta College in Kentucky, Bushnell of Yale, Stuart, Edwards, Herndon and Conkling.

Besides the Springfield lawyers, who have been discussed in connection with the circuit, McConnel, Williams, Higbee, Goudy, Browning, Koerner, Gillespie and Palmer served in the State Legislature. Palmer was later Governor; Browning became United States Senator and Secretary of the Interior; [and] Koerner had been Lieutenant-Governor in 1852. Some of these men, like the lawyers of the Eighth Circuit, played an active part in organizing the Republican Party in Illinois and in forwarding Lincoln's candidacy for the presidency. Lamon says that a caucus of lawyers, meeting in Springfield during the session of the Supreme Court, chose Lincoln as their candidate and secured his consent to their working for his nomination. Jackson Grimshaw was a delegate to the Bloomington Convention and a member of the State Central Committee in 1856. William A. Grimshaw was a delegate to the Republican National Convention in 1864, where he voted for Lincoln's renomination. Palmer, a former Democrat, presided at the Bloomington Convention, was temporary chairman at Decatur, and a presidential elector in 1860. Gillespie presided at the Decatur Convention. Koerner, originally a Democrat, became a leader of the Republican party and was a delegate to the Chicago Convention. Browning was a delegate at Bloomington, Decatur and Chicago. Williams was temporary chairman at Bloomington.

On the other hand, S. Corning Judd was a Democratic presidential elector in 1860, and a steadfast opponent of Lincoln's war policy. McConnel was a delegate to the Democratic National Convention in 1860, but supported the administration during the war. When Lincoln became President, he appointed Jackson Grimshaw Collector of Internal Revenue for the Quincy District, made Koerner Minister to Spain and selected Williams as United States District Judge for Kansas.

In the higher courts, as on the circuit, lawyers handled cases of all sorts. Take Lincoln's work before the Supreme Court for example. In 1854, he had one case involving the right of the trustees of the Illinois State Hospital for the Insane to remove the Superintendent, another involving the alleged conversion of a hog; in another the right of strict foreclosure was at issue. One case was an action of debt on a recognizance; *Illinois Central v. County of McLean* concerned the right of the county to tax the company's property within its limits. In another case Lincoln defended a tavernkeeper on a charge of selling whiskey without a license, and in still another he contested a decree of divorce. At other terms he argued cases involving patent rights, trust funds, ejectment proceedings, the legality of the removal of the county seat of Logan County from Mt. Pulaski to Lincoln, breach of contract, the method of assessing the property of the Illinois Central Railroad for taxation purposes, and others similarly heterogeneous.

In an article on "Lincoln in the United States Court 1855–1860," in the *Abraham Lincoln Association Bulletin,* Number 8, Paul M. Angle showed that in the Federal courts the business of Lincoln and Herndon was managed by the senior partner, although often transacted in the firm name. In "Abraham Lincoln: Circuit Lawyer," published in the Annual Papers of the Association for 1928, Mr. Angle demonstrated that Lincoln did most of the circuit work, that Herndon visited only the nearer counties, and that in those counties where both men practiced, each apparently handled his own cases and did his own preparatory work.

This differentiation of work extended to the Supreme Court also. The printed reports of that court usually give the firm name in cases in which they appeared. But the original written records show that they never apparently appeared together in the same case. Nor did Lincoln handle the court work and Herndon the pleadings. Each seems to have had his own clients, and to have prepared and argued his own cases. Lincoln had many more cases than Herndon; but Herndon conducted a number of cases which the printed reports assign to the firm. Indeed, in one case the printed report gives only Lincoln's name, whereas in the original record only Herndon's name appears. Herndon took charge of all business from Menard County. In 1847, when that county was dropped from the circuit, Lincoln stopped practicing there; but Herndon continued to attend court there, and naturally argued the cases that originated in that county.

So far as Lincoln was concerned, practice in the United States Courts and the Supreme Court—and in the Sangamon Circuit Court for that matter—differed in at least one respect from that away from home. In those courts he had time to prepare, which to him, according to Herndon, was essential to success. *Lincoln 1854–1861* shows that whenever possible he gave up outside activities for a week or two before the opening of the various Springfield courts. For instance, there is no record of any activity which would reveal his whereabouts for two weeks prior to the March term of the Sangamon Court in 1854. Similarly he cannot be located for the two weeks preceding the meeting of the Federal courts in July of that year. In 1855, there are only two entries for a week before the opening of the summer term of the Sangamon Circuit Court; and the ten days preceding the November term are blank. He cannot be located for eighteen days prior to the opening of the Supreme Court in 1856; and the week before the beginning of the Federal courts in March shows no activities. There are only three entries for the two weeks preceding the opening of the Supreme and Federal courts in January 1857; and for three weeks before the convening of the June term of the latter courts his whereabouts are known only on four days. Preceding the terms of the Supreme and Federal courts in January 1859, entries are few. Only one deduction is possible. During these periods Lincoln was in his office, or in the Supreme Court Library, hard at work.

Some phases of Lincoln's legal work during this period are still obscure. What, for instance, was the extent of his work in the Probate Court? Partial examination of the Probate Records has failed to show anything of importance. Have the papers drawn by Lincoln disappeared? Were estates settled, for the most part, without legal assistance? Or was this a type of work in which Lincoln did not engage? Further investigation will be necessary to answer these questions.

Did Lincoln do any amount of office work, such as drawing wills, advising clients, and other types of legal business which involve no appearance in court? From Browning's *Diary* we know that some lawyers at that time did much of that sort of thing; for in May 1855, while his partner Bushnell was away from home, Browning complains of the burden of office work. A few wills drawn by Lincoln have been discovered, and we know from letters that he often induced clients to settle out of court. Opinions written by him on such subjects as the legality of the charter of the Atlantic and Mississippi Railroad, the construction of the charter of the City of Springfield, the manner of settling the affairs of a partnership both members of which had died, the validity of preemptions of land on sections alternate to those owned by the Illinois Central Railroad, the possibility of breaking a will, and other matters are extant. In general, however, that type of work leaves little evidence; and the amount that Lincoln did may never be ascertained.

Again, what was the extent of Lincoln's practice in counties other than those of the Eighth Circuit? How often did he leave the circuit to try special cases elsewhere? Sometimes, as in his refusal to attend the courts in Edgar and Coles counties, November 14, 1857, he turned down business outside the circuit. On the other hand, during the period under consideration he did leave the circuit occasionally to conduct cases elsewhere. Thus, in March 1854, he tried the case of *Selby v. Dunlap* in Jacksonville. In September 1855, he went to Carlinville in connection with *Clark and Morrison v. Page and Bacon*, and to Cincinnati in connection with *McCormick v. Manny*. In May 1856, he was in Shelbyville for the case of *Terre Haute and Alton v. Earp*. November 20 and 21, 1857, we find him in Beardstown for the trial of *Gill v. Gill* and *Sprague v. Illinois River Railroad Company*; and the next year he was there again on May 5 and 6, to clear Duff Armstrong, son of an old friend, of a charge of murder. Discovery of such cases is more or less fortuitous, as it would be impracticable to make a special search in the archives of every county where he may have appeared. Undoubtedly his business outside the circuit was not large, although in time a few more such cases may come to light.

Many estimates of Lincoln's position as a lawyer have been attempted from criteria such as his legal education and experience, testimony of his colleagues, importance of cases in which he was retained and percentage of cases won and lost. Perhaps as satisfactory an indication as any— certainly one that must be taken into account in any final estimate—is the volume of his business as compared with that of other lawyers. From that point of view we find him, in the period from 1854 to 1861, undoubtedly one of the outstanding lawyers of central Illinois. Lack of records in some counties makes generalization about his circuit work somewhat difficult, but it appears that in each county there was at least one lawyer the number of whose cases exceeded his. He, however, was one of the few men who practiced in every county, and in every one his practice was large. In the Federal courts he was among the leaders, with a reputation which brought retainers in important cases in Chicago. In the Second Grand Division of the Supreme Court he and Herndon ranked third in number of cases, and got more than their proportionate share of business coming up from those counties where they were best known. Many of Lincoln's cases in the higher courts came to him through his colleagues, who either entrusted cases to him or engaged him to assist them. Their confidence in him is the best testimonial of his proficiency. Indeed, their trust went farther than that. Those of them with political opinions similar to his were willing to support him for the highest office in the land at a time of approaching stress.

Notes

1. Autobiography written for John L. Scripps, [ca. June 1860], in *The Collected Works of Abraham Lincoln*, ed. Roy P. Basler, Marion Dolores Pratt and Lloyd A. Dunlap, asst. eds., 8 vols plus index (New Brunswick: Rutgers University Press, 1953–55), 4:67.

2. Paul M. Angle, ed., *Lincoln, 1854–1861: Being the Day-by-Day Activities of Abraham Lincoln from January 1, 1854 to March 4, 1861* (Springfield: Abraham Lincoln Association, 1933).

3. *Thomas's note:* Insofar as this study is concerned, *Lincoln 1854–1861* has conclusively proved its worth. Not only has it enabled me to secure information more quickly and easily than before, but it has made possible the correlation and interpretation of many hitherto meaningless and apparently unrelated facts. Those who have read that book will recognize my indebtedness to it.

4. *Thomas's note:* The following is the court calendar for the Eighth Circuit for 1854, 1855 and 1856. 1854: Sangamon, March 20, June 12, November 20; Logan, April 3, September 4; McLean, April 10, September 11; Woodford, April 24, September 25; Tazewell, May 1, October 2; DeWitt, May 15, October 16; Champaign, May 22, October 23; Vermilion, May 26, October 27. 1855: Sangamon, March 19, June 11, November 19; Logan, April 2, September 3; McLean, April 9, September 10; Woodford, April 23, September 24; Tazewell, April 30, October 1; DeWitt, May 14, October 15; Champaign: May 21, October 22; Vermilion, May 25, October 26. 1856: Sangamon, March 17, June 9, November 17; Logan, March 31, September 1; McLean, April 7, September 8; Woodford, April 21, September 22; Tazewell, April 28, September 29; DeWitt, May 12, October 13; Champaign, May 19, October 20; Vermilion, May 23, October 24.

5. Orville H. Browning, *The Diary of Orville Hickman Browning*, 2 vols., ed. Theodore Calvin Pease and James G. Randall (Springfield: Illinois State Historical Library, 1925, 1933).

6. Henry C. Whitney, *Life on the Circuit with Lincoln*, ed. Paul M. Angle (Caldwell, Idaho: Caxton Printers, 1940), 436.

7. Whitney, *Life on the Circuit*, 62.

8. In the forgery case, tried in 1855, Lincoln successfully moved to have the indictment quashed.

9. Abraham Lincoln to Richard S. Thomas, Springfield, 24 Aug. 1854, and Lincoln to George P. Floyd, Springfield, 21 Feb. 1856, in *Collected Works*, ed. Basler et al., 2:226, 2:331.

10. Isaac N. Arnold, *Recollections of the Early Chicago and Illinois Bar*, Chicago Bar Association Lectures no. 22 (Chicago: Fergus, 1882), 12.

11. In 1838 New Jersey–born David B. Campbell, brother of Antrim Campbell, settled in Springfield, where he served as prosecutor (1848–56). In 1842 he was chosen mayor of Springfield. In 1846 he was attorney general of Illinois. He was noted for his prankish sense of humor.

12. Daniel Wolsey Voorhees (1827–97) represented his Indiana district in the U.S. House (1861–66, 1869–73) and served in the U.S. Senate (1877–97). Daniel Mace (1811–67), U.S. attorney for Indiana (1849–53), represented his district in the U.S. House (1851–57) James Wilson (1825–67) of Crawfordsville represented his district in the U.S. House (1857–61). John Pettit (1807–77), U.S. district attorney (1839–43), represented his district in the U.S. House (1853–55). John Palmer Usher (1816–89) served as Lincoln's secretary of the interior (1863–65).

13. Kentucky-born Usher F. Linder (1809–76), who settled in Coles County, Illinois, in 1835, was "a trifle vain, but just enough to spur him on." John M. Palmer, ed., *The Bench and Bar of Illinois: Historical and Reminiscent*, 2 vols. (Chicago: Lewis Publishing, 1899), 1:181.

14. *Thomas's note:* Pekin and Metamora still had no railroads, but Tazewell and Woodford counties were dropped from the circuit in 1857.

15. David Davis to Julius Rockwell, 27 Dec. 1855, Davis Papers, Illinois State Historical Library.

16. *Thomas's note:* The court calendar for 1857–1860 was as follows. 1857: DeWitt, March 2, October 5; Logan, March 16 and September 21; McLean, March 30, September 7; Champaign, April 13, October 19; Vermilion, April 17, October 26. 1858: DeWitt, March 1, October 4; Logan, March 15, September 20; McLean, March 29, September 6, December 13; Champaign, April 12, October 18; Vermilion, April 26, October 25. 1859: DeWitt, March 7, October 3; Logan, March 21, September 19; McLean, April 4, September 5, December 12; Champaign, April 18, October 17; Vermilion, May 2, November 7. 1860: DeWitt, March 5, October 1; Logan, March 19, September 17; McLean, April 2, September 3, December 10; Champaign, April 16, October 15; Vermilion, April 30, November 5.

17. *Thomas's note:* From 1857 to 1860 the Sangamon Court was scheduled to convene on the following dates. 1857: April 20, August 10; 1858: April 12, August 9, October 18; 1859: April 25, August 22, October 24; 1860: April 23, August 27, October 22.

18. Leonard Swett to Josiah H. Drummond, Bloomington, Ill., 27 May 1860, copy, Ida M. Tarbell Papers, Allegheny College.

19. New Hampshire–born Charles Emmerson (1811–70), who settled in Decatur, served in the Illinois House of Representatives (1850–52) and as a circuit court judge (1853–67).

20. In 1836 David Davis (1815–86) settled in Bloomington, Illinois. In 1862 Lincoln named him to the U.S. Supreme Court.

21. In 1833 German-born Gustave Koerner (1809–96) settled in Belleville, Illinois. A friend of Lincoln, he served as lieutenant governor (1856–60) and as U.S. minister to Spain (1862–65).

22. Edward Young Rice (1820–83) represented an Illinois district in the U.S. House (1871–73). In 1859 Lincoln erupted in anger at Rice. William Herndon recalled that it was "a terrible spectacle" when his partner denounced Rice's decision in a murder case, becoming "so angry that he looked like Lucifer in an uncontrollable rage." Carefully keeping "within the bounds of propriety just far enough to avoid a reprimand for contempt of court," Lincoln "was fired with indignation and spoke fiercely [and] strongly" of the decision of the judge, whom "he pealed . . . from head to foot." Lincoln "roared like a lion suddenly aroused from his lair," the court crier remembered. William H. Herndon interview with George Alfred Townsend, Springfield correspondence, 25 Jan. 1867, *New York Tribune*, 15 Feb. 1867; Herndon, "Analysis of the Character of Abraham Lincoln: A Lecture," address delivered in Springfield, 26 Dec. 1865, in *Abraham Lincoln Quarterly* 1 (Dec. 1941): 429; Herndon to Jesse Weik, Springfield, 20 Nov. 1885, Herndon-Weik Papers, Library of Congress; Paul M. Angle, ed., *Herndon's Life of Lincoln: The History and Personal Recollections of Abraham Lincoln as Originally Written by William H. Herndon and Jesse W. Weik* (Cleveland: World, 1942), 264–65; T. W. S. Kidd's lecture, "The Court Crier," excerpts in the Ida M. Tarbell Papers, Allegheny College.

23. John Todd Stuart, who regarded Logan (1800–1880) as the ablest attorney in the Sangamon County bar, said that the "rapidity of his intellectual perceptions were like flashes of lightning." On 13 April 1843 the *Sangamo Journal* (Springfield) reported that Logan "is regarded as perhaps the best lawyer in the State, and has undoubtedly a fine logical mind. His voice is not pleasant, but he has a most happy faculty of elucidating, and simplifying the most obstinate questions." John Hay thought him "one of the finest examples of the purely legal mind that the West has ever produced." Supreme Court justices John McLean and David Davis, as well as leading attorneys such as Gustave Koerner, Usher F. Linder, Elihu B. Washburne, Isaac N. Arnold, and Benjamin S. Edwards, all concurred. *Memorials of the Life and Character of Stephen T. Logan* (Springfield: H. W. Rokker, 1882), 16–17, 21–29; John Hay, "Colonel Baker," *Harper's New Monthly Magazine*, Dec. 1861, in *At Lincoln's Side: John Hay's Civil War Correspondence and Selected Writings*, ed. Michael Burlingame (Carbondale: Southern Illinois University Press, 2000), 154; David Davis to [William P. Walker], Springfield, 25 June 1847, David Davis Papers, Illinois State Historical Library, Springfield; Thomas J. McCormack, ed., *Memoirs of Gustave Koerner, 1809–1896*, 2 vols. (Cedar Rapids: Torch Press, 1909), 1:178–79; Usher F. Linder, *Reminiscences of the Early Bench and Bar of Illinois* (Chicago: Chicago Legal News Company, 1879), 155; Elihu Washburne in *Reminiscences of Lincoln by Distinguished Men of His Time*, ed. Allen Thorndike Rice (New York: North American Publications, 1886), 10–11; Isaac N. Arnold, *Reminiscences of the*

Illinois Bar Forty Years Ago: Lincoln and Douglas as Orators and Lawyers,
pamphlet (Chicago: Fergus, 1881), 4.

24. Caroline Owsley Brown, "Springfield Society before the Civil War," *Journal of the Illinois State Historical Society* 15 (1922): 490.

25. A colleague at the bar described the tall, slender Stuart as "the handsomest man in Illinois," with "the mildest and most amiable expression of countenance." He was ever "cheerful, social and good-humored" and "had the reputation of being the ablest and most efficient jury lawyer in the State." David Davis called Stuart a "Christian gentleman of the old school," a "generous man" with "polished manners and commanding presence" who served as a "peacemaker," fomenting "no litigation." David Davis ranked him "among the best *nisi prius* lawyers in the state," a man whose "persuasive address and captivating manner" went "to the heart of the average juryman." After graduating from Center College in 1826, Stuart studied law with Judge Daniel Breck in Kentucky. Two years later he settled in Springfield, where in 1833 he formed a partnership with Henry E. Dummer. The previous year Stuart entered politics, running successfully for the legislature, where he quickly became a Whig leader in the House of Representatives. There he was known as "Jerry Sly" for "his great powers of sly management and intrigue." William Herndon thought him "a sly one, tricky, [a] dodger." Stuart also served in the Black Hawk War, where he first met Lincoln. Linder, *Reminiscences of the Early Bench and Bar,* 348; David Davis, Address to the Illinois State Bar Association, 13 Jan. 1886, *Bloomington Pantagraph,* 6 Feb. 1886; C. C. Brown, "Major John T. Stuart," *Transactions of the Illinois State Historical Society* 7 (1902): 112; William H. Herndon to Jesse W. Weik, Springfield, 10 Dec. 1885, Herndon-Weik Papers, Library of Congress.

26. In 1853 T. G. Taylor, secretary of the Sangamon County Association, ran unsuccessfully for county judge on the Whig ticket. New Jersey–born Antrim Campbell (1814–68), who settled in Springfield in 1838, served as master in chancery of Sangamon County from 1849 to 1861, when he was appointed master in chancery of the U.S. Circuit Court for the Southern District of Illinois. New Jersey–born Charles S. Zane (1831–1915) attended McKendree College in Lebanon, Illinois, from 1853 to 1856 and was admitted to the bar in 1857. The following year he was elected city attorney for Springfield. Later he was a partner of William H. Herndon and later still of Shelby M. Cullom. Democrat Norman M. Broadwell (1825–93) studied with Lincoln and Herndon (1850–51) and served as a representative in the Illinois General Assembly (1860–62), as a county judge (1863–65), and as mayor of Springfield (1867–71). In 1855 Lincoln invited John E. Rosette (1823–81) to move from Ohio to Springfield, where he practiced law for thirty years. A Democrat when he came to Illinois, he switched to the Republican Party in 1856 and edited the *Springfield Republican,* which supported Lincoln for president.

27. James Cook Conkling (1816–99) was an active Whig leader who worked closely in politics with Lincoln.

28. Shelby Moore Cullom (1829–1914) served in the U.S. House (1865–71) and the U.S. Senate (1883–1913); he was also governor of Illinois (1877–83).

29. John A. McClernand (1812–1900) represented the Shawneetown district (1843–51) and the Springfield district (1859–61) in the U.S. House.

30. Elliott B. Herndon (1820–95) gave his brother, William, an unflattering assessment of Lincoln. Douglas L. Wilson and Rodney O. Davis, eds., *Herndon's Infor-*

mants: *Letters, Interviews, and Statements about Abraham Lincoln* (Urbana: University of Illinois Press, 1997), 459–60. In 1821 he moved with his family to Sangamon County, where he studied law and won admission to the bar. He held various posts, including Springfield city attorney, attorney for Sangamon County, U.S. attorney for the Southern District of Illinois, and disbursing agent for Illinois.

31. William Henry Herndon (1818–91) coauthored a celebrated biography of Lincoln based on his extensive interviews and correspondence with people who had known Lincoln.

32. Asahel Gridley (1810–81), a prominent merchant, banker, and lawyer in Bloomington, became a brigadier general of militia during the Black Hawk War and served in the state legislature.

33. Leonard Swett (1825–89) was a very close friend of Lincoln, whose presidential candidacy he championed at the 1860 Chicago convention and in the subsequent election campaign.

34. John M. Scott (1823–98) sat on the Illinois supreme court (1870–88).

35. Henry C. Whitney (*Life on the Circuit*, 243) called Orme "one of the most promising young lawyers in this state," a "many-sided man" whom David Twigg "properly denominated . . . as having 'more common sense than any man he ever knew.'"

36. William H. Hanna (1823–70) was born in Indiana and settled in Illinois in 1849. Amzi McWilliams (d. 1862) had a successful practice in Bloomington and then in Springfield. According to John M. Palmer (*Bench and Bar of Illinois*, 186), "Had it not been for an unfortunate temper he would have left a highly honorable and proud record." One day in court he shouted "No! No!! No!!!" at one of Lincoln's witnesses; Lincoln yelled back, "Oh! Yes! Yes!! Yes!!!" while "looking daggers at McWilliams, who quailed under Lincoln's determined look." Whitney, *Life on the Circuit*, 470. Pennsylvania-born John H. Wickizer (1821–89) settled in Bloomington in 1847. He served in the state legislature and was mayor of Bloomington.

37. Lionel P. Lacey (1819–66), a Democratic leader, had an unusually extensive practice.

38. William H. Young taught school in Postville, served in the Mexican War, ran as the American Party candidate for secretary of state in 1856, and served as district prosecuting attorney from 1861 until his death two years later.

39. Samuel C. Parks (1812–1917) at first settled in Springfield in 1840. Lincoln appointed him to the supreme court of Idaho in 1863.

40. E. H. Palmer became close to Lincoln in 1856 when the two were staying with other lawyers at a hotel in Clinton, Illinois. Because rooms were in short supply, Palmer was told that he must double up with someone. Lincoln said, "I will take the young stranger under my wing." They became fast friends. *History of DeWitt County, Illinois*, 2 vols. (Chicago: Pioneer, 1910), 1:255.

41. The first attorney to establish a practice in DeWitt County, Clifton H. Moore (1817–1901) collaborated with David Davis in highly successful land speculation. The only political post he held was as a delegate to the 1870 Illinois Constitutional Convention.

42. In 1861 Lincoln named his close friend Lawrence Weldon (1829–1905) U.S. district attorney for the Southern District of Illinois, a post he held until 1866, when he moved to Bloomington. In 1883 he became an associate justice of the U.S. Court of Claims in Washington, D.C.

43. Ezra G. Sanger served as a presidential elector in 1852. He died young of tuberculosis. Massachusetts-born Lincoln Brown Knowlton (1804–54) was known as "the Henry Clay of the Illinois bar." John M. Palmer portrayed him as "a stalwart man, above medium height, broad-shouldered, and raw-boned" (*Bench and Bar of Illinois*, 292). He served as a delegate to the Whig national convention in 1852 and won election to Congress the following year but died before he could take his seat. Amos L. Merriman served as judge of the Illinois Sixteenth Circuit Court from 1861 to 1863, when he moved to Washington, D.C., to prosecute war claims against the U.S. government. He was a partner first with his brother, Halsey O. Merriman, who died in 1854, and then with Julius Manning. He was an office lawyer, gifted at preparing papers. Julius Manning (d. 1862) settled in Knoxville, Illinois, in 1839 and moved to Peoria in 1853. A Democrat, he served in the lower house of the state legislature (1842–46).

44. Edward Jones, who served as circuit clerk in 1834, "died at an early age, the victim of those habits which are too frequently the accompaniment of brilliant and distinguishing qualities of mind." *History of Tazewell County* (Chicago: Chapman, 1879), 387. Pennsylvania-born George Forquer (1794–1837) moved to Illinois in 1804 and served as a state legislator, secretary of state, attorney general, and register of the Springfield land office.

45. Originally from Pennsylvania, Norman H. Purple (1803–63) had an extensive practice in Peoria. He served as state's attorney (1840–42) and justice of the supreme court of Illinois (1845–48). An active Democrat, he was in 1844 a presidential elector.

46. In 1850 Samuel W. Fuller (1822–73) migrated from New Hampshire to Pekin, Illinois, where he won election to the state senate in 1856 as a Democrat. Eleven years later, he moved to Chicago, where he joined the firm of Scammon and McCagg. William B. Parker (d. 1873) was a man "of fine education and good abilities," but he "lacked the perseverance so necessary to the success of a lawyer." *History of Tazewell County*, 388. In 1851, three years after being admitted to the Missouri bar, James Roberts moved to Pekin, where he established a large practice. His "career was cut short at the early age of thirty-three years by his death from overwork." *History of Tazewell County*, 388. Around 1838, New York–born Asa Lee Davidson settled in Canton, Illinois, for a few years. He then returned to New York before eventually settling in Peoria, Illinois.

47. Originally from Delaware, Benjamin S. Prettyman, Sr., (b. 1819) migrated to Illinois in 1831 and was admitted to the bar in 1845. He was renowned for his command of real estate law. He served as a delegate to every Democratic national convention from 1856 to 1892 (save 1876). He and Lincoln worked together on a number of Tazewell County cases.

48. Ohio-born Simeon P. Shope (b. 1837) settled in Ottawa, Illinois, was admitted to the bar in 1856, practiced first in Lewiston, Illinois, served as judge of the Tenth Circuit, and eventually sat on the state supreme court. In 1894 he moved to Chicago, where he became an eminent corporation lawyer. New York–born J. Albert Briggs (b. 1839) settled in Naperville, Illinois, in 1855; five years he later moved to Eureka, where he served as city attorney for more than a quarter of a century. John B. Holland, the first licensed attorney in Woodford County, Illinois, "became well known in the county, and served as probate justice for several years." Roy L. Moore, *History of Woodford County* (Eureka: Woodford County Republican, 1910), 245.

49. James D. Jaquith was a Republican leader in Champaign County.

50. In 1861 Lincoln appointed James W. Somers (1833–1904), an active Republican stump-speaker, to a post in the pension bureau, which he held for thirty-five years. Abraham Lincoln to James W. Somers, Springfield, 1 March 1860, and Lincoln's recommendation for Somers, 28 March 1860, both in *Collected Works*, ed. Basler et al., 4:33, 4:35. Henry C. Whitney described him as "engaging," "*debonair* and *suaviter in modo*, and bold and trenchant in debate." Somers combined "accurate and exhaustive knowledge of current politics" with "an exuberant imagination," which "rendered him one of the most captivating political speakers in the ranks of our young men." Whitney, *Life on the Circuit*, 243. Winston Somers (d. 1871) moved to Urbana in 1843 and practiced medicine over a wide area in eastern Illinois. The first lawyer to practice in Champaign County, William D. Somers had been a vehement supporter of Stephen A. Douglas, but he voted for Lincoln in 1864.

51. William Nichols Coler (b. 1827), a Democratic leader, served as colonel of the Twenty-fifth Illinois Infantry during the Civil War.

52. Joseph W. Sim served as judge of the county court. In 1857 James B. McKinley (1821–1903) settled in Champaign, where he practiced law until 1860, when he abandoned the profession to enter the banking business. James S. Jones, with his partner, established the first law firm in Champaign after Henry C. Whitney.

53. A close friend of Lincoln, Henry Clay Whitney (1831–1905) wrote *Life on the Circuit with Lincoln*. That volume contains his estimate of Davis and Moore (238–39).

54. Ibid., 238–39.

55. Oliver Lowndes Davis (d. 1892), who studied law with Isaac P. Walker, won election to the Seventh Circuit Court in 1861 and held that post until 1866. From 1873 to 1879 he served as judge of the Fifteenth Judicial Circuit. He eventually became a justice of the state supreme court. In 1860 he was a delegate to the Chicago convention that nominated Lincoln for president.

56. In 1832 John H. Murphy superintended the building of the Champaign County courthouse and participated as a soldier in the Black Hawk War, serving as an aide to Col. Isaac R. Moores. In 1841 he won admission to the bar after passing an examination that Lincoln helped administer. He was in partnership with John Kavanaugh until 1853. Civic-minded, he helped to promote schools and railroads. In 1840 Ohio-born Joseph Peters (1819–66) won admission to the bar of Illinois after being examined by Lincoln. Settling in Danville in 1845, he served as a county judge and as a member of the Illinois House of Representatives (1846–48). Democrat Samuel McRoberts (1799–1843) represented Illinois in the U.S. Senate (1841–43) after serving as a state circuit court judge (1824–27), state senator (1828–30), U.S. district attorney (1830–32), receiver of the general land office in Danville (1832–39), and solicitor of the general land office in Washington (1839–41).

57. E. B. Washburne first heard the sobriquet "Old Abe" applied to Lincoln when he was but thirty-eight. Lincoln himself at that age referred to his "old, withered, dry eyes" and at thirty-nine told Herndon, "I suppose I am now one of the old men." Allegedly he once said that "I . . . have been kept so crowded with the work of living that I felt myself comparatively an old man before I was forty." Washburne in *Reminiscences of Lincoln*, ed. Rice, 16; Abraham Lincoln to William H. Herndon, Washington, 2 Feb., 10 July 1848, both in *Collected Works*, ed. Basler

et al., 1:448, 1:497; Robert H. Browne, *Abraham Lincoln and the Men of His Time,* 2 vols. (Cincinnati: Jennings and Pye, 1901), 1:86.

58. Pennsylvania-born Jesse Wilson Fell (1808–87), who settled in Bloomington in 1833, sold his law practice to David Davis in 1836 to devote full time to land speculation. In the mid-1840s he resumed his law practice. The autobiographical sketch is enclosed in Abraham Lincoln to Jesse Fell, Springfield, 20 Dec. 1859, in *Collected Works,* ed. Basler et al., 3:511–12.

59. The *Springfield Republican* was founded in 1857.

60. *Thomas's note:* From 1854 to 1860 the Federal courts convened on the following dates: 1854: Chicago (April 18, October 3), Springfield (July 3, December 18); 1855: Northern District (July 2, December 17), Southern District (October 1); 1856: Northern District (July 7, December 15), Southern District (March 3, June 2); 1857: Northern District (July 6, December 21), Southern District (January 5, June 1); 1858: Northern District (July 5, December 20), Southern District (January 4, June 7); 1859: Northern District (July 4, December 19), Southern District (January 3, June 6); 1860: Northern District (July 2, December 17), Southern District (January 2, June 4). The courts for the Southern District did not meet in March, 1855, probably because the judicial appointment for that District was not made in time.

61. Thomas Drummond (1809–90) served as judge of the Northern Distict of Illinois (1855–69).

62. Samuel Treat (1815–1902) served as judge of the Southern District of Illinois (1855–87).

63. *Thomas's note:* In 1854 the Federal courts in Springfield were held in rented quarters on the second floor of the Tinsley Building on the southwest corner of Sixth and Adams streets. The next year the government rented new quarters—seven rooms in a three-story building on the northeast corner of Sixth and Washington streets belonging to Stephen T. Logan. Court was held on the second floor, in a small room heated by a great "cannon ball" stove in its center.

64. *Thomas's note:* Indirect rail communication to Chicago, by way of Bloomington and Mendota or LaSalle, was established in 1854.

65. In 1836 New York–born Isaac Newton Arnold (1815–85) settled in Chicago, where he won election to the U.S. House in 1860. During the Civil War he and Lincoln were close allies, and he published a biography of Lincoln in 1866. In 1836 New York–born Norman Buell Judd (1815–78) settled in Chicago, whose voters elected him to the state senate (1844–60). In 1860 he helped engineer the nomination of Lincoln, who appointed him U.S. minister to Prussia.

66. Walter Bennett Scates (1808–86) served on the Illinois supreme court (1841–47, 1854–57). New York–born Ozias C. Skinner (1817–77) served on the Illinois supreme court (1855–58).

67. John Dean Caton (1812–95) served on the Illinois supreme court (1842–64) and was president of the Illinois and Mississippi Telegraphic Company (1852–67).

68. Pinckney Houston Walker (1815–85) served on the Illinois supreme court (1858–85), where he allegedly wrote more opinions (three thousand) than any other judge in American history.

69. Sidney Breese (1800–78) had served briefly on the Illinois supreme court (1841–42) when he was elected a U.S. senator, a post he held until 1849. In the Senate he championed the Illinois Central and the Union Pacific railroads.

70. *Thomas's note:* The Second Grand Division of the Supreme Court was scheduled to meet as follows: December 11, 1854; December 10, 1855; December 8, 1856; January 5, 1858; January 4, 1859; January 3, 1860.

71. *Thomas's note:* In 1856 the Federal courts did not meet until March.

72. *Thomas's note:* Among others, Norman B. Judd, T. J. Henderson, T. J. Turner, Owen Lovejoy, James M. Ruggles, Robert Boal, I. N. Arnold, T. J. Pickett and H. E. Dummer came to Springfield to attend the Legislature at one time or another during these years.

73. Rollin Mears was the pastor of the Congregational Church in Griggsville.

74. The lecture was summarized in the *Illinois State Journal* (Springfield), 19 Jan. 1854.

75. Simeon Francis (1796–1872) owned and edited the *Illinois State Journal*, Springfield's Whig (later Republican) newspaper (1831–55). He and Lincoln were close friends.

76. Ninian W. Edwards (1809–89) was Lincoln's brother-in-law. Richard V. Dodge, minister of the Third Presbyterian Church, married Sarah Ridgely, daughter of the prominent banker Nicholas H. Ridgely.

77. Thomas Yeatman delivered a prohibition lecture.

78. In 1868 Mrs. Dwight Brown's husband was elected sheriff of Sangamon County.

79. Representative Hall was a part of the state capitol. George D. Prentice (1802–70) edited the *Louisville* (Ky.) *Journal.* Nicholas H. Ridgely (1800–88) was a prominent Springfield banker whose autocratic manner earned him the sobriquet "Czar Nicholas."

80. In 1840 Benjamin S. Edwards (1818–86), youngest son of the first territorial governor of Illinois, began practicing law. He paid little attention to politics, though he was elected judge of a circuit court in 1869.

81. Joseph Jackson Grimshaw (1820–75), an Illinois lawyer and Republican politician, had practiced law in Pittsfield (1843–57) and then moved to Quincy, where he ran unsuccessfully for Congress in 1856 and 1858.

82. William H. Bissell (1811–60) practiced law in Belleville, fought with distinction in the Mexican War, won election to the U.S. House (1848), and served as governor of Illinois (1857–60).

83. Mary Todd Lincoln to Emilie Todd Helm, Springfield, 16 Feb. 1857, in *Mary Todd Lincoln: Her Life and Letters*, ed. Justin G. Turner and Linda Levitt Turner (New York: Knopf, 1972), 48.

84. Springfield correspondence, *Democratic Press*, n.d., copied in the *Illinois State Register* (Springfield), 12 May 1854.

85. *Thomas's note:* During this period Roberts, Whitney, Parks, Fuller, Swett and Orme each had one case in the Supreme Court for the Second Grand Division; Lacey, Young and Manning each had two. From 1858 to 1860 Prettyman, Roberts and Davison had cases from Tazewell County, but it was not in the circuit at that time. Moore, Manning, Prettyman, Swett, Orme, Purple, Roberts, Parks and Scott appeared occasionally in the Federal courts.

86. Virginia-born David Allen Smith (1809–65) settled at first in Carlinville in 1837 before moving to Jacksonville two years later. In 1837 he emancipated the slaves he had inherited from his father.

87. Murray McConnel (1798–1869), one of the first lawyers to practice in Mor-

gan County, was a wealthy landowner who served as Democrat in the Illinois state legislature, where he championed the building of the Northern Cross Railroad connecting Jacksonville and Meredosia. In 1855 he became fifth auditor of the U.S. Treasury.

88. Archibald Williams (1801–63) was a Whig member of the Illinois legislature (1832–40) and a U.S. district attorney (1849–53). Chauncey Higbee served as a judge. Democrat Almeron Wheat, who served in the Illinois House of Representatives (1842–44), was "an able lawyer" with a "considerable practice" in Adams county. Palmer, ed., *Bench and Bar of Illinois,* 882. A good friend of John Hay, William N. Grover moved to St. Louis, where he became U.S. district attorney for the Eastern District of Missouri during the Civil War. Democrat William C. Goudy (1824–93), a graduate of Illinois College in Jacksonville, studied law with Stephen T. Logan and was admitted to the bar in 1847, when he settled in Lewistown. He served as state's attorney (1852–55) and as a state senator (1856–60). He later moved to Chicago, where he became a successful corporate attorney. New York–born S. Corning Judd (1827–95) settled in Lewistown in 1854. Nineteen years later, he moved to Chicago, where he served as postmaster (1885–89). Attorney and politician Joseph Gillespie (1809–85) was a good friend of Lincoln and a judge of the Illinois state circuit court (1861–73).

89. John M. Palmer (1817–1900), a leading Democrat in southern Illinois, broke with his party in 1854 over the Kansas-Nebraska Act and became a Republican.

90. An attorney in Pittsfield, William A. Grimshaw had been born and raised in Philadelphia, where his father William was a noted and prolific author. He served in the Illinois House of Representatives with Lincoln (1840–42).

12 *Edwin M. Stanton Takes Over the War Department*

When Edwin M. Stanton joined Lincoln's cabinet as Secretary of War in mid-January 1862, a New York doctor, who had known Stanton in California, commented ruefully: "He will tomahawk them all." People for the most part, however, thought Lincoln had made a wise choice. The New York diarist George Templeton Strong, treasurer of the United States Sanitary Commission, calling on Stanton with other members of that organization, reported that all of them were favorably impressed. At the lowest estimate, Stanton would be worth "a wagon load of Camerons," thought Strong. He was not handsome, as Strong saw him, in fact he was "rather pigfaced"—a robust, "Lutheroid" type of man. But he was prompt, intelligent, earnest, and warmhearted, "the reverse in all things of his cunning, coldblooded, selfish old predecessor." Stanton, at the moment, was the most popular man in Washington. But, asked Strong, "will it last?"[1]

Charles A. Dana, assistant editor of the *New York Tribune* and a close friend of Stanton, heralded his appointment to the war office with a glowing editorial. It was not true that the selection of a Democrat meant triumph for the policy of "border-State twaddling" on the slavery issue, Dana

Undated typescript, Benjamin P. Thomas Papers, Illinois State Historical Library, Springfield. Much of the material in this essay is not included in Thomas's biography of Stanton, which Harold Hyman completed after Thomas's death: *Stanton: The Life and Times of Lincoln's Secretary of War* (New York: Knopf, 1962).

wrote. Stanton was committed only to the maintenance of the Union. "If slavery or anti-slavery shall at any time be found obstructing or impeding the nation in its efforts to crush out this monstrous rebellion, he will walk straight on the path of duty, though that path should lead him over or through the impediment, and insure its annihilation." The public expected energy and vigor of Stanton, Dana said, and it would not be disappointed. Stanton would not dictate to McClellan, the general in chief of the armies. He would be a "zealous cooperator," not "a lordly superior."[2]

Stanton thanked Dana for his "admirable" editorial, "stating my position and purpose." He hoped that all loyal men would stand on watch and aid him. "Bad passions, and little passions, and mean passions gather around and hem in the great movement that should deliver this nation," he wrote. But he was not dismayed or disheartened. Already he felt a determined spirit growing up around him: "We have no jokes or trivialities," he told Dana, making an oblique thrust at Lincoln, "but all with whom I act show that they are now in dead earnest." Then, revealing a sterner attitude toward McClellan than that which Dana had ascribed to him, he added: "As soon as I get the machinery of the office working, the rats cleaned out, & the ratholes stopped, we shall move. This army has got to fight or run away; and while men are striving nobly in the West, the champagne and oysters on the Potomac must be stopped. But patience for a short while only is all I ask, if you and others like you will rally around me."[3]

Stanton immediately set himself to cleaning out the rats' nests in the old, dilapidated, four-story brick building at the corner of Pennsylvania Avenue and 17th Street that had housed the War Department for more than forty years. His problem was simpler than Simon Cameron's had been, for at least some progress had been made under the nine-months' stress of war toward bringing the personnel, equipment, and procedures of that department into line with vastly enlarged requirements. Cameron had had to start almost from scratch in providing clothes, food, weapons, and innumerable items of equipment for an army that now numbered more than half a million men. Stanton's task would be to augment, reform, and systematize, so as to enlist the country's manpower and economic resources in the efficient prosecution of the burgeoning war effort.

The War Department was still seriously undermanned for such an all-out effort, and still burdened with old functionaries. Unopened mail accumulated on tables and desktops. Letters got mixed up. Some duties needlessly overlapped, while others remained unassigned. Officers seeking promotions, soldiers wanting sick leave, [and] civilians on every imaginable sort of business thronged the rooms and hallways.

Before Stanton had been in office two weeks, he persuaded Congress to authorize the appointment of two more assistant secretaries, bringing the total to three, forty-nine clerks, four messengers, and two laborers, and the further addition of ten noncommissioned officers to the adjutant-general's staff. New jobs brought a rush of eager applicants, but Stanton gave preference to soldiers unfit for field service because of wounds or minor physical defects.

As his new assistant secretaries, Stanton chose Peter H. Watson, who had been associated with him in a number of important law cases, and John Tucker, a Pennsylvanian, who had assisted Cameron in organizing rail and water transportation in the East.[4] Since the holdover assistant secretary, Thomas A. Scott, formerly vice-president of the Pennsylvania Railroad, was also a Pennsylvanian, the appointment of Tucker brought outcries from political spoilsmen in New York.[5] Ex-President James Buchanan commented to Harriet Lane, his niece, that "with Scott & Tucker for assistant Secretaries the 'Ring' will probably still flourish & the buzzards which surrounded the War Department from Pennsylvania under Cameron will still find carrion under Stanton. But this must be without his knowledge."[6]

Stanton ordered the War Department closed to visitors on Tuesdays, Wednesdays, Thursdays, and Fridays, except for matters relating directly to active military operations. Saturdays were reserved for the business of senators and representatives. The public could call only on Mondays. He took over matters of internal security from the State Department. Under authorization of Congress, he assumed control of the telegraph system and stood ready, in case of necessity, to take over the railroads. He instituted rigid control of purchases.

Stanton organized a war board of his bureau chiefs: General Lorenzo Thomas, the Adjutant-General, General Montgomery C. Meigs, the Quartermaster General, General James W. Ripley, Chief of Ordnance, General James G. Totten, Chief Engineer, and Colonel Joseph P. Taylor, Commissary General.[7] The board met several times a week, and the verbatim reports of its sessions give penetrating insights into backstage happenings. Unfortunately they are available for a period of only a few weeks. The presence of the Confederate ironclad *Merrimac* at Norfolk, not far from McClellan's base at Fortress Monroe, caused Stanton constant worry. In fact, he was far more concerned about her than was Secretary Welles of the Navy, who seemed confident that the *Monitor*, having once worsted her, could keep her immobilized. Stanton often brought up the matter of the *Merrimac* at meetings of the war board. At one such session, General Totten wondered if she could be taken by boarding. "I do not see how they can get on her decks," Meigs said. "Capt. Wise, of the Navy, says that she is as high out of the water as the ceiling of the rooms in the President's House." Stanton commented: "It seems now as if the Navy is [as] determined to exaggerate her, as much as they underrated her before."[8] Stanton called Charles Ellet to a meeting of the board. Builder of the famous Wheeling Bridge, and a railroad expert, he had been called into consultation by both the British and the Russians during the Crimean War, and had long been advocating the use of steam rams in naval warfare.[9] Stanton had become acquainted with him as a hostile witness during a law case involving the Wheeling Bridge, and now wanted his opinion on the vulnerability of the *Monitor*. "I was engaged in a seven years' fight with him," Stanton told the members of the war board, "and there was not a single point, from coaling up to running an engine, that he did not bring up the strangest theories, and get men to swear to them. . . . He cannot be beat in figures. He would cipher anybody to death."[10] Ellet offered the opinion that the *Monitor* could not be relied on to hold the *Merrimac* in check. She could easily be boarded because of her low deck. Her revolving turret could be jammed with crowbars. She could be rammed and pierced below the waterline. General Totten said he had received a letter suggesting the use of a sort of raft alongside a vessel to ward off the attack of steam rams like the *Merrimac* and wondered whether he should refer it to the Navy Department. Stanton observed sourly: "It might as well be put in the fire."[11] It would appear that jealousy and rivalry between our armed services are not of modern vintage.

General John C. Fremont, who had botched up affairs at St. Louis by issuing an unauthorized emancipation proclamation and by favoring his friends with luscious contracts, had recently been appointed to a new command in western Virginia. When Fremont sent a list of proposed staff appointments to the War Department from New York City, the crusty Stanton said to General Thomas: "I will not allow Generals to carry on the war in New York. We have two Generals—Fremont and Hunter— holding court in New York, taking proposals from members of Congress for appointments on their staffs."[12] Nor would Stanton allow Fremont to appoint his own paymasters and quartermasters. "I see that they are organizing just such a gang as they had at St. Louis," he told Thomas, "and I intend to prevent it. . . . I want to hear of his being in his Department as soon as possible."[13]

A matter touching a close friend of the President arose when it was disclosed that Col. Edward D. Baker, killed at the battle of Ball's Bluff, had failed to account for $10,000, which he had been granted to raise a regiment.[14] A Philadelphia firm had submitted to the War Department a

bill for $600, duly attested, which they had spent on Baker's authoriza-
tion for newspaper advertisements soliciting recruits. Stanton told General Thomas to advise the firm to make claim against Baker's estate. "I
hear that Baker had an interest in contracts for clothing," Stanton said,
"and I would tell these parties that he had no lawful authority to bind
the United States. . . . I would just reject this account, and send the parties to the Court of Claims."[15]

Stanton noticed that generals often illegally enlarged their staffs by
having officers appointed to the staffs of McClellan, the commander in
chief, or Halleck, commander of the Western Department, and then seeing to it that they were reassigned to them. General "Jim" Lane, a Kansas senator, who had bivouacked a "Frontier Guard" in the East Room
of the White House during the first trying days of the war, was an outstanding offender in the matter of staff officers.[16] Leaving Washington
with a brigadier-general's commission and authority to raise two regiments, Lane, in western Missouri, had gained the reputation of an irre-
sponsible "jayhawker" by showing little respect for the property of civilians on either side. But his early manifestations of loyalty and his
infectious enthusiasm had won Lincoln's favor, and when he returned
again to Washington, Lincoln offered him the command of an expedition
into Arkansas.

At a meeting of the war board, General Thomas informed Stanton
that Lane had assured him he intended to accept the Arkansas assign-
ment, and that he had already brought about the reassignment of ten or
fifteen officers from McClellan's staff to his own. Since then, declared
Thomas, he had heard nothing further from him and did not know where
he was. The following colloquy took place:

Stanton: "I would not hunt for him or his staff."
Gen. Thomas: "But his staff are on duty."
Stanton: "I would stop their pay."
Gen. Thomas: "But I want to discharge them."
Stanton: "Well, strike them from the rolls."
Gen. Thomas: "One of the persons on the staff the President does not
want discharged. If I discharge one I must discharge all."
Stanton: "While I administer this office, I will not sanction an abuse
of that kind. Discharge them all. If the President don't like it, let him so
intimate, and I will retire."[17]

Before Stanton had been in the War Department a week, newsmen
and other callers noticed how his influence had permeated the place.
Joshua F. Speed, calling at the Department to obtain arms for use in Kentucky, wrote to Joseph Holt that he had "accomplished in a few days what

heretofore it would have taken as many weeks. . . . Instead of that loose shackeling way of doing business in the War Office, with which I have been so much disgusted & which I have had so good an opportunity of seeing—there is now—order regularity and precision." Speed expected Stanton to "infuse into the whole army an energy & activity which we have not seen heretofore."[18]

But old-timers in the Department were not so greatly impressed. Kermit Pritchett, a clerk, writing to let former War Secretary Cameron know how things were getting on without him, complained of "a general moan around the walls of the Department. It appears in truth as if daily, confusion grows worse confounded," he said. "The personnel of the Department is uppermost and the material business utterly neglected. We have orders upon orders, all seeming predicated upon the idea that every thing heretofore was disorder and fraud." Papers were now filed "under as many heads as the curiosities at Barnum's museum." To find anything was like "digging out a badger with the aid of a dozen ferrets and as many terriers."

To hear Jim Moore, another clerk, "describe the new order of *disorder*," continued Pritchett, "and his labors on his knees, with his nose in the pigeon holes would make a saint laugh." With Assistant Secretary Watson, formerly a lawyer, every letter was a "Declaration," every order an "Indictment." Quartermaster General Meigs was distressed at his inability "to penetrate the rubbish, and get at the new machinery to set his wheels a-going, which are all at a standstill for want of motion of the main shaft, the tinkering and oiling occupying all the time and nothing done." Clerks worked until midnight, sometimes until three in the morning. "Secretary Stanton is doubtless a great man, since you have endorsed him," observed Pritchett, but it seemed to persons in the Department that he displayed "but little sympathy and small appreciation for labors that are breaking many of us down."[19]

But Stanton did not ask more of others that he was willing to do himself. Seldom quitting before ten o'clock at night, he was the first to break down. One day, less than a month after taking over the Department, he keeled over in his office, apparently from a stroke, and had to be taken home in an ambulance. It turned out to be only vertigo, induced by exhaustion; he was back at work within four days.

Stanton's illness afforded the employees a chance to catch their breath. Samuel Wilkeson, a correspondent of the *New York Tribune,* wrote to Cameron that he had seized the opportunity to measure General Thomas's legs, and found them reduced to pipe stems from standing at Stanton's elbow answering questions hours on end.[20] "At Lochiel [Cameron's home in Pennsylvania]," breathed Wilkeson, "Thomas and I, un-burthened of work and spread meditatively each over his armchair, yes-terday compared the present with the past and we sighed for a good old gentleman that we wot of up in Pennsylvania, who delightfully mingled social courtesies with the intelligent and prompt dispatch of business, and who conferred benefits so gracefully that the receiver was never humiliated but yet was tenderly bound in a life long debt of gratitude. When the younger of these two regretful friends, arose with the benedic-tion, 'God bless Simon Cameron,' the Adjutant General piously added, 'aye, God bless him!'"[21]

Business in the War Department began officially at nine o'clock. As Stanton's carriage turned off Pennsylvania Avenue around that time, the doorkeeper would stick his head inside and announce: "The Secretary." The word spread; stragglers and loungers scurried to their desks and the place quivered with activity. Alighting from his carriage, Stanton was usually beset by favor-seekers, waiting on the sidewalk. He might stop for a word with a soldier or a needy-looking woman, but he would curtly tell the others to go to his reception room upstairs.

Proceeding to his private office on the second floor, in a corner over-looking the White House, Stanton immediately began pulling on the tas-selled cord that set a bell to jangling in the hallway and brought messen-gers on the run. All day that bell would jangle like a "moral tone," as one clerk put it, "filling the ears and minds of the working staff with lessons of duty and necessity." Sometimes Stanton sat at his desk, but quite as often he worked standing, at a large, high table as a means of getting exercise. Men close to Stanton believed that his irritability, which became more marked as the war wore on, came in large measure from poor health. Asthma, with which he had been afflicted from the age of ten, never ceased to rack him, sometimes to the point of strangulation, and he also developed a liver ailment. Whenever this complaint became acute, he was obliged to stop smoking the cigars that eased his asthma.

Stanton considered it a duty to see as many business-callers as he could, but it was impossible to give everyone a private audience, and even senators and representatives, sometimes finding it impossible to see him on the day set apart for them, took "potluck" with the crowd in the re-ception room. On Mondays, when the public was admitted, this room was always jammed, and Stanton, emerging from his office, walked across it with a somewhat awkward gait because of his stiff knee, and took his place behind a chest-high writing desk. He had injured the knee some years before at Pittsburgh, when he fell into the hold of an Ohio River boat while obtaining evidence for a law case.

Waving back those who approached him, Stanton would make a slow, deliberate scrutiny of the crowd, confer briefly with the officer in charge, to learn whether any cases merited special attention, then summon some-one forward. Soldiers usually got first chance, and then soldiers' wives and widows. If a soldier carried crutches or showed the marks of wounds, Stanton often left the desk and talked to him where he sat. Wounded officers were also granted solicitous attention; otherwise shoulder-straps were likely to meet a cool reception. Everyone was required to state his business quickly in the hearing of the others.

Stanton personified force and competence as he stood behind the tall desk, looking each visitor squarely, almost defiantly, in the eye, his own eyes glittering through polished steel-rimmed spectacles, his broad nos-trils tremulous when he became excited, his forehead wide though not especially high, his complexion dark and mottled as though from high living, his dark hair beginning to thin a bit, and his lips compressed above the immense black beard that gave off a mixed odor of tobacco and co-logne. Middle age had put considerable flesh on his short frame; his movements were deliberate, almost studied. He reminded General Wil-liam E. Doster, provost marshal of the District of Columbia, of a school-master who had had a poor night's sleep.[22]

At Stanton's entrance a hush fell on the room; people conversed under their breaths, and the clerks and orderlies moved about with soft-footed deference. So-called "influential people" tried their influence only once, Doster declared, "acquaintances at the bar tried it and were rebuffed, corrupt people found themselves suspected before they drew near. Women in tears, venerable old men, approached slowly—but withdrew quickly as if they had touched hot iron. A few got what they wanted and earned it in the getting. . . . But at bottom there was nothing terrible. Stanton was an able, overworked Pittsburgh lawyer, suddenly called on to play the combined roles of Carnot and Fouche, apparently utterly ignorant of both roles, and equipped with no special talents other than the profes-sional ones—ability to work, dogmatic temper, a bullying propensity. He was possessed of an assurance that lays hold of the most novel cases, a contempt for scientific training as compared with talent and labor, a keen insight into shams and disguises, an insensibility to all emotions except those of danger and bodily harm. This lawyer was really practicing law . . . a nation his client, but the difference was only in the size of the case. As in his law office, red tape, papers, precedents, decisions were his business here. As there he knew he could abuse his clerk as much as he chose, provided he won his case, so here he knew, no matter what he did, all would be right, if he secured the verdict. One thing was mandatory, he must not throw up the case—that no good lawyer does. Now let all the people stand aside and give him scope. . . . The verdict—victory—the suppression of Rebellion were the goal. Nothing else counted."[23]

Stanton's young cousin, William Stanton, appeared in the line of visitors one day to intercede for a good friend—a colonel seeking promotion. "Well, what do you want, William?" Stanton asked suspiciously. The young man told him briefly and handed up a sheaf of papers—the colonel's recommendations. Stanton wrote on the outside sheet: "The promotion cannot be made," signed his name, and handed them to his secretary, saying: "Send these papers back through the proper military channel." Then turning to the young man he asked in a softer tone: "How is your mother?" "Very well, thank you," he replied. "I'm glad to hear it," said Stanton; "come and breakfast with me at nine o'clock tomorrow morning." He prided himself on never allowing personal relationships or friendships to swerve him from duty; but he was not always cold. When General Frederick W. Lander died from wounds suffered in the field, soon after Stanton took office, the Secretary himself called on Mrs. Lander to tell her what had happened, trying to bring comfort along with the bad news.[24]

Stanton's hair-trigger temper would explode at a word or a gesture, and at such times he would dash the glasses before his eyes far up on his forehead, as though they pained him or obstructed his vision; the muscles of his face would twitch, and his voice would tremble with intensity, though he seldom raised its pitch. But the storm would pass away as quickly as it came, and be succeeded by an almost frightening calm. If the victim of Stanton's temper was a subordinate, the Secretary at their next meeting, would put his hand on the man's shoulder in a kindly and seemingly unconscious manner, or comment that he looked tired and must take a little rest. If the offended person stood high in the Department, the Secretary might confide an important piece of news to him. Though Stanton seemed incapable of offering an apology, he would find some means of expiation, if it amounted to no more than a word of appreciation for a new blotting-pad on his desk.

Stanton's intense emotions were always close to the surface. The news of Grant's victory at Fort Donelson arrived at the War Department on a Monday, when Stanton's reception room was filled with the usual crowd. When a dispatch was handed to the Secretary he held up his arms for silence, read it to the crowd, and, almost jumping with excitement, proposed three cheers and a tiger. They "were of course given with immense vigor," a clerk wrote, "which shook the old walls, broke all the spiders' webs, and set the rats scampering."

One indulgence Stanton allowed himself beside cigars. Three mornings a week, before going to the Department, he visited the city market, according to a practice he had begun before the war, to provide for the family table. He liked to exchange gossip and banter with the garrulous stallkeepers; the sights and smells of the market brought back memories of pleasant country living. A manservant accompanied him and took his purchases home.

The Stantons lived in splendid style in a large three-story brick house on H Street, spending far more than his salary as Secretary of War, for his pre-war earnings as a lawyer had put him in easy circumstances. The Stantons also did considerable entertaining, notwithstanding the long hours he put in at the War Department. Like the other cabinet ladies, Mrs. Stanton held a sort of open house on Monday, which was known as "cabinet calling day." An Iowa lady, attending one of these affairs, observed that Mrs. Stanton "is very handsome, and receives her friends with easy dignity." But John Hay, the President's young secretary, commented, after dining at the Stantons: "A pleasant little dinner, and a pretty wife as white and cold and motionless as marble whose rare smiles seemed to pain her."[25]

Like Lincoln, Stanton wore a stove-pipe hat, and, unlike the President, was particular about his clothes. He never carried money on his person, and never wore a watch. Twice a week a war department [messenger?] shaved his upper lip in his office. The Stantons were irregular attendants at the Episcopal church.

Stanton's appointment to the War Department caused mixed reactions among the members of Lincoln's cabinet. Secretary of the Treasury Salmon P. Chase had known Stanton intimately some years before in Ohio, when both men were rising young lawyers. At that time, Stanton was an outspoken antislavery man (his father had been an abolitionist); and Chase, veering ever more openly toward the Republican radicals since entering Lincoln's cabinet, and not realizing that Stanton's sentiments might have changed, thought he was gaining an ally. Secretary of State William H. Seward, on the other hand, leader of the moderates, having first met Stanton after the latter had become a Buchanan Democrat, supposed that he was opposed to drastic action against slavery, and expected him to line up on his side.

Chase, continuing to call regularly at the War Department, where he had exercised an important influence during Cameron's tenure, was disappointed to find that, though graciously received, he seemed unable to recapture the intimacy and influence with Stanton that he known in the Ohio days. The canny and cryptic Seward resorted to subtler methods. He seldom called at the War Department; but the Stantons were regularly invited to his frequent dinner parties, where he expounded his moderate views to the new Secretary while they lounged comfortably in his library, puffing their after-dinner Havanas and sipping Seward's vintage wines.

Attorney General Edward Bates, the oldest member of the cabinet, slim of body but rugged of face, a cautious and literal logician who had passed over Stanton in favor of another man, when selecting an attorney general for the District of Columbia a few months earlier, now sized up the newcomer as "a man of mind and action."[26] Stanton would have little personal contact with Caleb Smith, the Secretary of Interior. But in Postmaster-General Montgomery Blair, six feet tall, erect, a West Pointer turned lawyer, he would encounter a man of stubborn purpose and contriving mind, who questioned Stanton's personal honesty and political integrity. Montgomery's father, Frank P. Blair Sr., once a member of President Andrew Jackson's kitchen cabinet, now enjoying the role of elder statesman, felt that when Cameron left the War Department he himself had been turned out. "I have no acquaintance with Mr. Stanton," he wrote to Cameron, "& where I was wont to go at pleasure, the door is now shut."[27]

The cabinet member who regarded Stanton with the greatest aversion, however, was Navy Secretary Gideon Welles, onetime Jacksonian Democrat like Stanton himself, close friend of the Blairs, a former Connecticut editor whose sole experience in naval matters came from service as Chief of the Bureau of Provisions and Clothing in the Navy Department under Polk. Upright, plain-spoken, fearless, with the Puritan's proclivity for more readily discerning men's faults than recognizing their virtues, Welles was a shy, unsocial man, who toothsomely gossiped with himself during his leisure hours while recording his impressions of people and events in his voluminous and penetrating diary. He liked to "catch people in the suds," he said, "to fall upon them by surprise, when it is washing day." Welles's Olympian visage—long hair and magnificent gray beard, thick eyebrows, and commanding nose—caused Lincoln, out of Welles's hearing, to call him "Father Neptune," just as he would come to call Stanton "Mars."[28]

When Stanton entered the cabinet, Welles regarded him as a potential enemy; he suspected that Stanton had been predisposed against him by political rivals and disappointed contractors who had put Welles under fire in the press. Welles did not allow these suspicions to color his surface attitude, however, and met Stanton with formal courtesy. But Stanton forthwith stirred Welles's bile by taking it for granted that the army dog would wag the navy tail. Welles made it clear that the navy was a coordinate branch of the service, that it would cooperate with the land forces, but only on a basis of equality and not under army orders. The two men sparred and feinted, then clashed in a test of strength. Thereafter Stanton, somewhat chopfallen, sidestepped the peppery old shellback whenever he found it possible to do so.

Welles sized up Stanton as a man who loved the exercise of power. Granting that he was vigilant, devoted, and a dynamo for work, Welles thought he lacked moral courage and self-reliance under stress. "He took pleasure in being ungracious and rough towards those who were under his control," Welles wrote, "and when he thought his bearish manner would terrify or humiliate those who were subject to him. To his superiors or those who were his equals in position, and who neither needed nor cared for his violence, he was complacent, sometimes obsequious." During the pre-war political tussles, Welles had come to detest Seward as a man of slack principles, and he believed that Seward had brought Stanton into the cabinet under a pledge of fealty to himself. "The Secretary of State supposed," wrote Welles, "as did his predecessor Jeremiah S. Black under Buchanan, that Stanton was an appendage to him in the Administration, and they each, though diametrically opposed in their principles and views of government, had a common interest in all that took place." Welles believed too that Stanton toadied to the congressional committee on the conduct of the war, so that it would help cover up the War Department's shortcomings.[29]

The President, who found himself in the middle of all this cabinet hassling, revealed his attitude toward Stanton when Congressman Henry L. Dawes of Massachusetts came to the White House to congratulate him on selecting such an able man to head the War Department. Lincoln agreed that Stanton was making a grand beginning, although people had warned him that the vigorous new Secretary might "run away with the whole concern."[30] Stanton reminded Lincoln of an old Methodist preacher he had heard about out West, who performed so energetically in the pulpit that some of his parishioners feared that it might become necessary to put bricks in his pockets to hold him down. Lincoln said: "We may be obliged to serve Stanton that same way; but I guess we'll just let him jump a while first.'"[31]

Notes

1. George Templeton Strong, *The Diary of George Templeton Strong*, 4 vols., ed. Allan Nevins and Milton Halsey Thomas (New York: Macmillan, 1952), 3:203 (entry for 29 Jan. 1862).

2. George C. Gorham, *Life and Public Services of Edwin M. Stanton*, 2 vols. (Boston: Houghton Mifflin, 1899), 1:243.

3. Edwin M. Stanton to Charles A. Dana, Washington, 24 Jan. 1862, Charles A. Dana Papers, quoted in Benjamin P. Thomas and Harold M. Hyman, *Stanton: The Life and Times of Lincoln's Secretary of War* (New York: Knopf, 1962), 170.

4. "He appointed his trusted friend Peter Watson to one of the new assistant secretary posts; he had promised to take on this responsibility before Stanton had been willing to join Lincoln's cabinet, and Stanton now insisted that he redeem this pledge. Short, stout, with red hair and beard, a man of business acumen whose driving energy matched that of Stanton, Watson, like Stanton, sacrificed an income amounting to many times his government salary in accepting the post. The country's leading patent attorney, Watson had an expert knowledge of mechanical principles and devices." Thomas and Hyman, *Stanton*, 152–53. On May 8, 1861, Cameron named as general agent in charge of transportation John Tucker, a civilian who had no background in the field. One historian commented that although "there might have been some justification for his appointment for the first flush of war work, it is difficult to see why such an unqualified person was entrusted with this responsible task long after that time had passed." A. Howard Meneely, *The War Department, 1861: A Study in Mobilization and Administration* (New York: Columbia University Press, 1928), 130.

5. In 1861 Thomas Alexander Scott (1823–81) was appointed assistant secretary of war in charge of all government railroads and transportation lines.

6. James Buchanan to Harriet Lane, Wheatland, near Lancaster, 16 Jan. 1862, Buchanan Papers, Historical Society of Pennsylvania.

7. Lorenzo Thomas (1804–75) served as adjutant general of the army (1861–69). Montgomery Cunningham Meigs (1816–92) served as quartermaster general (1861–82). James Wolfe Ripley (1794–1870) served as chief of ordnance from 1861 to 1863, when he was forced to step down because of his opposition to the introduction of breech-loading rifles. Joseph Gilbert Totten (1788–1864) served as chief engineer of the army from 1838 until his death. Joseph Pannell Taylor (1796–1864), brother of President Zachary Taylor, served as commissary general from 1861 until his death.

8. Proceedings of the War Board, stenographic minutes of a meeting held on 13 March 1862, Stanton Papers, Library of Congress. Lt. Henry Augustus Wise, USN (1819–69), author of *Los Gringos* (1849) and *Tales from the Marines* (1855), became chief of the Bureau of Ordnance and Hydrography. He published under the pen name Harry Gringo. John Hay enjoyed what he called Wise's "fantastic fun." Hay to Harriet Loring, Madrid, 30 June 1870, Hay Papers, Brown University. William Howard Russell called Wise "really smart clever quick." Martin Crawford, ed., *William Howard Russell's Civil War: Private Diary and Letters, 1861–1862* (Athens: University of Georgia Press, 1992), 114 (entry for 31 Aug. 1861).

9. Pennsylvania-born Charles Ellet, Jr., (1810–62) also designed suspension bridges for Philadelphia, which opened in 1842, and the international railroad bridge that opened in 1855 at Niagara Falls. His advice about steam rams was ignored until the success of the *Merrimac*. Thereafter he was commissioned to create a steam-ram fleet in the West. He died of a wound received while commanding his makeshift flotilla.

10. Proceedings of the War Board, stenographic minutes of a meeting held on 20 March 1862, Stanton Papers, Library of Congress.

11. Ibid.

12. Minutes of a War Board meeting on 25 March 1862, Stanton Papers, Library of Congress.

13. Minutes of a War Board meeting on 21 March 1862, Stanton Papers, Library of Congress.

14. Ibid. In 1875 Stephen T. Logan told John G. Nicolay, "My partnership with him [Baker] in the practice of law was formed in 1841. I had had Baker before that. But I soon found I could not trust him in money matters. He got me into some scrapes by collecting and using money though he made it all right afterwards. You know Baker was a perfectly reckless man in matters of money." Nicolay's conversation with S. T. Logan at Springfield, 6 July 1875, in *An Oral History of Abraham Lincoln: John G. Nicolay's Interviews and Essays*, ed. Michael Burlingame (Carbondale: Southern Illinois University Press, 1996), 38.

15. Minutes of a War Board meeting on 21 March 1862, Stanton Papers, Library of Congress.

16. James H. Lane (1814–66) represented Kansas in the U.S. Senate (1861–66). When Virginia adopted a secession ordinance on April 17, 1861, authorities in Washington, fearing for the safety of the capital, took emergency measures. After consulting with Gen. Winfield Scott and Secretary of War Simon Cameron, Maj. David Hunter, in charge of security for the president, appealed to Senator Lane to organize a special White House guard. Lane immediately gathered a force of fifty to a hundred men, dubbed them the Frontier Guard, and led them to the Executive Mansion. Later Nicolay and Hay described the scene: "After spending the evening in an exceedingly rudimentary squad drill, under the light of the gorgeous gas chandeliers, they disposed themselves in picturesque bivouac on the brilliant-patterned velvet carpet—perhaps the most luxurious cantonment which American soldiers have ever enjoyed. Their motley composition, their anomalous surroundings, the extraordinary emergency, their mingled awkwardness and earnestness, rendered the scene a medley of bizarre contradictions—a blending of masquerade and tragedy, of grim humor and realistic seriousness—a combination of Don Quixote and Daniel Boone altogether impossible to describe." John G. Nicoly and John Hay, *Abraham Lincoln: A History*, 10 vols. (New York: Century, 1890), 4:107.

17. Minutes of a War Board meeting on 21 March 1862, Stanton Papers, Library of Congress.

18. J. F. Speed to Joseph Holt, Washington, 4 Feb. 1862, Holt Papers, Library of Congress.

19. K. Pritchett to Simon Cameron, 2 Feb. 1862, Cameron Papers, Library of Congress.

20. Samuel Wilkeson, a native of Buffalo and a graduate of Union College, headed the Washington bureau of the *Tribune*. Before the war he had been an editor and part owner of Thurlow Weed's *Albany Evening Journal*, but after a falling out with Weed, Wilkeson joined forces with Horace Greeley, Weed's nemesis in New York politics.

21. Samuel Wilkeson to Simon Cameron, 12 Feb. 1862, Cameron Papers, Library of Congress.

22. William E. Doster, *Lincoln and Episodes of the Civil War* (New York: G. P. Putnam's Sons, 1915), 115.

23. Doster, *Lincoln and Episodes of the Civil War,* 116–17. Lazare Carnot (1753–1823), Napoleon's minister of war, earned the sobriquet "the organizer of victory." Joseph Fouche (1759–1815) was Napoleon's minister of police.

24. Gen. Frederick West Lander (1821–62), well known for his work on transcontinental surveys in the 1850s, died on March 2, 1862. He had in the spring of 1861 assisted McClellan in the campaigns in West Virginia. In charge of a division, he successfully defended Hancock, Maryland, from a Confederate assault in January 1862 and the following month led an attack near Bloomery Gap. Jean Margaret Davenport Lander (1829–1903), a celebrated, English-born actress, took over the direction of Union hospitals in Port Royal, S.C., shortly after the death of her husband, Gen. Frederick Lander, on March 2, 1862. After the war she returned to the stage, where she won acclaim.

25. John Hay, *Inside Lincoln's White House: The Complete Civil War Diary of John Hay,* ed. Michael Burlingame and John R. Turner Ettlinger (Carbondale: Southern Illinois University Press, 1997), 37 (entry for 1 Sept. 1862).

26. Edward Bates, *The Diary of Edward Bates, 1859–1866,* ed. Howard K. Beale, vol. 4 of the Annual Report of the American Historical Association for the Year 1930 (Washington: Government Printing Office, 1933), 228 (entry for 2 Feb. 1862).

27. F. P. Blair to Simon Cameron, Silver Spring, Md., 30 Jan. 1862, Cameron Papers, Library of Congress. Francis P. Blair, Sr. (1791–1876) edited the *Washington Globe,* a Democratic journal, but became a Free-Soiler in 1848 and a Republican in the following decade.

28. Lincoln's endorsement on an envelope forwarded to Welles and Stanton, 7 March 1863, in *Collected Works,* ed. Basler et al., 8:512. Gideon Welles (1802–78) received unusually competent help from Assistant Secretary Gustavus V. Fox and Chief Clerk William Faxon.

29. Gideon Welles, *The Diary of Gideon Welles, Secretary of the Navy under Lincoln and Johnson,* 3 vols., ed. Howard K. Beale (New York: W. W. Norton, 1960), 1:67–69.

30. H. L. Dawes, "Recollections of Stanton under Lincoln," *Atlantic Monthly* 73 (Feb. 1894): 163. Henry Laurens Dawes (1816–1903) of North Adams represented his district in the U.S. House (1857–75). He also served in the U.S. Senate (1875–93).

31. Dawes, "Recollections of Stanton under Lincoln," 163.

PART 3

The Biographers of Lincoln

13   *Backstage with the Lincoln Biographers*

So many people have yielded to that seemingly irresistible impulse to write books about Abraham Lincoln that a few years ago a certain individual took it upon himself to write a sort of biography of the Lincoln biographers. If that strikes you as being funny, it is even funnier than you think; because I was that individual.[1] And yet there was ample justification for my doing what I did.

A man develops his own character, but if he becomes sufficiently prominent for the world to want to know him, he is portrayed for posterity by his biographers. And what the man really was, and what his image comes to be, after it has been reflected and refracted through the minds of others, may be extremely different.

This is especially so in the case of a man like Lincoln, where each generation of biographers has built upon the work of its predecessors, and where the groundwork was laid by persons who wrote from their own recollections or from the recollections of others. For a person writing history from what he remembers of it, or from what he did to shape it, history becomes an extremely subjective matter; whereas the aim of the modern historian is to view his characters objectively.

So a major task of recent Lincoln scholarship has been to discount the subjective bias of the early Lincoln writers.

Undated manuscript, Benjamin P. Thomas Papers, Illinois State Historical Library, Springfield.

Nowhere are a writer's slants, conceits, and prejudices so well revealed as in his personal letters, and with this thought in mind I began, several years ago, to ransack the libraries for the personal correspondence of the big names in Lincoln literature. And I reaped a plentiful harvest, though the quest took me from coast to coast. The Library of Congress has hundreds of letters written by and to William H. Herndon, who was Lincoln's law partner for sixteen years, and who furnished the material for two biographies of Lincoln.[2] In the Huntington Library at San Marino, California, there is an enormous collection of letters to and from Ward Hill Lamon, whose name appeared as author of one of the first important Lincoln biographies, although he did not actually write it.[3] The Allegheny College Library, at Meadville, Pennsylvania, has the letters of Ida M. Tarbell, the first person to write an important biography of Lincoln without having known him personally.[4] At the University of Chicago are the letters of William E. Barton, a clergyman, who was recognized as an eminent Lincoln biographer some twenty years ago.[5] In the Illinois State Historical Library are many letters of John George Nicolay and John Hay, who were Lincoln's private secretaries, and who spent fifteen years writing a ten-volume life of Lincoln.[6] Also in Springfield are a large number of letters to and from Jesse W. Weik, who was the actual writer of the life of Lincoln that bore William H. Herndon's name.[7] And in all these collections, letters from other Lincoln authors of minor stature are also to be found.

These letters really take you behind the scenes of Lincoln authorship, and when I had exhausted these collections I felt that I had come to know these people pretty well, that, in coming to recognize their quirks and preconceptions, I could judge their work much better than I could before, and, furthermore, that I had come to a better understanding of Lincoln in the process.

Time will not permit me to go into the story very fully, but perhaps I can share with you some of the interesting tidbits I picked up.

You all know the story of Lincoln and Ann Rutledge. William H. Herndon, Lincoln's law partner, originated it in a lecture that he delivered in Springfield in November 1866, about a year and a half after Lincoln's death.[8] And he depicted it not merely as a casual love affair in Lincoln's early life, but—and this was the shocking part—he declared that Ann Rutledge was the only woman Lincoln ever really loved, which was saying that he never loved his wife, who was still living at the time the story was broadcast. Moreover, Herndon made Lincoln's remembrance of this early sweetheart the determining factor throughout the rest of Lincoln's life. Nobody seemed to recall anything about the alleged affair until Herndon broke the story, and, as you know, it has never been proved true.[9] So it is enlightening to know how men who had known Lincoln personally reacted to it.

Just before Herndon delivered his Ann Rutledge lecture, he sent advance copies of it to several of Lincoln's former friends. Among them was Isaac N. Arnold, who had known Lincoln as a fellow lawyer for twenty years and had served him faithfully as a congressman. Arnold was a cautious, conscientious, scholarly sort of man, who had already written a biography of Lincoln himself. He was not the sort to welcome anything sensational.[10]

"I have just read *hastily, rapidly,* because I could not read *slowly,* your paper," gasped Arnold as he replied. "This is a strange chapter in Mr. Lincoln's history—very strange—. Of absorbing interest. You verify what I have said of Mr. Lincoln, had he lived in the days of mythology he would have been placed among the Gods. I know nothing of your facts. I think your treatment of them incomparably . . . poetic! . . . I mean 'poetic,' but if you read the word *pathetic* it will still be true."

He closed on a warning note.

"I have looked to you to give the world a picture of Mr. Lincoln's life. Especially his private life. You are wiser than I have been in taking more time. You do not need the caution, I know, but yet I cannot forbear, saying you are dealing with the fame of the greatest, take him all in all, the best man, our country has produced. I hope you will not intentionally do him injustice. I shall read your paper again."[11]

Joshua F. Speed, who had befriended Lincoln when he moved from New Salem to Springfield as a penniless young man, and who was probably closer to him than anyone else in the early Springfield years, was now living in Kentucky.[12] "It is new to me," he avowed. "But so true is my appreciation of Lincoln's character that independent of my knowledge of you I could almost swear to it."[13]

But T. Lyle Dickey, a fellow lawyer and political friend of Lincoln's, until he refused to follow him into the Republican party, was cynical. "Thank you for the copy of that fancy lecture" he wrote Herndon. "Romance is not your forte. The few grains of history stirred into that lecture—in a plain narrative would be interesting—but I don't like the garnishments."[14]

Especially interesting were the comments of Francis Bicknell Carpenter, whose book, *Six Months at the White House,* appearing just a few weeks before this, had described Carpenter's experiences at the White House while he painted his famous picture of the signing of the Emancipation Proclamation.[15] Carpenter had printed a large part of a previous lecture of Herndon's in his book, and the two men began a friendly correspondence when Carpenter wrote to Herndon to apologize for using his material without first asking his permission. Carpenter had enjoyed Herndon's other lectures—he had given three before the one on Ann Rutledge—but when he read this last lecture he was not sure as to just how he felt about it.[16]

"I was a good deal *disturbed* by it, I will frankly confess," he wrote. "It seemed to me an intrusion of a sacred *chamber*—a tearing away of the veil which conceals the 'holy of holies.' I could see the reason for this—the necessity the author felt of showing the secret springs of action in Mr. Lincoln's life—feeling as he did, that this unrevealed history was the key to his character. But it seemed to me that the *fact* of this experience might have been given without treading so far upon ground which all felt intuitively to be sacred."[17]

Herndon took this criticism in good part. "I like your style of a man," he told Carpenter; and then he proceeded fully to explain his purpose. His passion was for truth, and he wanted the facts about Lincoln to come out under the auspices of his friends and not his enemies. "The great, keen, shrewd, boring, patient, philosophical, critical and remorseless world will find out all things, and bring them to light" he wrote, "and the question is now: who shall do that—a man's friends or his enemies? Shall it be done now or left for the future world to wrangle over, and yet forever debate. . . . The very existence of Christ is denied because he had no good truthful biographers. . . . I want, and intend to have, the generous broad and deep sympathies of the universal heart for good and noble Abraham. . . . My philosophy is to sink a counter nail and blow up my enemies—Lincoln's future traducers."[18]

Carpenter was convinced. "I think you are right," he replied. "The *truth* is what the world wants. Lincoln's love for Ann Rutledge may yet loom up in history like Dante's for Beatrice, or Petrarch's for Laura."[19]

Herndon received a good deal of criticism for sponsoring the Ann Rutledge story; but he did not become unduly concerned about it until he received a blistering letter from Grant Goodrich, a Chicago lawyer.[20] Herndon, trying to research every scrap of biographical material about his former law partner, had written to Goodrich for information about a patent case in which Goodrich and Lincoln had been associated; and Goodrich replied with the desired facts. Then, without warning, he swung on Herndon from his heels.

"In my opinion," he wrote, "you are the last man who ought to attempt to write a life of Abraham Lincoln. Your long and intimate association with him, unfits you for the task. No one holding the intimate relations to another which you did to him ever has succeeded. There may be exceptions, but I cannot remember one. . . . In intimate association, we fix upon some characteristics or peculiarity, and fail to catch other lineaments. We can only regard them as the kind friend, amusing companion, & generous mind. In the *distance* we see the bold outline of the mountain; its summits wrapped in sunshine, or swathed in cloud. When we *approach* it, we catch a view of the deep, it may be dark gorges, the rugged cliffs, the lean rocks, and distorted outlines. So in the characters of our dearest friends. See how Boswell, with all his literary abilities failed in his Life of Johnson. No blow so severe was ever struck at Johnson. Think of these things.

"If I am to judge of what your production will be by the publication of your . . . Ann Rutledge lecture, I am more solicitous still. I fear you did not realize what an injury and injustice you did to the memory of your friend, and mortification you caused his friends, but especially his widow and children. Ask yourself, if he was living, whether he would not have revolted at the uncovering to the public gaze that drama of his life? And shall his friends exhibit what we know he would have preserved in sacred privacy. . . . I should as soon think of exposing his dead body, uncoffined, to the public eye. It should never have been dug up from the grave, where time had buried it.

"Besides, your style is not well adapted to such an undertaking. The want of practice is palpable. Your style is purely legal, such an one as is acquired by drawing legal documents and pleadings, and is decidedly different from one formed by familiarity with the best writers. It is rugged, abounding in adjectives and explications—full of climaxes and hard dry words. It reads as if it had been jerked out word by word—it gives one the sense you have in riding in a lumber wagon over a frozen road—or the noise made in machinery when a cog is broken.

"Now my friend, I have spoken plainly, but sincerely. I may do you injustice, but it is not intentional. I may lose your friendship by it, but I have only done what I would wish one to do to me under the same circumstances. And I have noticed in myself and others, that the very points in which strength is supposed, are the very points of weakness."[21]

William H. Herndon was never a man to take a punch without retaliating. His counterblow was short, sharp, and devastating. "Mr. Goodrich, Sir," he replied. "I thank you for the first part of your letter giving me an account of the patent case Mr. Lincoln tended to. I say I thank you for it. As to the second part of your letter, I guess I shall have to treat you as Lincoln always did treat you, as an exceedingly weak-headed brother. The more he kicked you, the closer you clung to him. Do you remember? Analyze yourself."[22]

One of the earliest biographies of Lincoln was that which bore the name of Ward Hill Lamon, a big, blustering Virginian, who had moved to Danville, Illinois, where he formed a limited law partnership with Lincoln. When Lincoln became President, Lamon accompanied him to Washington, and as marshal of the District of Columbia, constituted himself as a sort of personal bodyguard to Lincoln. As I have said, his biography of Lincoln was ghost-written. And the ghost was Chauncey Black, a Democrat, and son of Jeremiah S. Black, who had been a member of President James Buchanan's cabinet.[23] This biography which was written by Black under Lamon's name resulted from a deal with Herndon whereby Black and Lamon had acquired copies of Herndon's Lincoln material, so that in a way it, too, was Herndon's product.

Black started out with the preconceived notion that the way to write the life of Lincoln was to contrast his humble beginnings with his later greatness, and the blacker he could paint the Lincoln family and the conditions of Lincoln's early life, the greater he could make Lincoln's achievements appear by contrast. "It is our duty," Black wrote to Lamon, "to show the world the majesty and beauty of his character as it grew by itself and unassisted out of this unpromising soil. We must point mankind to the diamond glowing on the dunghill and then to the same resplendent jewel in the future setting of great success and brilliant achievements."[24]

Now, as you know, it is dangerous for a biographer to begin a work with preconceived ideas. He should always be open-minded, and let his story develop as it will. So, in judging Lamon's biography of Lincoln, it is well for present-day historians to bear in mind that it was written from this point of view.

When Lamon and Black conceived the idea of this book, they signed a contract providing, among other things, that in case they disagreed about what should go into it, the matter was to be referred to arbitrators. But Black was so stubborn about making changes, and some of the things he said were so derogatory to Lincoln that Lamon and the publishers made some last minute alterations without getting his consent. Black was so enraged by this that he threatened suit and he and Lamon became bitter enemies. Black always blamed these changes for the book's failure to sell, for as a publishing venture it was completely unsuccessful. He gave his version of what happened to the book in a letter he wrote to Herndon on August 18, 1873:

"A large mass of very valuable material was excluded by the treachery of the publishers and the timidity of Lamon," he complained. "The last chapter giving the startling secret history of the closing months of Mr. Buchanan's administration, drawn from papers in the handwriting of Stanton, my Father, Gen'l Scott and others was suppressed wholly, and also a most precious and graphically written diary of Donn Piatt, which covers the sayings, doings and surroundings of Mr. Lincoln between the election and the inauguration. Many of the chapters were shamefully mutilated and the most creditable as well as the most interesting parts ruthlessly struck out. In some instances they contented themselves with merely mutilating or corrupting the text. In others they blotted it out altogether, and in others still, committed the intolerable outrage of intermingling their own base hogwash with my honest narrative."[25]

Of course the publishers were wise to act as they did. Black never was able to overcome his partisan hostility to Lincoln, and he depicted Lincoln's background and his early years as having been much cruder than they really were, in accordance with his preconceived notion of making Lincoln's later achievements appear more magnificent by contrast. This volume concluded with Lincoln's accession to the presidency. If Black had gone on to finish the second volume of the book, as he and Lamon had planned to do, and had published the two volumes together, the book would not have seemed so hostile to Lincoln. But this first volume, appearing by itself, was extremely heady stuff. Even today, parts of it have an unpleasant tang; and to the mid-Victorian idealists of his own day, who had become accustomed to an unvaried diet of eulogy about Lincoln, the book reeked; and the critics tore into it unmercifully.

One of the most persistent critics of this book was the Reverend James A. Reed, pastor of the First Presbyterian Church of Springfield, who made a tour of the West, lecturing on Lincoln's religion—something which Black, prompted by Herndon, had said that Lincoln lacked. Another critic of the Black-Lamon book was Josiah G. Holland, who wrote the first important biography of Lincoln—a biography in the current eulogistic vein—and who was now editor of *Scribner's Monthly.*[26] Holland had flayed the Lamon book in a review, and he thought so highly of Mr. Reed's defense of Lincoln's religion that he printed Reed's lecture in *Scribner's Magazine.*[27]

Now, as you know, the matter of Lincoln's religion, or lack of it, has been one of the great controversies in Lincoln literature. We know today that Lincoln was deeply religious, in his presidential years, at any rate. No man could have written and spoken as Lincoln did, unless he had profound religious convictions. But Lincoln did not belong to any church, and like so many other features of this character, his religious feelings were a matter of growth over the years. Very probably, in the days when Herndon knew Lincoln, and the time that Black wrote about, Lincoln's faith was entirely different (and far less strong) from what it became later.

At any rate, the Reverend Mr. Reed belabored both Herndon and Lamon for what Black had said on this score. Black himself, the real culprit, escaped the criticism, because his role of ghost was unknown.

But Black smarted just as much as though the criticism had been directed at him, and he thought Reed and Holland should be answered. Lamon was sulky and refused to be smoked out, and since Black couldn't defend the book himself without revealing himself as its author, he tried to drag Herndon into the controversy as his mouthpiece. "The Rev. J. A. Reed of Springfield," Black wrote to Herndon, "has it appears been delivering to numerous audiences in the West, a lecture on the 'Life of Lincoln,' which paints *Lamon* as a mercenary libeler, and you as the forger of the documents paraded in support of the libels. . . . The substance and effect of Mr. Reed's elaborate performance is that you, being an infidel and therefore an immoral man yourself, have resorted to the basest means of proving that Mr. Lincoln was like you. . . . But I do not propose to review Mr. Reed; you will do that better than I can.

"Now this lecture is to be sure a flimsy, fraudulent concern. But it is well calculated to deceive the public mind . . . and unless it is answered and exposed it disgraces us all. Lamon as you know is incapable of writing anything—or conducting any controversy, however trivial; and he has taken away from me all the books and papers we got from you, or anybody else, and thus left me as helpless as himself. . . . The responsibility of meeting this flood of falsehoods . . . rests therefore upon you. . . . Unless you rise to the occasion Mr. Lincoln's real character will be lost in oblivion, and a false one will live in its stead. You are the only person living who can rescue us from destruction. They are combining against us everywhere—Holland, Arnold, the preachers and the press. They mean to drown us out with false clamors. They will suborn half of Springfield, where public opinion terrorizes the truth; and they will get all the preachers who ever saw Lincoln to lie about his supposed religion. . . . Our publishers are no better than our avowed enemies; and Lamon, whose name is on the book, being an imbecile from the first, and wheedled into emasculating his text, now cowers before the storm, as useless as a cross baby."[28]

In dragging Herndon into this controversy, Black was motivated by something more than zeal for truth. He still believed that there was money to be made from the book, and he conceived the idea of getting control of it away from Lamon and the publishers, and bringing it out in a revised form under his and Herndon's names. Consequently he welcomed any sort of publicity for it—good or bad—as something that would increase sales.

Herndon did finally come to Black's support by delivering a lecture on Lincoln's religion in Springfield, on December 12, 1873, and with that the controversy took on greater virulence.[29] Poor Herndon became the target for newspaper criticism from all over the country, a result which pleased Black no end. He was like the prize fight manager who safely outside the ropes himself, urges his battered protégé to greater efforts with assurance: "They ain't laid a glove on us."

When the *New York Herald* accused Herndon of betraying Lincoln as Judas betrayed his Master, Black thought this presented a wonderful opportunity for Herndon to reply; and he even took the liberty of penning the reply himself, and of sending it to Springfield for Herndon to sign. Black had a novel approach.[30] If Herndon must be a Judas, Black would put Judas in a new and favorable light. So the letter which Herndon was to send to the Herald's editor began thus:

"Do you know that there is a lingering question about the nature of Judas's heart, and that it is maintained with some show of reason that he was the most devoted and most loving of the apostles? It is said by some that poor Judas believed that his Master should never die, and he betrayed him to the law merely to see the decisive test applied, the welcome triumph achieved, and the perfect day dawn."[31]

As the controversy continued, even Mrs. Lincoln got into it. Herndon had quoted a conversation he claimed to have had with her about Lincoln's religion, and she now denied that any such conversation had ever taken place. Herndon answered her in the *Illinois State Register*, a Springfield newspaper.[32] Doctor William Jayne, who had been a close friend of both Lincoln and Herndon, and who had been appointed Governor of Dakota Territory by Lincoln, liked the way Herndon answered Mrs. Lincoln and congratulated him on his restraint. "In this affair with the 'First Ladie of the Land' you do not act like a clod hopper a d——d old liar & hussy," he commended, "but like a country gentleman and lawyer you say that the good poor woman. . . . is not altogether a competent and trustworthy witness. William, your intellect & diplomacy does not seem to have rusted by a few years of country life."[33]

But despite all of Black's conniving, the Rev. Mr. Reed and Doctor Holland thinking that enough rancor had been generated, decided to hold their peace, and the controversy gradually died out, only to break out afresh, however, when Herndon's own book was published several years later. Black never got control of the Lamon book and eventually drifted out of Lincoln authorship into newspaper work and politics. And it was not until many years later that it became generally known that he was the real author of Lamon's life of Lincoln.

I think you will agree, even from the few examples I have given, that Lincoln students of the early days—of what we might call the reminiscent period of Lincoln study—were a blustery, vehement group; and a major task of modern Lincoln scholarship has been to clear away the myths, the half-truths, and the untruths that they originated. Among these are the un-proved story of Lincoln and Ann Rutledge, the erroneous notion that Lincoln was of illegitimate birth, the too-deeply shadowed picture of his boyhood and family background, the false story of his losing his nerve and hiding out on the day he was to be married, the view that his marriage was nothing more than an unmitigated trial and torment to him.[34]

Most of these stories had their origin in the mercurial mind of William H. Herndon, and some modern Lincoln students have been pretty severe on Herndon for sending Lincoln scholarship away on these false trials. But Herndon did not do this intentionally. He was a sincere seeker for the truth; and his historical waywardness resulted not from an intention to deceive, but from his inability properly to assess conflicting evidence, and from a belief in his own clairvoyance.[35]

Yet we must be eternally grateful to Herndon for giving us an intimate, first-hand picture of Lincoln the human being—how he looked and walked, his love of fun, his melancholy, the slow and careful working of his mind, his personal habits and idiosyncrasies. And above all we are indebted to Herndon for his refusal to handle Lincoln with kid gloves. If his approach was sometimes overly realistic, he at least kept Lincoln from becoming the same sort of cold, too-perfect figure that George Washington became at the hands of Parson Weems, who, as you all know, originated the famous story of Washington and the cherry tree, along with others which were calculated to depict Washington as the perfect human being from the cradle to the grave.

If the sentimental eulogists of the Mid-Victorian era had been allowed to work their will with Lincoln, they would have prettified him at the cost of all his human qualities. He too would have become the perfect man from birth, instead of a man whose human faults and frailties give ordinary people a feeling of kinship with him. To Herndon we must ever be grateful for keeping Lincoln real.

For the grandeur of Lincoln's life lies in his conquest of the human imperfections that all of us are heir to. Ida M. Tarbell gave a pretty good summation of Lincoln when she wrote: "His life was a call to self-training—of training of the mind until it can form sound, workmanlike, trustworthy conclusions, training of the moral nature to justness and rightness—training of the will until it can be counted on to back up the conclusions of the mind and heart. It is a call to openness of mind, willingness to learn.

"His method is a constant lesson in liberality towards others, to a recognition that there may be something to be said for the other man's point of view as well as yours, that you no more see all the truth than he does, and that if what each of you see can be fused, a larger amount of truth will result. Above all, his method is a revelation of what a man can make of himself if he will. Indeed, I am sometimes inclined to feel that the greatest service Lincoln has done this country was to demonstrate what could be made of a mind by passionate, persistent effort. What moral heights the nature would rise to if dealt with in perfect candor."[36]

At one time Ida Tarbell ranked as the foremost of Lincoln biographers. Today her books have been largely superseded, but she deserves not to be forgotten.[37] For her work was characterized by that combination of realism and imagination that makes for great biography. She had the vision to see beyond the documents in trying to get at Lincoln.

In this Miss Tarbell foreshadowed our best modern historians. For the imaginative quality is something which for a time American historians seemed to lose. Now, happily, they are recapturing it, and are no longer afraid of venturing beyond strict documentation. Francis Parkman wrote that a historian "must himself be . . . a sharer or a spectator of the action he describes," and in his own volumes Parkman so shared in the wilderness drama of Jesuit missionaries and explorers, of Wolfe and Montcalm, that the reader finds himself transposed to those times and places.[38] Yet Parkman was also a stickler for scrupulous accuracy, so that his work exemplifies, as well as that of any historian, the legitimate place of properly controlled imagination in historical writing. In fact, I wonder if history can be properly written without imagination—without the historian or the biographer placing himself in the position of the characters he writes about, so as to feel the tensions and the pressures under which those persons acted. Speaking of Lincoln in this connection, the late Lloyd Lewis once remarked that it is doubtful if we can really get to know Lincoln solely through prosaic documentation, and I wonder if that same observation does not hold true of any of our great historical characters.[39]

To be sure, the use of imagination in historical writing is a tricky technique, which, if misapplied, can deprive a book of all value. Facts come first, and they must never be distorted. But it takes imagination to give facts the breath of life. Imagination, properly applied, can result in more vivid writing without sacrifice of truth.

Ida Tarbell, besides possessing this imaginative quality, was also the first of the Lincoln biographers to approach her subject with an open mind. When Paul Angle, during his years as executive-secretary of the Abraham Lincoln Association, in Springfield, wrote to tell her that he was about to publish an article which would disprove some of her conclusions, she told him to go ahead. "I think you are rendering the Lincoln public a real service in this case as you have in so many others," she asserted. "It is a consolation to have a watchdog, like yourself, at the door in Springfield."[40]

As Miss Tarbell's wisdom ripened with age, she came to realize that her work was perhaps too uncritically laudatory by the new standards which college-trained historians were bringing to Lincoln research. "I am afraid I am over-lenient towards mistakes, having made so many myself," she admitted.[41] And when her books came under fire she could say with all sincerity: "It is a deep satisfaction to me that the work has become gradually so thorough and so scientific."[42]

And those have become the hallmarks of modern Lincoln writing— thoroughness and the impartial spirit of scientific inquiry. Not that we Lincoln writers no longer have our controversies. And not that our personal relations are always like milk and honey. But the backstage story of the present-day Lincoln biographers is a matter I had better not go into.

Notes

1. Benjamin P. Thomas, *Portrait for Posterity: Lincoln and His Biographers* (New Brunswick: Rutgers University Press, 1947).

2. William Henry Herndon (1818–91) conducted correspondence and extensive interviews with people who knew Lincoln. Those became the basis of *The Life of Abraham Lincoln* (Boston: Osgood, 1872) by Ward Hill Lamon (and his ghost-writer, Chauncey F. Black) and *Herndon's Lincoln: The True Story of a Great Life,* 3 vols. (Chicago: Belford Clarke, 1889) by Herndon and Jesse W. Weik.

3. On the authorship of Lamon's biography of Lincoln, see Albert V. House, Jr., "The Trials of a Ghost-Writer of Lincoln's Biography: Chauncey F. Black's Authorship of Lamon's Lincoln," *Journal of the Illinois State Historical Society* 31 (Sept. 1938): 262–96.

4. Ida Minerva Tarbell (1857–1944) wrote *The Early Life of Abraham Lincoln* (New York: S. S. McClure, 1895), *The Life of Abraham Lincoln,* 2 vols. (New York: Doubleday and McClure, 1900), and *In the Footsteps of the Lincolns* (New York: Harper and Brothers, 1924).

5. Between 1920 and 1930 William Eleazer Barton (1891–1930), a retired Congregational minister based in Chicago, published several books on Lincoln.

6. John George Nicolay (1832–1901) and John Milton Hay (1838–1905) served as Lincoln's private secretaries in the White House and wrote *Abraham Lincoln: A History* (New York: Century, 1890).

7. Jesse William Weik (1857–1930) was a freelance writer based in Greencastle, Indiana.

8. On November 16, 1866, Herndon delivered a lecture in Springfield: "Abraham Lincoln. Miss Ann Rutledge. New Salem. Pioneering, and THE Poem."

9. Modern scholars do not agree with this judgment. See John Y. Simon, "Abraham Lincoln and Ann Rutledge," *Journal of the Abraham Lincoln Association* 11 (1990): 13–33, and Douglas L. Wilson, "Abraham Lincoln, Ann Rutledge, and the Evidence of Herndon's Informants," in *Lincoln before Washington: New Perspectives on the Illinois Years*, ed. Douglas L. Wilson (Urbana: University of Illinois Press, 1998), 74–98, which effectively rebut James G. Randall's argument in "Sifting the Ann Rutledge Evidence," in Randall, *Lincoln the President: From Springfield to Gettysburg*, 2 vols. (New York: Dodd, Mead, 1945), 2:321–42. See also John Evangelist Walsh, *The Shadows Rise: Abraham Lincoln and the Ann Rutledge Legend* (Urbana: University of Illinois Press, 1993).

10. Isaac Newton Arnold (1815–85) of Chicago served in Congress (1861–65) and wrote two biographies of Lincoln: *The History of Abraham Lincoln and the Overthrow of Slavery* (Chicago: Clarke, 1866) and *The Life of Abraham Lincoln* (Chicago: Jansen, McClurg, 1885). See James A. Rawley's introduction to the reprint of the fourth edition of Arnold's *Life of Lincoln* (Lincoln: University of Nebraska Press, 1994), v–xvi.

11. Isaac N. Arnold to William H. Herndon, Chicago, 16 Nov. 1866, Herndon-Weik Papers, Library of Congress.

12. Joshua Fry Speed (1814–82) of Kentucky was Lincoln's closest friend; they were bunkmates in Springfield from 1837 to 1841.

13. Joshua F. Speed to William H. Herndon, Louisville, 30 Nov. 1866, in *Herndon's Informants: Letters, Interviews, and Statements about Abraham Lincoln*, ed. Douglas L. Wilson and Rodney O. Davis (Urbana: University of Illinois Press, 1997), 431.

14. Theophilus Lyle Dickie (1811–85) was a prominent attorney in Ottawa, Illinois. In 1858 he switched his allegiance from the Republican to the Democratic party. Dickey to William H. Herndon, 8 Dec. 1866, in *Herndon's Informants*, ed. Wilson and Davis, 505.

15. In 1864 Francis Bicknell Carpenter (1830–1900) painted the huge picture *First Reading of the Emancipation Proclamation of President Lincoln* and two years later published *Six Months in the White House with Abraham Lincoln: The Story of a Picture* (New York: Hurd and Houghton, 1866).

16. On December 12 and 26, 1865, Herndon delivered "Analysis of the Character of Abraham Lincoln: A Lecture," which was eventually published in the *Abraham Lincoln Quarterly* 1 (Sept. 1941): 343–83, and 1 (Dec. 1941): 403–41. On January 23, 1866, Herndon spoke in Springfield on "Facts Illustrative of Mr. Lincoln's Patriotism and Statesmanship," also published in the *Abraham Lincoln Quarterly* 3 (Dec. 1944): 178–203.

17. Francis B. Carpenter to William H. Herndon, 4 Dec. 1866, in *Herndon's Informants*, ed. Wilson and Davis, 495.

18. William H. Herndon to Francis B. Carpenter, Springfield, 11 Dec. 1866, in *The Hidden Lincoln: From the Papers and Letters of William H. Herndon*, ed. Emanuel Hertz (New York: Viking, 1938), 46–49.

19. Francis B. Carpenter to William H. Herndon, 15 Feb. 1867, Herdnon-Weik Papers, Library of Congress.

20. In 1834, New York–born Grant Goodrich (1811–89) settled in Chicago, where he practiced law with Lincoln in the federal courts. He had offered Lincoln a partnership in his law firm; Lincoln "refused the offer, giving as a reason that he tended to consumption, and, if he removed to a city like Chicago, he would have to sit down and study harder than ever." Angle, ed., *Herndon's Lincoln*, 247.

21. Grant Goodrich to William H. Herndon, 9 Dec. 1866, in *Herndon's Informants*, ed. Wilson and Davis, 511–12.

22. William H. Herndon to Grant Goodrich, 10 Dec. 1866, copy, Herndon-Weik Papers, Library of Congress.

23. Jeremiah Sullivan Black (1810–83) served as attorney general (1857–60) and secretary of state (1860–61).

24. Jeremiah S. Black to William H. Herndon, 8 March 1870, Herndon-Weik Papers, Library of Congress.

25. Jeremiah S. Black to William H. Herndon, 18 Aug. 1873, Herndon-Weik Papers, Library of Congress. Donn Piatt (1819–91) of Ohio was a journalist who during the Civil War served as chief of staff to Gen. Robert Schenck.

26. Josiah Gilbert Holland (1819–81), an editor of the *Springfield* (Mass.) *Republican*, wrote *The Life of Abraham Lincoln* (Springfield: Gurdon Bill, 1866).

27. James A. Reed, "The Later Life and Religious Sentiments of Abraham Lincoln," *Scribner's Monthly* (Nov. 1873): 333–43.

28. Jeremiah S. Black to William H. Herndon, 23 June 1873, Herndon-Weik Papers, Library of Congress.

29. The text of Herndon's lecture is in William Henry Herndon, *Lincoln's Religion*, ed. Douglas C. McMurtrie (Chicago: Black Cat Press, 1936), 13–44.

30. *New York Herald*, 15 Dec. 1873.

31. Jeremiah S. Black to William H. Herndon, 18 and 19 Dec. 1873, Herndon-Weik Papers, Library of Congress.

32. In the issue of 14 Jan. 1874.

33. William Jayne to William H. Herndon, Springfield, 19 Jan. 1874, Herndon-Weik Papers, Library of Congress. Jayne (1826–1916) had been mayor of Springfield and a member of the Illinois legislature before moving to Dakota.

34. Lincoln thought his early life on the frontier background was grimmer than Thomas suggests. See Mark E. Neely, Jr., "Lincoln's Peculiar Relationship with Indiana," *Inland: The Magazine of the Middle West* (1980): 4–7. This brilliant article was reprinted in pamphlet form and entitled *Escape from the Frontier: Lincoln's Peculiar Relationship with Indiana* (Fort Wayne: Lincoln National Life Insurance Company, n.d.).

In fact, the marriage was indeed a trial and torment to Lincoln. See Michael Burlingame, *The Inner World of Abraham Lincoln* (Urbana: University of Illinois Press, 1994), 268–326.

35. On Herndon's reliability as an interviewer, see Wilson, ed., *Lincoln before Washington*, 21–52, 74–98.

36. Ida M. Tarbell to George P. Hambrecht, 30 Jan. 1922, Hambrecht Collection, Illinois State Historical Library, Springfield.

37. See "Our Lincoln Heritage from Ida Tarbell," chapter 15 of this volume.

38. Parkman, introduction to *France and England in North America*, 2 vols. (1865, repr. New York: Library of America, 1983), 1:16.

39. Lloyd Lewis (1891–1949) was a Chicago journalist who wrote biographies of William T. Sherman and Ulysses S. Grant.

40. Ida M. Tarbell to Paul M. Angle, 4 Dec. 1936, copy, Ida M. Tarbell Papers, Allegheny College.

41. Ida M. Tarbell to Oliver R. Barrett, 25 February 1936, copy, Ida M. Tarbell Papers, Allegheny College.

42. Ida Tarbell to Harry E. Pratt, 24 Jan. 1940, copy, Ida M. Tarbell Papers, Allegheny College.

14   Harry Edward Pratt

Many persons experienced a sense of personal bereavement and scholarship suffered a severe loss when Harry Edward Pratt, Illinois State Historian and one of the nation's foremost Lincoln authorities, died in Springfield on February 12, 1956.

He was born in Cambridge, Illinois, on December 16, 1901, the second child of Edward and Katie (Hall) Pratt. His father died in October 1903, at the age of thirty-two; his mother lived until November 1948. His sister Sue was graduated from MacMurray College and married Harold Ward.

On the paternal side, Harry's ancestry traced back to Thomas Pratt who came to Massachusetts from England about 1640, and to Revolutionary soldier Ephraim. Later their descendants moved to Pennsylvania, then to Ohio, and in 1855 to Knox County, Illinois. Harry's grandfather, Elihu Austin Pratt, served four years in the Union Army and in 1875 moved to Henry County, where he died in 1912. The Halls were among the early settlers of the county.

Harry had the advantages of travel to different parts of the United States while attending the Cambridge public schools, and was an enthusiastic reader and collector from an early age. While in high school he was chosen a delegate to Boys State and was active in Boy Scout work.

He was graduated from the University of Illinois in 1923. He taught history at Athens High School in Ohio, became director of student enterprises at Moraine Park High School in Dayton, then moved to Cody, Wyoming, where he was senior master at the Valley Ranch School. A basket-

Journal of the Illinois State Historical Society 49 (1956): 135–43.

ball star in high school and a crack tennis player at Illinois, he coached those sports and track at these secondary schools. Also keenly interested in baseball and football, he thought seriously of making coaching his career. Throughout his life Dr. Pratt continued to be an ardent sports fan, following his favorite teams closely in the newspapers and on the radio.

At Illinois, however, he had developed another enthusiasm that eventually became uppermost in his mind. As a sophomore he had taken a course in history under Dr. J. G. Randall, an outstanding authority on Lincoln and the Civil War.[1] Under this stimulus he became an avid student of history, serving as unofficial research assistant to Dr. Randall and tracking down clues for him in the Illinois State Historical Library and other repositories. This interest soon became so consuming that it would not be denied.

He enrolled at Illinois as one of Dr. Randall's first graduate students, receiving his master's degree in 1927 and his Ph.D. in history in 1930. His doctoral dissertation on David Davis, presiding judge of the old Eighth Circuit, brought him close to Lincoln; the intimacy would ripen into knowledge and understanding with the passing years.

While still doing graduate work at Illinois, Harry Pratt married Hjordis Lind on July 3, 1927. They had one child, Patty Ellen, now Mrs. DeVere R. Boyd, Jr.

After obtaining his doctorate Harry Pratt served for four years as dean at Blackburn College, Carlinville. He was beloved for his friendly interest in the students' problems, and his enthusiasm made history live in and out of the classroom. Then in the fall of 1934 he moved to Illinois Wesleyan University at Bloomington to become associate professor of history. Here, as at Blackburn, he made lasting friendships with members of the faculty and the student body. A turning point in his life came two years later, however, when he was offered and accepted the position of executive secretary of the Abraham Lincoln Association in Springfield.

President and energizing spirit of the Abraham Lincoln Association was Logan Hay, prominent Springfield lawyer, unselfish civic leader and a man steeped in the Lincoln tradition.[2] Under his guidance the Association had won national recognition in scholarly circles for the work it had done and was doing in clearing away the myths that had beclouded Lincoln and in reconstructing the true story of his life, especially his Illinois years.

The Association's first executive secretary, Paul M. Angle, had resigned in 1932 to become head of the Illinois State Historical Library, and had been succeeded by the writer of this article.[3] In the autumn of 1936 I decided to resign, and Mr. Hay, Paul Angle and I held a consultation concerning the selection of my successor. We were of one mind: Harry

Pratt was by all odds the man best qualified for the job. The directors of the Association concurred in our judgment, and Angle and I were delegated to go to Bloomington and broach the matter to him. We called him away from his duties and conferred with him in my car.

I can remember yet how Harry's eyes lighted up when we offered him the position; for it involved a great deal of historical research, and research was his forte. He also knew what a privilege it was for a young man to work under Logan Hay's tutelage. There have been no better preceptors in the Lincoln field than "Jim" Randall and Logan Hay. Three of the books which Dr. Pratt wrote during the seven years (1936–1943) that he served as executive secretary of the Abraham Lincoln Association are basic Lincoln literature. *Lincoln 1840–1846* (1939) and *1809–1839* (1941) completed a four-volume set—begun with Angle's *Lincoln 1854–1861* (1933) and my own *Lincoln 1847–1853* (1936)—covering Lincoln's day-by-day activities from his birth to his inauguration as president. It would be difficult for anyone except the compilers of these books to realize how much meticulous and often dirty work their preparation involved. To amass the material that went into them meant spending long, solitary hours turning the pages of yellowing newspapers, examining old letters, searching grimy court records undisturbed for years—in short, uncovering every possible bit of information bearing on Lincoln's pre-presidential years. Though Paul Angle and I both thought we had become proficient at that sort of historical detective work, we agreed before long that Harry Pratt had no equal in turning up historical source material in obscure and unlikely places. It was a talent that distinguished his work then and ever afterward.

Dr. Pratt's *The Personal Finances of Abraham Lincoln* (1943) was a truly original contribution to our knowledge of Lincoln. Dispelling the legend of Lincoln's lifelong poverty, it proved that after paying off the heavy debt incurred in his early venture as a storekeeper he quickly improved his financial status, and during his career as a lawyer not only provided comfortably for his family, but also accumulated surplus funds that he invested mostly in notes and mortgages. Worth approximately $15,000 in 1860, he invested most of his presidential salary of $25,000 a year in government bonds and left an estate of some $83,000, which under the administration of David Davis had increased to about $111,000 when it was distributed to his heirs.

But these three books were only a part of Dr. Pratt's contribution to Lincoln scholarship during those years; for he was a prodigious and tireless worker. In 1938 he edited the Association's facsimile publication of William Dean Howells' campaign biography of Lincoln which Lincoln had corrected in his own handwriting.[4] In 1944 he published *Concern-*

ing Mr. Lincoln, an annotated compilation of letters revealing Lincoln as contemporaries saw and described him.[5] From the time he assumed the executive secretaryship most of the articles in the Association's quarterly *Bulletin* were from his pen; and when that publication was superseded in 1940 by the *Abraham Lincoln Quarterly* he became associate editor of the new periodical, with Angle as editor. And all the while, largely through his efforts, an enormous mass of information about Lincoln was accumulating in the Association's files.[6] Its membership more than doubled, and Dr. Pratt's correspondence was now on a national scale. The visitors who came to see the Lincoln shrines were given memorable personally conducted tours.

World War II came and brought with it a scarcity of college instructors. In 1943 Dr. Pratt left the Association to teach history at Ball State Teachers' College in Muncie, Indiana. Then because of his wife's ill health he had to put his scholarly interests aside, and took a position with Sears, Roebuck & Company. Assigned first to Beloit, Wisconsin, he was later transferred to Muskegon, Michigan, where in addition to his business duties he took an active part in the organization of Goodwill Industries in that city. There his wife "Yordie" Lind Pratt died on September 3, 1949.[7]

The academic world had not forgotten him, and the following year, the position of Illinois State Historian became vacant with the resignation of Jay Monaghan.[8] The position carried with it the directorship of the Illinois State Historical Library, and had always meant election as secretary-treasurer of the Illinois State Historical Society, owing to the close relationship between the Library and the Society.

Alfred W. Stern, Clarence P. McClelland and I were the trustees of the Library at that time, and we consulted with Governor Adlai E. Stevenson and the directors of the Society.[9] Again, as had been the case when Dr. Pratt was selected as executive secretary of the Abraham Lincoln Association, he was the immediate and unanimous choice of those entrusted with the decision. He was offered and accepted the post.

It was as though Harry Pratt had been foreordained for the position he now held. Already well versed in Illinois history, his knowledge of it became encyclopedic. Already an authority on Lincoln, he gained still greater stature in that field. His knack for finding historical source material brought rich accessions to the Library. Its collection of Lincoln manuscripts almost doubled, passing the one thousand mark in 1953; numerous collections of manuscripts of other prominent Illinoisans were added to its resources; and many files of Illinois newspapers were rescued from obscurity and made available for research in the Library. He edited the *Journal of the Illinois State Historical Society* with outstanding competence, and under his leadership the Junior Historian program and the *Illinois Junior Historian* magazine took on new life. A fluent speaker, and able to entertain and hold the attention of his audience while always leaving something worthwhile with them, he appeared frequently before local historical societies, civic groups and professional and scholarly organizations, and on radio and television programs. His infectious enthusiasm inspired and invigorated statewide interest in history. His quiet but warm personality won him a multitude of friends. To him the sort of work he was now doing was scarcely work at all—he called the Historical Library the "fun house."

From the beginning of the Abraham Lincoln Association's research program in 1925 a close relationship had existed between the Association and the Historical Library. When Dr. Pratt became State Historian, the Association was fully embarked on its most ambitious undertaking— the preparation of the monumental nine-volume *The Collected Works of Abraham Lincoln* (1953). In this project the Historical Library, a treasure house of Lincoln material, was an indispensable adjunct, and the relationship between the two institutions became still closer. Dr. Pratt aided greatly in bringing the *Collected Works* to reality not only by making available all the facilities of the Library, but also through his personal help and counsel.

Serving as assistant editor in the preparation of the *Collected Works* was Marion Dolores Bonzi.[10] A mutual interest in Lincoln drew her and Dr. Pratt together, and on October 1, 1950, they were married. Almost at once the Pratts became a husband-and-wife historical partnership. They both began to be mentioned in authors' acknowledgments. Dr. Randall wrote in his *Lincoln the President: Midstream:* "The Pratts—Harry E. Pratt of the Illinois State Historical Library and Mrs. Marion Bonzi Pratt of the Abraham Lincoln Association—stand high among the author's distinguished benefactors by reason of their incomparable knowledge, able guidance, and unstinting service." Carl Sandburg dedicated his *Abraham Lincoln: The Prairie Years and the War Years*, a one-volume abridgment and revision of his massive six-volume biography, to Harry and Marion Pratt, among others, and characterized them as "a handsome team of Lincoln scholars, who gave time and care to the new manuscript of the Prairie Years."

In 1953, with the *Collected Works* finished and published, the Abraham Lincoln Association discontinued its work and turned over to the Historical Library the tremendous store of Lincoln material that it had accumulated over almost thirty years. With this accession to the Library's already enormous resources, one of the largest working collections of Lincolniana in the world came under Dr. Pratt's supervision.

Dr. Pratt was a member of Sigma Pi fraternity and Phi Delta Kappa, Kappa Phi Kappa and Delta Theta Epsilon. He was also a member of such organizations as the American Historical Association, the American Association of State and Local History, the Illinois Library Association, the Caxton Club, and the national Manuscript Society. He was a life member of the Mississippi Valley Historical Association and the Illinois State Historical Society, and an honorary member of the Lincoln Fellowships of Wisconsin and Southern California and the Civil War Round Tables of Chicago and New York. He served on the advisory board of the Lincoln National Life Foundation and the Lincoln Memorial Garden Foundation. His connection with the Methodist Church was more than nominal affiliation, for he led Sunday School and Bible classes from Cambridge to Muskegon.

Lincoln Memorial University at Harrogate, Tennessee, awarded him its Lincoln Diploma of Honor, and it gave him pride and satisfaction when his wife received the same honor in 1953. Lincoln College at Lincoln, Illinois, conferred in 1954 the honorary degree of Doctor of Literature on both Harry and Marion Pratt with a unique joint citation.

Over the years Dr. Pratt wrote the impressive list of books, monographs and articles, most of which are included in the appended bibliography. He also reviewed many books for newspapers, historical and literary journals.[11] But the works that bear his name by no means measure his activities as a scholar; for no man gave more generously of his time and talents to others. Local historians and writers of magazine and newspaper articles constantly came to him for help. And few indeed are the Lincoln books of consequence published during his years with the Abraham Lincoln Association and as Illinois State Historian in which the author does not acknowledge his indebtedness to Harry Pratt. Thus the public appreciated his work, but his colleagues appreciated it still more. He deserved the title "a historian's historian."

In the spring of 1955 Dr. Pratt suffered a coronary thrombosis. It came on April 15—the anniversary of Lincoln's death. After a number of weeks in the hospital, quietly carrying on various duties of the State Historian, Dr. Pratt returned to the Library, trying to take things a little easier until he had fully regained his health. But to work at anything less than full thrust was difficult for a man of his intensive drive; and to lose touch with happenings at the "fun house" would have been worse to him than death itself. Ten months after the first attack another heart spasm struck him, this time a fatal one. He passed away on the one hundred and forty-seventh anniversary of the day that Abraham Lincoln entered the world. His resting place is Oak Ridge Cemetery, in the shadow of Lincoln's tomb.[12]

Notes

1. James Garfield Randall (1881–1953) wrote *Lincoln the President*, 4 vols. (New York: Dodd, Mead, 1945–55), *Constitutional Problems under Lincoln* (New York: Appleton, 1926), and *The Civil War and Reconstruction* (Boston: D. C. Heath, 1937), among other books. He taught for many years at the University of Illinois.

2. Republican Logan Hay (1871–1942) served as an Illinois state senator and as president of the Illinois Bar Association.

3. Paul McClelland Angle (1900–1975) served as the head of the Illinois State Historical Library from 1932 to 1945, when he became director of the Chicago Historical Society.

4. William Dean Howells, *Life of Abraham Lincoln* (Springfield: Abraham Lincoln Association, 1938).

5. Harry E. Pratt, *Concerning Mr. Lincoln: In Which Abraham Lincoln Is Pictured as He Appeared to Letter Writers of His Time* (Springfield: Abraham Lincoln Association, 1944).

6. This invaluable material in the Illinois State Historical Library, Springfield.

7. Hjordis Lind Pratt committed suicide. Margaret A. Flint to Ernest E. East, Springfield, 13 Sept. 1949, Ernest E. East Papers, Illinois State Historical Library.

8. Pennsylvania-born James Monaghan (1891–1980) was appointed Illinois state historian in 1946 after serving as a research editor for the Illinois State Historical Society since 1939. When he stepped down in 1951, he took a post with the Henry E. Huntington Library in San Marino, California. He edited *Bibliography of Lincolniana* (1945) and wrote a study of Lincoln's handling of foreign relations (*Diplomat in Carpet Slippers*) among other books.

9. Alfred W. Stern (1881–1960) was a prominent businessman and collector of Lincolniana. Clarence P. McClelland (1883–1974) served as president of MacMurray College in Jacksonville (1925–52).

10. Marion Dolores Bonzi Pratt (1907–63) also served as Illinois state historian and editor of the *Abraham Lincoln Quarterly*.

11. The bibliography has been omitted from this volume.

12. Upon receiving the proofs of this article, Thomas wrote to Pratt's widow complaining about textual alterations she had made in her capacity as editor of the *Journal of the Illinois State Historical Society:* "I am extremely troubled and unhappy about the unauthorized changes that have been made in the article on Harry that I prepared for the *Journal.* I went to great pains in that article to write accurately and with good taste and literary artistry and I think that in the revision all those qualities have been impaired. I also tried to bring a touch of personal intimacy into it, and it seems to me that that too has been largely lost. In other words, neither the present content nor the style are mine.

"On the score of accuracy, for example, it is not true to say or give the impression that Harry was Governor Stevenson's personal choice for State Historian. Stevenson did not know Harry either personally or by reputation, and he simply approved the judgment of the trustees. Nor do I think that Harry's prestige needs to be enhanced by making it appear that he had Stevenson's personal endorsement; Harry can stand on his own feet.

"Similarly, on the score of accuracy, I do not regard Harry as a 'preceptor' in the Lincoln field in the same sense that Logan Hay and Jim Randall were preceptors. Perhaps this is a quibble, but if this article is to bear my name I must be permitted to say things in my own way and according to my own conceptions.

"Examples of what I consider questionable taste are the reference to Harry's listing in *Who's Who* and the long quote from the joint citation at Lincoln College [omitted in the final version of the article]. Inclusion in or omission from *Who's Who* is a poor measure of a man, as I see it. Many stuffed shirts manage to get into *Who's Who*, whereas many able men are omitted; and to cite a man of Harry's unquestionable attainments as being listed in *Who's Who* seems like reaching a long way to find something more to say about him, as though you hadn't been able to find enough to say already. To my mind it is a mistake to say too much in an article of this sort, for in doing so you are likely to cheapen the tribute by creating the impression of a false build-up. That is why I disapprove of quoting the joint citation. Everything it says has been said already.

"Insofar as artistry is concerned, I prided myself on having worked conscientiously to say just what I wanted to say in the best way I could say it. My sentences expressed exactly the idea that I wished to convey. And though someone else might very well be able to say the same thing better, that was my way of saying it. But now in many cases the sentences are no longer mine. They have lost their personal character and anyone familiar with my style would scarcely attribute them to me. And in at least one instance where new material has been added—Harry and his sister at the time of their father's death [also omitted]—the meaning isn't even comprehensible.

"In short, the article in its present form is not my work at all and it would be misrepresentation for it to go out under my name. I must ask that you do one of two things. Either print it as I wrote it or remove my name from it. Perhaps the latter course would be simpler and better since the article is already in print. No author's name is needed on the article; it can stand as a tribute from the staff, which in its present form it is. Of course, if you take the latter course, you will have to make revisions wherever I have introduced a personal touch and used the pronoun 'I,' but that should not be difficult.

"I hope you understand that this letter is not written in ill-will. Whatever choice you make in the matter will be perfectly agreeable with me. Nor is there any necessity for discussing it." Benjamin P. Thomas to Marion Pratt, Springfield, 28 Sept. 1956, copy, Benjamin P. Thomas Papers, Illinois State Historical Library.

15 Our Lincoln Heritage from Ida Tarbell

Fourteen years ago I had just made my bow to the Lincoln audience with a book entitled *Lincoln's New Salem*.[1] I had been in Lincoln work for two years, but the Lincoln field is too complicated and controversial for one to claim authority in it with only two years' study. Moreover, while Lincoln himself was the most tolerant of men, some Lincoln scholars have not exhibited the same tolerance. Lincoln scholarship has known some bitter grapples in which few holds were barred. So it was with not a little trepidation that I awaited the critics' reaction to my work.

Within a week of my book's appearance, however, I received a most gracious letter; and it came from the best known Lincoln student of that day. "It is just the kind of a book I have been hoping for many a day somebody would write," the letter said, "but I confess I did not conceive that anybody would ever do it as well as you have done it. You have put so much sober care into it and shown what is dear to me—an appreciation of the reality and dignity of life in that little settlement."

My fears were immediately dispelled. If that was what Ida Tarbell thought about the book, I did not care what others might say. Perhaps

An address delivered at Allegheny College, 26 February 1948, under the auspices of the Reis Library of that institution in recognition of Ida Tarbell's gift of her personal Lincoln collection and the correspondence relating to her Lincoln work. Published in *Abraham Lincoln Quarterly* 6 (March 1950): 3–23.

she was a little fulsome in her praise, for she always tried to encourage younger Lincoln writers and make them feel at home in the Lincoln field, an attitude which was in marked contrast to that which she encountered when she was just a neophyte.

She began her Lincoln studies when the Lincoln generation was shuffling off. Those who had known Lincoln and cared to write about him had had their say. The reminiscent epoch was passing. The groundwork of Lincoln biography had been laid. The modern age of Lincoln scholarship was in the offing. The technique of our present historical method had not yet been brought to bear. It was a transitional period and Miss Tarbell's work was destined to be typical of her age.

When Miss Tarbell began her Lincoln studies, William H. Herndon, Lincoln's law partner, had been dead for three years—Billy Herndon who did not like the legendary figure of Lincoln and who aspired to set the world right about the Lincoln he had known. Herndon had died in poverty, reviled, denounced and hated because he tried to tell the truth, although it must be granted that he had not always been able to recognize it.

Jesse Weik, who did the actual writing for Herndon, was living quietly at Greencastle, Indiana, smarting under the obloquy he shared with Herndon, disappointed in the financial failure of what he still insisted was a great book, selling an occasional Lincoln article to a magazine to provide himself with a precarious livelihood, cherishing the documentary material that Herndon had left.

John Hay, who had served as one of Lincoln's private secretaries, and who had helped create a magnificent figure of Lincoln with a monumental ten-volume biography, was surfeited with Lincoln authorship and ready to move into broader fields of literature and statesmanship. His collaborator, John George Nicolay, also secretary to Lincoln, was still vigorous at sixty. He and Hay had labored on their biography of Lincoln off and on for fifteen years. It had run serially in the *Century* magazine and had appeared in book form four years before Miss Tarbell began her Lincoln work, bringing the authors fame and money. About the same time she began her Lincoln studies, Nicolay and Hay brought out an edition of Lincoln's speeches and writings. Nicolay lived in Washington now, a slight[,] frail man with pale, ascetic face, lean nose, thin hair, and long whiskers shedding forth luxuriant from his chin. Plagued by eye strain and uncertain health, he was sometimes tart and testy. Unlike Hay, he regarded Lincoln as his life's work, and he watched like a sentinel over the portrait of Lincoln that he and Hay had drawn. He looked upon the Lincoln field as his demesne and trespassers were unwelcome.

Robert Todd Lincoln, son of the president, was living too, and at fifty-three had already been secretary of war and minister to England. Wealthy, powerful in political and business circles, mentioned as a candidate for president, soon to become president of the Pullman Company, he was a proud, shy, sensitive sort of man who never willfully capitalized upon his father's fame but had benefited from his father's eminence none the less. Never very intimate with his father, he had probably never really understood him, nor did he feel obliged to aid others to understanding. He preferred not to recall his father's humble beginnings and his blue pencil had been applied freely to the work of Nicolay and Hay. Unobtrusive in the field of Lincoln writing, but ever watchful, he sometimes acted privily but no less effectively to see that posterity got what he conceived to be the proper concept of his father. Satisfied with what Nicolay and Hay had done, he was uncooperative with other aspiring students.

Also living was Henry Clay Whitney, a lawyer friend of Lincoln's whose *Life on the Circuit with Lincoln* had been published two years before.[2] A young man of twenty-three when he first met Lincoln, Whitney was now a crusty, disillusioned man of sixty-three. Proud of his intimacy with Lincoln, hypercritical of those who tried to write about Lincoln without having known him personally, Whitney was not averse to making a little money from his Lincoln knowledge when chance offered.

With Herndon's realism discredited, the world had a distorted conception of Lincoln, an image compounded of reminiscences which had not always escaped the inaccuracies that come from failing memories or uninhibited imaginations. It was not essentially untrue; but it was colored by the quirks and preconceptions and idiosyncrasies of individuals, and by sectional bias. It lacked perspective and adequate background, and it had been smudged in certain detail by unskilled hands. Even Herndon, with all his good intentions, had contributed to the distortion when lack of critical acuteness, misplaced trust in the memories of others and undue reliance on his own clairvoyance sometimes led him astray.

What remained to be done in the Lincoln field? In the first place, a wealth of documents that would resolve moot points in the Lincoln story and provide clarifying detail for almost every phase of Lincoln's life had been largely ignored. They would be richly rewarding to anyone willing to take the trouble to dig them out. And then there was the matter of interpretation—the need for explanation of the why and wherefore of Lincoln's actions, of appraising his successes and failures, of estimating the true meaning of his life. A person who had not known Lincoln personally would lack the firsthand knowledge the men of the reminiscent school enjoyed, but conversely, such a person would have the advantage of perspective and detachment that those men so conspicuously lacked. The Lincoln field offered a challenge to an unbiased, critical mind.

Was Miss Tarbell qualified to undertake this work? Did she have the patience and persistence required of one who does worthwhile research? Was there any reason to think she could understand or interpret Lincoln better than those who had actually known him? Could she draw meaning from things that were meaningless or unintelligible to them? Did she have anything in common with Lincoln? As she set herself to this new task, what was there in her background that might help?

So far she had written a number of feature stories for newspapers and magazines and two biographies—one dealing with Madame Roland and the other with Napoleon Bonaparte.[3] Her interests had originally been scientific, and after she took up writing it was the figures of the French Revolutionary period that attracted her. It was through Samuel S. McClure, editor of *McClure's* magazine, and his partner, John S. Phillips, that she was induced to enter the Lincoln field when the partners conceived the idea of setting up a sort of Lincoln bureau in their editorial rooms.[4] Their original plan was to put her in charge of an organized search for unpublished Lincoln material with the idea of popularizing Lincoln in the magazine.

A career woman in an age when such women were rare, she was now thirty-seven years old. Tall and slim, she was attractive and well-poised, with clear eyes, soft brown hair and a wistful smile. Gracious, eager to make her mark in the literary world, quick to learn, and talented with a pen, she was to be a fortunate find for McClure.

It probably never occurred to her that her background had anything in common with Lincoln's beyond the fact that she was born in a log house and he was born in a log cabin. Yet both had a rugged childhood. His was characterized by poverty; hers by ugly surroundings. She was brought up in the oil country, in a valley disfigured by sludge and tar and the refuse of the drills, where trees and vegetation were smothered by the greasy seepage of the pumps and the pungent petroleum odor that permeated everything; where man took nature's wealth and left his benefactress defaced and scarred. Yet, just as Lincoln aspired to rise above his humble beginnings, Ida Tarbell looked above the ugly valley to the hills, where trees and grass and flowers were still beautiful.

It was not that she held herself aloof from life. She never did that, any more than Lincoln did. She liked the mystery, the struggle, the excitement of it, just as he did. An oil community of the pioneer days was a tough and boisterous place, tougher, perhaps—certainly with a more wicked toughness—than the frontier where Lincoln grew up. Being a man, compelled to make his living among men, Lincoln was touched by the rugged influences around him, whereas Ida Tarbell was not, although she was not oblivious of them. She herself tells of coming across a copy of the *Police Gazette* that belonged to the Tarbell hired man, and of devouring its racy contents eagerly. But she saw no indecency in the pictures of the scantily clad women and she admired the swaggering sportiness of the men.

By the time she was a young lady, Miss Tarbell's family moved to a community not quite so raw, where they lived in a house her father had built with his own hands from the salvage of a dismantled hotel. This was the town of Titusville, a center of supply for the oil industry, and a place that tried to keep its old-time order and decency when the rigging crews and roustabouts moved in. Here Ida Tarbell headed the honor roll in high school, finding her greatest joy in scientific subjects—biology, geology, zoology, chemistry—finding a new world under the lens of a microscope. She had been given intensive religious instruction as a girl, but she found it hard to reconcile what science taught her with the scriptural account of creation. She compared the scientific explanation of the origins of the earth and its creatures, evolving through long periods of time, with the account of the creation in Genesis, where the whole process was supposedly the work of six days. And when her teachers tried to explain that the days of the Bible might mean periods of time, like the day of Rome and the day of Greece, she was shocked that she must either reject the scientific explanation or cease to take the Bible literally. Like Lincoln she was beset with doubt, but with her usual levelheadedness she decided that the hereafter, if there was such a thing, would be assured to one who lived a decent, useful life. Like Lincoln she had a sense of frustration when dealing with abstractions, like him she had little patience with dogma and creeds. But also like him, she came eventually to realize that the incomprehensible could still be true and real, that above and beyond what men could understand there was something that seemed to order their destiny.

Like Lincoln, Miss Tarbell had consuming ambition. His was for political advancement and the esteem of his fellow men. Hers was for independence. Lincoln had to make his way without benefit of formal education, learning from life; whereas Miss Tarbell saw education as the path of realization for her hopes. That is how she came to Allegheny College.

Can you imagine this eager, zestful girl enrolling here, the only woman in a class of forty, with only five girls including herself in the entire student body? How such an attractive girl escaped matrimony under such circumstances will always be a mystery to me. Did I hear some young lady sigh for the good old days? Well, there were some wonderful things about them, to be sure. Miss Tarbell thought Bentley Hall was the most beautiful building she had ever seen. But looking back later, she also remembered the pot-bellied stove that was the only source of heat in Bentley Hall in winter, the hard chairs, the kerosene lamps, the bare floors always cold and wet from the snow that was continually tracked in.

She remembered some great teachers, too. Jeremiah Tingley, head of the science department, effervescing with enthusiasm, consecrated to his profession; George Haskins, brackish and crusty, hard to satisfy, but a great Latin scholar.[5] Even in Miss Tarbell's day, Allegheny was an old college in an old town. She loved it from the first, and she took away with her a precious thing, a thing which kept her life from ever being lonely— a lasting sense of the companionship of books.

Out in the world and on her own at last, she was to discover, as most of us do, that a diploma does not guarantee success. Her first job was in a seminary at Poland, Ohio, where all she was supposed to teach was Greek, Latin, French, German, geology, botany, geometry, trigonometry, and two strange subjects known as "verb grammar" and "percentage arithmetic." Her salary was five hundred dollars a year and "board yourself," so she was not insensitive to Lincoln's early struggles to make a living. One wonders how she had time for observation with such a teaching schedule, but she was always keenly sensitive to the ways of people around her, just as Lincoln was. There in Poland, fifteen miles from Youngstown, she saw industry impinging on a rural way of life, destroying its beauty, breaking down its standards of conduct, [and] bringing a love of money for the sake of money to those who had hitherto regarded affluence as a way to a satisfying life. She became conscious of the problem of race adjustment as foreign workers moved in. She saw the enormous wealth that industry could create and also the instability and despair it brought to workers with its periodic depressions, when it came to an unexpected, puzzling stop, then spun and skidded and ground and screeched like an overloaded train that was trying to get a new grip on the rails to drive on irresistibly again.

Miss Tarbell did not stay at Poland long. Her next job was with the *Chautauquan,* the house organ, we might say, of the Chautauqua Literary and Scientific Circle—a plan of adult education sponsored by the Chautauqua Association and numbering some twenty thousand members. Its headquarters were here at Meadville, so Miss Tarbell returned to the college atmosphere. At last she was in the field of literature that would become her life work. In the office of the *Chautauquan* she handled the correspondence, edited articles, and contributed an occasional one herself. She learned the art of self-expression and the mysteries of printing. She made stimulating acquaintances. She was always making acquaintances, just as Lincoln was, for she was simple and easy to know, and people did not forget her. But she was dissatisfied with the limitations of her job. She was secure, in a sense, but she was not independent, and she was beginning to believe that the only real security is in the mind, that the only certainties in life are the things you know, and the only worthwhile achievement is not how much you can make, but what you can make of yourself.

With not a little foreboding, Miss Tarbell decided to resign from her job and set out on her own, to study in France, and sustain herself with her pen. It was a daring decision, for she had no standing in literary circles. She was not a finished writer, although she had learned what good writing is; and she had habits of order, industry and painstaking care which are useful tools in any craft.

Her years in France were fruitful, as all her experiences were. She liked the French scholars whom she met, especially Charles Seignobos, the medievalist. He held his learning as she came to hold her talents, not as an accomplishment in which to take a smug and selfish satisfaction, but as an endowment to be put to public use.[6] Although she would not realize it until much later, it was just such a renunciation of selfishness that brought Abraham Lincoln fame, that enabled a self-centered small-town politician to grow to be a great statesman.

Miss Tarbell earned some money from newspaper pieces while she studied in France. But before the first of her two biographies was finished she was obliged to pawn her sealskin coat. Parisian pawnbrokers were fearful of becoming the unwitting purchasers of stolen goods, and Miss Tarbell was asked to furnish evidence of good character. As proof of this she showed the skeptical pawnbroker her Allegheny College diploma.

This, then, was the young woman who turned her talents to the Lincoln story, and who set out to track down the clues that *McClure's* appeal for unpublished Lincoln material began to bring to light. She picked up the Lincoln trail in Kentucky, and as she followed it, she examined court records, talked to old people who had known the Lincolns, ransacked houses for letters and pictures. It was mid-February when she started out and the weather was bitter and blustery. She was obliged to put up at wretched hotels, with cheerless, dirty lobbies, cold bedrooms and poor cooking. She traveled by train when she could, but sometimes had to hire a hack or buggy.

And the results were disappointing. She found much new material, but it was too fragmentary and disconnected for publication. To have meaning it must be correlated with the pattern already worked out. So, unwittingly almost, Miss Tarbell became a Lincoln biographer instead of an editor.

Her immediate success went beyond her own or McClure's most optimistic hopes. Within ten days of the appearance of her first Lincoln article *McClure's* gained ten thousand new subscribers, and within three months one hundred thousand new subscriptions had been received. But the old-guard Lincoln men were provoked. John G. Nicolay refused to help Miss Tarbell and complained that she had no right to invade his field. Whitney called her "an obscure Bohemian," a "bluestocking" whose series in McClure's was "a weary & oft told and plagiarized narrative," "sponged" and "cribbed" from others, and written in the style of a kindergarten teacher. Robert Lincoln was friendly but not enthusiastic. Only Jesse Weik was helpful, just as Herndon had tried to be helpful to other writers.

Having once taken up the study of Lincoln, Miss Tarbell was never able to put it down. It was not always her major literary interest, but it was her only continuing one. Out of her articles in *McClure's* came her *Early Life of Abraham Lincoln* to be followed by a two-volume *Life.*[7] When she was sidetracked temporarily by her work on the *History of the Standard Oil Company,* Jesse Weik wrote to ask her if she had given up her Lincoln work. "Of course, I have not dropped Lincoln," she replied. "I intend to keep hold of him as long as I live."[8] Even when she was at work on other matters there was always a manuscript of a Lincoln article or book upon her desk, and she was always glad to get back to it. At the age of eighty-four she wrote: "Anyone who really takes up seriously the study of . . . [Lincoln's] life is never willing to lay it down. He is companionable as no public mind that I've ever known anything about, you feel at home with him, he never high hats you and he never bores you which is more than I can say of any public man living or dead with whom I have tried to get well acquainted. . . . An impressive part of this acquaintance with him as a man is watching him grow, expand. Nothing was ever finished for Lincoln."[9]

What did Miss Tarbell contribute to what we know of Lincoln? Of course she added detail. Her *Life of Abraham Lincoln* contains an appendix of some two hundred pages of new documents she brought to light. She was especially interested in the physical setting of events and her work is replete with photographs, many of which she took with her own camera on her trips through the Lincoln country. The people and many of the structures that she photographed are gone and we would have no record of them now, but for her work. Besides the documents and pictures she contributed, she clarified disputed points. But her greatest Lincoln legacy was understanding of the man and his environment, and of how his environment shaped him.

It had been the fashion of earlier biographers to make Lincoln's early life as unattractive as possible in order that they might contrast his humble beginnings with his later greatness. Chauncey Black, who was ghostwriter for Ward Hill Lamon's *Life of Lincoln*, wrote to Lamon while he was working on the book: "We must point mankind to the diamond glowing on the dunghill and then to the same resplendent jewel in the future setting of great events and brilliant achievements."[10] Herndon described Lincoln as rising from "a stagnant, putrid pool."[11] There is evidence to indicate that both Herndon and Black rather welcomed the false notion that Lincoln was of illegitimate birth, since this enabled them to make a more startling contrast between his beginnings and his achievements.

But Miss Tarbell looked at Lincoln's background differently. She suspected that Lincoln's parents and the conditions of his early life had been purposely written down. Actually he was a typical pioneer child of typical pioneer parents. There was poverty, to be sure, but it was not the degrading sort of poverty. And to overdraw the picture was to miss the point; for what Miss Tarbell saw in Lincoln's story was the power of the American West and what it could do in the way of fashioning a man. Lincoln did not become what he did in spite of his background. He became what he did because of it. Here was a man who was denied the advantages of formal education, but absorbed his education largely from his surroundings. Here was a product of the American way of life. Here was a man who epitomized American characteristics. This was the real meaning of Lincoln's story, and to overdraw the hardships and sordidness was to make it unreal and unconvincing.

Although Miss Tarbell's mature life was spent in cities—Paris, New York, Washington—she never lost contact with the people of the country and small towns, for she traveled often and extensively on lecture tours. Thus, like Lincoln, she never lost her feeling for the common folk. She saw in the naturalness of America's rural people rather than in the veneer of city life the true manifestations of Americanism. She liked the way Chic Sale depicted the rural character she had drawn, "The Man Who Knew Lincoln," in one of his vaudeville skits. "I know of no one on our stage that interprets with so much sympathy, humor, and understanding the honest-to-God American of our country towns and corners," she wrote to Sale. "You catch his shrewdness, independence of spirit, his love of fun and its practice. I always laugh at your characters and love them because they are so entirely themselves."[12]

She thought the people's love of Lincoln came largely from the fact that he was a true American type, exemplifying the American characteristics of common sense, directness, humor, and tenacious determination. He spoke the common language. His very speech took flavor from the elements of life. "The horse, the dog, the ox, the chin fly, the plow, the hog, these companions of his youth became interpreters of his meaning" when he tried to make men understand him.[13] He had the common touch. In his triumph over adversity the people saw a realization of the same hopes and aspirations they entertained for themselves.

Miss Tarbell was never able to suppress the womanly romanticism of her fervent feminine nature. She hoped, for example, that the story of Lincoln's love for Ann Rutledge would never be proved untrue and she defended it from the attacks of skeptics. Nor can we say she was wrong. The story is one of those incidents of Lincoln's life about which we are not yet certain, and probably never shall be.[14] Perhaps Miss Tarbell had a feminine intuition that it was true. To her it seemed that a man like Lincoln, who had known so much sadness, so much of disappointment and tragedy, deserved to have his life enriched by such a romance.

But her romanticism never tempted her into sickly sentimentality. Her Lincoln was altogether a man. To her his life presented an example of what a man can do to overcome handicaps and the frailties of human nature. Her Lincoln was not perfect. He was a man like other men. To deny his human attributes was to sunder the subtle communion that the people held with him. To depict him as a God or superman would make him a counterpart of the statuesque, too perfect Washington of Parson Weems.

Miss Tarbell's life was characterized by a stanch idealism, and this idealism is manifest throughout her work. But it never led her to reject the truth. The ideal of scholarship is absolute impartiality, but too often scholars have their own peculiar hobbies to ride. The search for truth is too often hindered by unwillingness to confess mistakes, or give up preconceived ideas, and this has been especially true of Lincoln students. But it was surely not the case with Ida Tarbell. She recognized that setting out to prove certain things, instead of drawing conclusions from the facts, was dangerous in any investigation. She was the first person to bring to the study of Lincoln an open mind. She had no false pride and no illusions of infallibility. Always and sincerely she expressed gratitude when anyone exposed an error in her work, and if something was proved to be so, she accepted it, whether it accorded with what she would like to believe or not. She became involved in a bitter controversy over the legitimacy or illegitimacy of Lincoln's mother, a controversy that shook the world of Lincoln scholarship for years and left rancor which still manifests itself occasionally today. But Miss Tarbell was good-tempered through the whole thing, and when the preponderance of evidence pointed to illegitimacy, she did not try to go counter to the facts, although she had hoped fervently that the matter would turn out differently. When I wrote my *Portrait for Posterity* and tried to give her her proper place among the Lincoln biographers, I debated with myself whether to call her an idealistic realist or a realistic idealist, and I am not yet sure which best describes her. Perhaps this doubt is flattering to her, for both realism and idealism have their place in Lincoln biography. The realists' ruthless searching gives the necessary facts; but the realist is ill-advised to scorn those soul qualities in Lincoln that documentary evidence, which is the chief reliance of the realist, may not always disclose.

Will Miss Tarbell take rank as one of the great Lincoln scholars of all time? I am afraid I must conclude that she will not. She lacked the cold impartiality of the scholar. She admitted this herself. As her wisdom ripened with age she realized that she was too uncritically laudatory by modern standards of scholarship. "I am afraid I am over-lenient with mistakes," she said, "having made so many myself." At the age of eighty-four she wrote: "As one of the old guard, about the oldest, I think, I am never very sure of my standing with the younger Lincoln students, but I am thankful for them. They are constantly unearthing things that I never found and enabling me to correct what are supposed to be facts."[15]

Primarily Miss Tarbell was a popularizer and with the passing years her books are becoming outmoded. But this is not to detract from what she did. A popularizer is an interpreter—one who aids others to understanding. That was her role. "I have never had illusions about the value of my individual contribution!" she asserted in her *Autobiography*. "I realized early that what a man or a woman does is built on what those who have gone before have done, that its real value depends on making the matter in hand a little clearer, and a little sounder for those who come after. Nobody begins or ends anything."[16]

This is especially true of Lincoln biography. Not yet has anyone been able to give us a completely satisfactory life of Lincoln, rounded, sufficient, definitive. Our portrait of Lincoln is a composite, touched by many brushes, the joint product of many different draughtsmen whose combined efforts have given us an essentially faithful portrayal of a subject so difficult to comprehend that no one artist could have done the job alone, although each has made some brush marks that endure. Whatever of value each searcher has contributed has been incorporated in the work of those who followed, so that the process has been like the building of an edifice.

Miss Tarbell's work is incorporated in it for all time, not readily recognizable as hers perhaps, but there, nevertheless, helping to hold it together, contributing to its stability. And if some realist should demand documentary proof of this, it can readily be adduced.

No other writer compares with Carl Sandburg in giving us the true feel of the man Lincoln and of the times in which he moved. And Sandburg acknowledges that he derived his greatest stimulus from the work of Ida Tarbell. Sending her page proofs of his *Abraham Lincoln: The Prairie Years,* he wrote: "Yourself and Oliver R. Barrett are the only persons receiving advance sheets, as you are the two who have helped me most"; and in his preface Sandburg credited her with putting fresh color into what had heretofore been pictured as "drab and miserable beyond the fact."[17] In another letter, Sandburg told her how he and Barrett "talked long this evening about how much less of *fresh glint* there would be on the Lincoln legend without your work"; and when his *Abraham Lincoln: The War Years* was published he sent her a copy "not merely with my compliments, but with respect and affection—and something like reverence for a wisdom and integrity that have lasted so well across the years."

As this tall, gaunt product of the blending of Sweden and the American mid-West, with his almost boyish face, and his two locks of stiff gray hair that persist in falling across his forehead, sought for the real Lincoln; as Sandburg sat on a small chair with his typewriter before him on a crackerbox—because Grant and Sherman had conducted their campaigns from a crackerbox and there was something uniquely American about a crackerbox—and as his gaze swept over his notes that were pinned to an upright screen beyond his typewriter, Miss Tarbell's books were always close at hand. When he took time out from his Lincoln studies to write his long poem, *The People, Yes,* he wrote to her that he was sure the work held some of her heartbeats about democracy and these times. Another time, Sandburg wrote to tell her that her *History of the Standard Oil Company* had a prominent place on his front room bookshelf. "Perhaps every two years," he said, "I reread that classic commentary: Commercial Machiavellianism. So you are never forgotten here and there are brightnesses you might not know of about this note of yours fluttering out of the day's mail yesterday."[18] Sandburg and Ida Tarbell enjoyed close kinship through their feeling for Lincoln. Both saw him as a truly American product, combining the rugged independence, the easy freedom, the boisterous humor, the loamy philosophy of the frontier plains with the stern, strong, rocky fibre of the mountains.

If one reads Miss Tarbell's books and then reads Sandburg, he will sense a similarity of feeling. There is much of Ida Tarbell in Sandburg's product, not always readily recognizable, perhaps, but filtered out to us through the mind of one who excels in the poet's talent to translate what he feels within him.

When Sandburg's *War Years* began to appear serially in *The Red Book* magazine, Oliver Barrett, who has been one of Sandburg's closest friends for years, wrote to tell Miss Tarbell: "I presume you have noticed the early chapters of Carl's latest work in the Red Book. It must be very pleasing to you who must realize how much of the good work that has been done later has been due to the impetus of your early researches."

Probably Ida Tarbell was too warm, too human, too graciously impulsive to take permanent rank as a great scholar. But what of that? She will be remembered rather as a woman of surpassing wisdom, as one who had a wonderful understanding of a man not easy to understand.

It has been asserted that one cannot live in close contact with Lincoln's life without coming under its influence. One reviewer of Sandburg's *Prairie Years* asserted that "We doubt not that it has done Carl Sandburg much good to write it. Such is the blessing that Abraham Lincoln bestows on his biographers." And another reviewer "liked Lincoln the better for the book and Carl Sandburg and myself and my neighbor. And that result," he said, "is the living virtue that streams out of Lincoln forever." Did Lincoln do anything to Ida Tarbell's personality? I am sure he did.

In her autobiography she says that study of Lincoln restored her esteem for her American citizenship, which had lost some of its meaning to her during the years she spent in France. And it gave her a new appreciation of democracy and its ideals. She was sometimes discouraged by the shortcomings and seeming failures of democracy, just as Lincoln must have been at times. But she held to her faith in it when others wished to change the system. The faults of democracy were those of human nature, and human nature would be no better and would probably be worse under fascism or communism. "You don't change human nature by changing the machinery," she wrote. "Under freedom human nature has the best chance for growth, for correcting its weaknesses and failures, for developing its capacities. It is on these improvements in men that the future of the world depends."[19]

Miss Tarbell saw democracy as a spiritual faith, not as a matter of law or system. And if there was something wrong with the America of her age, the remedy that she would prescribe was more, not less, democracy. If a few rich individuals and corporations were plundering the poor and driving weaker competitors to the wall with a purpose to establish monopoly, and if alliance between selfish and unscrupulous business men and bribe-seeking politicians made these practices possible, Miss Tarbell did not blame democracy. This was a negation of democracy. As has too often been the case throughout our history, selfish interests were using democratic catchwords to cloak renunciation of democracy. If the people could only be awakened and persuaded to use the powers democracy gave them, the abuses could be alleviated speedily. Miss Tarbell's faith in democracy was no less strong than Lincoln's, and he saw it as "the last, best hope of earth."

Mapping out her work in the latter part of her life, Miss Tarbell said: "I wanted to do my part toward making the world acquainted with the man who I believed had best shown how to carry out a program of cooperation based on consideration of others—that was Abraham Lincoln. . . . The more people who know about Lincoln, the more chance democracy has to destroy its two enemies, privilege and militancy. I proposed to take every chance I had to talk about him."

People were continually asking Miss Tarbell what Lincoln would do about specific problems of their own day. But she realized the futility of speculations of that nature. This was not to say that Lincoln had nothing to offer them. They could profit immeasurably by studying and following his methods, by learning patience, by probing to the essentials of a problem, by forswearing vanity, false pride and partisan malice, by training the will to follow the dictates of the mind and conscience regardless of criticism. And above all there was his tolerance, his willingness to see an opponent's point of view and recognize that right was not always altogether on one side. These were lessons Ida Tarbell learned from Lincoln.

In her investigation of the Standard Oil Company, for example, she always tried to be scrupulously fair. She always gave the officials of the company a chance to present their side, and often let them read what she had written before it went to press. If they could convince her that she was mistaken or unfair, she would revise her work accordingly; but it was up to them to prove that she was wrong. And in the very men she criticized so unflinchingly she often found much to admire.

Yes, Ida Tarbell's wisdom and understanding came in no small measure from her study of Lincoln.

She wanted others to learn these lessons, too. Lincoln and Allegheny College were her two abiding loves; and how appropriate it is that she bequeathed her Lincoln treasures and that part of her correspondence that deals with her Lincoln work to this institution. Now, students who follow her footsteps here can draw from Lincoln the same inspiration that was vouchsafed to her. The strength and wisdom and goodness that came to her from Lincoln, may also come to them. How wonderful for any college to be permeated with a Lincoln atmosphere, to diffuse the influence of Lincoln through its teaching, to infuse its traditions with Lincoln's spirit.

Do not be disturbed or disappointed if the tough realists of the future detract from Ida Tarbell's stature as a Lincoln scholar. Her place in the Lincoln story will not be that of a great scholar. She will be known rather as a wise and wholesome influence. Her impress on our Lincoln portrait is ineffaceable. Yet, her writings, however influential, may prove to be by no means her greatest glory. Her Lincoln legacy to Allegheny College, exerting a calm, sure, subtle influence through coming years, may turn out to be our richest heritage.[20]

Notes

1. Published in 1934 by the Abraham Lincoln Association.

2. Henry Clay Whitney (1835–1905) was a lawyer who saw much of Lincoln on the circuit from 1854 to 1861.

3. Ida M. Tarbell, *Madame Roland: A Biographical Study* (New York: C. Scribner's Sons, 1896). Tarbell's *A Life of Napoleon Bonaparte, with a Sketch of Josephine, Empress of the French* (New York: McClure, Phillips, 1901) originally appeared in *McClure's Magazine* in 1895.

4. Samuel Sidney McClure (1857–1949) founded *McClure's Magazine* in 1893. John Sanburn Phillips (b. 1861), co-founder of *McClure's Magazine*, established his own publication, the *American Magazine*, in 1906.

5. Ida M. Tarbell, *All in the Day's Work: An Autobiography* (New York: Macmillan, 1939), 41–45.

6. Tarbell, *All in the Day's Work*, 132–36.

7. Ida M. Tarbell, *The Early Life of Abraham Lincoln* (New York: McClure, 1896); Tarbell, *The Life of Abraham Lincoln*, 2 vols. (New York: McClure, Phillips, 1900).

8. Ida M. Tarbell, *The History of the Standard Oil Company*, 2 vols. (New York: Macmillan, 1904).

9. Ida M. Tarbell to John W. Starr, Jr., 10 March 1941, copy, Ida M. Tarbell Papers, Allegheny College.

10. Chauncy Black to William H. Herndon, 8 March 1870, Herndon-Weik Papers, Library of Congress.

11. Paul M. Angle, ed., *Herndon's Life of Lincoln: The History and Personal Recollections of Abraham Lincoln as Orginally Written by William H. Herndon and Jesse Weik* (Cleveland: World, 1942), vii.

12. Charles P. ("Chic") Sale (1885–1936) acted in vaudeville.

13. Ida M. Tarbell, *In the Footsteps of the Lincolns* (New York: Harper and Brothers, 1924), 137.

14. More recent scholarship suggests that the story of Lincoln's romance with Ann Rutledge was true. John Y. Simon, "Abraham Lincoln and Ann Rutledge," *Journal of the Abraham Lincoln Association* 11 (1990): 13–33; Douglas L. Wilson, "Abraham Lincoln, Ann Rutledge, and the Evidence of Herndon's Informants," in *Lincoln before Washington: New Perspectives on the Illinois Years,*

ed. Douglas L. Wilson (Urbana: University of Illinois Press, 1997), 74–98; John Evangelist Walsh, *The Shadows Rise: Abraham Lincoln and the Ann Rutledge Legend* (Urbana: University of Illinois Press, 1993).

15. Ida M. Tarbell to Oliver R. Barrett, 25 Feb. 1936, copy, Tarbell Papers, Allegheny College.

16. Tarbell, *All in the Day's Work*, 400.

17. Carl Sandburg, *Abraham Lincoln: The Prairie Years*, 2 vols. (New York: Harcourt Brace, 1926), 1:viii. Chicago attorney Oliver Rogers Barrett (1873–1950) was a prominent Lincoln collector.

18. Carl Sandburg to Ida M. Tarbell, [Herbert, Mich.], 19 May 1935, in *The Letters of Carl Sandburg*, ed. Herbert Mitgang (New York: Harcourt, Brace and World, 1968), 329–30.

19. Tarbell, *All in the Day's Work*, 179–80.

20. Tarbell's legacy is the treasure trove of information that she gathered from people who had known Lincoln. In her papers at Allegheny College are a wealth of interviews and correspondence that sheds much light on the Sixteenth President. Some of that valuable material found its way into her books; a great deal did not. Like William Herndon, she deserves the gratitude of all Lincoln students for having assiduously gathered and preserved data.

16   The Art of Biography

To make one not-too-important criticism of Mr. Garraty's paper, I question whether a valid distinction can be made between academic and non-academic biographers on the basis of technique. [Douglas Southall] Freeman, [Albert J.] Beveridge, Irving Brant, Ray Stannard Baker, and Marquis James come to mind as non-academic biographers who belong in the academic fellowship in so far as technique is concerned.[1]

A more realistic differentiation might be made by distinguishing between those biographers who regard themselves primarily as scholars and those to whom biography is first of all a literary form. And it is in the latter group that we find the experimenters with new techniques— invented conversation, imaginary incidents, false climaxes, [and] psychoanalysis. To the literary artist such devices are a harmless means of heightening reader interest. To the historian they are breeders of inaccuracy and myth. The literary biographer sees no harm in such freewheeling provided the overall impression that he or she creates is essentially accurate. The scholarly biographer insists that the details be accurate too.

Mr. Garraty makes the extremely significant point that there is something to be said for the purpose if not the practices of many of these experimenters. The scholarly biographer has too often fallen victim to an inhibiting technique. He has become a slave to historical method instead of making it serve him. I go along with Professor Frederick Tolles, whom Mr. Garraty quotes to the effect that research and scholarship are not at

---

Undated typescript written sometime between 1952 and 1956, Benjamin P. Thomas Papers, Illinois State Historical Library, Springfield.

all incompatible with the imaginative and artistic qualities that make for readability.[2]

One student of biographical writing, Edward H. O'Neill, goes so far as to suggest that the scientific historian should not attempt to write biography at all. "There can be no purely scientific life-writing," he claims.[3] The biographer to be successful must have feelings as well as opinions about his subject; and when the biographer allows feeling or emotion to influence him, he ceases to be scientific. I beg to differ. Take Frank Freidel's *Roosevelt: The Ordeal*.[4] There you have an example of excellent biography, written in the scientific spirit. But there is plenty of feeling in it, plenty of sentiment. Not cheap sentimentality, but a strong undercurrent of sympathy.

Dwight MacDonald, a reviewer for the *New Yorker*, also takes a dim view of the scholar as biographer.[5] In a recent review of Lord David Cecil's biography of Lord Melbourne, he wrote: "After the usual scholarly biography, written in barbarous academese and presenting huge chunks of raw data untouched by human thought, it is a relief to come on something that has some form and style."[6] That is pretty severe, and certainly inapplicable to many scholarly biographies. Yet, all too often, academic biographers, and academic historians, too refuse to face up to the fact that they work in a literary medium, and pay far too little attention to literary craftsmanship.

It would seem that even some academic historians are inclined to look down their noses at their colleagues who write biography. Professor Caughey, in the article in the *Mississippi Valley Historical Review* referred to by Mr. Garraty, states that biography is simpler than history, and (I quote): "It may be less exacting. Or perhaps it is just that it exerts a greater appeal to miscellaneous scholars and writers who could also turn out first-class histories if they wanted to."[7] I don't know exactly what a "miscellaneous" scholar or writer is; but this patronizing attitude would seem to be a corollary of the notion that biography is a mere by-product of history. Not being entirely unbiased in the matter, I prefer to accept Marquis James' statement that biography is "a more personal and individual thing" than history, "and more difficult to do well."

Modern biography began with Boswell's *Life of Johnson*; for Boswell lifted biography above the level of historical hackwork and marked it as a form of literature. And what are the *requirements* of biography as a literary form? Among other things, it must give the reader a complete reading experience; that is, it must be entirely comprehensible and enjoyable to a person who has no prior knowledge of the subject. It must explain and interpret. Explanation shows how a man acted, how he succeeded, how he failed. Interpretation shows *why* he acted, *why* he succeeded or failed. Biography must present not only the physical but also the mental aspects of the man, showing how he grew in mind and character, or how he stagnated or regressed. One might say that biography is cumulative characterization.

The quality of controlled imagination that Mr. Garraty mentioned is fundamental to good biography. This sort of imagination is not fictionalizing; it is enrichment. Without it a biographical character remains cold, flat, and unreal. For bare facts are not enough to give a true picture of a man.

Let me show you what I mean. And please pardon me for using an example from one of my own books. I do it because I know in this instance what went on in my mind, and the impression I hoped to convey to the reader.

Sometime during the late summer of 1862, when Lee and his army were thrusting into Maryland, Lincoln wrote a memorandum. You are familiar with it. It begins: "The will of God prevails. In great contests each party claims to act in accordance with the will of God. Both *may* be, and one *must* be wrong. God can not be *for,* and *against,* the same thing at the same time." Then he goes on, wondering why God, who, by his mere quiet power over the minds of men could stop the war at any time, allows it to continue; trying to find out what God's purpose is.[8] Those are all the facts we have. But here is where the imagination comes in.

Lincoln must have been alone. He couldn't have thought out and penned such a memorandum except in solitude. But he was an extremely busy man. If he was alone, he must have written it late at night. Why was he up late and not working? He must have been waiting for news. What was his mood? Solemn, obviously, from the nature of the memorandum. Anxious, inevitably, with the enemy on Northern soil and a great battle impending. And so I introduced the memorandum this way: "The lonely man in the White House found time for meditation as he waited for news night after night. With his strong sense of fatalism, he felt a Power beyond himself shaping the nation's destiny, and in an hour of anxiety he solemnly penned his thoughts." Those sentences are largely imaginative. Yet I am convinced that they portray the situation accurately, and that something would have been lost in the telling without the use of imagination. In other words, the use of imagination does not necessarily result in inaccuracy. It can be an aid to accuracy.

William E. Barton, a leading Lincoln authority of the 'twenties, once wrote: "I am working very hard to make a real contribution to the world's knowledge of Lincoln. . . . I feel that somehow Lincoln has eluded the biographers. I wish I might hope that I could interpret him. I have been so occupied with gathering facts, I sometimes think I am farther from my real goal than I was when I began." Similarly, Ida Tarbell once admitted: "I am such a slave to facts, dates and things, I mean, that I fail to see the greater facts often." It goes without saying that the biographer must always build his characterization of a man upon a basis of pure fact. But the man comes alive only when imagination and intellect have played upon those facts.

Many techniques, constantly employed by the novelist, are available to the biographer—suspense, accelerated or retarded pace, the foreshadowing of things to come, the evoking of mood. And he can use them without violating the canons of historical method or the dictates of scholarship. The canon of objectivity—when objectivity is interpreted as meaning that a historian must divorce himself from all feeling or passion when he writes—is responsible for a lot of dull and deceptive history. Is historical accuracy achieved by the undramatic portrayal of a dramatic event? Is truth served when none of the excitement in an exciting situation comes through in the writing? Is it served when the life story of a man never takes on life?

Now, to be sure, all historians can't be expected to write for the popular market. Many extremely important books, by their very mass and the nature of their subject matter, will be read by few persons except historians. We shall always have historians' historians, just as we have ballplayers' ballplayers—outstanding performers whose excellence is appreciated chiefly within the profession. It is sometimes said that they lack glamour. In biography, as Mr. Garraty has pointed out, only the lives of a few great men command a mass market. But I'm not pleading for more best sellers. I simply want to see academic historians and biographers widen their sights and cater more generally to the reading public with an unadulterated, but more attractively prepared and packaged product that will drive the cheap synthetics off the market and acquaint more people with history as it happened and as it *can* be written.

Background is always a problem for the biographer—collateral events, forces in the making, the tide of the times. How are these to be presented? In how much detail *can* they be presented without shifting the focus too far from the central character or leaving him in the shadows for too long a time? Freeman, pondering this problem when writing his life of Lee, decided that, paradoxically, biography may fail to be instructive because it is too informative. In dealing with Lee's campaigns and battles, he chose to give the reader no information beyond what Lee himself possessed. In his life of Washington, or in parts of it, at any rate, he swung to the opposite extreme, and ignored Washington completely while dealing lengthily with background.

Nicolay and Hay in their monumental biography frequently lost Lincoln in the military details of the Civil War; and realizing, perhaps, that they had done so, called their book a history rather than a biography.[9] In my own biography of Lincoln I tried to keep the focus on Lincoln by seeing the war as he saw it—from the White House or the War Department telegraph office as news of battles came in.

There can be no hard and fast rule about this problem. And yet a satisfactory solution of it lies at the very heart of good biographical writing. Oscar Handlin recognizes this fact, when, setting forth the editorial specifications for the new Library of American Biography series, he proposed to depict "not the complete man or the complete society, but the points at which the two interact," hoping in so doing to enlarge our understanding "both of our past and the men in our past."[10]

I subscribe to all of Mr. Garraty's objections to multi-volume biographies. Few historical figures are worthy of them. Some are. And every writer of a multi-volume biography whom Mr. Garraty mentioned has enriched or is enriching our historical knowledge. Some historical figures are so massive that massive treatment is a prerequisite of a satisfactory *one volume* life. I know how much my own one volume biography of Lincoln owes to the extended treatments of Lincoln, and especially to the hundreds of solid monographic studies that preceded it. And I'll say also that the one volume biographer can do a better and surer job if he has done some of this spade work himself. Surely, however, the multi-volume biography should not be the last word written about our most prominent men. The detail becomes overpowering. In each case a synthesis is needed, whether it be done by the author of the multi-volume work or by someone else.

I favor the use of biographical subjects for doctoral dissertations within the limits of the student's potentialities. It could serve especially as a means of obtaining biographies of persons whose careers impinged on the larger careers of larger men, or on important events, but who are of insufficient importance to command the talents of the full-statured historian. But let's insist that these studies be biographies in the true sense, not mere tabulations of fact. And let's begin at the grass roots level of the graduate school to teach our future historians how to write. Unless things have changed since my days in graduate school, it might almost be said that a man must slough off the ponderosity that adheres to him from graduate training before he can hope to write well.

Shortly after my biography of Abraham Lincoln was published I received a letter from a graduate student which I shall always prize. "A little while ago I finished your *Abraham Lincoln*," he wrote. "I am at present working wearily toward a Ph.D., and most of the reading I must do is like eating shredded wheat by the bathtub full and without benefit of milk. Your book has at once roused afresh my enthusiasm for Lincoln, enlarged my understanding of his times and thus of ours; and heartened me to continue my labors in the craft. Thanks for writing it."

But let me close on a happy note. I see signs of a change. It is encouraging to note the number of men in the profession, especially the younger ones, who are pocketing the royalty checks from those most ruthless critics, the commercial publishers. I think it can be stated without question that the literary quality of books and articles by academic historians and biographers has improved immensely during the last decade. And as for that graduate student, he is like a man going swimming in cold water. He'll enjoy it after he gets wet all over.

Notes

1. John A. Garraty (b. 1920) wrote *The Nature of Biography* (1957) and biographies of Silas Wright (1949), George W. Perkins (1960), Henry Cabot Lodge (1953), and Woodrow Wilson (1956). The Virginia journalist Douglas Southall Freeman (1886–1953) wrote multivolume studies of Robert E. Lee (1934–35), Lee's lieutenants (1942–44), and George Washington (1948–54). The Indiana politician Albert J. Beveridge (1862–1927) wrote multivolume studies of John Marshall and Lincoln. Irving Newton Brant (1885–1976), a midwestern journalist, wrote a multivolume biography of James Madison (1941–61). Ray Stannard Baker (1870–1946), also a journalist, wrote many studies of Woodrow Wilson, including a multivolume biography (1927–39). Marquis James (1891–1955), a journalist as well, published many biographies, including studies of Sam Houston and Andrew Jackson.

2. Frederick Barnes Tolles (1915–75) taught history at Swarthmore College and wrote extensively about the history of Quakers in America.

3. Edward H. O'Neill wrote *A History of American Biography, 1800–1935* (Philadelphia: University of Pennsylvania Press, 1935).

4. Frank Burt Freidel, *Franklin D. Roosevelt: The Ordeal*, vol. 2 of a 4-vol. biography (Boston: Little, Brown, 1954).

5. The literary and cultural critic Dwight McDonald (1906–82) was a staff writer for *The New Yorker* from 1951 to 1971.

6. Lord David Cecil, *Melbourne* (Indianapolis: Bobbs Merrill, 1954).

7. John Walton Caughey, "Historians' Choice: Results of a Poll on Recently Published American History and Biography," *Mississippi Valley Historical Review* 39 (Sept. 1952): 295.

8. Meditation on the Divine Will, [2 Sept. 1862?], in *The Collected Works of Abraham Lincoln*, ed. Roy P. Basler, Marion Dolores Pratt and Lloyd A. Dunlap,

asst. eds., 8 vols. plus index (New Brunswick: Rutgers University Press, 1953–55), 5:403–4.

9. John G. Nicolay and John Hay, *Abraham Lincoln: A History*, 10 vols. (New York: Century, 1890).

10. Oscar Handlin, *Truth in History* (Cambridge: Harvard University Press, 1979), 276. Handlin (b. 1915) taught at Harvard University and edited the Library of American Biography.

Index

abolitionists, 65, 93; BPT on, xxv–xxvi

Abraham Lincoln: A Biography (Thomas), xi–xl; assessments of, xxx–xxxiii, 251; genesis of, xxviii; reception of, xxxiii–xxxiv; revision, xxxi–xxxii; writing of, xxix–xxx

Abraham Lincoln Association, xix, xxi, xxii, xxiii, xxviii, xxx, xxxv, 55, 153, 157, 223, 224, 225, 226

Abraham Lincoln: The Prairie Years (Sandburg), 242

Abraham Lincoln Quarterly, xxiii, xxvii

Abrams, Gordon, 11

Abzug, Robert H., xxviii

Adams, John Quincy, 54, 55, 97

Adams et al. v. Logan County, 123

Addison, John, 116

Allegheny College, 234–35, 243

Allen, John, 73, 74

Alton and Bloomington Railroad, 126

Alton and Mississippi Rail Road, 178

Alton and Sangamon Railroad, 121, 123

American House, 174

American System, 105

Angle, Paul M., xvi, xx, xxiii, xxiv, xxv, xxxii; and the Abraham Lincoln Association, xix, 223; on BPT, xiii, xv, xvii; on BPT's writings, xii, xxii, xxvi, xxxiii; writings of, 153, 176

Anti-Nebraska editors' meeting, 12

Anti-Slavery Impulse, The (Barnes), xxvi

Armstrong, Duff, 178

Arnold, Isaac Newton, 3, 170; 209; on circuit court life, 158

Ashmun, George, 97, 100

Atchison, David Rice, 97

"Aunt Becca," 10

Austria, 56, 57

Baker, Edward D., 62, 63, 90, 111, 112, 141; financial irregularities of, 192–93

Baldwin, J. G., 31

Baringer, William E., xxx

Barnes, Gilbert H., xxvi

Barrett, Oliver R., 241, 242

Barton, William E., 208, 248–49

Basler, Roy P., xxiv, xxxviii

Bates, Edward, 91, 199

Battery, The, 110

Bell, John, 97

Benson, Godfrey Rathbone. *See* Charnwood, Lord

Benton, Thomas Hart, 97, 147

Beveridge, Albert J., 246

Bigelow, John, 55, 56

Birch, Jesse, 165

BENJAMIN P. THOMAS (1902–56) wrote *Abraham Lincoln: A Biography* (1952), *Portrait for Posterity: Lincoln and His Biographers* (1947), *Lincoln, 1847–1853* (1946), and *Lincoln's New Salem* (1934), among other books.

MICHAEL BURLINGAME, the Sadowski Professor of History Emeritus, Connecticut College, has had nine books on Lincoln published, including *The Inner World of Abraham Lincoln* (1994). He is at work on a multivolume biography of Abraham Lincoln.

The University of Illinois Press
is a founding member of the
Association of American University Presses.

———————————————————

University of Illinois Press
1325 South Oak Street
Champaign, IL 61820-6903
www.press.uillinois.edu